CSS124

The
PSALTER

WITH DOCTRINAL STANDARDS,
LITURGY, CHURCH ORDER,
AND ADDED CHORALE SECTION

WM. B. EERDMANS PUBLISHING COMPANY
Grand Rapids, Michigan

The metrical versions of the Psalms in this Psalter, copyrighted in 1912 by the United Presbyterian Board of Publication and Bible School Work, Pittsburgh, Pa., are used by permission.

PHOTOLITHOPRINTED BY EERDMANS PRINTING COMPANY
GRAND RAPIDS, MICHIGAN, UNITED STATES OF AMERICA

INTRODUCTION

This new edition of The Psalter is issued in response to repeated requests from churches which continue to use this metrical version of the Psalms in public worship. This version was first published in 1912 by the United Presbyterian Church, based on the work of a joint committee representing nine American and Canadian denominations, and was afterward adopted by several other church groups. As in the previous edition, the Doctrinal Standards, Liturgy, and Church Order are retained in this volume, and there has been added a special Chorale Section containing versions of many of the best-loved Dutch Psalms.

THE PUBLISHERS

CONTENTS

THE PSALTER

The Blessedness of the Godly

PSALM 1 C. M.   MEDITATION   John H. Gower

1. That man is blest who, fear - ing God, From sin re - strains his feet, Who will not stand with wick - ed men, Who shuns the scorn - ers' seat.

2. Yea, blest is he who makes God's law His por - tion and de - light, And med - i - tates up - on that law With glad - ness day and night.

3. That man is nour - ished like a tree Set by the riv - er's side; Its leaf is green, its fruit is sure, And thus his works a - bide.

4. The wick - ed like the driv - en chaff Are swept from off the land; They shall not gath - er with the just, Nor in the judg - ment stand.

5. The Lord will guard the right - eous well, Their way to Him is known; The way of sin - ners, far from God, Shall sure - ly be o'er - thrown.

Copyright, 1890, by John H. Gower. Used by per.

2   The Righteous and Unrighteous

PSALM 1   8s and 7s   REDEEMER   Luther O. Emerson

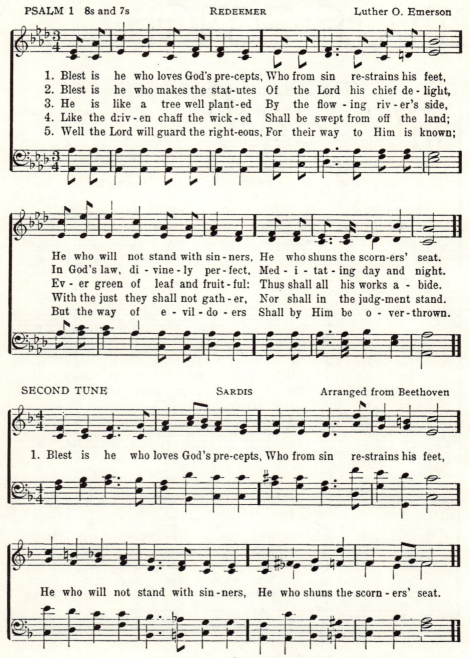

1. Blest is   he who loves God's pre-cepts, Who from sin   re-strains his feet,
2. Blest is   he who makes the stat-utes Of   the Lord   his chief de - light,
3. He is   like a   tree well plant-ed   By   the flow - ing   riv - er's side,
4. Like the driv - en chaff the wick - ed   Shall be swept from off   the land;
5. Well the Lord will guard the right-eous, For   their way   to   Him is known;

He who will   not stand with sin - ners, He   who shuns the scorn-ers'   seat.
In God's law, di - vine - ly per - fect, Med - i - tat - ing day and   night.
Ev - er green of   leaf and fruit - ful: Thus shall all   his works a - bide.
With the just they shall not gath - er,   Nor shall in   the judg-ment stand.
But the way of   e - vil - do - ers   Shall by Him be   o - ver - thrown.

SECOND TUNE   SARDIS   Arranged from Beethoven

1. Blest is   he   who loves God's pre-cepts, Who from sin   re-strains his feet,

He who will   not stand with sin - ners, He   who shuns the scorn - ers'   seat.

8

The Kingship of Jesus Christ

PSALM 2 7s   HERALD ANGELS   Arranged from Mendelssohn

1. Where-fore do the na-tions rage And the peo-ple vain-ly dream That in tri-umph
2. But the Lord will scorn them all, Calm He sits enthroned on high; Soon His wrath will
3. This His word shall be made known, This Je-ho-vah's firm de-cree: Thou art My be-
4. Therefore, kings, be wise, give ear; Hearken, judg-es of the earth; Learn to serve the

they can wage War a-gainst the King su-preme? Christ His Son a scoff they make,
on them fall, Sore displeased He will re-ply: Yet ac-cord-ing to My will
lov-ed Son, Yea, I have be-got-ten Thee. All the earth at Thy re-quest
Lord with fear, Min-gle trembling with your mirth. Kiss the Son, lest o'er your way

And the rul-ers plot-ting say: Their do-min-ion let us break, Let us cast their
I have set My King to reign, And on Zi-on's ho-ly hill My A-noint-ed
I will give Thee for Thy own; Then Thy might shall be confessed And Thy foes be
His consuming wrath should break; But su-preme-ly blest are they Who in Christ their

yoke a-way, Their do-min-ion let us break, Let us cast their yoke a-way.
I main-tain; And on Zi-on's ho-ly hill My A-noint-ed I main-tain.
o-ver-thrown; Then Thy might shall be confessed And Thy foes be o-ver-thrown.
ref-uge take; But su-preme-ly blest are they Who in Christ their ref-uge take.

9

4

Christ's Inheritance

PSALM 2 L. M. UXBRIDGE Lowell Mason

1. O where - fore do the na - tions rage, And
2. Their strength is weak - ness in the sight Of
3. By God's de - cree His Son re - ceives The
4. Be wise, ye rul - ers of the earth, And
5. De - lay not, lest His an - ger rise, And

kings and rul - ers strive in vain, A - gainst the Lord of
Him Who sits en - throned a - bove; He speaks, and judg-ments
na - tions for His her - it - age; The con-qu'ring Christ su-
serve the Lord with god - ly fear; With rev - 'rent joy con-
ye should per - ish in your way; Lo, all that put their

earth and heav'n To o - ver - throw Mes - si - ah's reign?
fall on them Who tempt His wrath and scorn His love.
preme shall reign As King of kings, from age to age.
fess the Son While yet in mer - cy He is near.
trust in Him Are blest in - deed, and blest for aye.

5

God Our Guardian

PSALM 3 C. M. DALEHURST Arthur Cottman

1. O Lord, how are my foes in-creased! A - gainst me man - y rise;
2. Thou art my shield and glo - ry, Lord, My Sav-iour, O Most High.
3. I laid me down and slept, I waked, Be - cause the Lord sus - tains;
4. A - rise, O Lord; save me, my God; For Thou hast owned my cause,
5. Sal - va - tion to the Lord be - longs, In Him His saints are blest;

God Our Guardian

How man-y say, In vain for help He on his God re-lies!
The Lord from out His ho-ly hill Gives an-swer when I cry.
Tho' man-y thou-sands com-pass me, Un-moved my soul re-mains.
And oft hast beat-en down my foes Who scorn Thy right-eous laws.
O let Thy bless-ing ev-er-more Up-on Thy peo-ple rest.

6   A Trustful Appeal to God

PSALM 4 L. M.   REST   William B. Bradbury

1. My right-eous God, Who oft of old Hast saved from
2. How long, O men, will ye de-fame, How long my
3. But know, the Lord has set a-part The man of
4. In rev-'rence wait, from sin de-part, In med-i-
5. O who will show us an-y good, Ex-claims the
6. More joy from Thee has filled my heart Than great a-

troub-les man-i-fold, Give an-swer when I call to
glo-ry turn to shame, How long will ye vain fol-lies
god-ly life and heart To be His fa-vored one for
ta-tion calm your heart; Hold fast the right, be true and
faith-less mul-ti-tude; But lift on us, O Lord, we
bun-dance could im-part; I lay me down to peace-ful

Thee, Be gra-cious now and hear my plea.
prize, How long pur-sue de-ceit and lies?
aye; Je-ho-vah hears me when I pray.
just, And in Je-ho-vah put your trust.
pray, The bright-ness of Thy face this day.
sleep, For Thou, O Lord, dost safe-ly keep.

7

Quieting Thoughts

PSALM 4 6s and 5s   PENITENCE   Spencer Lane

1. On the good and faith-ful God has set His love; When they call He
2. Lay up-on God's al-tar Good and lov-ing deeds, And in all thing
3. In God's love a-bid-ing, I have joy and peace More than all the

sends them Bless-ings from a-bove. Stand in awe, and sin not, Bid your
trust Him To sup-ply your needs. Anx-ious and de-spair-ing, Man-y
wick-ed, Tho' their wealth in-crease. In His care con-fid-ing, I will

heart be still;...... Thro' the si-lent watch-es Think up-on His will.
walk in night;.... But to those that fear Him God will send His light.
sweet-ly sleep,...... For the Lord, my Sav-iour, Will in safe-ty keep.

By per of C L. Hutchins   [Selected Stanzas]

8

Faith and Peace

PSALM 4 6s and 5s   MERRIAL.   Joseph Barnby

1. On the good and faith-ful God has set His love;....
2. Stand in awe, and sin not, Bid your heart be still;....
3. Anx-ious and de-spair-ing, Man-y walk in night;...
4. In His care con-fid-ing, I will sweet-ly sleep....

Faith and Peace

When they call He sends them Bless-ings from a-bove.
Through the si-lent watch-es Think up-on His will.
But to those that fear Him God will send His light.
For the Lord, my Sav-iour, Will in safe-ty keep.

[Selected Stanzas]

9   An Entreaty for Guidance

PSALM 5 7s   COMFORT   English Melody

1. O Je-ho-vah, hear my words, To my tho'ts at-ten-tive be; Hear my cry, my
2. Thou, Je-ho-vah, art a God Who de-light-est not in sin; E-vil shall not
3. In the full-ness of Thy grace To Thy house I will re-pair, Bowing tow'rd Thy

King, my God, I will make my prayer to Thee. With the morning light, O Lord, Thou shalt
dwell with Thee, Nor the proud Thy fa-vor win. E-vil-do-ers Thou dost hate, Ly-ing
ho-ly place, In Thy fear will worship there. Lead me in Thy righteousness, Let my

hear my voice a-rise, And ex-pect-ant I will bring Prayer as morning sac-ri-fice.
tongues Thou wilt defeat; God abhors the man who loves Vi-o-lence and base de-ceit.
foes as-sail in vain; Lest my feet be turned a-side, Make Thy way be-fore me plain.

13

10 Confident Access to God

PSALM 5 7s   MARTYN   Simeon B. Marsh

1. { In the full-ness of Thy grace   To Thy house I will re - pair,
     Bow - ing tow'rd Thy ho - ly place,   In Thy fear will wor - ship there. }
2. { False and faith - less are my foes,   In their mouth no truth is found;
     Dead - ly are the words they speak,   All their tho'ts with sin a - bound. }
3. { O let all that trust Thy care   Ev - er glad and joy - ful be;
     Let them joy who love Thy Name,   Safe - ly guard - ed, Lord, by Thee. }

Lead me in Thy right-eous - ness,   Let my foes as - sail in vain!
Bring, O God, their plans to nought,   Hold them guilt-y in Thy sight,
For a bless - ing from Thy store   To the right-eous Thou wilt yield;

Lest my feet be turned a - side,   Make Thy way be - fore me plain.
For a-gainst Thee and Thy law   They have set them-selves to fight.
Thou wilt com-pass him a - bout   With Thy fa - vor as a shield.

[Stanzas 3 5]

11 Prayer and Protection

PSALM 5 7s   REDHEAD   Richard Redhead

1. O Je - ho - vah, hear my words,   To my tho'ts at - ten - tive be;
2. With the morn-ing light, O Lord,   Thou shalt hear my voice a - rise,
3. O let all that trust Thy care   Ev - er glad and joy - ful be;
4. For a bless - ing from Thy store   To the right-eous Thou wilt yield;

Prayer and Protection

Hear my cry, my King, my God, I will make my prayer to Thee.
And ex-pect-ant I will bring Prayer as morn-ing sac-ri-fice.
Let them joy who love Thy Name, Safe-ly guard-ed, Lord, by Thee.
Thou wilt com-pass him a-bout With Thy fa-vor as a shield.

[Selected Stanzas]

12 Divine Chastisement

PSALM 6 8s and 7s   ZENO   Alexander B. Morton

1. Lord, re-buke me not in an-ger; Chas-tened
2. Come, O Lord, my soul de-liv-er, In Thy
3. Pit-y, Lord, my sad con-di-tion; I am
4. Now the foes that seek to harm me, Quick-ly

sore I waste a-way; Pit-y my dis-tress and
lov-ing-kind-ness save. Shall the dead Thy Name re-
wea-ry and dis-tressed; Man-y ad-ver-sa-ries
put to shame, shall flee, For the Lord hath heard my

hear me; Lord, how long wilt Thou de-lay?
mem-ber? Who shall praise Thee in the grave?
vex me, Weep-ing, I can find no rest.
weep-ing, And He will re-gard my plea.

Confidence in Divine Justice

PSALM 7 11s   PAULINA   Arranged from Donizetti

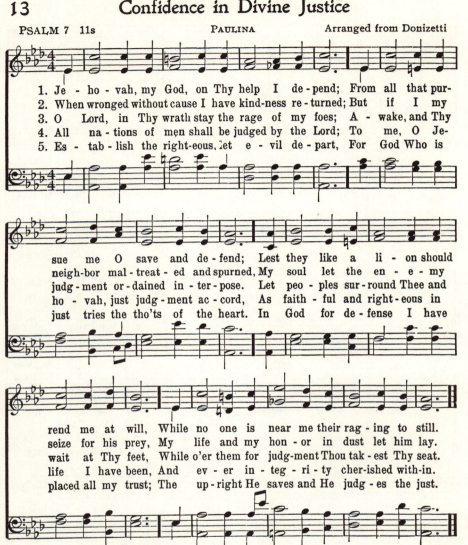

1. Je - ho - vah, my God, on Thy help I de - pend; From all that pur-
2. When wronged without cause I have kind-ness re - turned; But if I my
3. O Lord, in Thy wrath stay the rage of my foes; A - wake, and Thy
4. All na - tions of men shall be judged by the Lord; To me, O Je-
5. Es - tab - lish the right-eous, let e - vil de - part, For God Who is

sue me O save and de - fend; Lest they like a li - on should
neigh-bor mal - treat - ed and spurned, My soul let the en - e - my
judg - ment or - dained in - ter - pose. Let peo - ples sur - round Thee and
ho - vah, just judg - ment ac - cord, As faith - ful and right - eous in
just tries the tho'ts of the heart. In God for de - fense I have

rend me at will, While no one is near me their rag - ing to still.
seize for his prey, My life and my hon - or in dust let him lay.
wait at Thy feet, While o'er them for judg-ment Thou tak - est Thy seat.
life I have been, And ev - er in - teg - ri - ty cher-ished with-in.
placed all my trust; The up - right He saves and He judg - es the just.

6 The Lord with the wicked is wroth every day,
And if they repent not is ready to slay;
By manifold ruin for others prepared
They surely at last shall themselves be ensnared.

7 Because He is righteous His praise I will sing,
Thanksgiving and honor to Him I will bring,
Will sing to the Lord on Whose grace I rely,
Extolling the Name of Jehovah Most High.

14 The Name of the Lord

PSALM 8 C. M.   CLINTON   Joseph P. Holbrook

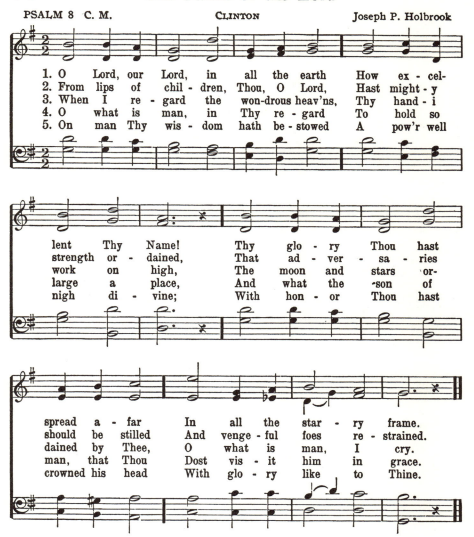

1. O Lord, our Lord, in all the earth How ex-cel-
2. From lips of chil-dren, Thou, O Lord, Hast might-y
3. When I re-gard the won-drous heav'ns, Thy hand-i
4. O what is man, in Thy re-gard To hold so
5. On man Thy wis-dom hath be-stowed A pow'r well

lent Thy Name! Thy glo-ry Thou hast
strength or-dained, That ad-ver-sa-ries
work on high, The moon and stars or-
large a place, And what the son of
nigh di-vine; With hon-or Thou hast

spread a-far In all the star-ry frame.
should be stilled And venge-ful foes re-strained.
dained by Thee, O what is man, I cry.
man, that Thou Dost vis-it him in grace.
crowned his head With glo-ry like to Thine.

6 Thou has subjected all to him,
    And lord of all is he,
Of flocks and herds, and beasts and birds,
    And all within the sea.

7 Thy mighty works and wondrous grace
    Thy glory, Lord, proclaim.
O Lord, our Lord, in all the earth
    How excellent Thy Name.

God's Glory in His Works

PSALM 8 7s   THANKSGIVING   Walter B. Gilbert

1. Lord, our Lord, Thy glo - rious Name All Thy won-drous works pro-claim;
2. Moon and stars in shin-ing height Night-ly tell their Mak-er's might;
3. With do - min - ion crowned he stands O'er the crea-tures of Thy hands;

In the heav'ns with ra - diant signs Ev - er-more Thy glo - ry shines.
When Thy won-drous heav'ns I scan, Then I know how weak is man.
All to him sub - jec - tion yield In the sea and air and field.

In - fant lips Thou dost or - dain Wrath and venge-ance to re - strain,
What is man that he should be Loved and vi - sit - ed by Thee,
Lord, our Lord, Thy glo - rious Name All Thy won-drous works pro - claim,

Weak - est means ful - fill Thy will. Might - y en - e - mies to still.
Raised to an ex - alt - ed height, Crowned with hon-or in Thy sight?
Thine the Name of match-less worth, Ex - cel - lent in all the earth.

16 The Lord the Righteous Judge

PSALM 9 11s   FREDERICK   George Kingsley

1. Whole-heart-ed thanks-giv-ing to Thee will I bring, In praise of Thy
2. My en - e - mies turn and are scat-tered in fear, They stum-ble and
3. Re - buked are the na - tions, the wick - ed de-stroyed, Their mem-o - ry
4. Thou, Lord, art a ref - uge for all the op-pressed; All trust Thee who

mar - vel - ous deeds I will sing, In Thee I will joy and ex-
per - ish be - cause Thou art near; For Thou hast de - fend - ed my
per - ished, their dwell - ing-place void; En-throned and e - ter - nal, Je-
know Thee, and trust - ing are blest; For nev - er, O Lord, did Thy

ult - ing-ly cry, Thy Name I will praise, O Je - ho - vah Most High.
right and my cause, Thou sit - test in judg-ment, up - hold - ing Thy laws.
ho - vah shall reign, The peo - ples to judge and the right to main-tain.
mer - cy for - sake The soul that has sought of Thy grace to par-take.

5 Give praise to Jehovah, the mighty deeds tell
Of Him Who has chosen in Zion to dwell,
Of Him to Whom justice and vengeance belong,
Who visits the lowly and overthrows wrong.

6 Behold my affliction, Thy mercy accord,
And back from death's portals restore me, O Lord,
That I in the gates of Thy Zion may raise
My song of salvation and show forth Thy praise.

7 The sins of the nations their ruin have wrought,
Their own evildoing destruction has brought;
In this the Lord's justice eternally stands,
That sinners are snared in the work of their hands.

8 The wicked shall perish, the nations shall fall,
Forgetting their God, Who is God over all;
But God will remember the prayer of the weak,
Most surely fulfilling the hope of the meek.

9 Arise in Thy justice, O Lord, and Thy might,
No longer let sinners prevail in Thy sight;
Great Judge of the nations, in judgment appear
To humble the proud and to teach them Thy fear.

17 Whole-Hearted Praise

PSALM 9 L. M.   ANVERN   Arranged by Lowell Mason

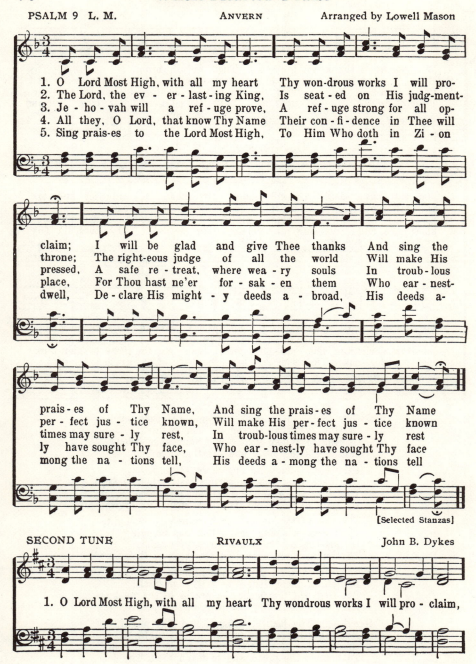

1. O Lord Most High, with all my heart Thy won-drous works I will pro-
2. The Lord, the ev - er - last-ing King, Is seat - ed on His judg-ment-
3. Je - ho - vah will a ref - uge prove, A ref - uge strong for all op-
4. All they, O Lord, that know Thy Name Their con - fi - dence in Thee will
5. Sing prais-es to the Lord Most High, To Him Who doth in Zi - on

claim; I will be glad and give Thee thanks And sing the
throne; The right-eous judge of all the world Will make His
pressed, A safe re - treat, where wea - ry souls In troub - lous
place, For Thou hast ne'er for - sak - en them Who ear - nest-
dwell, De - clare His might - y deeds a - broad, His deeds a-

prais - es of Thy Name, And sing the prais - es of Thy Name
per - fect jus - tice known, Will make His per - fect jus - tice known
times may sure - ly rest, In troub-lous times may sure - ly rest
ly have sought Thy face, Who ear - nest-ly have sought Thy face
mong the na - tions tell, His deeds a - mong the na - tions tell

[Selected Stanzas]

SECOND TUNE   RIVAULX   John B. Dykes

1. O Lord Most High, with all my heart Thy wondrous works I will pro - claim,

20

Whole-Hearted Praise

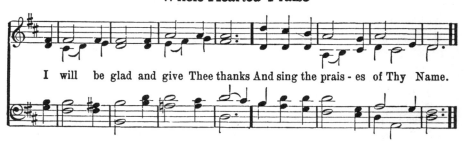

I will be glad and give Thee thanks And sing the prais-es of Thy Name.

18 Complaint Against the Wicked

PSALM 10 L. M.   BRIGGS   William A. Tarbutton

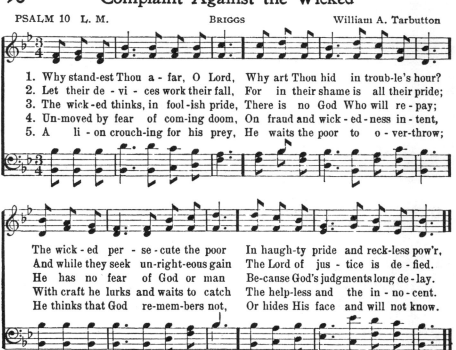

1. Why stand-est Thou a - far, O Lord, Why art Thou hid in troub-le's hour?
2. Let their de - vi - ces work their fall, For in their shame is all their pride;
3. The wick-ed thinks, in fool-ish pride, There is no God Who will re - pay;
4. Un-moved by fear of com-ing doom, On fraud and wick - ed-ness in - tent,
5. A li - on crouch-ing for his prey, He waits the poor to o - ver-throw;

The wick - ed per - se - cute the poor In haugh-ty pride and reck-less pow'r,
And while they seek un-right-eous gain The Lord of jus - tice is de - fied.
He has no fear of God or man Be-cause God's judgments long de - lay.
With craft he lurks and waits to catch The help-less and the in - no - cent.
He thinks that God re-mem-bers not, Or hides His face and will not know.

6 Arise, O Lord, lift up Thy hand,
 O God, protect the poor and meek;
Why should the proud Thy justice doubt,
 And words of bold defiance speak?

7 O Lord, Thou wilt indeed requite,
 The sin and sorrow Thou dost see;
The helpless and the fatherless
 Commit themselves, O Lord, to Thee.

8 Break Thou the pow'r of wicked men
 And let their works no longer stand;
The Lord is King for evermore,
 Who drove the nations from His land.

9 Lord, Thou hast heard the lowly prayer,
 The fainting heart Thou wilt restore,
The helpless cause Thou wilt maintain,
 That mortal man may boast no more.

19 Prayer for the Oppressed

PSALM 10 S. M.   CLIFTON   C. Warwick Jordan

1. Why dost Thou stand a-far, O Lord, in our dis-tress?
2. Do Thou, O Lord, a-rise; O God, lift up Thy hand;
3. Their foes Thou dost be-hold, Their wrongs Thou wilt re-pay;
4. Thou, Lord, hast heard their prayer When hum-ble hearts drew nigh;
5. De-fend the fa-ther-less And all who are op-pressed,

And why dost Thou con-ceal Thy-self When troub-lous times op-press?
For-get Thou not the suf-f'ring poor, The hum-ble in the land.
The poor com-mit them-selves to Thee, Thou art the or-phans' stay.
Thou al-so wilt re-vive their strength And ev-er hear their cry.
That they by hu-man pride and pow'r May be no more dis-tressed.

[Selected Stanzas]

20 Unshaken Faith Amid Danger

PSALM 11 11s   PROTECTION   Anonymous

1. In God will I trust, tho' my coun-sel-ors say, O flee as a
2. The Lord in His tem-ple shall ev-er a-bide; His throne is e-
3. The Lord is most right-eous, the Lord loves the right, The e-vil He

bird to your moun-tain a-way; The wick-ed are strong and the
ter-nal, what-ev-er be-tide. The chil-dren of men He be-
hates and will sure-ly re-quite; The wick-ed His an-ger will

Unshaken Faith Amid Danger

right-eous are weak, Foun - da - tions are shak - en, yet God will I seek.
holds from on high, The wick - ed to pun - ish, the right-eous to try.
drive from their place, The up - right in rap - ture shall gaze on His face.

21 Assurances for Evil Days

PSALM 12 C. P. M.   BREMEN   Thomas Hastings

1. O Lord, be Thou my help - er true, For just and god - ly men are few;
2. The lips that speak, the truth to hide, The tongues of ar - ro-gance and pride,
3. Be-cause the poor are sore oppressed, Be - cause the need - y are dis-tressed,
4. Je - ho - vah's prom-ise - es are sure, His words are true, His words are pure

The - faith - ful who can find?   From truth and wis - dom men de - part,
That boast-ful words em - ploy,   False-speak-ing tongues that boast their might,
And bit - ter are their cries,   The Lord will be their help - er strong;
As sil - ver from the flame.   Tho' base men walk on ev - 'ry side,

With flat-t'ring lips and doub - le heart They speak their e - vil mind.
That own no law, that know no right, Je - ho - vah will de - stroy.
To save them from con-tempt and wrong Je - ho - vah will a - rise.
His saints are safe, what-e'er be - tide, Pro - tect - ed by His Name.

22 Trust in the Mercy of God

PSALM 13 7s and 6s OLIVA Alexander B. Morton

1. How long wilt Thou for-get me, O Lord, Thou God of grace?
2. O Lord my God, be-hold me, And hear my ear-nest cries;
3. But I with ex-pec-ta - tion Have on Thy grace re - lied;

How long shall fears be-set me While dark - ness hides Thy face?
Lest sleep of death en-fold me, En - light - en Thou my eyes;
My heart in Thy sal-va-tion Shall still with joy con - fide.

How long shall griefs dis-tress me And turn my day to night?
Lest now my foe in-sult-ing Should boast of his suc - cess,
And I with voice of sing-ing Will praise the Lord a - bove,

How long shall foes op - press me And tri - umph in their might?
And en - e - mies ex - ult - ing Re - joice in my dis - tress.
Who, rich - est boun-ties bring-ing, Has dealt with me in love.

Human Corruption

PSALM 14 L. M. BLACKBURN William M. H. Aitken

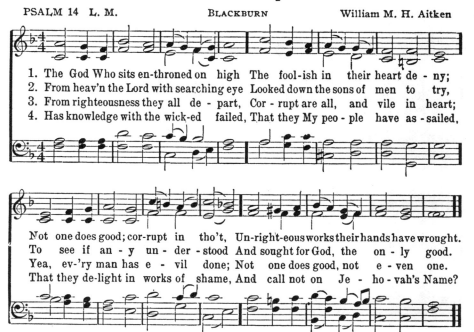

1. The God Who sits en-throned on high The fool-ish in their heart de - ny;
2. From heav'n the Lord with searching eye Looked down the sons of men to try,
3. From righteousness they all de - part, Cor - rupt are all, and vile in heart;
4. Has knowledge with the wick-ed failed, That they My peo - ple have as - sailed,

Not one does good; cor-rupt in tho't, Un-right-eous works their hands have wrought.
To see if an - y un - der - stood And sought for God, the on - ly good.
Yea, ev-'ry man has e - vil done; Not one does good, not e - ven one.
That they de-light in works of shame, And call not on Je - ho-vah's Name?

5 Thy lowly servant they despise,
Because he on the Lord relies;
But they shall tremble yet in fear,
For to the righteous God is near.

6 O that from Zion His abode
Salvation were on us bestowed!
When God His exiles shall restore,
They shall in song His grace adore.

SECOND TUNE LAUDS Arranged by Richard Redhead

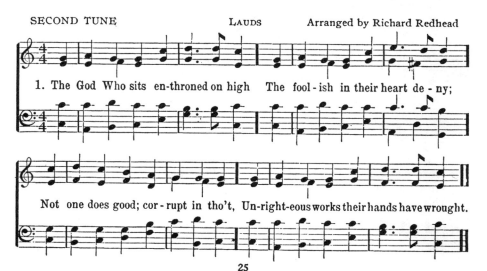

1. The God Who sits en-throned on high The fool-ish in their heart de - ny;

Not one does good; cor-rupt in tho't, Un-right-eous works their hands have wrought.

24 Tests of Christian Character

PSALM 15 8s and 7s   HELEN   Silas J. Vail

1. Who, O Lord, with Thee a-bid-ing, In Thy house shall be Thy guest?
2. He that slan-ders not his broth-er, Does no e-vil to a friend;
3. Free-ly to the need-y lend-ing, No ex-cess he asks a-gain;

Who, his feet to Zi-on turn-ing, In Thy ho-ly hill shall rest?
To re-proach-es of an-oth-er He re-fus-es to at-tend.
And the in-no-cent be-friend-ing, He de-sires not praise of men.

He that ev-er walks up-right-ly, Does the right with-out a fear,
Wick-ed men win not his fa-vor, But the good who fear the Lord;
Do-ing this, and e-vil spurn-ing, He shall nev-er-more be moved:

When he speaks, he speaks not light-ly, But with truth and love sin-cere.
From his vow he will not wav-er, Tho' it bring him sad re-ward.
This the man with Thee so-journ-ing, This the man by Thee ap-proved.

25 The Godly Man

PSALM 15 S. M. LISBON Daniel Read

1. Lord, who shall come to Thee, And stand be - fore Thy face?
2. The man of up - right life, Sin - cere in word and deed,
3. Who hon - ors god - ly men, But scorns the false and vile,
4. Who loves not u - su - ry, Nor takes a base re - ward;

Who shall a - bide, a wel-come guest, With - in Thy ho - ly place?
Who slan-ders nei - ther friend nor foe, Nor i - dle tales will heed.
Who keeps his prom - ised word to all, Tho' loss be his the while.
Un - moved for - ev - er he shall be, And stand be - fore the Lord.

26 An Ideal Worshiper

PSALM 15 7s INNOCENTS The Parish Choir

1. Who, O Lord, shall dwell with Thee In the tem - ple of Thy grace?
2. He who walks in right-eous - ness, All his ac - tions just and clear;
3. He to whom does not be - long Tongue of mal - ice or de - ceit;
4. Who the wick - ed man will spurn, Hon - or those that fear the Lord;
5. Who no u - su - ry will claim, Nor with bribes pol-lute his hand:

Who Thy con-stant guest shall be In Thy high and ho - ly place?
He whose words the truth ex - press, Spo - ken from a heart sin - cere.
Who will not his neigh - bor wrong, Nor a slan-derous tale re - peat.
Nor will from his prom - ise turn Tho' but loss be his re - ward.
He who thus his life shall frame Shall un-moved for - ev - er stand.

27 God the Highest Good

PSALM 16 C. M.   ST. PETER   Alexander R. Reinagle

1. O God, pre-serve me, for in Thee A - lone my trust has stood;
2. I love Thy saints, who fear Thy Name And walk as in Thy sight;
3. Their sor - rows shall be mul - ti - plied Who wor-ship aught but Thee;
4. The Lord is my in - her - it - ance, The Lord a - lone re - mains
5. The lines are fall - en un - to me In pla - ces large and fair;

My soul has said, Thou art my Lord, My chief and on - ly good.
They are the ex - cel - lent of earth, In them is my de - light.
I share not in their of - fer - ings, Nor join their com - pa - ny.
The full - ness of my cup of bliss; The Lord my lot main - tains.
A good - ly her - it - age is mine, Marked out with gra - cious care.

28 Fellowship with God

PSALM 16 C. M.   MAITLAND   George N. Allen

1. When in the night I med - i - tate On mer - cies mul - ti - plied,
2. For - ev - er in my thou't the Lord Be - fore my face shall stand;
3. My in - most be - ing thrills with joy And glad-ness fills my breast;
4. I know that I shall not be left For - got - ten in the grave,
5. The path of life Thou show-est me; Of joy a bound-less store

My grate - ful heart in - spires my tongue To bless the Lord, my Guide.
Se - cure, un-moved, I shall re - main, With Him at my right hand.
Be - cause on Him my trust is stayed, My flesh in hope shall rest.
And from cor - rup - tion, Thou, O Lord, Thy ho - ly one wilt save.
Is ev - er found at Thy right hand, And pleas-ures ev - er - more.

28   [Stanzas 6-10]

Immortality and Resurrection

PSALM 16 S. M.   LEOMINSTER   George William Martin

1. To Thee, O Lord, I fly And on Thy help de - pend;
2. I keep be - fore me still The Lord Whom I have proved;
3. My soul in death's dark pit Shall not be left by Thee;

Thou art my Lord and King Most High; Do Thou my soul de - fend.
At my right hand He guards from ill, And I shall not be moved.
Cor - rup - tion Thou wilt not per - mit Thy ho - ly one to see.

I praise the Lord a - bove Whose coun - sel guides a - right;
My heart is glad and blest, My soul its joy shall tell;
Life's path - way Thou wilt show, To Thy right hand wilt guide,

My heart in-structs me in His love In sea - sons of the night.
And, lo, my flesh in hope shall rest, And still in safe - ty dwell.
Where streams of pleas-ure ev - er flow, And bound-less joys a - bide.

[Selected Stanzas]

30 The Lord Our Inheritance

PSALM 16 S. M.   MARY   Henry A. Lewis

1. To Thee, O Lord, I fly And on Thy help de - pend;
2. The lot to me that fell Is beau - ti - ful and fair;
3. I keep be - fore me still The Lord Whom I have proved;

Thou art my Lord and King Most High; Do Thou my soul de - fend.
The her - it - age in which I dwell Is good be - yond com - pare.
At my right hand He guards from ill, And I shall not be moved.

A her - it - age for me Je - ho - vah will re - main;
I praise the Lord a - bove Whose coun - sel guides a - right;
Life's path-way Thou wilt show, To Thy right hand wilt guide,

My por - tion rich and full is He, My right He will main - tain.
My heart in-structs me in His love In sea - sons of the night.
Where streams of pleas-ure ev - er flow, And bound - less joys a - bide.

The Prayer of the Righteous

PSALM 17 C. H. M.   CALM   Thomas Hastings

1. Lord, hear the right, re - gard my cry, My prayer from lips sin - cere;
2. With stead-fast cour-age I de - sign No wrong to speak or do;
3. O Thou that ev - er sav - est those Whose trust on Thee is stayed,
4. O guard me well as one doth guard The ap - ple of the eye;
5. My en - e - my, grown strong in pride, Would take my life a - way,

Send Thy ap - prov - al from on high, My right-eous-ness make clear.
Thy path of life I choose for mine And walk with pur - pose true.
Pre - serv - ing them from all their foes By Thy al - might - y aid,
While dead-ly foes are press-ing hard, To Thee, to Thee I cry.
A li - on lurk - ing by my side, Most greed-y for his prey.

Thou in the night my heart hast tried, Nor found it turned from Thee a - side.
For help, O God, I cry to Thee, As-sured that Thou wilt an - swer me.
Let me Thy lov - ing-kind-ness see, Thy won-drous mer-cy, full and free.
Do Thou my rest and ref - uge be, O let Thy wings o'er-shad-ow me.
Con-front and cast him down, O Lord, From e - vil save me by Thy sword.

6 Defend me from the men of pride,
  Whose portion is below,
Who, with life's treasures satisfied,
  No better portion know;
They, with earth's joys and wealth content,
Must leave them all when life is spent.

7 When I in righteousness at last
  Thy glorious face shall see,
When all the weary night is past,
  And I awake with Thee
To view the glories that abide,
Then, then I shall be satisfied.

32 Our Need of Divine Help

PSALM 17 C. H. M. LONGFELLOW Frederic F. Bullard

1. Lord, hear the right, re - gard my cry, My prayer from
2. With stead - fast cour - age I de - sign No wrong to
3. O Thou that ev - er sav - est those Whose trust on
4. When I in right - eous - ness at last Thy glo - rious

lips sin - cere; Send Thy ap - prov - al from on high,
speak or do; Thy path of life I choose for mine
Thee is stayed, Pre - serv - ing them from all their foes
face shall see, When all the wea - ry night is past,

My right - eous - ness make clear. Thou in the night my
And walk with pur - pose true. For help, O God, I
By Thy al - might - y aid, Let me Thy lov - ing-
And I a - wake with Thee To view the glo - ries

heart hast tried, Nor found it turned from Thee a - side.
cry to Thee, As - sured that Thou wilt an - swer me.
kind - ness see, Thy won - drous mer - cy, full and free.
that a - bide, Then, then I shall be sat - is - fied.

[Selected Stanzas]

Copyright, 1902, by Congregational Sunday-School and Publishing Society. Used by per.

33 Our Refuge in the Lord

PSALM 17 C. M.　　　　　AGAWAM　　　　　William B. Bradbury

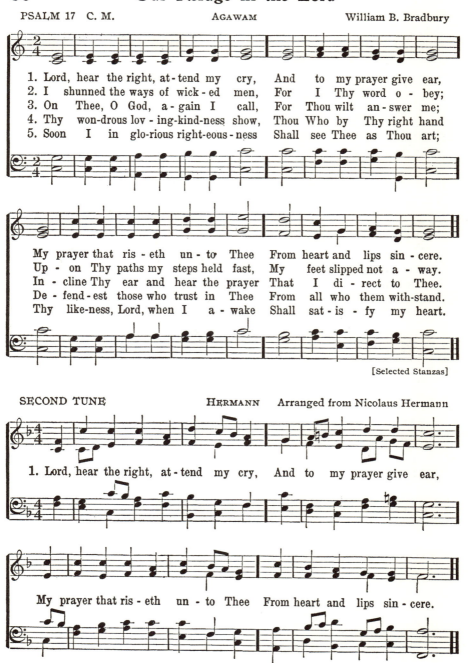

1. Lord, hear the right, at-tend my cry, And to my prayer give ear,
2. I shunned the ways of wick-ed men, For I Thy word o-bey;
3. On Thee, O God, a-gain I call, For Thou wilt an-swer me;
4. Thy won-drous lov-ing-kind-ness show, Thou Who by Thy right hand
5. Soon I in glo-rious right-eous-ness Shall see Thee as Thou art;

My prayer that ris-eth un-to Thee From heart and lips sin-cere.
Up-on Thy paths my steps held fast, My feet slipped not a-way.
In-cline Thy ear and hear the prayer That I di-rect to Thee.
De-fend-est those who trust in Thee From all who them with-stand.
Thy like-ness, Lord, when I a-wake Shall sat-is-fy my heart.

[Selected Stanzas]

SECOND TUNE　　　　　HERMANN　　Arranged from Nicolaus Hermann

1. Lord, hear the right, at-tend my cry, And to my prayer give ear,

My prayer that ris-eth un-to Thee From heart and lips sin-cere.

God's Strength Our Protection

PSALM 18 L. M. MENDON German Melody

1. I love the Lord, His strength is mine; He is my
God, I trust His grace; My for - tress high, my
shield di - vine, My Sav - iour and my hid - ing - place.

2. My prayer to God shall still be raised When troub-les
thick a - round me close; The Lord, most wor - thy
to be praised, Will res - cue me from all my foes.

3. When, floods of e - vil rag - ing near, Down nigh to
death my soul was brought, I cried to God in
all my fear; He heard and great de - liv - 'rance wrought.

4. He came: the earth's foun - da - tions quake, The hills are
shak - en from their place, Thick smoke and fire devour - ing break In an - ger dread be - fore His face.

5 Descending through the bending skies,
  With gloom and darkness under Him,
Forth through the storm Jehovah flies
  As on the wings of cherubim.

6 Thick darkness hides Him from the
    view,
  And swelling clouds His presence veil,
Until His glorious light breaks through
  In lightning flash and glistening hail.

7 Jehovah's thunders fill the heaven,
  The dreadful voice of God Most High;
With shafts of light the clouds are riven,
  His foes, dismayed, in terror fly.

8 The raging torrents overflow,
  And sweep the world's foundations
    bare,
Because Thy blasts of anger blow,
  O Lord of earth and sea and air.

9 He took me from the whelming waves
  Of bitter hate and sore distress;
The Lord, my stay and helper, saves,
  Though mighty foes around me press.

10 From direful straits He set me free,
  He saved the man of His delight;
For good the Lord rewarded me,
  Because I kept His ways aright.

35 Holiness and Divine Favor

PSALM 18 L. M. CLOLATA W. St. Clair Palmer

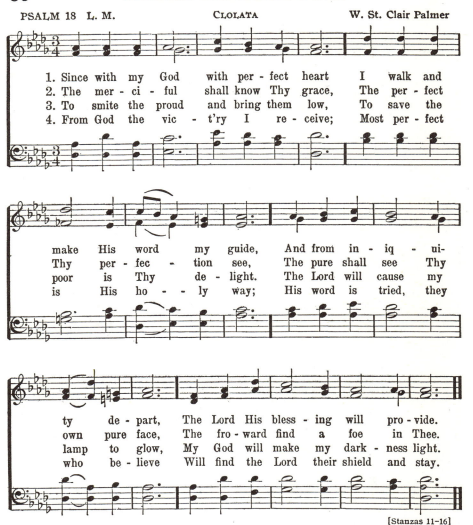

1. Since with my God with per - fect heart I walk and make His word my guide, And from in - iq - ui - ty de - part, The Lord His bless - ing will pro - vide.
2. The mer - ci - ful shall know Thy grace, The per - fect Thy per - fec - tion see, The pure shall see Thy own pure face, The fro - ward find a foe in Thee.
3. To smite the proud and bring them low, To save the poor is Thy de - light. The Lord will cause my lamp to glow, My God will make my dark - ness light.
4. From God the vic - t'ry I re - ceive; Most per - fect is His ho - ly way; His word is tried, they who be - lieve Will find the Lord their shield and stay.

[Stanzas 11–16]

5 For who is God, and strong to save,
　Beside the Lord, our God of might?
'Tis He that makes me strong and brave,
　The Lord Who guides my steps aright.

6 Thy free salvation is my shield,
　My sure defense in every strait;
Thy hand upholds me, lest I yield;
　Thy gentleness has made me great.

Our Source of Strength

PSALM 18   L. M.   MOZART   Arranged from Mozart

1. As Thou, O Lord, hast made me strong To o - ver-
2. From strife Thou wilt de - liv - er me, And make the
3. Je - ho - vah lives, and blest is He, My rock, my

come my might - y foe, So now to fight a-
na - tions own my sway; Strange peo - ples, when my
ref - uge and de - fense, My Sav - iour Who de-

gainst the wrong And con - quer in Thy Name I go.
pow'r they see, Shall come with trem - bling and o - bey.
liv - ers me, And will the wick - ed rec - om - pense.

4 For grace and mercy ever near,
    For foes subdued and victories won,
All nations of the earth shall hear
    My praise for what the Lord has done.

5 To David, His anointed king,
    And to his sons upon his throne,
The Lord will great salvation bring
    And ever make His mercy known.

37 Nature's Tribute to God

PSALM 19 H. M.   ARTHUR'S SEAT   Arranged from John Goss

1. The spa-cious heav'ns de-clare The glo-ry of our God, The fir-ma-ment dis-plays.... His hand-i-work a-broad; Day un-to day pro-claims His might, And night His wis-dom tells to night.

2. A-loud they do not speak, They ut-ter forth no word, Nor in-to lan-guage break,... Their voice is nev-er heard; Yet through the world the truth they bear And their Cre-a-tor's pow'r de-clare.

3. The clouds of heav'n are spread, A tent to hold the sun, And like a bride-groom fair..... Comes forth the might-y one, Re-joic-ing in his strength and grace To run his won-drous dai-ly race.

4. His dai-ly go-ing forth Is from the end of heav'n; The firm-a-ment to him..... Is for his cir-cuit giv'n; His journ-ey reach-es to its ends, And ev-'ry-where his heat ex-tends.

38 The Perfect Law of God

PSALM 19 H. M.   HADDAM   Arranged by Lowell Mason

1. Je - ho - vah's per-fect law   Re - stores the soul a - gain;   His
2. The Lord's commands are pure,   They light and joy re - store;   Je-
3. They are to be de - sired   A - bove the fin - est gold;   Than
4. His er - rors who can know?   Cleanse me from hid - den stain;   Keep
5. When Thou dost search my life,   May all my tho'ts with - in   And

tes - ti - mo - ny sure   Gives wis - dom un - to men;   The pre - cepts
ho - vah's fear is clean,   En - dur - ing ev - er - more;   His stat - utes,
hon - ey from the comb   More sweet-ness far they hold;   With warn - ings
me from will - ful sins,   Nor let them o'er me reign;   And then I
all the words I speak   Thy full ap - prov - al win.   O Lord, Thou

of the Lord are right,   And fill the heart with great de - light.
let the world con - fess,   Are whol - ly truth and right-eous-ness.
they Thy serv - ant guard,   In keep - ing them is great re - ward.
up - right shall ap - pear   And be from great trans-gres-sions clear.
art a rock to me,   And my Re - deem - er Thou shalt be.

[Stanzas 5–9]

39 The Witness of Nature to God

PSALM 19 8s   OLENA   John B. Herbert

1. The heav'ns in their splendor de - clare   The might and the glo - ry of God;
2. They speak not with aud - i - ble word,   Yet clear is the mes-sage they send;
3. For - sak - ing his tent in the sky,   Ar - rayed as a bridegroom, the sun
4. He tells thro' the length of the heav'ns   His Mak-er's great wisdom and might,

Copyright, 1912, by United Presbyterian Board of Publication. Used by per.

The Witness of Nature to God

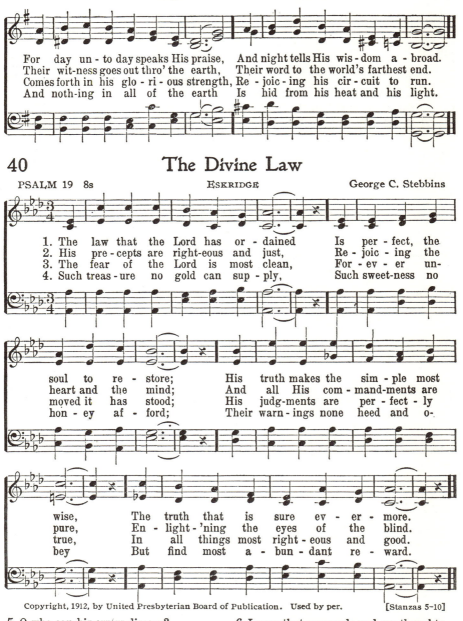

For day un-to day speaks His praise, And night tells His wis-dom a-broad.
Their wit-ness goes out thro' the earth, Their word to the world's farthest end.
Comes forth in his glo-ri-ous strength, Re-joic-ing his cir-cuit to run.
And noth-ing in all of the earth Is hid from his heat and his light.

40   The Divine Law

PSALM 19   8s   ESKRIDGE   George C. Stebbins

1. The law that the Lord has or-dained   Is per-fect, the
2. His pre-cepts are right-eous and just,   Re-joic-ing the
3. The fear of the Lord is most clean,   For-ev-er un-
4. Such treas-ure no gold can sup-ply,   Such sweet-ness no

soul to re-store;   His truth makes the sim-ple most
heart and the mind;   And all His com-mand-ments are
moved it has stood;   His judg-ments are per-fect-ly
hon-ey af-ford;   Their warn-ings none heed and o-

wise,   The truth that is sure ev-er-more.
pure,   En-light-'ning the eyes of the blind.
true,   In all things most right-eous and good.
bey   But find most a-bun-dant re-ward.

Copyright, 1912, by United Presbyterian Board of Publication. Used by per.   [Stanzas 5-10]

5 O who can his errors discern?
    From hidden faults, Lord, keep me free;
Let pride never reign in my heart,
    And clear of great sin I shall be.

6 I pray that my words and my thoughts
    May all with Thy precepts accord,
And ever be pleasing to Thee,
    My rock, my Redeemer, my Lord.

The Value of Holy Scripture

PSALM 19 C. M. MOUNT AUBURN George Kingsley

1. Most per - fect is the law of God, Re-
2. The pre - cepts of the Lord are right; With
3. The fear of God is un - de - filed And
4. They warn from ways of wick - ed - ness Dis-
5. What man can know his e - vil heart, Dis-

stor - ing those that stray; His tes - ti - mo - ny
joy they fill the heart; The Lord's com - mand - ments
ev - er shall en - dure; The stat - utes of the
pleas - ing to the Lord, And in the keep - ing
cern - ing all his sin? O cleanse me, Lord, from

is most sure, Pro - claim - ing wis - dom's way.
all are pure, And clear - est light im - part.
Lord are truth And right - eous - ness most pure.
of His word There is a great re - ward.
hid - den faults, And make me pure with - in.

[Selected Stanzas]

6 From willful sins Thy servant keep,
   No vantage let them gain;
From great transgression thus made free,
   I upright shall remain.

7 The words which from my mouth proceed,
   The thoughts within my heart,
Accept, O Lord, for Thou my Rock
   And my Redeemer art.

42 Love for God's Word

PSALM 19 C. M.   KINSMAN   James McGranahan

1. Most per - fect is the law of God, Re - stor - ing those that stray;
2. The pre - cepts of the Lord are right; With joy they fill the heart;
3. The fear of God is un - de - filed And ev - er shall en - dure;
4. They warn from ways of wick - ed - ness Dis - pleas-ing to the Lord,

His tes - ti - mo - ny is most sure, Pro - claim-ing wis - dom's way.
The Lord's com-mand-ments all are pure, And clear - est light im - part.
The stat - utes of the Lord are truth And right-eous-ness most pure.
And in the keep - ing of His word There is a great re - ward.

CHORUS

O how love I Thy law! O how love I Thy law! It is my med - i -
ta - tion all . . . the day. . . O how love I Thy law! O how
all the day. . .

love I Thy law! It is my med - i - ta - tion all the day, (all the day).

     [Selected Stanzas]

43 Mutual Intercession

PSALM 20 L. M. WARD Arranged by Lowell Mason

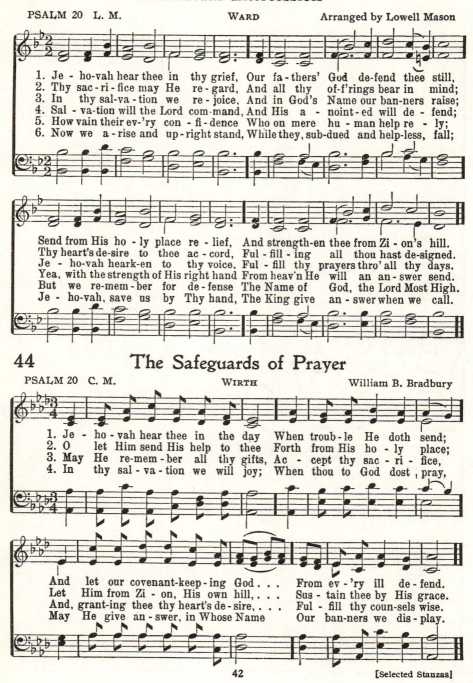

1. Je - ho-vah hear thee in thy grief, Our fa - thers' God de-fend thee still,
2. Thy sac - ri - fice may He re - gard, And all thy of-f'rings bear in mind;
3. In thy sal-va - tion we re - joice, And in God's Name our ban-ners raise;
4. Sal - va - tion will the Lord com-mand, And His a - noint-ed will de - fend;
5. How vain their ev-'ry con - fi - dence Who on mere hu - man help re - ly;
6. Now we a - rise and up-right stand, While they, sub-dued and help-less, fall;

Send from His ho - ly place re - lief, And strength-en thee from Zi - on's hill.
Thy heart's de-sire to thee ac - cord, Ful - fill - ing all thou hast de-signed.
Je - ho-vah heark-en to thy voice, Ful - fill thy prayers thro' all thy days.
Yea, with the strength of His right hand From heav'n He will an an - swer send.
But we re-mem - ber for de - fense The Name of God, the Lord Most High.
Je - ho-vah, save us by Thy hand, The King give an - swer when we call.

44 The Safeguards of Prayer

PSALM 20 C. M. WIRTH William B. Bradbury

1. Je - ho - vah hear thee in the day When troub - le He doth send;
2. O let Him send His help to thee Forth from His ho - ly place;
3. May He re - mem - ber all thy gifts, Ac - cept thy sac - ri - fice,
4. In thy sal - va - tion we will joy; When thou to God dost pray,

And let our covenant-keep-ing God . . . From ev - 'ry ill de - fend.
Let Him from Zi - on, His own hill, . . . Sus - tain thee by His grace.
And, grant-ing thee thy heart's de - sire, . . . Ful - fill thy coun-sels wise.
May He give an - swer, in Whose Name Our ban-ners we dis - play.

[Selected Stanzas]

45   Jesus Crowned and Triumphant

PSALM 21   12s and 9s   LATAKIA   E. G. Taylor

1. Now the King in Thy strength shall be joy - ful, O Lord,
2. All the bless - ings of good - ness Thou free - ly didst give;
3. Thro' sal - va - tion from Thee hath His fame spread a - broad,
4. For the King in the strength of Je - ho - vah Most High
5. By the hand of Thy might and Thy an - ger de - stroyed,
6. Thou wilt speed - i - ly make them turn back - ward in flight,

Thy sal - va - tion shall make Him re - joice;
With the pur - est of gold He is crowned;
Thou didst glo - ry and hon - or im - part;
Did un - wav - er - ing con - fi - dence place;
All Thy foes and their off - spring shall fail;
When Thy ar - rows are aimed to de - stroy.

For the wish of His heart Thou didst free - ly ac - cord,
When He asked of Thee life Thou hast made Him to live
Thou hast made Him most bless - ed for - ev - er, O God,
On the Name of Je - ho - vah He still will re - ly,
By the e - vil they planned and the craft they em - ployed
O Je - ho - vah, be Thou far ex - alt - ed in might,

The re - quest of His sup - pli - ant voice.
While the a - ges shall cir - cle a - round.
And Thy pres - ence hath glad - dened His heart.
And shall stand ev - er - more in His grace.
They shall nev - er a - gainst Thee pre - vail.
And Thy pow'r shall our prais - es em - ploy.

46 The Coronation of Jesus Christ

PSALM 21 L. M.   FALCONER   Alexander B. Morton

1. The King re - joic-eth in Thy strength, In Thy sal-va - tion, Lord Most High,
2. A king - ly crown Thou giv-est Him, Thy blessings meet Him on His ways;
3. With maj - es - ty and hon - or crowned, How great His glo-ry in Thy grace!
4. The King doth in Je - ho - vah trust, His lov-ing-kind-ness He hath proved;

For Thou hast filled His heart's de - sire, His prayer Thy love doth not de - ny.
He asked for life, and un - to Him Thou gav-est end - less length of days.
For - ev - er blest, Thou mak-est Him With joy to live be - fore Thy face.
Con - fid - ing in the Lord Most High He stand-eth ev - er - more un-moved.

Copyright, 1901, by United Presbyterian Board of Publication. Used by per.   [Selected Stanzas]

SECOND TUNE   ST. DROSTANE   John B. Dykes

1. The King re - joic-eth in Thy strength, In Thy sal - va - tion, Lord Most High,

For Thou hast filled His heart's de - sire, His prayer Thy love doth not de - ny.

47 The Cross of Calvary

PSALM 22 L. M.   HEBRON   Lowell Mason

1. My God, My God, I cry to Thee; O why hast Thou for-sak-en Me? A - far from Me, Thou dost not heed, Though day and night for help I plead.
2. But Thou art ho - ly in Thy ways, En-throned up - on Thy peo-ple's praise; Our fa - thers put their trust in Thee, Be - lieved, and Thou didst set them free.
3. They cried, and, trust - ing in Thy Name, Were saved, and were not put to shame; But in the dust My hon - or lies, While all re - proach and all de - spise.
4. My words a cause for scorn they make, The lip they curl, the head they shake, And, mock - ing, bid Me trust the Lord Till He sal - va - tion shall af - ford.
5. My trust on Thee I learned to rest When I was on My moth - er's breast; From birth Thou art My God a - lone, Thy care My life has ev - er known.

6 O let Thy strength and presence cheer,
For trouble and distress are near;
Be Thou not far away from Me,
I have no source of help but Thee.

7 Unnumbered foes would do Me wrong,
They press about Me, fierce and strong,
Like beasts of prey their rage they vent,
My courage fails, My strength is spent.

8 Down unto death Thou leadest Me,
Consumed by thirst and agony;
With cruel hate and anger fierce
My helpless hands and feet they pierce.

9 While on My wasted form they stare,
The garments torn from Me they share,
My shame and sorrow heeding not,
And for My robe they cast the lot.

10 O Lord, afar no longer stay;
O Thou My helper, haste, I pray;
From death and evil set Me free;
I live, for Thou didst answer Me.

11 I live and will declare Thy fame
Where brethren gather in Thy Name;
Where all Thy faithful people meet,
I will Thy worthy praise repeat.

48

A Call to Praise

PSALM 22 L. M. PARK STREET Frederick M. A. Venua

1. All ye that fear Je - ho - vah's Name, His glo - ry tell, His
2. The suf-f'ring one He has not spurned Who un - to Him for
3. O Lord, Thy good - ness makes me raise A - mid Thy peo - ple
4. For all the meek Thou wilt pro - vide, They shall be fed and
5. The ends of all the earth shall hear And turn un - to the
6. For His the king - dom, His of right, He rules the na - tions

praise pro - claim; Ye chil - dren of His cho - sen race, Stand ye in
suc - cor turned; From him He has not hid His face, But an-swered
songs of praise; Be - fore all them that fear Thee, now I wor - ship
sat - is - fied; All they that seek the Lord shall live And nev - er-
Lord in fear; All kin - dreds of the earth shall own And wor - ship
by His might; All earth to Him her hom-age brings, The Lord of

awe be - fore His face, Stand ye in awe be - fore His face.
his re - quest in grace, But an-swered his re - quest in grace.
Thee and pay my vow, I wor - ship Thee and pay my vow.
end - ing prais - es give, And nev - er - end - ing prais - es give.
Him as God a - lone, And wor - ship Him as God a - lone.
lords, the King of kings, The Lord of lords, the King of kings.

[Stanzas 12–19]

7 Both rich and poor, both bond and free,
  Shall worship Him with bended knee,
  And children's children shall proclaim
  The glorious honor of His Name.

8 The Lord's unfailing righteousness
  All generations shall confess,
  From age to age shall men be taught
  What wondrous works the Lord has wrought.

49 The Triumphs of the Gospel

PSALM 22 L. M.　　　　　VISION　　　　　　　William H. Doane

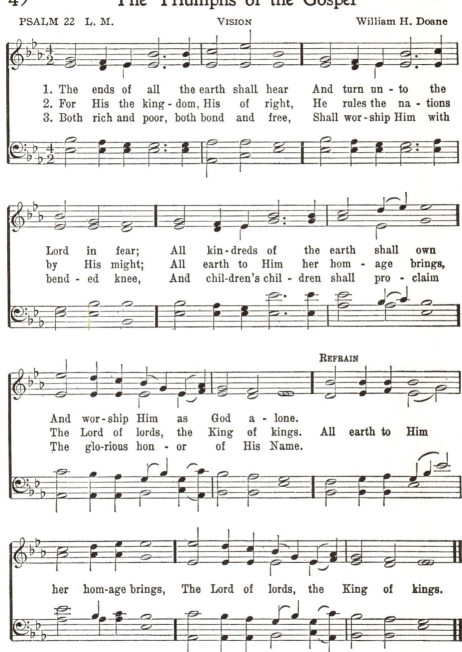

1. The ends of all the earth shall hear And turn un - to the
2. For His the king - dom, His of right, He rules the na - tions
3. Both rich and poor, both bond and free, Shall wor - ship Him with

Lord in fear; All kin - dreds of the earth shall own
by His might; All earth to Him her hom - age brings,
bend - ed knee, And chil-dren's chil - dren shall pro - claim

REFRAIN

And wor - ship Him as God a - lone.
The Lord of lords, the King of kings. All earth to Him
The glo-rious hon - or of His Name.

her hom-age brings, The Lord of lords, the King of kings.

[Selected Stanzas]

50 The Dominion of Jesus Christ

PSALM 22 7s and 6s   TOURS   Berthold Tours

1. Come, ye that fear Je - ho - vah, Ye saints, your voi - ces raise;
2. All kin-dreds of the na - tions To Christ the Lord shall turn,
3. Both high and low shall wor - ship, Both strong and weak shall bend,

Come, stand in awe be - fore Him, And sing His glo - rious praise.
Thro' earth's re - mot - est re - gions His al - tar - fires shall burn.
A faith - ful Church shall serve Him Till gen - er - a - tions end.

Ye low - ly and af - flict - ed Who on His word re - ly,
All king-dom, pow'r, and glo - ry Be - long to Him a - lone;
His praise shall be re - count - ed To na - tions yet to be,

Your heart shall live for - ev - er, The Lord will sat - is - fy.
He rul - eth o'er the na - tions, Kings bow be - fore His throne.
The tri - umphs of His jus - tice A new - born world shall see.

[Selected Stanzas]

Witness-Bearing and Grateful Praise

PSALM 22 C. M.   BOVINA   Laura A. Tate

1. A - mid the throng-ing wor - ship-ers Je - ho - vah will I bless;
2. The bur - den of the sor - row - ful The Lord will not de - spise;
3. He feeds with good the hum - ble soul And sat - is - fies the meek,

Be - fore my breth - ren, gath - ered there, His Name will I con - fess.
He has not turned from those that mourn, He heark - ens to their cries.
And they shall live and praise the Lord Who for His mer - cy seek.

Come, praise Him, ye that fear the Lord, Ye chil - dren of His grace;
His good - ness makes me join the throng Where saints His praise pro - claim,
The ends of all the earth take tho't, The na - tions seek the Lord;

With rev - 'rence sound His glo - ries forth And bow be - fore His face.
And there will I ful - fill my vows 'Mid those who fear His Name.
They wor - ship Him, the King of kings, In earth and heav'n a - dored.

[Selected Stanzas]

The Guardian Care of God

PSALM 23 8s, 7s, 4   CORONÆ   William H. Monk

1. Thou, Je - ho - vah, art my Shep-herd, There-fore I no want shall know;
2. For Thy Name's sake Thou dost guide me In the paths of right-eous-ness;
3. Thou pre - par - est me a ta - ble In the pres-ence of the foe;
4. Sure - ly grace and lov-ing-kind-ness Shall for - ev - er fol - low me,

In green pas - tures Thou dost rest me, Lead - est where still wa-ters flow,
Tho' I walk the vale of shad-ows, Fears no more my soul op - press;
Thou my head with oil a - noint-est, Yea, my cup doth o - ver - flow.
Till, my days of life all end - ed, Ev - er-more my home shall be,

And, when faint - ing, Sweet re - fresh-ment dost be - stow.
Thou art with me, With Thy rod and staff to bless.
O my Sav - iour, Hav - ing Thee, no want I know.
O Je - ho - vah, In Thy ho - ly house with Thee.

53

The Lord Our Shepherd

PSALM 23 C. M.   EVAN   William H. Havergal

1. The Lord's my Shep-herd, I'll not want; He makes me down to lie
2. My soul He doth re - store a - gain, And me to walk doth make
3. Yea, though I walk thro' death's dark vale, Yet will I fear no ill,
4. A ta - ble Thou hast fur-nished me In pres-ence of my foes;
5. Good-ness and mer - cy all my life Shall sure-ly fol - low me,

The Lord Our Shepherd

In pas-tures green; He lead-eth me   The qui-et wa-ters by.
With-in the paths of right-eous-ness, E'en for His own Name's sake.
For Thou art with me, and Thy rod   And staff me com-fort still.
My head Thou dost with oil a-noint, And my cup o-ver-flows.
And in God's house for-ev-er-more   My dwell-ing-place shall be.

54 Jesus Our Shepherd

PSALM 23 C. M.   HERMON   Lowell Mason

1. My faith-ful Shep-herd is the Lord, Sup-ply-ing
2. He ten-der-ly re-stores my soul When I am
3. Thro' death's dark val-ley though I walk, No e-vil
4. A ta-ble Thou dost spread for me In pres-ence
5. Thro' life Thy good-ness and Thy grace Shall dai-ly

all . . . . . my needs; In pas-tures green He
in . . . . . dis-tress, And for His Name's sake
will . . . . . I fear; Thy rod and staff will
of . . . . . my foes; Thou hast a-noint-ed
fol - - - - low me; And I, with-in Thy

makes me rest, By qui-et wa-ters leads.
guides my feet, In paths of right-eous-ness.
com-fort me, For Thou art ev-er near.
me with oil, My cup of joy o'er-flows.
house, O Lord, Shall ev-er dwell with Thee.

The Good Shepherd

PSALM 23 7s and 6s   EWING   Alexander Ewing

1. The Lord my Shep-herd holds me With-in His ten-der care,
2. What-ev-er ill be-tides me, He will re-store and bless;
3. My food Thou dost ap-point me, Sup-plied be-fore my foes;

And with His flock He folds me, No want shall find me there.
For His Name's sake He guides me In paths of right-eous-ness.
With oil Thou dost a-noint me, My cup of bliss o'er-flows.

In pas-tures green He feeds me, With plen-ty I am blest;
Thy rod and staff shall cheer me In death's dark vale and shade,
Thy good-ness, Lord, shall guide me, Thy mer-cy cheer my way;

By qui-et streams He leads me And makes me safe-ly rest.
For Thou wilt then be near me: I shall not be a-fraid.
A home Thou wilt pro-vide me With-in Thy house for aye.

56 The Saviour's Constant Presence

PSALM 23 10s and 4s · LUX BENIGNA · John B. Dykes

1. My Shep-herd is the Lord Who knows my needs, And I am
2. Tho' in death's vale and shad-ow be my way I fear no
3. The good-ness and the mer-cy that have aye Up-on me

blest; By qui-et streams, in pas-tures green, He leads
ill, For Thou art near, Thy rod and staff my stay
shone Shall sure-ly fol-low me thro' all the way

And makes me rest. My soul He saves and for His own Name's
And com-fort still. My ta-ble Thou dost spread be-fore my
Till life is done; And ev-er-more Je-ho-vah's house shall

sake .... He guides my feet the paths of right to take.
foes, ... My head Thou dost a-noint, my cup o'er-flows.
be .... My dwell-ing-place thro' all e-ter-ni-ty.

57   Conditions of Approach to God

PSALM 24 11s

ADESTE FIDELES

Anonymous

1. The earth and the full-ness with which it is stored, The world and its dwell-ers be-
2. What man shall the hill of Je-ho-vah as-cend, And who in the place of His
3. That man ev-er blest of Je-ho-vah shall live, The God of sal-va-tion shall

long to the Lord; For He on the seas its foun-da-tions has laid, And firm on the
pres-ence at-tend? The man of pure heart, and of hands without stain, Who swears not to
righteousness give; For this is the peo-ple, yea, this is the race, The Is-ra-el

wa-ters its pil-lars has stayed, And firm on the wa-ters its pil-lars has stayed.
falsehood nor loves what is vain, Who swears not to falsehood nor loves what is vain.
true that are seek-ing His face, The Is-ra-el true that are seek-ing His face.

58   The Triumphal Ascension of Christ

PSALM 24 11s

LANSING

Charles H. Gabriel

1. Ye gates, lift your heads, the glad sum-mons o-bey, Ye doors ev-er-
2. What King of all glo-ry is this that ye sing? The Lord, strong and
3. The King of all glo-ry high hon-ors a-wait, The King of all

54

The Triumphal Ascension of Christ

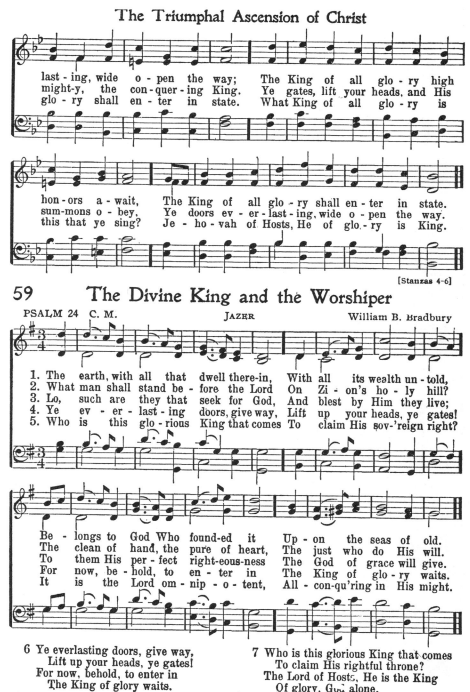

last-ing, wide o-pen the way; The King of all glo-ry high
might-y, the con-quer-ing King. Ye gates, lift your heads, and His
glo-ry shall en-ter in state. What King of all glo-ry is

hon-ors a-wait, The King of all glo-ry shall en-ter in state.
sum-mons o-bey, Ye doors ev-er-last-ing, wide o-pen the way.
this that ye sing? Je-ho-vah of Hosts, He of glo-ry is King.

[Stanzas 4-6]

59 The Divine King and the Worshiper

PSALM 24 C. M.   JAZER   William B. Bradbury

1. The earth, with all that dwell there-in, With all its wealth un-told,
2. What man shall stand be-fore the Lord On Zi-on's ho-ly hill?
3. Lo, such are they that seek for God, And blest by Him they live;
4. Ye ev-er-last-ing doors, give way, Lift up your heads, ye gates!
5. Who is this glo-rious King that comes To claim His sov-'reign right?

Be-longs to God Who found-ed it Up-on the seas of old.
The clean of hand, the pure of heart, The just who do His will.
To them His per-fect right-eous-ness The God of grace will give.
For now, be-hold, to en-ter in The King of glo-ry waits.
It is the Lord om-nip-o-tent, All-con-qu'ring in His might.

6 Ye everlasting doors, give way,
   Lift up your heads, ye gates!
For now, behold, to enter in
   The King of glory waits.

7 Who is this glorious King that comes
   To claim His rightful throne?
The Lord of Hosts, He is the King
   Of glory, God alone.

55

60 Prayer for Defense and Guidance

PSALM 25 S. M.   DENNIS   Arranged from Hans G. Nägeli

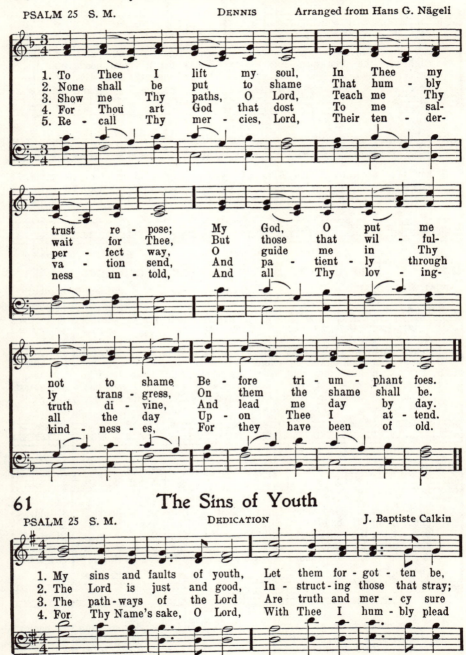

1. To Thee I lift my soul, In Thee my
2. None shall be put to shame That humbly
3. Show me Thy paths, O Lord, Teach me Thy
4. For Thou art God that dost To me sal-
5. Re - call Thy mer - cies, Lord, Their ten - der-

trust re - pose; My God, O put me
wait for Thee, But those that wil - ful-
per - fect way, O guide me in Thy
va - tion send, And pa - tient - ly through
ness un - told, And all Thy lov - ing-

not to shame Be - fore tri - um - phant foes.
ly trans - gress, On them the shame shall be.
truth di - vine, And lead me day by day.
all the day Up - on Thee I at - tend.
kind - ness - es, For they have been of old.

61 The Sins of Youth

PSALM 25 S. M.   DEDICATION   J. Baptiste Calkin

1. My sins and faults of youth, Let them for - got - ten be,
2. The Lord is just and good, In - struct - ing those that stray;
3. The path - ways of the Lord Are truth and mer - cy sure
4. For Thy Name's sake, O Lord, With Thee I hum - bly plead

The Sins of Youth

And for Thy ten-der mer-cies' sake, O Lord, re-mem-ber me.
The meek He will in judg-ment guide And make them know His way.
To such as keep His cov-e-nant And test-ti-mo-nies pure.
To par-don my in-iq-ui-ty, For it is great in-deed.

[Stanzas 6–9]

62   The Friendship of the Lord

PSALM 25 S. M.   THATCHER   Arranged from Handel

1. The man that fears the Lord God's way shall
2. The friend-ship of the Lord Is ev-er
3. My eyes are ev-er-more Tow'rd Thee, O
4. O turn to me Thy face, To me Thy

un-der-stand; His soul shall ev-er
with His own, And un-to those that
Lord, Whose care Shall sure-ly save my
mer-cy show, For I am ver-y

dwell at ease, His chil-dren rule the land.
fear His Name His faith-ful-ness is shown.
heed-less feet From ev-'ry hid-den snare.
des-o-late And brought ex-ceed-ing low.

57   [Stanzas 10–13]

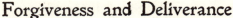

63 Forgiveness and Deliverance

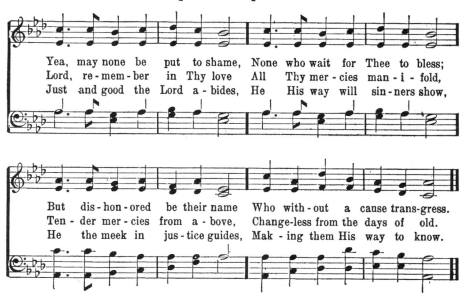

Yea, may none be put to shame, None who wait for Thee to bless;
Lord, re-mem-ber in Thy love All Thy mer-cies man-i-fold,
Just and good the Lord a-bides, He His way will sin-ners show,

But dis-hon-ored be their name Who with-out a cause trans-gress.
Ten-der mer-cies from a-bove, Change-less from the days of old.
He the meek in jus-tice guides, Mak-ing them His way to know.

65 The Blessings of the God-Fearing

PSALM 25 7s   EVENING PRAYER   Alberto Randegger

1. Grace and truth shall mark the way Where the Lord His own will lead,
2. For Thy Name's sake hear Thou me, For Thy mer-cy, Lord, I wait;
3. He who walks in god-ly fear In the path of truth shall go;
4. They that fear and love the Lord Shall Je-ho-vah's friend-ship know;

If His word they still o-bey And His tes-ti-mo-nies heed.
Par-don my in-iq-ui-ty, For my sin is ver-y great.
Peace shall be his por-tion here, And his sons all good shall know.
He will grace to them ac-cord, And His faith-ful cov-enant show,

[Stanzas 7-10]

66 The Look of Faith

PSALM 25 7s   HOLLEY   George Hews

1. Ev - er are my long - ing eyes Tow'rd the
2. Turn to me, Thy grace im - part, I am
3. Look on my af - flict - ed state, Free - ly
4. Shame me not, I hide in Thee; Truth and

Lord, Whose watch - ful care, When my foes their
des - o - late in - deed; Great the troub - les
all my sins for - give, Mark my foes, their
right - pre - serve me still; Let, O God, Thy

plots de - vise, Keeps my feet from ev - 'ry snare.
of my heart; Save Thou me, O Lord, I plead.
cru - el hate, Keep my soul and let me live.
peo - ple be Now re - deemed from ev - 'ry ill.

[Stanzas 11–14]

67 Aspiration and Supplication

PSALM 25 7s   SEYMOUR   Arranged from von Weber.

1. Lord, to me Thy ways make known, Guide in truth and teach Thou me;
2. Lord, re - mem - ber in Thy love All Thy mer - cies man - i - fold,
3. Sins of youth re - mem - ber not, Nor my tres - pass - es re - cord;
4. Just and good the Lord a - bides, He His way will sin - ners show,
5. Grace and truth shall mark the way Where the Lord His own will lead,

Thou my Sav-iour art a - lone, All the day I wait for Thee.
Ten - der mer - cies from a - bove, Change-less from the days of old.
Let not mer - cy be for - got, For Thy good-ness' sake, O Lord.
He the meek in jus - tice guides, Mak - ing them His way to know.
If His word they still o - bey And His tes - ti - mo - nies heed.

[Selected Stanzas]

68   The Paths of the Lord

PSALM 25   7s   DALLAS   Arranged from Cherubini

1. Grace and truth shall mark the way Where the
2. For Thy Name's sake hear Thou me, For Thy
3. He who walks in god - ly fear In the
4. They that fear and love the Lord Shall Je-

Lord His own will lead, If His word they
mer - cy, Lord, I wait; Par - don my in-
path of truth shall go; Peace shall be His
ho - vah's friend - ship know; He will grace to

still o - bey, And His tes - ti - mo - nies heed.
iq - ui - ty, For my sin is ver - y great.
por - tion here, And His sons all good shall know.
them ac - cord, And His faith - ful cov - enant show.

     [Selected Stanzas]

69 The Petition of a Good Conscience

PSALM 26 C. M. BELIEF English Melody

1. Be Thou my judge, O right-eous Lord, Try Thou my in-most heart;
2. O search me, Lord, and prove me now; Thy mer-cy I a-dore;
3. My hands I wash in in-no-cence And seek Thy al-tar, Lord,
4. The hab-i-ta-tion of Thy house Is ev-er my de-light;
5. Let not the judg-ment fall on me For e-vil men de-creed,

I walk with stead-fast trust in Thee, Nor from Thy ways de-part.
I choose Thy truth to be my guide, And sin-ful ways ab-hor.
That there I may with thank-ful voice Thy won-drous works re-cord.
The place where dwells Thy glo-ry, Lord, Is love-ly in my sight.
For cru-el men and vi-o-lent, In-spired by bribes and greed.

6 But I in my integrity
Will humbly walk with Thee;
O my Redeemer and my Lord,
Be merciful to me.

7 Redeemed by Thee, I stand secure
In peace and happiness;
And in the Church, among Thy saints,
Jehovah I will bless.

70 Integrity of Character

PSALM 26 S. M. ELIZABETH Ernest R. Kroeger

1. Judge my in-teg-ri-ty, The right-eous judge Thou art;
2. Thy mer-cy and Thy grace I love to con-tem-plate;
3. Clean hands, O Lord, I raise As I Thy al-tars seek,
4. O Lord, Thy house I love, Where glo-ry dwells with-in;
5. Re-deem-ing love and grace Be-stow, O Lord, on me;

Prove me, O Lord, ex-am-ine me, And try my in-most heart.
Thy paths of truth my foot-steps trace, And wick-ed men I hate.
Where I may sing in grate-ful praise, And of Thy won-ders speak
O keep my heart se-cure a-bove All fel-low-ship with sin.
A-mong Thy saints how blest my place, For-ev-er prais-ing Thee.

71 The Fearlessness of Faith

PSALM 27 H. M.   MILLENNIUM   Anonymous

1. Je - ho - vah is my light, And my sal - va - tion
2. When e - vil - do - ers came To make my life their
3. My one re - quest has been, And still this prayer I
4. When troub - les round me swell, When fears and dan - gers
5. Up - lift - ed on a rock A - bove my foes a -

near; Who shall my soul af - fright, Or cause my
prey, They stum - bled in their shame And fell in
raise, That I may dwell with - in God's house through
throng, Se - cure - ly I will dwell In His pa -
round, A - mid the bat - tle shock My song shall

heart to fear? While God my strength, my life sus -
sore dis - may; Though hosts make war on ev - 'ry
all my days, Je - ho - vah's beau - ty to ad -
vil - ion strong; With - in the cov - ert of His
still re - sound; Then joy - ful of - f'rings I will

tains, Se - cure from fear my soul re - mains.
side, Still fear - less I in God con - fide.
mire, And in His tem - ple to in - quire.
tent He hides me till the storm is spent.
bring, Je - ho - vah's praise my heart shall sing.

63

72 Entreaty and Hopeful Trust

PSALM 27 H. M. SAMUEL Arthur S. Sullivan

1. Lord, hear me when I pray, And an - swer
2. Hide not Thy face from me, In wrath turn
3. Teach me, O Lord, Thy way, Make plain to
4. Faint - heart - ed would I be, Didst Thou not

me in grace; Oft as I hear Thee say,
not a - way, My help and Sav - iour be,
me my path; Be - cause of foes, I pray,
prom - ise, Lord, I shall Thy good - ness see

Come ye and seek My face, My heart and lips their
For - sake me not, I pray; Should fa - ther, moth - er,
Pro - tect me from their wrath; To false ac - cus - ers,
While Thou dost life ac - cord. Wait on the Lord, nor

an - swer speak, Thy face, Je - ho - vah, will I seek.
both for - sake, The Lord on me will pit - y take.
cru - el foes, O Lord, do not my soul ex - pose.
faint, nor fear, Yea, trust and wait, the Lord is near.

[Stanzas 6–9]

73 The Confidence of Faith

PSALM 27   8s and 6   ST. MARGARET   Albert L. Peace

1. The Lord Al-might-y is my light, He is my
Sav-iour ev-er near, And, since my strength is in His might
Who can dis-tress me or af-fright? What e-vil shall I fear?

2. O Lord, re-gard me when I cry, In mer-cy
hear me when I speak; Thou bidst me seek Thy face, and I,
O Lord, with will-ing heart re-ply, Thy face, Lord, will I seek.

3. Hide not Thy face a-far from me, For Thou a-
lone canst help af-ford; O cast me not a-way from Thee
Nor let my soul for-sak-en be, My Sav-iour and my Lord.

4. Though earth-ly friends no pit-y take, Yet Thy com-
pas-sion knows no end; E'en tho' my fa-ther shall for-sake,
E'en tho' my moth-er's love shall break, The Lord will be my friend.

[Selected Stanzas]

5 My heart had failed in fear and woe
   Unless in God I had believed,
   Assured that He would mercy show
   And that my life His grace should know,
   Nor was my hope deceived.

6 Fear not, though succor be delayed,
   Still wait for God, and He will hear;
   Be strong, nor be thy heart dismayed,
   Wait, and the Lord shall bring thee aid,
   Yea, trust and never fear.

Desire After God

74

PSALM 27 C. M.   NAOMI   Arranged from Hans G. Nägeli

1. O Lord, give ear when with my voice I cry a-loud to Thee;
2. When Thou didst say, Seek ye My face, My answering heart re-plied,
3. Hide not Thy face, nor in Thy wrath Thy serv.- ant put a - way;
4. O God, my Sav - iour, leave me not; Tho' par - ents should for-sake,

Have mer - cy al - so. I en - treat, Give an - swer un - to me.
Thy face, Je - ho - vah, will I seek A - bove all else be - side.
Thou hast a help - er been to me In ev - 'ry troub-lous day.
The Lord, with-in His arms of love, His child will sure - ly take.

[Selected Stanzas]

Invocation and Confident Petition

75

PSALM 28 S. M.   WOOD   Darius E. Jones

1. O Lord, to Thee I cry; Thou art my rock and trust;
2. O hear me when in prayer Thy fa - vor I en - treat;
3. O let me have no part With those that hate the right;
4. But bless - ed be the Lord Who heark - ens when I cry;
5. His help makes glad my heart, And songs of praise I sing;
6. Bless Thy in - her - it - ance, Our Sav - iour be, I pray;

O be not si - lent, lest I die And slum-ber in the dust.
Hear, while I lift im - plor-ing hands Be - fore Thy mer - cy - seat.
For as their works, so their re - ward: Je - ho - vah will re - quite.
The Lord, my strength, my help, my shield, On Him will I re - ly.
Je - ho - vah is His people's strength, The strong-hold of their king.
Sup - ply Thou all Thy peo - ple's need, And be their con - stant stay.

Divine Power in Manifestation

PSALM 29 12s and 11s ARLES Charles H. Gabriel

1. Now un-to Je-ho-vah, ye sons of the might-y,
2. The voice of Je-ho-vah, the God of all glo-ry,
3. His voice makes the moun-tains and des-erts to trem-ble,
4. The Lord ruled in might at the flood of great wa-ters,

All glo-ry and strength and do-min-ion ac-cord;
Rolls o-ver the wa-ters, the thun-ders a-wake;
Wild beasts are af-fright-ed, the for-ests laid bare,
A King Whose do-min-ion is nev-er to cease;

As-cribe to Him glo-ry, and ren-der Him hon-or,
The voice of Je-ho-vah, ma-jes-tic and might-y,
And thro' all cre-a-tion, His won-der-ful tem-ple,
The Lord will give bless-ing and strength to His peo-ple,

In beau-ty of ho-li-ness wor-ship the Lord.
Is heard, and the ce-dars of Leb-a-non break.
All things He has fash-ioned His glo-ry de-clare.
The Lord all His peo-ple will com-fort with peace.

77

Commemoration and Praise

PSALM 30   7s and 6s   CRUCIFIX   Greek Melody

1. O Lord, by Thee de-liv-ered, I Thee with songs ex-tol; My foes Thou hast not
2. His ho-ly Name re-mem-ber, Ye saints, Je-ho-vah praise; His an-ger lasts a
3. In prosp'rous days I boast-ed, Unmoved I shall re-main, For, Lord, by Thy good
4. What prof-it if I per-ish, If life Thou dost not spare? Shall dust repeat Thy
5. My grief is turned to glad-ness, To Thee my thanks I raise, Who hast removed my

suf-fered To glo-ry o'er my fall. O Lord, my God, I sought Thee, And Thou didst
mo-ment, His fa-vor all our days; For sor-row, like a pil-grim, May tar-ry
fa-vor My cause Thou didst maintain; I soon was sore-ly troub-led, For Thou didst
prais-es, Shall it Thy truth de-clare? O Lord, on me have mer-cy, And my pe-
sor-row And gird-ed me with praise; And now, no lon-ger si-lent, My heart Thy

heal and save; Thou, Lord, from death didst ransom And keep me from the grave.
for a night, But joy the heart will glad-den When dawns the morning light.
hide Thy face; I cried to Thee, Je-ho-vah, I sought Je-ho-vah's grace.
ti-tion hear; That Thou mayst be my help-er, In mer-cy, Lord, ap-pear.
praise will sing; O Lord, my God, for-ev-er My thanks to Thee I bring.

By permission of C. C. Converse

78

Grateful Praise

PSALM 30   H. M.   AVALON   Arranged by William H. Doane

1. Lord, I will praise Thy Name, For Thou hast set me free, Nor suf-fered foes to
2. Thou hast my soul re-stored When I was near the grave, And from the depths, O
3. His wrath is quick-ly past, His fa-vor lives for aye; Tho' grief a night may

By permission of W. H. Doane

68

Grateful Praise

claim A tri-umph o - ver me; O Lord, my God, to Thee I cried
Lord, Thou gra-cious-ly didst save; O ye His saints, sing to the Lord,
last, Joy comes at break of day; In my pros - per - i - ty se - cure

And Thou hast health and strength supplied, And Thou hast health and strength supplied.
With thanks His ho - li - ness re - cord, With thanks His ho - li - ness re - cord.
I said, My peace shall still en - dure; I said, My peace shall still en-dure.

79 Thoughts on God's Loving-Kindness

PSALM 30 H. M.   CLARKSVILLE   William B. Bradbury

1. My God, it was Thy grace That did my strength sup - ply;
2. What prof - it can it bring If life Thou dost not spare?
3. With grief to glad - ness turned, With sor - row changed to joy,

When Thou didst hide Thy face, Sore troub - led then was I. To
Shall dust Thy prais - es sing, Shall it Thy truth de - clare? Je -
Thy prais - es I have learned, And songs my lips em - ploy; So

Thee I cried, O Lord; to Thee I made my sup - pli - cat - ing plea.
ho - vah hear, in mer - cy hear, My Help - er, Sav-iour, now ap - pear.
shall my tongue thro' life a - dore And praise Thy Name for ev - er-more.

69   [Stanzas 4-6]

80 God Our Resort in Trouble

PSALM 31 C. M. BRECON Nicholas Heins

1. In Thee, O Lord, I put my trust, I call up-on Thy Name;
2. Bow down Thy ear to my re-quest, And swift de-liv-'rance send;
3. Since Thou my rock and for-tress art, My lead-er be, and guide;
4. To Thee my spir-it I com-mend; Re-demp-tion is with Thee,
5. I hate all those that love the false, My trust is in the Lord;
6. For my af-flic-tion Thou hast seen, And known my man-y woes;

O save me in Thy right-eous-ness, Nor let me suf-fer shame.
Be Thou to me a rock of strength, A for-tress to de-fend.
From all temp-ta-tion res-cue me, Thou dost my strength a-bide.
O Thou Je-ho-vah, God of truth, Who hast de-liv-ered me.
I will be glad, and joy-ful-ly Thy mer-cy will re-cord.
Thou hast not let me be en-slaved, But freed me from my foes.

7 Show mercy, Lord, to me distressed,
   And send my soul relief;
My life is spent with bitterness,
   My strength consumed with grief.

8 I mourn and fail because of sin,
   Friends turn in dread away;
Reproached am I and terrified,
   While foes conspire to slay.

9 But, Lord, in Thee is all my trust,
   Thou art my God, I cried;
My life, my times are in Thy hand,
   I in Thy strength confide.

10 From all that persecute my soul
   Thy gracious help I crave;
O smile upon Thy servant, Lord,
   And in Thy mercy save.

11 Let me not be ashamed, O Lord,
   I plead with Thee to save;
But let the wicked be ashamed,
   And silent in the grave.

12 Yea, let their lips henceforth be mute
   Who words of falsehood seek,
The lips which with contempt and pride
   Against the righteous speak.

81 The Riches of God's Goodness

PSALM 31 C. P. M. ARIEL Arranged from Mozart

1. How great the good - ness kept in store For
2. Se - cured by Thy un - fail - ing grace, In
3. Blest be the Lord, for He hath showed, While
4. Ye saints, Je - ho - vah love and serve, For

those who fear Thee and a - dore In meek hu - mil - i - ty. How
Thee they find a hid - ing-place When foes their plots de - vise; A
giv - ing me a safe a - bode, His love be - yond com - pare; Al-
He the faith-ful will pre-serve, And shield from men of pride; Be

great the deeds with mer - cy fraught Which o - pen - ly Thy hand hath wrought
sure re-treat Thou wilt pre-pare, And keep them safe - ly shel-tered there,
tho' His face He seemed to hide, He ev - er heard me when I cried,
strong and let your hearts be brave, All ye that wait for Him to save,

For those who trust in Thee, For those who trust in Thee.
When strife of tongues shall rise, When strife of tongues shall rise.
And made my wants His care, And made my wants His care.
In God the Lord con - fide, In God the Lord con - fide.

[Stanzas 13-16]

Security in God

PSALM 31 S. M.   LEBANON   John Zundel

1. De - fend me, Lord, from shame, For still I trust in Thee;
2. Thee for my rock I take, My for - tress and my stay;
3. My spir - it un - to Thee I trust - ful - ly com - mend;

Since just and right-eous is Thy Name, From troub - le set me free.
O lead me for Thy own Name's sake And guide me in Thy way.
Je - ho - vah, God of truth, to me Thou didst re - demp - tion send.

O Lord, in mer - cy hear, De - liv - er me with speed;
Lord, Thou dost strength im - part; Then free me from the snare
I hate the false and vain, My trust is in the Lord,

Be my de - fense and ref - uge near, My help in time of need.
Which foes for me, with wick - ed art, Did se - cret - ly pre - pare.
And still my heart in joy - ous strain Thy mer - cy will re - cord.

[Selected Stanzas]

83 Sin and Forgiveness

PSALM 32 7s and 6s   RUTHERFORD   Arranged from Chrétien Urhan

1. How blest is he whose tres - pass Hath free - ly been for - giv'n,
2. While I kept guilt - y si - lence My strength was spent with grief,
3. So let the god - ly seek Thee In times when Thou art near;

Whose sin is whol - ly cov - ered Be - fore the sight of heav'n.
Thy hand was heav - y on me, My soul found no re - lief;
No whelm - ing floods shall reach them, Nor cause their hearts to fear.

Blest he to whom Je - ho - vah Im - put - eth not his sin,
But when I owned my tres - pass, My sin hid not from Thee,
In Thee, O Lord, I hide me, Thou sav - est me from ill,

Who hath a guile - less spir - it, Whose heart is true with - in.
When I con - fessed trans - gres - sion, Then Thou for - gav - est me.
And songs of Thy sal - va - tion My heart with rap - ture thrill.

84 ## Gracious Guidance

PSALM 32   7s and 6s   MODENA   Isaac B. Woodbury

1. I gra-cious-ly will teach thee The way that thou shalt go,
2. The sor-rows of the wick-ed In num-ber shall a-bound,

And with My eye up-on thee My coun-sel make thee know.
But those that trust Je-ho-vah, His mer-cy shall sur-round;

But be ye not un-ru-ly, Or slow to un-der-stand,
Then in the Lord be joy-ful, In song lift up your voice;

Be not per-verse, but will-ing To heed My wise com-mand.
Be glad in God, ye right-eous, Re-joice, ye saints, re-joice.

[Stanzas 4 and 5]

85 ## The Praise of Almighty God

PSALM 33 C. P. M.   ANNETTA   William J. Kirkpatrick

1. Ye right-eous, in the Lord re-joice; 'Tis come-ly that with joy-ful voice
2. For up-right is Je-ho-vah's word, And all the do-ings of the Lord
3. Je-ho-vah speaks, the heav'ns ap-pear; He breathes, and, lo, each shining sphere

The Praise of Almighty God

God's saints His Name should praise. With harp and hymn of glad - ness sing,
In jus - tice have their birth; In judg-ment and in deeds of right
In splen-dor stands ar - rayed; He rolls the wa - ters heap on heap,

Your gift of sweet-est mu - sic bring. To Him a new song raise.
The Lord for - ev - er takes de - light, His good - ness fills the earth.
He stores a - way the might - y deep In gar - ners for it made.

86   The God of Providence and Grace

PSALM 33   C. P. M.   FRANCES   James McGranahan

1. Let all the earth Je - ho - vah fear, Let all that dwell both far and near
2. He makes the na tions' coun-sels vain, The plans the peo-ples would maintain
3. O tru - ly is the na - tion blest Whose God be-fore the world con-fessed

In awe be-fore Him stand; For, lo, He spake and it was done,
Are thwart-ed by His hand; Je - ho-vah's coun-sel stands se - cure,
Je - ho - vah is a - lone; And blest the peo - ple is whom He

And all with sov-'reign pow'r be - gun Stood fast at His com - mand.
His pur - pos - es of heart en - dure, For ev - er - more they stand.
Has made His her - it - age to be, And cho - sen for His own.

     [Stanzas 4-6]

87 God the Only Deliverer

PSALM 33 C. P. M.   WESTMINSTER COLLEGE   German Melody

1. Je - ho - vah from His throne on high Looks down with clear and searching eye
2. Not hu-man strength or mighty hosts, Not charg-ing steeds or war-like boasts
3. Our hope is on Je - ho - vah stayed, In Him our hearts are joy - ful made,

On all that dwell be - low; . . . And He that fashioned heart and mind
Can save from o - ver - throw; . . . But God will save from death and shame
Our help and shield is He; . . . Our trust is in His ho - ly Name,

Looks ev - er down on all man-kind, The works of men to know.
All those who fear and trust His Name, And they no want shall know.
Thy mer - cy, Lord, in faith we claim, As we have hoped in Thee.

[Stanzas 7–9]

88 The Goodness of God Proved

PSALM 34 C. M.   EUPHEMIA   Benjamin C. Unseld

1. The Lord I will at all times bless, In praise my mouth em - ploy;
2. We looked to Him and light re-ceived, A - shamed we shall not be;
3. O taste and see that God is good To all that seek His face;

My soul shall in Je - ho - vah boast, The meek shall hear with joy.
Our hum - ble cry Je - ho - vah heard, From troub - le set us free.
Yea, blest the man that trusts in Him, Con - fid - ing in His grace.

The Goodness of God Proved

O mag-ni-fy the Lord with me, Let us ex-alt His Name;
The an-gel of the Lord en-camps A-round a-bout His own,
O fear the Lord, all ye His saints; No want shall bring dis-tress;

When in dis-tress on Him I called, He to my res-cue came.
De-liv-ers them from all their foes, Lest they be o-ver-thrown.
The li-ons young may pine for food, The saints all good pos-sess.

89 The Secret of a Happy Life

PSALM 34 C. M. ALEXANDRIA William Arnold

1. Ye chil-dren, come, give ear to me And learn Je-ho-vah's fear;
2. Re-strain thy lips from speak-ing guile, From wick-ed speech de-part,
3. Je-ho-vah's eyes are on the just, He heark-ens to their cry;
4. The Lord may suf-fer man-y griefs Up-on the just to fall,
5. By e-vil are the e-vil slain, And they that hate the just;

He who would long and hap-py live, Let him my coun-sel hear.
From e-vil turn and do the good, Seek peace with all thy heart.
A-gainst the wick-ed sets His face, Their ver-y name shall die.
But He will bring them safe-ly through, De-liv-'ring them from all.
But all His serv-ants God re-deems, And safe in Him they trust.

77

[Stanzas 7-11]

90 Testimony and Praise

PSALM 34 L. M. AMES Sigismund Neukomm

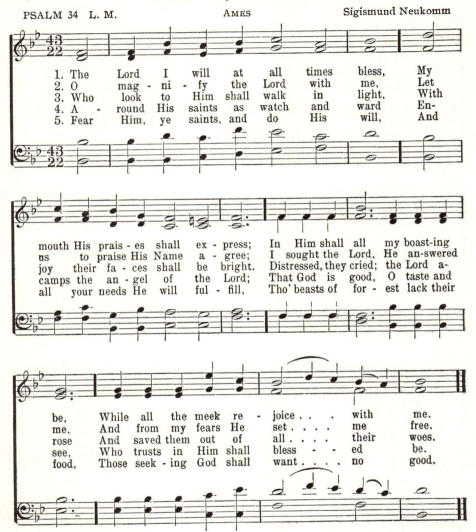

1. The Lord I will at all times bless, My
2. O mag-ni-fy the Lord with me, Let
3. Who look to Him shall walk in light, With
4. A-round His saints as watch and ward En-
5. Fear Him, ye saints, and do His will, And

mouth His prais-es shall ex-press; In Him shall all my boast-ing
us to praise His Name a-gree; I sought the Lord, He an-swered
joy their fa-ces shall be bright. Distressed, they cried; the Lord a-
camps the an-gel of the Lord; That God is good, O taste and
all your needs He will ful-fill, Tho' beasts of for-est lack their

be, While all the meek re-joice . . . with me.
me, And from my fears He set . . . . me free.
rose And saved them out of all . . . . their woes.
see, Who trusts in Him shall bless - ed be.
food, Those seek-ing God shall want . . . . no good.

6 Ye children, come and hear my voice,
And learn to make God's fear your choice;
Who seek long life and happy days
Must learn to walk in wisdom's ways.

7 Who fears the Lord must keep his tongue
From evil and his lips from wrong,
Must do the good, from evil cease,
And ever seek and follow peace.

91 The Safety of Believers

PSALM 34 L. M.　　　　　ABENDS　　　　　Herbert S. Oakeley

1. God guards the good with watch-ful eye, His ear at-ten-tive to their cry,
2. The right-eous cry, Je-ho-vah hears, And rescues them from all their fears;
3. Af-flic-tions on the good must fall, But God will bring them safe thro' all;
4. By e-vil are the e-vil slain, The hope of sin-ful men is vain;
5. The Lord re-demp-tion will pro-vide For all who in His grace con-fide;

A-gainst the wick-ed sets His face, From earth their mem'ry to e-rase.
The Lord draws nigh to bro-ken hearts, To con-trite spir-its help im-parts.
From harmful stroke He will de-fend, And sure and full de-liv-'rance send.
The wick-ed, who the right-eous hate, Their con-dem-na-tion shall be great.
From con-dem-na-tion they are clear Who trust in Him with ho-ly fear.

[Stanzas 8-12]

SECOND TUNE　　　　　PENTECOST　　　　　William Boyd

1. God guards the good with watch-ful eye, His ear at-ten-tive to their cry,
2. The right-eous cry, Je-ho-vah hears, And res-cues them from all their fears;
3. Af-flic-tions on the good must fall, But God will bring them safe thro' all;
4. By e-vil are the e-vil slain, The hope of sin-ful men is vain;
5. The Lord re-demp-tion will pro-vide For all who in His grace con-fide;

A-gainst the wick-ed sets His face, From earth their mem'ry to e-rase.
The Lord draws nigh to bro-ken hearts, To con-trite spir-its help im-parts.
From harm-ful stroke He will de-fend, And sure and full de-liv-'rance send.
The wick-ed, who the right-eous hate, Their con-dem-na-tion shall be great.
From con-dem-na-tion they are clear Who trust in Him with ho-ly fear.

God Our Advocate and Judge

PSALM 35 L. M. CATHERINE E. M. Clark

1. Be Thou my help - er in the strife, O Lord, my
2. A - shamed, con - found - ed let them be Who seek my
3. My soul is joy - ful in the Lord, In His sal-
4. Un - right - eous wit - ness - es have stood And told of
5. O Lord, how long wilt Thou de - lay? My soul for

strong de - fend - er be; Thy might - y shield pro - tect my
ru - in and dis - grace; O let Thy an - gel fight for
va - tion I re - joice; To Him my heart will praise ac-
crimes be - yond be - lief; Re - turn - ing e - vil for my
Thy sal - va - tion waits; My thank - ful - ness I will dis-

life, Thy spear con - front the en - e - my.
me. And drive my foes be - fore his face.
cord And bless His Name with thank - ful voice.
good, They o - ver - whelm my soul with grief.
play A - mid the crowds that throng Thy gates.

A - mid the con - flict, O my Lord, Thy pre - cious
With-out a cause my life they sought, With - out a
For who, O Lord, is like to Thee, De - fend - er
When in af - flic - tion they were sad, I wept and
Let not my en - e - mies re - joice And wrong - ful-

God Our Advocate and Judge

prom - ise	let	me	hear,	The	faith - ful,	re	-	as - sur - ing
cause	their	plots	they	laid;	Them-selves with - in		their	snares be
of	the	poor	and	meek?	The	need - y	Thy	sal - va - tion
made	their	grief	my	own;	But	in	my	troub - le	they	are
ly	ex - ult	o'er	me;	They	speak	not	peace,	but	lift	their

word:	I	am	thy	Sav - iour,	do	not	fear.
caught,	And	be	my	craft - y	foes	dis - mayed.
see	When might - y	foes	their	ru - in	seek.
glad	And	strive	that	I	may	be	o'er - thrown.
voice	To	troub - le	those	that	peace - ful	be.

6 My foes with joy my woes survey,
    But Thou, O Lord, hast seen it all;
O be no longer far away,
    Nor silent when on Thee I call.
O haste to my deliverance now,
    O Lord, my righteous cause maintain;
My Lord and God alone art Thou;
    Awake, and make Thy justice plain.

7 O Lord my God, I look to Thee,
    Be Thou my righteous Judge, I pray;
Let not my foes exult o'er me
    And laugh with joy at my dismay.
With shame and trouble those requite
    Who would my righteous cause destroy;
But those who in the good delight,
    Let them be glad and shout for joy.

8 Yea, let the Lord be magnified,
    Because Thy servants Thou dost bless;
And I, from morn till eventide,
    Will daily praise Thy righteousness.
My soul is joyful in the Lord,
    In His salvation I rejoice;
To Him my heart will praise accord
    And bless His Name with thankful voice.

81

93 · A Wicked Life

PSALM 36 C. M. CHIMES Lowell Mason

1. The tres - pass of the wick - ed man Most
2. He cher - ish - es the emp - ty hope, Al-
3. The words he ut - ters with his mouth Are
4. While on his bed his thought he gives To

plain - ly tes - ti - fies That fear of God's most
though his sin be great, It nev - er shall be
wick - ed - ness and lies; He keeps him - self from
plan - ning wick - ed - ness; He sets him - self in

ho - ly Name Is not be - fore his eyes.
brought to light And viewed with right - eous hate.
do - ing good, And ceas - es to be wise.
e - vil ways, He shuns not to trans - gress.

94 The Love and Justice of God

PSALM 36 C. M. CADDO William B. Bradbury

1. Thy mer - cy and Thy truth, O Lord, Tran-scend the loft - y sky;
2. Lord, Thou pre - serv - est man and beast; Since Thou art ev - er kind,
3. With the a - bun-dance of Thy house We shall be sat - is - fied,
4. The foun-tain of e - ter - nal life Is found a - lone with Thee,
5. From those that know Thee may Thy love And mer - cy ne'er de - part,
6. The work-ers of in - iq - ui - ty Are fall - en ut - ter - ly;

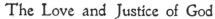

The Love and Justice of God

Thy judg-ments are a might-y deep, And as the moun-tains high.
Be - neath the shad - ow of Thy wings We may a ref - uge find.
From riv - ers of un - fail - ing joy Our thirst shall be sup-plied.
And in the bright-ness of Thy light We clear - ly light shall see.
And may Thy jus - tice still pro - tect And bless the up - right heart.
They shall not tri - umph in their pride, Or drive my soul from Thee.

[Stanzas 5-10]

95 An Answer to Distrust

PSALM 37 C. P. M.   JOSEPHINE   Ernest R. Kroeger

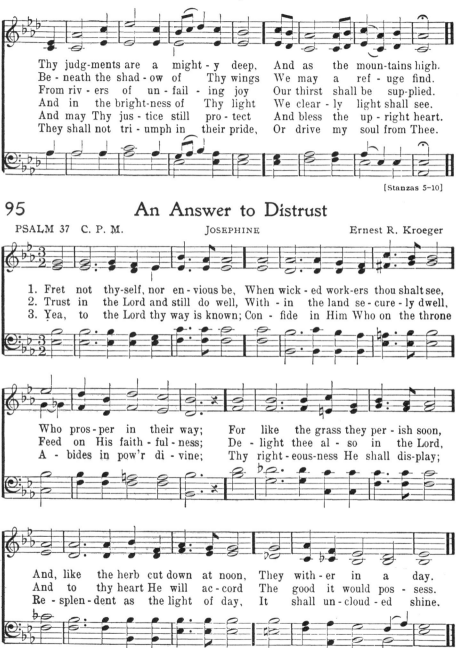

1. Fret not thy-self, nor en - vious be, When wick - ed work-ers thou shalt see,
2. Trust in the Lord and still do well, With - in the land se - cure - ly dwell,
3. Yea, to the Lord thy way is known; Con - fide in Him Who on the throne

Who pros-per in their way; For like the grass they per - ish soon,
Feed on His faith - ful - ness; De - light thee al - so in the Lord,
A - bides in pow'r di - vine; Thy right-eous-ness He shall dis-play;

And, like the herb cut down at noon, They with - er in a day.
And to thy heart He will ac - cord The good it would pos - sess.
Re - splen - dent as the light of day, It shall un - cloud - ed shine.

96   Contrasted Characters

PSALM 37   C. P. M.   KINGSTON   William Hayes

1. Rest in the Lord and be thou still, With pa-tience wait His ho-ly will,
2. The e-vil-do-er soon shall die, But those that on the Lord re-ly
3. Yea, thou shalt soon con-sid-er well The place where they were wont to dwell,
4. The vile may plot a-gainst the just Who in the Lord Je-ho-vah trust,

En-dur-ing to the end. Fret not tho' sin-ners' gains in-crease;
Shall all the land ob-tain; A lit-tle while and thou shalt see
And it shall not be found; But saints shall all the land pos-sess,
But God will scorn them all; The Lord their com-ing day shall see,

For-sake thy wrath, from an-ger cease; It will to e-vil tend.
That wick-ed men cut off shall be, They shall be sought in vain.
And find de-light and hap-pi-ness Where fruits of peace a-bound.
When bro-ken all their pow'r shall be, And ru-in on them fall.

[Stanzas 4-7]

97   Well-Doing and Well-Being

PSALM 37   C. P. M.   GANGES   S. Chandler

1. A lit-tle that the right-eous hold Is bet-ter far than wealth un-told
2. He knows the days the per-fect live, To them a her-it-age will give
3. Al-though the wick-ed pros-pered seem, At last they van-ish like a dream
4. They bor-row oft and pay not back, But right-eous men do noth-ing lack,

84

Well-Doing and Well-Being

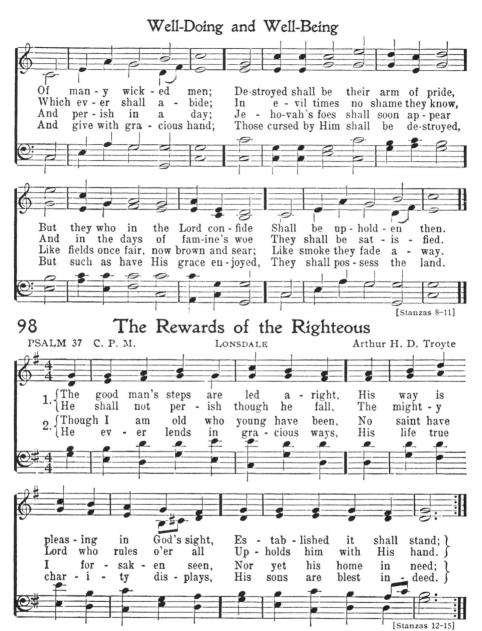

Of man-y wick-ed men; De-stroyed shall be their arm of pride,
Which ev-er shall a - bide; In e - vil times no shame they know,
And per-ish in a day; Je - ho-vah's foes shall soon ap-pear
And give with gra - cious hand; Those cursed by Him shall be de-stroyed,

But they who in the Lord con-fide Shall be up-hold-en then.
And in the days of fam-ine's woe They shall be sat - is - fied.
Like fields once fair, now brown and sear; Like smoke they fade a - way.
But such as have His grace en-joyed, They shall pos-sess the land.

[Stanzas 8–11]

98 The Rewards of the Righteous

PSALM 37 C. P. M. LONSDALE Arthur H. D. Troyte

1. { The good man's steps are led a - right, His way is
   { He shall not per - ish though he fall, The might - y

2. { Though I am old who young have been, No saint have
   { He ev - er lends in gra - cious ways, His life true

pleas - ing in God's sight, Es - tab - lished it shall stand; }
Lord who rules o'er all Up - holds him with His hand. }
I for - sak - en seen, Nor yet his home in need; }
char - i - ty dis - plays, His sons are blest in - deed. }

[Stanzas 12–15]

3 Depart from evil, do thou well,
  And evermore securely dwell;
   Jehovah loves the right.
His faithfulness His saints have proved,
Forever they shall stand unmoved,
   But sinners God will smite.

4 The righteous, through His favoring hand,
  Shall yet inherit all the land
   And dwell therein for aye;
He talks of wisdom and of right,
In God's pure law is his delight,
   His steps go not astray.

The Righteous and the Evil-Doer

PSALM 37 C. P. M. RAPTURE Edward Harwood

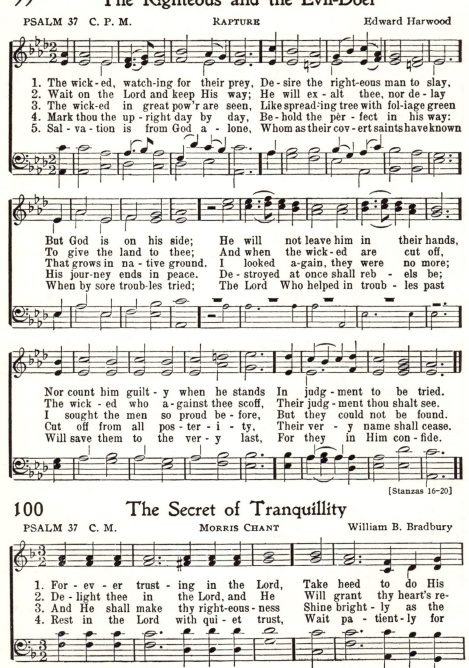

1. The wick-ed, watch-ing for their prey, De-sire the right-eous man to slay,
2. Wait on the Lord and keep His way; He will ex-alt thee, nor de-lay
3. The wick-ed in great pow'r are seen, Like spread-ing tree with fol-iage green
4. Mark thou the up-right day by day, Be-hold the per-fect in his way:
5. Sal-va-tion is from God a-lone, Whom as their cov-ert saints have known

But God is on his side; He will not leave him in their hands,
To give the land to thee; And when the wick-ed are cut off,
That grows in na-tive ground. I looked a-gain, they were no more;
His jour-ney ends in peace. De-stroyed at once shall reb-els be;
When by sore troub-les tried; The Lord Who helped in troub-les past

Nor count him guilt-y when he stands In judg-ment to be tried.
The wick-ed who a-gainst thee scoff, Their judg-ment thou shalt see.
I sought the men so proud be-fore, But they could not be found.
Cut off from all pos-ter-i-ty, Their ver-y name shall cease.
Will save them to the ver-y last, For they in Him con-fide.

[Stanzas 16-20]

100 The Secret of Tranquillity

PSALM 37 C. M. MORRIS CHANT William B. Bradbury

1. For-ev-er trust-ing in the Lord, Take heed to do His
2. De-light thee in the Lord, and He Will grant thy heart's re-
3. And He shall make thy right-eous-ness Shine bright-ly as the
4. Rest in the Lord with qui-et trust, Wait pa-tient-ly for

The Secret of Tranquillity

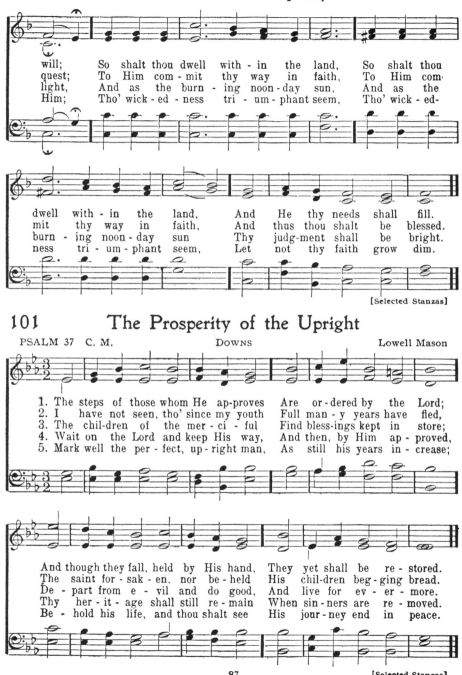

will; | So shalt thou dwell with-in the land, | So shalt thou
quest; | To Him com-mit thy way in faith, | To Him com-
light, | And as the burn-ing noon-day sun, | And as the
Him; | Tho' wick-ed-ness tri-um-phant seem, | Tho' wick-ed-

dwell with-in the land, | And He thy needs shall fill.
mit thy way in faith, | And thus thou shalt be blessed.
burn-ing noon-day sun | Thy judg-ment shall be bright.
ness tri-um-phant seem, | Let not thy faith grow dim.

[Selected Stanzas]

101 The Prosperity of the Upright

PSALM 37 C. M.   DOWNS   Lowell Mason

1. The steps of those whom He ap-proves | Are or-dered by the Lord;
2. I have not seen, tho' since my youth | Full man-y years have fled,
3. The chil-dren of the mer-ci-ful | Find bless-ings kept in store;
4. Wait on the Lord and keep His way, | And then, by Him ap-proved,
5. Mark well the per-fect, up-right man, | As still his years in-crease;

And though they fall, held by His hand, | They yet shall be re-stored.
The saint for-sak-en, nor be-held | His chil-dren beg-ging bread.
De-part from e-vil and do good, | And live for ev-er-more.
Thy her-it-age shall still re-main | When sin-ners are re-moved.
Be-hold his life, and thou shalt see | His jour-ney end in peace.

87   [Selected Stanzas]

102 Penitential Grief and Supplication

PSALM 38   8s and 7s   ST SYLVESTER   John B. Dykes

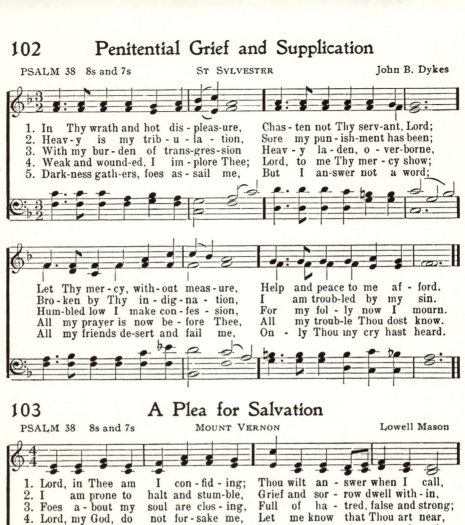

1. In Thy wrath and hot dis-pleas-ure,   Chas-ten not Thy serv-ant, Lord;
2. Heav-y is my trib-u-la-tion,   Sore my pun-ish-ment has been;
3. With my bur-den of trans-gres-sion   Heav-y la-den, o-ver-borne,
4. Weak and wound-ed, I im-plore Thee;   Lord, to me Thy mer-cy show;
5. Dark-ness gath-ers, foes as-sail me,   But I an-swer not a word;

Let Thy mer-cy, with-out meas-ure,   Help and peace to me af-ford.
Bro-ken by Thy in-dig-na-tion,   I am troub-led by my sin.
Hum-bled low I make con-fes-sion,   For my fol-ly now I mourn.
All my prayer is now be-fore Thee,   All my troub-le Thou dost know.
All my friends de-sert and fail me,   On-ly Thou my cry hast heard.

103 A Plea for Salvation

PSALM 38   8s and 7s   MOUNT VERNON   Lowell Mason

1. Lord, in Thee am I con-fid-ing;   Thou wilt an-swer when I call,
2. I am prone to halt and stum-ble,   Grief and sor-row dwell with-in,
3. Foes a-bout my soul are clos-ing,   Full of ha-tred, false and strong;
4. Lord, my God, do not for-sake me,   Let me know that Thou art near,

Lest my foes, the good de-rid-ing,   Tri-umph in Thy serv-ant's fall.
Shame and guilt my spir-it hum-ble,   I am sor-ry for my sin.
Choos-ing good, I find op-pos-ing   All who love and do the wrong.
Un-der Thy pro-tec-tion take me,   As my Sav-iour now ap-pear.

88   [Stanzas 6–9]

104 The Frailty of Life

PSALM 39 L. M.   BERA   John E. Gould

1. With firm re-solve I held my peace And spake not
   ei-ther bad or good, Lest I should ut-ter sin-ful
   thoughts While wick-ed men be-fore me stood.

2. While I was dumb my grief was stirred, My heart grew
   hot with thought sup-pressed; The while I mused the fire in-
   creased, Then to the Lord I made re-quest.

3. Make me, O Lord, to know my end, Teach me the
   meas-ure of my days, That I may know how frail I
   am, And turn from pride and sin-ful ways.

4. My time is noth-ing in Thy sight, Be-hold, my
   days are but a span; Yea, tru-ly at his best estate, A breath, a fleet-ing breath, is man.

5. Man's life is passed in vain de-sire If troub-led
   years be spent for gain; He knows not whose his wealth shall
   be, And all his toil is but in vain.

6. And now, O Lord, what wait I for? I have no
   hope ex-cept in Thee; Let not un-god-ly men re-
   proach. From all trans-gres-sion set me free.

7 Because Thou didst it I was dumb,
   I spoke no word of rash complaint;
Remove Thy stroke away from me,
   Beneath Thy chastisement I faint.

8 When Thou for his iniquity
   Rebukest and correctest man,
His beauty is consumed away,
   How weak his strength, how vain his plan.

9 Lord, hear my prayer, regard my cry,
   I weep, be Thou my comforter;
I am a stranger here below,
   A pilgrim as my fathers were.

10 O spare me, Lord, avert Thy wrath
   Deal gently with me, I implore,
That I may yet recover strength
   Ere I go hence and be no more.

105 The Brevity of Human Life

PSALM 39 S. M.　　　　　AYLESBURY　　　　　Harvey Camp

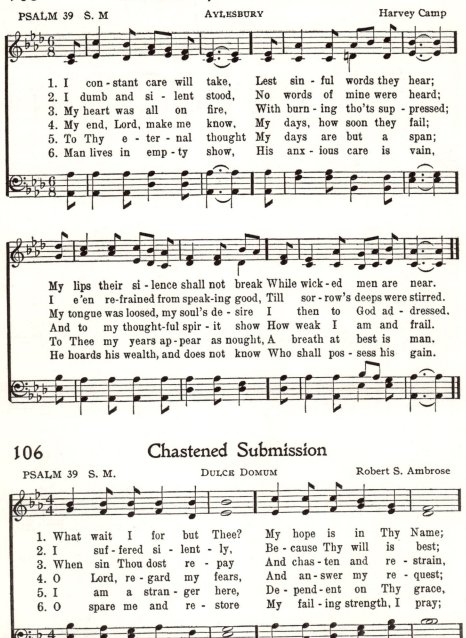

1. I con-stant care will take, Lest sin-ful words they hear;
2. I dumb and si-lent stood, No words of mine were heard;
3. My heart was all on fire, With burn-ing tho'ts sup-pressed;
4. My end, Lord, make me know, My days, how soon they fail;
5. To Thy e-ter-nal thought My days are but a span;
6. Man lives in emp-ty show, His anx-ious care is vain,

My lips their si-lence shall not break While wick-ed men are near.
I e'en re-frained from speak-ing good, Till sor-row's deeps were stirred.
My tongue was loosed, my soul's de-sire I then to God ad-dressed.
And to my thought-ful spir-it show How weak I am and frail.
To Thee my years ap-pear as nought, A breath at best is man.
He hoards his wealth, and does not know Who shall pos-sess his gain.

106 Chastened Submission

PSALM 39 S. M.　　　　　DULCE DOMUM　　　　　Robert S. Ambrose

1. What wait I for but Thee? My hope is in Thy Name;
2. I suf-fered si-lent-ly, Be-cause Thy will is best;
3. When sin Thou dost re-pay, And chas-ten and re-strain,
4. O Lord, re-gard my fears, And an-swer my re-quest;
5. I am a stran-ger here, De-pend-ent on Thy grace,
6. O spare me and re-store My fail-ing strength, I pray;

Chastened Submission

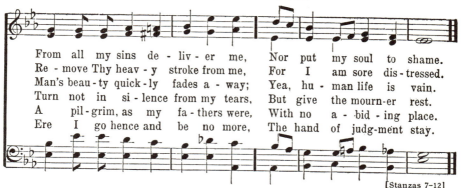

From all my sins de-liv-er me, Nor put my soul to shame.
Re-move Thy heav-y stroke from me, For I am sore dis-tressed.
Man's beau-ty quick-ly fades a-way; Yea, hu-man life is vain.
Turn not in si-lence from my tears, But give the mourn-er rest.
A pil-grim, as my fa-thers were, With no a-bid-ing place.
Ere I go hence and be no more, The hand of judg-ment stay.

[Stanzas 7–12]

107 A Mourner's Entreaties

PSALM 39 S. M.   GREENWOOD   Joseph E. Sweetser

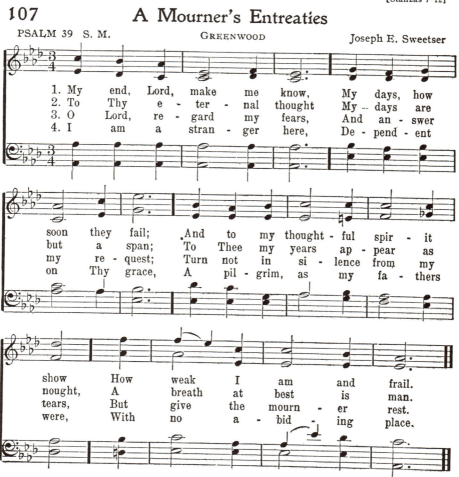

1. My end, Lord, make me know, My days, how
2. To Thy e-ter-nal thought My days are
3. O Lord, re-gard my fears, And an-swer
4. I am a stran-ger here, De-pend-ent

soon they fail; And to my thought-ful spir-it
but a span; To Thee my years ap-pear as
my re-quest; Turn not in si-lence from my
on Thy grace, A pil-grim, as my fa-thers

show How weak I am and frail.
nought, A breath at best is man.
tears, But give the mourn-er rest.
were, With no a-bid-ing place.

[Selected Stanzas]

108 A Recital of Gracious Experience

PSALM 40 C. M. ELIZABETHTOWN George Kingsley

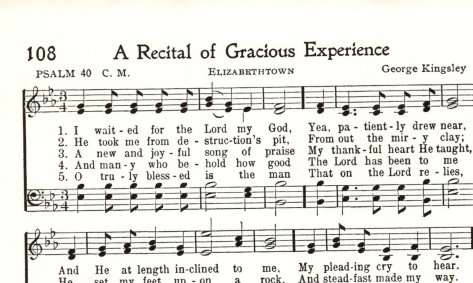

1. I wait - ed for the Lord my God, Yea, pa - tient - ly drew near,
2. He took me from de - struc-tion's pit, From out the mir - y clay;
3. A new and joy - ful song of praise My thank - ful heart He taught,
4. And man - y who be - hold how good The Lord has been to me
5. O tru - ly bless - ed is the man That on the Lord re - lies,

And He at length in-clined to me, My plead-ing cry to hear.
He set my feet up - on a rock, And stead-fast made my way.
A song of glo - ry to our God For all that He has wrought.
Shall learn to fear, and in His Name Their trust hence-forth shall be.
Re - spect-ing not the proud, nor such As turn a - side to lies.

6 O Lord my God, how manifold
  The works which Thou hast wrought,
Ofttimes Thou hast bestowed on us
  Thy care and gracious thought.

7 Thy works and thoughts most wonderful,
  If I of them would speak,
Cannot be numbered, and in vain
  To set them forth I seek.

109 Personal Devotion to God

PSALM 40 C. M. BELMONT William Gardiner

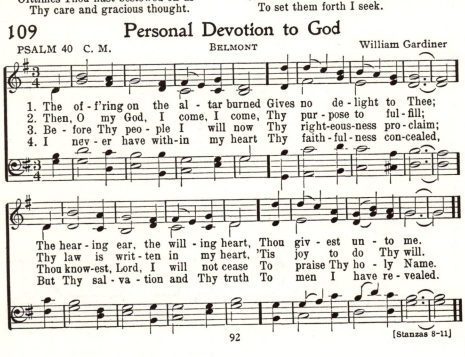

1. The of - f'ring on the al - tar burned Gives no de - light to Thee;
2. Then, O my God, I come, I come, Thy pur - pose to ful - fill;
3. Be - fore Thy peo - ple I will now Thy right-eous-ness pro - claim;
4. I nev - er have with-in my heart Thy faith - ful - ness con-cealed,

The hear - ing ear, the will - ing heart, Thou giv - est un - to me.
Thy law is writ - ten in my heart, 'Tis joy to do Thy will.
Thou know-est, Lord, I will not cease To praise Thy ho - ly Name.
But Thy sal - va - tion and Thy truth To men I have re - vealed.

[Stanzas 8-11]

110 The Mercy of God Besought

PSALM 40 C. M.   RUTH   W. Irving Hartshorn

1. Thy ten-der mer-cies, O my Lord, With-hold not, I im-plore;
2. My sins are more than I can count, My heart has failed for grief;
3. Let all who seek Thee now re-joice, Yea, glad in Thee a-bide,

But let Thy kind-ness and Thy truth Pre-serve me ev-er-more.
Be pleased, O Lord, to res-cue me, O haste to my re-lief.
And, lov-ing Thy sal-va-tion, say, The Lord be mag-ni-fied.

For count-less ills have com-passed me, My sin-ful deeds a-rise;
Be those who seek to hurt my soul Dis-mayed and put to flight,
My low-ly state and bit-ter need The Lord has not for-got;

Yea, they have o-ver-tak-en me; I dare not raise my eyes.
And they them-selves be put to shame Who in my woe de-light.
Thou art my Sav-iour and my help, Come, Lord, and tar-ry not.

93   [Stanzas 12-17]

111 Grace and Gratitude

PSALM 40 L. H. M. DUNSTAN Joseph Barnby

1. I wait-ed for the Lord Most High, And He in-clined to hear my cry; He took me from de-struc-tion's pit And from the mir-y clay; Up-on a rock He set my feet, And stead-fast made my way.

2. A new and joy-ful song of praise He taught my thank-ful heart to raise; And man-y, see-ing me re-stored, Shall fear the Lord and trust; And blest are they that trust the Lord, The hum-ble and the just.

3. O Lord my God, how man-i-fold Thy won-drous works which I be-hold, And all Thy lov-ing, gra-cious thought Thou hast be-stowed on man; To count Thy mer-cies I have sought, But bound-less is their span.

4. Not sac-ri-fice de-lights the Lord, But he who hears and keeps His word; Thou gav-est me to hear Thy will, Thy law is in my heart; I come the Scrip-ture to ful-fill, Glad ti-dings to im-part.

112 An Entreaty for Mercy

PSALM 40 L. H. M.   FLEMMING   Arranged from F. F. Flemming

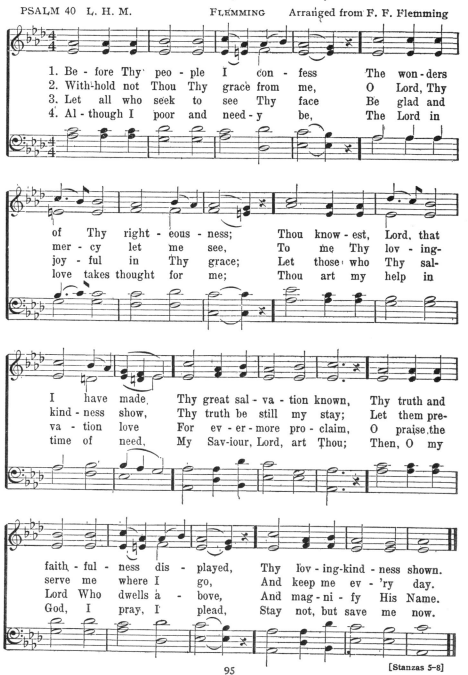

1. Be - fore Thy peo - ple I con - fess The won - ders of Thy right - eous - ness; Thou know - est, Lord, that I have made, Thy great sal - va - tion known, Thy truth and faith - ful - ness dis - played, Thy lov - ing-kind - ness shown.

2. With-hold not Thou Thy grace from me, O Lord, Thy mer - cy let me see, To me Thy lov - ing-kind - ness show, Thy truth be still my stay; Let them pre - serve me where I go, And keep me ev - 'ry day.

3. Let all who seek to see Thy face Be glad and joy - ful in Thy grace; Let those who Thy sal - va - tion love For ev - er - more pro - claim, O praise the Lord Who dwells a - bove, And mag - ni - fy His Name.

4. Al - though I poor and need - y be, The Lord in love takes thought for me; Thou art my help in time of need, My Sav - iour, Lord, art Thou; Then, O my God, I pray, I plead, Stay not, but save me now.

95

[Stanzas 5-8]

113 The Friend of the Poor

PSALM 41 C. M.   SOUTHPORT   George Kingsley

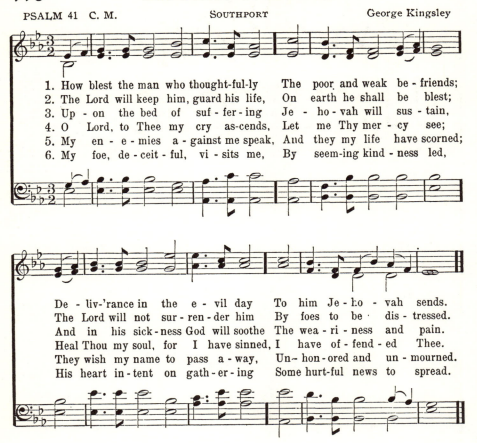

1. How blest the man who thought-ful-ly The poor and weak be-friends;
2. The Lord will keep him, guard his life, On earth he shall be blest;
3. Up-on the bed of suf-fer-ing Je-ho-vah will sus-tain,
4. O Lord, to Thee my cry as-cends, Let me Thy mer-cy see;
5. My en-e-mies a-gainst me speak, And they my life have scorned;
6. My foe, de-ceit-ful, vi-sits me, By seem-ing kind-ness led,

De-liv-'rance in the e-vil day To him Je-ho-vah sends.
The Lord will not sur-ren-der him By foes to be dis-tressed.
And in his sick-ness God will soothe The wea-ri-ness and pain.
Heal Thou my soul, for I have sinned, I have of-fend-ed Thee.
They wish my name to pass a-way, Un-hon-ored and un-mourned.
His heart in-tent on gath-er-ing Some hurt-ful news to spread.

7 My foes, together whispering,
　Their evil plans devise;
Disease, they say, cleaves fast to him,
　Laid low, he shall not rise.

8 Yea, he who was my chosen friend,
　In whom I put my trust,
Who ate my bread, now turns in wrath
　To crush me in the dust.

9 Do Thou, Jehovah, show me grace,
　And raise me up again,
That I with justice may requite
　These base and wicked men.

10 By this I know assuredly
　That I am loved by Thee,
Because my foe does not exult
　In triumph over me.

11 And as for me, in uprightness
　Thou dost uphold me well,
And settest me before Thy face
　For evermore to dwell.

12 Blest be Jehovah, Israel's God
　For evermore. Amen.
Let age to age eternally
　Repeat His praise. Amen.

114 Thirstings for God

PSALM 42 L. M. BACA William B. Bradbury

1. As thirsts the hart for wa-ter brooks, So thirsts my soul, O God, for Thee; It seeks for God, and ev-er looks And longs the liv-ing God to see, And longs the liv-ing God to see.

2. Far from the courts of God, my tears Have been my food by night and day, While con-stant-ly with bit-ter sneers, Where is thy God, the scoff-ers say, Where is thy God, the scoff-ers say.

3. With grief I think of days gone by, When oft I trod the hal-lowed way To Zi-on, prais-ing God on high With throngs who kept the ho-ly day, With throngs who kept the ho-ly day.

4. O why art thou cast down, my soul, And why so troub-led shouldst thou be? Hope thou in God, and Him ex-tol, Who gives His sav-ing help to me, Who gives His sav-ing help to me.

5. Since, O my God, my soul is bowed, In ex-ile far, with bit-ter grief, I turn my thoughts to Thy a-bode For con-so-la-tion and re-lief, For con-so-la-tion and re-lief.

6. With might-y voice deep calls to deep, While rag-ing storms Thy judg-ments tell; The an-gry bil-lows o'er me leap, The waves of sor-row near me swell, The waves of sor-row near me swell.

7 Though troubles surge, yet through the day
   The Lord His gracious help will give,
   And in the night my heart shall pray
   And sing to Him in Whom I live.

8. To God my Rock I cry and say,
   O why hast Thou forgotten me?
   Why go I mourning on my way,
   Oppressed by foes that know not Thee?

9 With anguish as from piercing sword
   Reproach of bitter foes I hear,
   While day by day, with taunting word
   Where is thy God, the scoffers sneer.

10 O why art thou cast down, my soul,
   And why so troubled shouldst thou be?
   Hope thou in God, and Him extol,
   Who gives His saving help to me.

115 Longing After God

PSALM 42 11s and 10s   SANDRINGHAM   Arranged from Joseph Barnby

1. As pants the hart for streams of liv-ing wa-ter,
2. O Lord my God, o'er-whelmed in deep af-flic-tion,
3. Thou wilt com-mand Thy serv-ant's con-so-la-tion,
4. Why, O my soul, art thou cast down with-in me,

So longs my soul, O liv-ing God, for Thee;
Far from Thy rest, to Thee I lift my soul;
Thy lov-ing-kind-ness yet shall cheer my day,
Why art thou troub-led and op-pressed with grief?

I thirst for Thee, for Thee my heart is yearn-ing;
Deep calls to deep and storms of troub-le thun-der,
And in the night Thy song shall be my com-fort;
Hope thou in God, the God of thy sal-va-tion,

When shall I come Thy gra-cious face to see?
While o'er my head the waves and bil-lows roll.
God of my life, to Thee I still will pray.
Hope, and thy God will sure-ly send re-lief.

98   [Selected Stanzas]

116 Remembrance of God

PSALM 42 C. M.
KATHRINE

Charles H. Gabriel

Slowly

1. As pants the hart for cool-ing streams, When heat-ed in the chase,
2. For Thee, my God, the liv-ing God, My thirst-y soul doth pine;
3. Why rest-less, why cast down, my soul? Trust God, Who will em-ploy
4. Why rest-less, why cast down, my soul? Hope still, and thou shalt sing

So longs my soul, O God, for Thee And Thy re-fresh-ing grace.
O when shall I be-hold Thy face, Thou Maj-es-ty Di-vine?
His aid for thee, and change these sighs To thank-ful hymns of joy.
The praise of Him Who is thy God, Thy health's e-ter-nal spring.

Copyright, 1901, by United Presbyterian Board of Publication. Used by per.　[Selected Stanzas]

SECOND TUNE　　　SPOHR　　　Arranged from Spohr

1. As pants the hart for cool-ing streams, When heat-ed in the chase,
2. For Thee, my God, the liv-ing God, My thirst-y soul doth pine;
3. Why rest-less, why cast down, my soul? Trust God, Who will em-ploy
4. Why rest-less, why cast down, my soul? Hope still, and thou shalt sing

So longs my soul, O God, for Thee, And Thy re-fresh-ing grace.
O when shall I be-hold Thy face, Thou Maj-es-ty Di-vine?
His aid for thee, and change these sighs To thank-ful hymns of joy.
The praise of Him Who is thy God, Thy health's e-ter-nal spring.

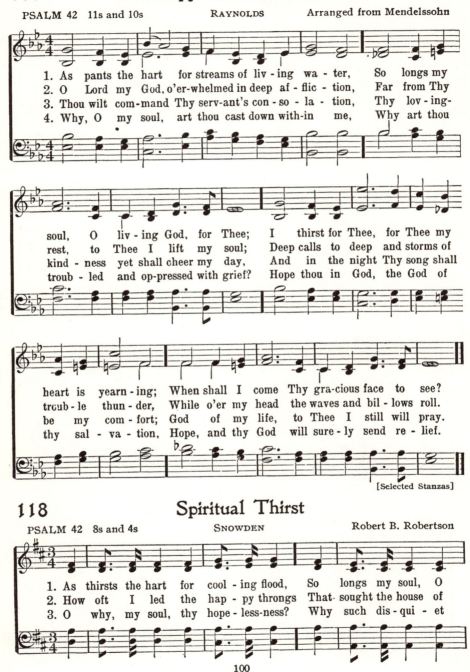

117

Our Support Amidst Distress

PSALM 42   11s and 10s   RAYNOLDS   Arranged from Mendelssohn

1. As pants the hart for streams of liv-ing wa-ter, So longs my
2. O Lord my God, o'er-whelmed in deep af-flic-tion, Far from Thy
3. Thou wilt com-mand Thy serv-ant's con-so-la-tion, Thy lov-ing-
4. Why, O my soul, art thou cast down with-in me, Why art thou

soul, O liv-ing God, for Thee; I thirst for Thee, for Thee my
rest, to Thee I lift my soul; Deep calls to deep and storms of
kind-ness yet shall cheer my day, And in the night Thy song shall
troub-led and op-pressed with grief? Hope thou in God, the God of

heart is yearn-ing; When shall I come Thy gra-cious face to see?
troub-le thun-der, While o'er my head the waves and bil-lows roll.
be my com-fort; God of my life, to Thee I still will pray.
thy sal-va-tion, Hope, and thy God will sure-ly send re-lief.

[Selected Stanzas]

118

Spiritual Thirst

PSALM 42   8s and 4s   SNOWDEN   Robert B. Robertson

1. As thirsts the hart for cool-ing flood, So longs my soul, O
2. How oft I led the hap-py throngs That sought the house of
3. O why, my soul, thy hope-less-ness? Why such dis-qui-et

100

Spiritual Thirst

liv - ing God, To taste Thy grace; When un - to Thee shall I draw near,
God with songs Of joy and praise; I ev - er joined with true de - light
and dis-tress? On God re - ly; For I shall yet be - hold His face,

O when with - in Thy courts ap - pear, And see Thy face?
The mul - ti - tude that kept a - right The ho - ly days.
Who is my God, and I His grace Will mag - ni - fy.

[Selected Stanzas]

119 Devout Longings

PSALM 43 C. M. EDMESTON Isaac B. Woodbury

1. Judge me, O God, and plead my cause A - gainst a god - less race; From men de-
2. O Thou the God of all my strength, Why hast Thou cast me off? Why go I
3. O send Thou forth Thy light and truth, Let them be guides to me, And bring me
4. Then will I to God's al - tar go, To God, my bound-less joy; Yea, God, my
5. Why art thou then cast down, my soul, What should dis-cour-age thee? And why with
6. Hope thou in God; His praise shall yet My thank-ful lips em-ploy; He is the

ceit - ful and un - just De - liv - er in Thy grace, De - liv - er in Thy grace.
mourn-ing all the day, While foes op-press and scoff, While foes op-press and scoff?
to Thy ho - ly hill, Thy dwell-ing-place to see, Thy dwell-ing-place to see.
God, Thy Name to praise My harp I will em-ploy, My harp I will em - ploy.
vex - ing tho'ts art thou Dis-qui - et - ed in me, Dis-qui - et - ed in me?
spring of all my health, My God, my bound-less joy, My God, my bound-less joy.

120 Hope and Trust

PSALM 43 8s and 7s AMARA William O. Perkins

1. Judge me, God of my sal-va-tion, Plead my cause, for Thee I trust;
2. On Thy strength a-lone re-ly-ing, Why am I cast off by Thee,
3. Light and truth, my way at-tend-ing, Send Thou forth to be my guide,
4. At Thy sa-cred al-tar bend-ing, God, my God, my bound-less joy,

Hear my ear-nest sup-pli-ca-tion, Save me from my foes un-just.
In my help-less sor-row sigh-ing, While the foe op-press-es me?
Till Thy ho-ly mount as-cend-ing, I with-in Thy house a-bide.
Harp and voice, in wor-ship blend-ing, For Thy praise will I em-ploy.

CHORUS

O my soul, why art thou griev-ing? What dis-qui-ets and dis-mays?

Hope in God; His help re-ceiv-ing, I shall yet my Sav-iour praise.

102

God the Giver of Victory

PSALM 44 11s   RESIGNATION   Anonymous

1. O God, we have heard and our fa-thers have told
2. They gained not the land by the edge of the sword,
3. Com-mand, and Thy word shall de-liv-er-ance bring,
4. No trust will I place in my strength to de-fend,

What won-ders Thou didst in the great days of old;
Their own arm to them could no safe-ty af-ford,
O God, to Thy cho-sen, for Thou art our King;
Nor yet on my sword as a safe-guard de-pend;

The na-tions were crushed and ex-pelled by Thy hand,
But Thy right hand saved, and the light of Thy face,
Thro' Thee we will sure-ly de-feat all our foes,
In Thee, Who hast saved us and put them to shame,

Cast out that Thy peo-ple might dwell in their land.
Be-cause of Thy fa-vor and won-der-ful grace.
Thro' Thy Name will tri-umph o'er those that op-pose.
We boast all the day, ev-er prais-ing Thy Name.

The Martyr Church

PSALM 44   11s

GOOD SHEPHERD

Joseph Barnby

1. Thou, Lord, hast for-sak-en, to shame brought our boasts;
2. Like sheep to the slaugh-ter Thy peo-ple are giv'n,
3. Thou mak-est our neigh-bors re-proach us in pride,
4. Yea, all the day long I be-hold my dis-grace,
5. All this have we suf-fered, and nev-er for-got

No more to the field dost Thou go with our hosts;
Dis-persed through the na-tions a-far we are driv'n;
And those that are near us to scoff and de-ride;
And cov-ered am I with con-fu-sion of face;
To serve Thee, Je-ho-vah, nor false-ly have wrought;

Thou turn-est us back from the foe in dis-may,
Thou sell-est Thy peo-ple to stran-gers for naught,
A. by-word the na-tions have made of our name,
The voice of blas-phem-ers and scoff-ers I hear,
Our heart is not turned and our steps have not strayed,

And spoil-ers who hate us have made us their prey.
Their price to Thy treas-ure no in-crease has brought.
With scorn and de-ri-sion they put us to shame.
The foe and a-ven-ger a-gainst me ap-pear.
Tho' crushed a-mid ru-ins and un-der death's shade.

[Stanzas 5–9]

123 An Importunate Prayer

PSALM 44 11s   MAGNUS   John B. Herbert

Slowly

1. If we have for-got-ten the Name of our God, Or un-to an
2. We all the day long for Thy sake are con-sumed, De-feat-ed and
3. O why art Thou hid-ing the light of Thy face, For-get-ting our

i - dol our hands spread a - broad, Shall not the Al-might-y un-
help-less, to death we are doomed; Then why dost Thou tar - ry? Je-
bur-den of grief and dis-grace? Our soul is bowed down, yea, we

cov - er this sin? He knows all our hearts and the se - crets with-in.
ho - vah, a-wake, Nor spurn us for - ev - er; a - rise for our sake.
cleave to the dust; Rise, help, and re - deem us, Thy mer - cy we trust.

CHORUS

Rise, help, and re - deem us, Thy mer - - cy we trust;
Thy mer - cy we trust;

Rise, help, and re - deem us, Thy mer - cy we trust.

[Stanzas 10-12]

124 The Royal Majesty of Christ

PSALM 45 S. M.   MORNINGTON   Earl of Mornington

1. My heart doth o - ver - flow, A good - ly
2. Su - preme - ly fair Thou art, Thy lips with
3. Now gird Thee with Thy sword, O strong and
4. Tri - um - phant - ly ride forth For meek - ness,
5. Thy strength shall o - ver - come All those that

theme is mine; My ea - ger tongue with joy - ful
grace o'er - flow; His rich - est bless - ings ev - er -
might - y One, In splen - did maj - es - ty ar -
truth, and right; Thy arm shall gain the vic - to -
hate the King, And un - der Thy do - min - ion

song Doth praise the King Di - vine.
more Doth God on Thee be - stow.
rayed, More glo - rious than the sun.
ry In won - drous deeds of might.
strong The na - tions Thou shalt bring.

6 Thy royal throne, O God,
    For evermore shall stand;
Eternal truth and justice wield
    The sceptre in Thy hand.

7 Since Thou art sinless found,
    The Lord, Thy God confessed,
Anointeth Thee with perfect joy,
    Thou art supremely blest.

8 Thy garments breathe of myrrh
    And spices sweet and rare;
Glad strains of heavenly music ring
    Throughout Thy palace fair.

9 Amid Thy glorious train
    King's daughters waiting stand,
And fairest gems bedeck Thy bride,
    The queen at Thy right hand.

125 The Church the Bride of Christ

PSALM 45 S. M. GERAR Lowell Mason

1. O Roy-al Bride, give heed, And to my
2. Thy beau-ty and thy grace Shall then de-
3. To thee, since thou art His, Great hon-or
4. En-throned in roy-al state, All glo-rious
5. And they that hon-or thee Shall in thy

words at-tend; For Christ the King for-sake the
light the King; He on-ly is thy right-ful
shall be shown; The rich shall bring their gifts to
thou shalt dwell, With gar-ments fair, in-wrought with
train at-tend; And to the pal-ace of the

world .... And ev-'ry for-mer friend.
Lord, ... To Him thy wor-ship bring.
thee, ... Thy glo-ry they shall own.
gold, ... The Church He lov-eth well.
King .... Shall joy-ful-ly as-cend.

[Stanzas 10-16]

6 O King of royal race,
  Thy sons of heavenly birth
Thou wilt endow with kingly gifts
  As princes in the earth.

7 Thy Name shall be proclaimed
  Through all succeeding days,
And all the nations of the earth
  Shall give Thee endless praise.

126 God a Very Present Help

PSALM 46 C. M. MATERNA Samuel A. Ward

1. God is our ref-uge and our strength, Our ev-er pres-ent aid,
2. A riv-er flows whose streams make glad The cit-y of our God,
3. The na-tions raged, the king-doms moved, But when His voice was heard
4. O come, be-hold what won-drous works Je-ho-vah's hand has wrought;
5. Be still and know that I am God, O'er all ex-alt-ed high;

And, there-fore, though the earth re-move, We will not be a-fraid;
The ho-ly place where-in the Lord Most High has His a-bode;
The troub-led earth was stilled to peace Be-fore His might-y word.
Come, see what des-o-la-tion great He on the earth has brought.
The sub-ject na-tions of the earth My Name shall mag-ni-fy.

Though hills a-midst the seas be cast, Though foam-ing wa-ters roar,
Since God is in the midst of her, Un-moved her walls shall stand,
The Lord of Hosts is on our side, Our safe-ty to se-cure,
To ut-most ends of all the earth He caus-es war to cease;
The Lord of Hosts is on our side, Our safe-ty to se-cure;

Yea, though the might-y bil-lows shake The moun-tains on the shore.
For God will be her ear-ly help, When troub-le is at hand.
The God of Ja-cob is for us A ref-uge strong and sure.
The weap-ons of the strong de-stroyed, He makes a-bid-ing peace.
The God of Ja-cob is for us A ref-uge strong and sure.

127 The Protective Power of God

PSALM 46 L. M.　　　　WALTHAM　　　　J. Baptiste Calkin

1. God will our strength and ref - uge prove, In all dis-
2. Our trust in God shall still a - bide Tho' hills be
3. A riv - er flows, whose liv - ing streams Make glad the
4. God has in her His dwell - ing made, And she shall
5. The kings and na - tions raged in pride; He spake, the
6. Come, see the works of God dis - played, The won - ders

tress a pres - ent aid, And, though the trem - bling
shak - en from their seat, And though the o - cean's
cit - y of our God, The ho - ly place where
nev - er - more be moved; Her God shall ear - ly
earth did melt a - way; The Lord of Hosts is
of His might - y hand, What des - o - la - tions

earth re - move, We will not fear nor be dis - mayed.
swell - ing tide ·A - gainst the trem - bling moun - tains beat.
glo - ry beams, Where God Most High has His a - bode.
give her aid, Her con - stant help - er He has proved.
on our side, Our fa - thers' God, our strength and stay.
He has made, What ru - in spread through all the land.

7 Through all the peopled earth He makes
　　The dreadful scourge of war to cease,
　The implements of battle breaks,
　　And makes the nations dwell in peace.

8 Be still, ye nations, bow in fear,
　　And know that I alone am God;
　To us the Lord of Hosts is near,
　　Our fathers' God is our abode.

128   The Lord of Hosts

PSALM 46   8s, 7s, 6s   EIN' FESTE BURG   Martin Luther

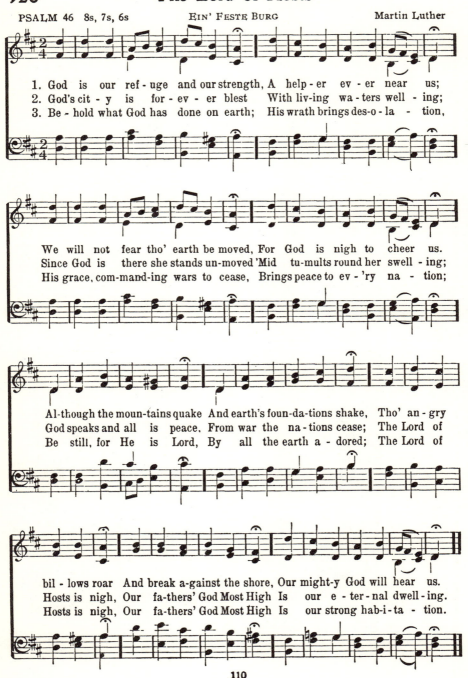

1. God is our ref-uge and our strength, A help-er ev-er near us;
2. God's cit-y is for-ev-er blest With liv-ing wa-ters well-ing;
3. Be-hold what God has done on earth; His wrath brings des-o-la-tion,

We will not fear tho' earth be moved, For God is nigh to cheer us.
Since God is there she stands un-moved 'Mid tu-mults round her swell-ing;
His grace, com-mand-ing wars to cease, Brings peace to ev-'ry na-tion;

Al-though the moun-tains quake And earth's foun-da-tions shake, Tho' an-gry
God speaks and all is peace, From war the na-tions cease; The Lord of
Be still, for He is Lord, By all the earth a-dored; The Lord of

bil-lows roar And break a-gainst the shore, Our might-y God will hear us.
Hosts is nigh, Our fa-thers' God Most High Is our e-ter-nal dwell-ing.
Hosts is nigh, Our fa-thers' God Most High Is our strong hab-i-ta-tion.

129 The Universal Sovereignty of Christ

PSALM 47 L. M. TRURO Charles Burney

1. Re-joice, ye peo-ple, hom-age give, To God with voice of tri-umph sing;
2. He put-teth na-tions un-der us And mak-eth us tri-um-phant stand;
3. God hath as-cend-ed with a shout, Je-ho-vah with the trump-et's sound.
4. Our God is King of all the earth, With tho't-ful heart His praise make known;
5. To praise and serve our cov-enant God The princ-es of the earth draw nigh;

He rul-eth in dread maj-es-ty, The great, the u-ni-ver-sal King.
He giv-eth for our her-it-age His prom-ised rest, a good-ly land.
Sing praise to God our King, sing praise, Yea, let His glo-rious praise a-bound.
O'er all the na-tions God doth reign, Ex-alt-ed on His ho-ly throne.
All king-ly pow'rs be-long to Him, He is ex-alt-ed, God Most High.

130 The Ascended King

PSALM 47 S. M. SILVER STREET Isaac Smith

1. All na-tions, clap your hands, Let shouts of tri-umph ring,
2. A-bove our might-y foes He gave us pow'r to stand,
3. With shouts as-cends our King, With trump-et's stir-ring call;
4. O sing in joy-ful strains, And make His glo-ry known;
5. Our fa-thers' God to own The kings of earth draw nigh,

For might-y o-ver all the lands The Lord Most High is King.
And as our her-it-age He chose The good-ly prom-ised land.
Praise God, praise God, His prais-es sing, For God is Lord of all.
God o-ver all the na-tions reigns, And ho-ly is His throne.
For none can save but God a-lone, He is the Lord Most High.

131 The Glory of the Church

PSALM 48 L. M.   OTTERBOURNE   Arranged from Haydn

1. The Lord is great; with wor - thy praise Pro - claim His
2. Mount Zi - on, glo - ri - ous and fair, Gives joy to
3. With - in her dwell - ings for de - fense Our God has
4. With our own eyes we have be - held What oft our

pow'r, His Name con - fess, With - in the cit - y
peo - ple in all lands; The cit - y of the
made His pres - ence known, And hos - tile kings, in
fa - thers told be - fore, That God Who in His

of our God, Up - on His mount of ho - li - ness.
might - y King In maj - es - ty se - cure - ly stands.
sud - den fear, Have fled as ships by tem - pests blown.
Zi - on dwells Will keep her safe - ly ev - er - more.

132 Meditation and Joyful Gratitude

PSALM 48 L. M.   ST. JOHN'S HIGHLANDS   Anonymous

1. With - in Thy tem - ple's sa - cred courts, With lov - ing and a - dor - ing tho't,
2. Wher - e'er Thy Name, O God, is known, Wher - e'er Thy glorious fame ex - tends,
3. Thy hand is full of right - eous - ness; Let Zi - on's glad - ness then be great,
4. En - com - pass Zi - on, count her tow'rs, And mark her strong de - fens - es well;
5. This might - y God for - ev - er lives Our God and Sav - iour to a - bide,

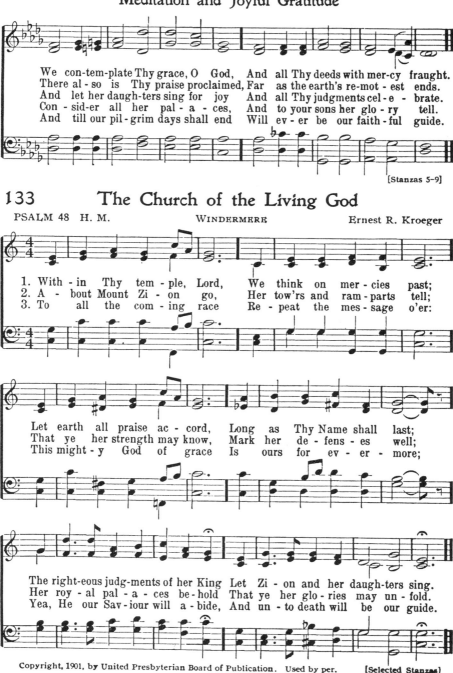

We con-tem-plate Thy grace, O God, And all Thy deeds with mer-cy fraught.
There al-so is Thy praise proclaimed, Far as the earth's re-mot-est ends.
And let her daugh-ters sing for joy And all Thy judgments cel-e-brate.
Con-sid-er all her pal-a-ces, And to your sons her glo-ry tell.
And till our pil-grim days shall end Will ev-er be our faith-ful guide.

[Stanzas 5-9]

133   The Church of the Living God

PSALM 48   H. M.   WINDERMERE   Ernest R. Kroeger

1. With-in Thy tem-ple, Lord, We think on mer-cies past;
2. A-bout Mount Zi-on go, Her tow'rs and ram-parts tell;
3. To all the com-ing race Re-peat the mes-sage o'er:

Let earth all praise ac-cord, Long as Thy Name shall last;
That ye her strength may know, Mark her de-fens-es well;
This might-y God of grace Is ours for ev-er-more;

The right-eous judg-ments of her King Let Zi-on and her daugh-ters sing.
Her roy-al pal-a-ces be-hold That ye her glo-ries may un-fold.
Yea, He our Sav-iour will a-bide, And un-to death will be our guide.

Copyright, 1901, by United Presbyterian Board of Publication. Used by per.   [Selected Stanzas]

134 Praise and Trust

PSALM 48 S. M. DIADEMATA George J. Elvey

1. With - in Thy tem - ple, Lord, In that most ho - ly place,
2. Let Zi - on now re - joice, And all her chil - dren sing;
3. Ob - serve her pal - a - ces, Mark her de - fens - es well,

We on Thy lov - ing - kind - ness dwell, The won - ders of Thy grace.
Let them with thank - ful - ness pro - claim The judg - ments of their King.
That to the sons that fol - low you Her glo - ries you may tell;

Men sing Thy praise, O God, Wher - e'er Thy Name is known;
Mount Zi - on's walls be - hold, A - bout her ram - parts go,
For God as our own God For - ev - er will a - bide,

By ev - 'ry deed Thy hand hath wrought Thy right - eous - ness is shown.
And num - ber ye the loft - y tow'rs That guard her from the foe.
And till life's jour - ney close in death Will be our faith - ful guide.

114   [Selected Stanzas]

The Vanity of Trust in Riches

PSALM 49 7s   FISK   Calvin S. Harrington

1. Hear this, all ye peo - ple, hear, Earth's in - hab - it - ants, give ear;
2. Truth with all my heart I seek, And my mouth shall wis - dom speak;
3. Why should I to fear give way When I see the e - vil day,
4. They that trust in treas-ured gold, Tho' they boast of wealth un-told,
5. If from death one would be free And cor - rup - tion nev - er see,

All of high and low de - gree, Rich and poor, give heed to me.
Heark-en while in lyr - ic strain I make hid - den wis - dom plain.
When with wick - ed - ness my foes Shall sur-round me and op - pose?
None can bid his broth - er live, None to God a ran - som give.
Cost - ly is life's ran - som price, Far be - yond all sac - ri - fice.

SECOND TUNE   FERRIER   John B. Dykes

1. Hear this, all ye peo - ple, hear, Earth's in - hab - it - ants, give ear;
2. Truth with all my heart I seek, And my mouth shall wis - dom speak;
3. Why should I to fear give way When I see the e - vil day,
4. They that trust in treas-ured gold, Tho' they boast of wealth un - told,
5. If from death one would be free And cor - rup - tion nev - er see,

All of high and low de - gree, Rich and poor, give heed to me.
Heark-en while in lyr - ic strain I make hid - den wis - dom plain.
When with wick-ed - ness my foes Shall sur-round me and op - pose?
None can bid his broth - er live, None to God a ran - som give.
Cost - ly is life's ran - som price, Far be - yond all sac - ri - fice.

136 The Issues of Life

PSALM 49 7s   WATCHMAN   Lowell Mason

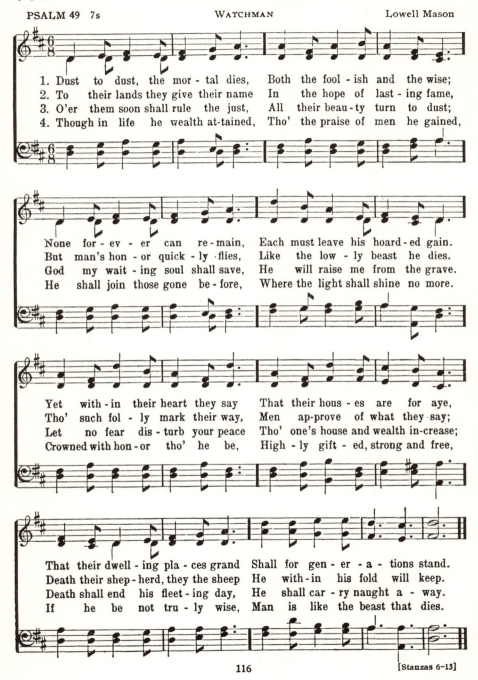

1. Dust to dust, the mor-tal dies, Both the fool-ish and the wise;
2. To their lands they give their name In the hope of last-ing fame,
3. O'er them soon shall rule the just, All their beau-ty turn to dust;
4. Though in life he wealth at-tained, Tho' the praise of men he gained,

None for-ev-er can re-main, Each must leave his hoard-ed gain.
But man's hon-or quick-ly flies, Like the low-ly beast he dies.
God my wait-ing soul shall save, He will raise me from the grave.
He shall join those gone be-fore, Where the light shall shine no more.

Yet with-in their heart they say That their hous-es are for aye,
Tho' such fol-ly mark their way, Men ap-prove of what they say;
Let no fear dis-turb your peace Tho' one's house and wealth in-crease;
Crowned with hon-or tho' he be, High-ly gift-ed, strong and free,

That their dwell-ing pla-ces grand Shall for gen-er-a-tions stand.
Death their shep-herd, they the sheep He with-in his fold will keep.
Death shall end his fleet-ing day, He shall car-ry naught a-way.
If he be not tru-ly wise, Man is like the beast that dies.

       [Stanzas 6-13]

Acceptable Worship

PSALM 50 L. M. ST. PETERSBURG Arranged from Bortniansky

1. The might-y God, Je-ho-vah, speaks And calls the earth from sea to sea;
2. He calls a-loud to heav'n and earth That He may just-ly judge His own;
3. Hear, O my peo-ple, I will speak, A-gainst thee I will tes-ti-fy;
4. I will re-ceive from out thy fold No of-f'ring for My ho-ly shrine;

From beau-teous Zi-on God shines forth, He comes and will not si-lent be;
My cho-sen saints to-geth-er bring Who sac-ri-fice to Me a-lone;
Give ear to me, O Is-ra-el, For God, thy cov-enant God, am I;
The cat-tle on a thou-sand hills And all the for-est beasts are Mine;

De-vour-ing flame be-fore Him goes, And dark the tem-pest round Him grows.
The heav'ns His right-eous-ness de-clare, For God Him-self as Judge is there.
I do not spurn thy sac-ri-fice, Thy of-f'rings are be-fore My eyes.
Each mountain bird to Me is known, What-ev-er roams the field I own.

5 Behold, if I should hungry grow,
  I would not tell My need to thee,
For all the world itself is Mine,
  And all its wealth belongs to Me;
Why should I aught of thee receive,
  My thirst or hunger to relieve?

6 Bring thou to God the gift of thanks,
  And pay thy vows to God Most High;
Call ye upon My holy Name
  In days when sore distress is nigh;
Deliverance I will send to thee,
  And praises thou shalt give to Me.

Sins of Hypocrisy

PSALM 50   L. M.   RAKEM   Isaac B. Woodbury

1. Thus speaks the Lord to wick-ed men: My stat-utes
2. Ye have con-sent-ed with the thief, Ye have par-
3. Thus have ye done; I si-lence kept, And this has
4. Con-sid-er this, who God for-get, Lest I de-

why do ye de-clare? Why take My cov-enant in your mouth,
tak-en with the vile, Your mouths to e-vil words ye give,
been your se-cret thought, That I was whol-ly as your-selves,
stroy with none to free; Who of-fers sac-ri-fice of thanks,

Since ye for wis-dom do not care? For ye My
Your tongues pro-claim de-ceit and guile, Ye glo-ry
To take your e-vil deeds as nought; I will re-
He glo-ri-fies and hon-ors Me; To him who

ho-ly words pro-fane And cast them from you in dis-dain.
in your broth-er's shame, Your moth-er's son do ye de-fame.
prove you and ar-ray Your deeds be-fore your eyes this day.
or-ders well his way Sal-va-tion free I will dis-play.

[Stanzas 7-10]

The Eternal Judgment

PSALM 50 S. M. BOYLSTON Lowell Mason

1. The might-y God, the Lord, Has
2. From Zi-on His a-bode, Where
3. Our God shall sure-ly come, Nor
4. Then to the heav'ns a-bove He

spo-ken un-to all; From ris-ing to the
per-fect beau-ty dwells, The Lord His glo-ry
si-lence shall He keep; De-vour-ing fire shall
from His throne shall call, The earth His king-ly

set-ting sun The na-tions hear His call.
has dis-played In bright-ness that ex-cels.
her-ald Him, A-bout Him storms shall sweep.
voice shall hear, He is the Judge of all.

[Selected Stanzas]

5 Let all My chosen saints
   Before Me gathered be,
Those that by sacrifice have sealed
   Their promise unto Me.

6 Then shall the heavens declare
   His righteousness abroad,
Because the Lord Himself is Judge,
   Yea, none is Judge but God.

140 Penitential Prayers

PSALM 51 7s   AJALON   Richard Redhead

1. God be mer-ci-ful to me, On Thy grace I rest my plea;
2. My trans-gres-sions I con-fess, Grief and guilt my soul op-press;
3. I am e-vil, born in sin; Thou de-sir-est truth with-in.
4. Bro-ken, hum-bled to the dust By Thy wrath and judg-ment just,

Plen-teous in com-pas-sion Thou, Blot out my trans-gres-sions now;
I have sinned a-gainst Thy grace And pro-voked Thee to Thy face;
Thou a-lone my Sav-iour art, Teach Thy wis-dom to my heart;
Let my con-trite heart re-joice And in glad-ness hear Thy voice;

Wash me, make me pure with-in, Cleanse, O cleanse me from my sin.
I con-fess Thy judg-ment just, Speech-less, I Thy mer-cy trust.
Make me pure, Thy grace be-stow, Wash me whit-er than the snow.
From my sins O hide Thy face, Blot them out in bound-less grace.

SECOND TUNE   TOPLADY   Thomas Hastings

1. God be mer-ci-ful to me, On Thy grace I rest my plea;

Plen-teous in com-pas-sion Thou, Blot out my trans-gres-sions now;

120

Penitential Prayers

Wash me, make me pure with-in, Cleanse, O cleanse me from my sin.

141 Gracious Renewal and Testimony

PSALM 51 7s GETHSEMANE John B. Dykes
Slowly

1. Gra-cious God, my heart re-new, Make my spir-it right and true;
2. Sin-ners then shall learn from me And re-turn, O God, to Thee;
3. Not the for-mal sac-ri-fice Hath ac-cept-ance in Thy eyes;
4. Pros-per Zi-on in Thy grace And her bro-ken walls re-place;

Cast me not a-way from Thee, Let Thy Spir-it dwell in me;
Sav-iour, all my guilt re-move, And my tongue shall sing Thy love;
Bro-ken hearts are in Thy sight More than sac-ri-fi-cial rite;
Then our right-eous sac-ri-fice Shall de-light Thy ho-ly eyes;

Thy sal-va-tion's joy im-part, Stead-fast make my will-ing heart.
Touch my si-lent lips, O Lord, And my mouth shall praise ac-cord.
Con-trite spir-it, plead-ing cries, Thou, O God, wilt not de-spise.
Free-will of-f'rings, glad-ly made, On Thy al-tar shall be laid.

[Stanzas 5-8]

142 A Penitent's Plea

PSALM 51 7s REFUGE Joseph P. Holbrook

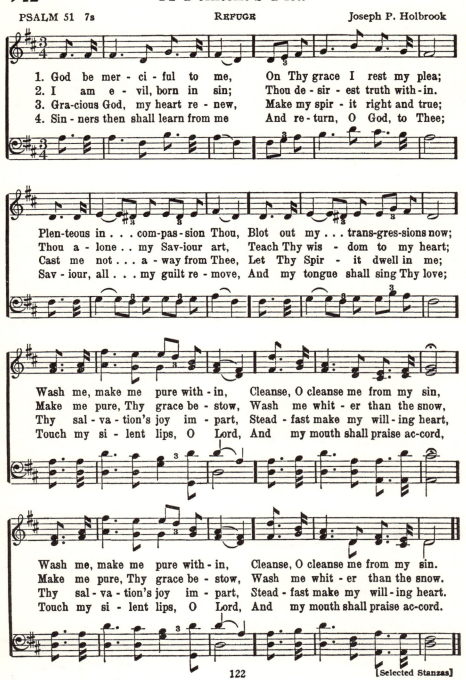

1. God be mer - ci - ful to me, On Thy grace I rest my plea;
2. I am e - vil, born in sin; Thou de - sir - est truth with - in.
3. Gra-cious God, my heart re - new, Make my spir - it right and true;
4. Sin - ners then shall learn from me And re - turn, O God, to Thee;

Plen-teous in . . . com-pas-sion Thou, Blot out my . . . trans-gres-sions now;
Thou a - lone . . my Sav-iour art, Teach Thy wis - dom to my heart;
Cast me not . . . a - way from Thee, Let Thy Spir - it dwell in me;
Sav - iour, all . . . my guilt re - move, And my tongue shall sing Thy love;

Wash me, make me pure with - in, Cleanse, O cleanse me from my sin,
Make me pure, Thy grace be - stow, Wash me whit - er than the snow,
Thy sal - va - tion's joy im - part, Stead - fast make my will - ing heart,
Touch my si - lent lips, O Lord, And my mouth shall praise ac-cord,

Wash me, make me pure with - in, Cleanse, O cleanse me from my sin.
Make me pure, Thy grace be - stow, Wash me whit - er than the snow.
Thy sal - va - tion's joy im - part, Stead - fast make my will - ing heart.
Touch my si - lent lips, O Lord, And my mouth shall praise ac-cord.

122

[Selected Stanzas]

143   Prayer for Pardon and Cleansing

PSALM 51 C. M.   VOX DILECTI   John B. Dykes

1. O God, ac-cord-ing to Thy grace Be mer-ci-ful to me,
2. A-gainst Thee on-ly have I sinned, Done e-vil in Thy sight;
3. From all pol-lu-tion make me clean, Yea, whit-er than the snow;
4. From out Thy pres-ence cast me not, Thy face no more to see;

In Thy a-bound-ing love blot out All my in-iq-ui-ty;
Lord, in Thy judg-ment Thou art just, And in Thy sen-tence right.
O let my bro-ken heart re-joice And glad-ness make me know;
Thy Ho-ly Spir-it and His grace Take not a-way from me.

O wash me whol-ly from my guilt And make me clean with-in,
Be-hold, in e-vil I was formed, And I was born in sin,
Blot out all my in-iq-ui-ties, And hide my sins from view;
Re-store me Thy sal-va-tion's joy, My will-ing heart up-hold;

For my trans-gres-sions I con-fess, I ev-er see my sin.
But Thou wilt make me wise in heart, Thou seek-est truth with-in.
Cre-ate in me a spir-it right, O God, my heart re-new.
Then sin-ners shall be turned to Thee When I Thy ways un-fold.

123

144 Pardon and Testimony

PSALM 51 C. M.   COOLING   Alonzo J. Abbey

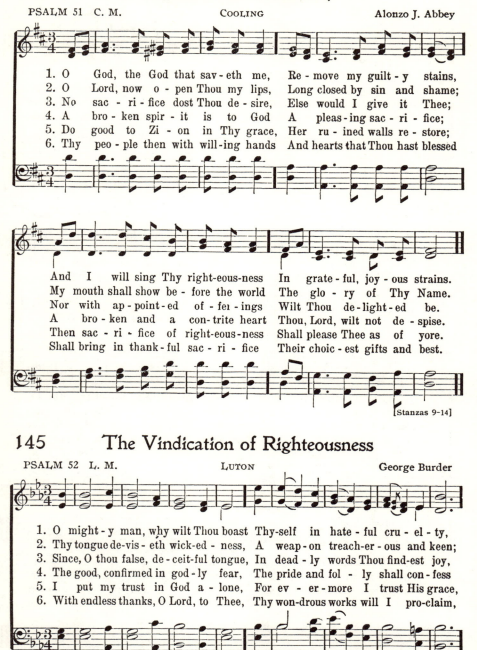

1. O God, the God that sav-eth me, Re-move my guilt-y stains,
2. O Lord, now o-pen Thou my lips, Long closed by sin and shame;
3. No sac-ri-fice dost Thou de-sire, Else would I give it Thee;
4. A bro-ken spir-it is to God A pleas-ing sac-ri-fice;
5. Do good to Zi-on in Thy grace, Her ru-ined walls re-store;
6. Thy peo-ple then with will-ing hands And hearts that Thou hast blessed

And I will sing Thy right-eous-ness In grate-ful, joy-ous strains.
My mouth shall show be-fore the world The glo-ry of Thy Name.
Nor with ap-point-ed of-fer-ings Wilt Thou de-light-ed be.
A bro-ken and a con-trite heart Thou, Lord, wilt not de-spise.
Then sac-ri-fice of right-eous-ness Shall please Thee as of yore.
Shall bring in thank-ful sac-ri-fice Their choic-est gifts and best.

[Stanzas 9-14]

145 The Vindication of Righteousness

PSALM 52 L. M.   LUTON   George Burder

1. O might-y man, why wilt Thou boast Thy-self in hate-ful cru-el-ty,
2. Thy tongue de-vis-eth wick-ed-ness, A weap-on treach-er-ous and keen;
3. Since, O thou false, de-ceit-ful tongue, In dead-ly words Thou find-est joy,
4. The good, confirmed in god-ly fear, The pride and fol-ly shall con-fess
5. I put my trust in God a-lone, For ev-er-more I trust His grace,
6. With endless thanks, O Lord, to Thee, Thy won-drous works will I pro-claim,

124

The Vindication of Righteousness

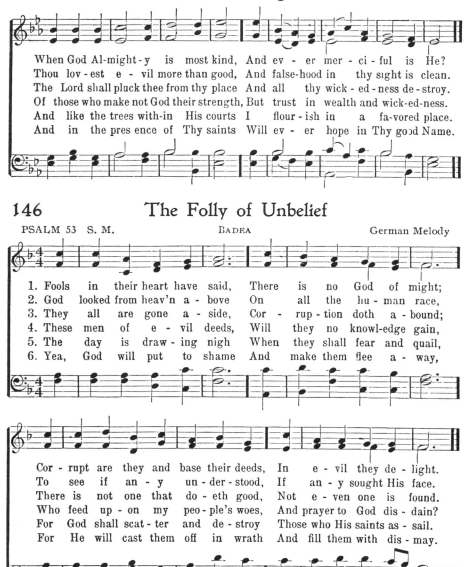

When God Al-might-y is most kind, And ev - er mer - ci - ful is He?
Thou lov - est e - vil more than good, And false-hood in thy sight is clean.
The Lord shall pluck thee from thy place And all thy wick - ed - ness de - stroy.
Of those who make not God their strength, But trust in wealth and wick-ed-ness.
And like the trees with-in His courts I flour - ish in a fa-vored place.
And in the pres ence of Thy saints Will ev - er hope in Thy good Name.

146   The Folly of Unbelief

PSALM 53 S. M.   BADEA   German Melody

1. Fools in their heart have said, There is no God of might;
2. God looked from heav'n a - bove On all the hu - man race,
3. They all are gone a - side, Cor - rup - tion doth a - bound;
4. These men of e - vil deeds, Will they no knowl-edge gain,
5. The day is draw - ing nigh When they shall fear and quail,
6. Yea, God will put to shame And make them flee a - way,

Cor - rupt are they and base their deeds, In e - vil they de - light.
To see if an - y un - der - stood, If an - y sought His face.
There is not one that do - eth good, Not e - ven one is found.
Who feed up - on my peo - ple's woes, And prayer to God dis - dain?
For God shall scat - ter and de - stroy Those who His saints as - sail.
For He will cast them off in wrath And fill them with dis - may.

7 O would that Israel's help
   Were out of Zion come!
  O would that God might early bring
   His captive people home!

8 When God from distant lands
   His exiled ones shall bring,
  His people shall exultant be,
   And gladly they shall sing.

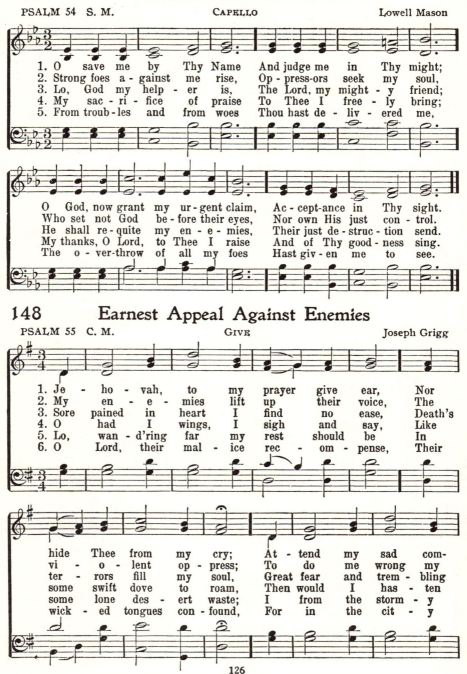

147   Our Saviour in Trial

PSALM 54 S. M.   CAPELLO   Lowell Mason

1. O save me by Thy Name And judge me in Thy might;
2. Strong foes a-gainst me rise, Op-press-ors seek my soul,
3. Lo, God my help-er is, The Lord, my might-y friend;
4. My sac-ri-fice of praise To Thee I free-ly bring;
5. From troub-les and from woes Thou hast de-liv-ered me,

O God, now grant my ur-gent claim, Ac-cept-ance in Thy sight.
Who set not God be-fore their eyes, Nor own His just con-trol.
He shall re-quite my en-e-mies, Their just de-struc-tion send.
My thanks, O Lord, to Thee I raise And of Thy good-ness sing.
The o-ver-throw of all my foes Hast giv-en me to see.

148   Earnest Appeal Against Enemies

PSALM 55 C. M.   GIVE   Joseph Grigg

1. Je-ho-vah, to my prayer give ear, Nor
2. My en-e-mies lift up their voice, The
3. Sore pained in heart I find no ease, Death's
4. O had I wings, I sigh and say, Like
5. Lo, wan-d'ring far my rest should be In
6. O Lord, their mal-ice rec-om-pense, Their

hide Thee from my cry; At-tend my sad com-
vi-o-lent op-press; To do me wrong my
ter-rors fill my soul, Great fear and trem-bling
some swift dove to roam, Then would I has-ten
some lone des-ert waste; I from the storm-y
wick-ed tongues con-found, For in the cit-y

Earnest Appeal Against Enemies

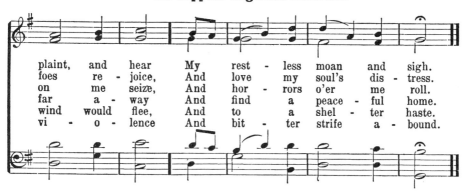

plaint, and hear My rest - less moan and sigh.
foes re - joice, And love my soul's dis - tress.
on me seize, And hor - rors o'er me roll.
far a - way And find a peace - ful home.
wind would flee, And to a shel - ter haste.
vi - o - lence And bit - ter strife a - bound.

7 They walk her walls both night and day,
   Within all vices meet;
Oppression, fraud, and crime hold sway,
   Nor leave the crowded street.

8 No foreign foe provokes alarm,
   But enemies within;
May God destroy their power to harm
   And recompense their sin.

149   Confession of Trust

PSALM 55 C. M.   ASCRIPTION   Luther O. Emerson

1. On God a - lone my soul re - lies, And He will soon re - lieve;
2. He has re-deemed my soul in peace, From con-flict set me free;
3. The liv - ing God in right-eous-ness Will rec - om-pense with shame
4. All treach'rous friends who o - ver - reach And break their plight-ed troth,
5. Up - on the Lord thy bur - den cast, To Him bring all thy care;
6. God will not let His saints be moved; Pro - tect - ed, they shall see

The Lord will hear my plain-tive cries At morn-ing, noon, and eve.
My man - y foes are made to cease, And strive no more with me.
The men who, hard-ened by suc - cess, For - get to fear His Name.
Who hide their hate with hon-eyed speech, With such the Lord is wroth.
He will sus - tain and hold thee fast, And give thee strength to bear.
Their foes cut off and sin re-proved; O God, I trust in Thee.

[Stanzas 9–14]

127

150 Desire for Rest

PSALM 55 8s   ASSIUT   George C. Stebbins

1. O God, give Thou ear to my plea, And hide not Thy-self from my cry;
2. O that I had wings like a dove, For then I would fly far a-way
3. Nay, soul, call on God all the day; The Lord for Thy help will ap-pear;
4. Thy bur-den now cast on the Lord, And He shall thy weak-ness sus-tain;

O heark-en and an-swer Thou me, As rest-less and wea-ry I sigh.
And seek for the rest that I love, Where troub-le no more could dis-may.
At eve, morn, and noon hum-bly pray, And He thy pe-ti-tion will hear.
The right-eous who trust in His word Un-moved shall for-ev-er re-main.

[Selected Stanzas]

151 Prayer for Deliverance

PSALM 56 6s   CANA   Anonymous

1. O God, be mer-ci-ful, Be mer-ci-ful to me,
2. What time I am a-fraid I put my trust in Thee;
3. All day they wrest my words, Their tho'ts are full of hate;
4. Thou know-est all my woes, O treas-ure Thou my tears;
5. In God, the Lord, I rest, His word of grace I praise,
6. Up-on me are Thy vows, O God, in Whom I live;

For man, with con-stant hate, Would fain my ru-in see.
In God I rest, and praise His word, so rich and free;
They meet, they lurk, they watch, As for my soul they wait;
Are they not in Thy book, Where all my life ap-pears?
His prom-ise stands se-cure, Nor fear nor foe dis-mays;
The sac-ri-fice of praise To Thee I now will give;

Prayer for Deliverance

My man - y en - e - mies   A - gainst me proud - ly fight;
In   God   I   put   my   trust,   I   nei - ther doubt nor   fear,
Shall they by   wick - ed - ness   Es - cape Thy judg-ment right?
My   foes shall back - ward turn   When I   ap - peal to   Thee,
In   God   I   put   my   trust,   I   nei - ther doubt nor   fear,
For Thou hast saved from death,   From fall - ing kept me   free,

To   o - ver - whelm my   soul   They watch from morn to   night.
For   man can nev - er   harm   With   God   my   help - er   near.
O   God   of right - eous - ness,   De - stroy them in Thy might.
For this   I   sure - ly   know,   That   God   is   still   for   me.
For   man can nev - er   harm   With   God   my   help - er   near.
That in   the   light of   life   My   walk   may be   with Thee.

152   Fear and Faith

PSALM 56   6s   HOLY GUIDE   Uzziah C. Burnap

1. What time   I   am a - fraid   I   put my trust in   Thee;
2. In   God   I   put   my   trust,   I   nei - ther doubt nor   fear,
3. In   God, the Lord, I   rest,   His   word   of grace I   praise,
4. Up - on   me are Thy   vows,   O   God, in Whom I   live;
5. For Thou hast saved from death,   From fall - ing kept me   free,

In   God   I   rest, and   praise   His   word,   so   rich and   free.
For   man can nev - er   harm   With   God   my   help - er   near.
His prom - ise stands se - cure,   Nor   fear nor   foe dis - mays.
The sac - ri - fice of   praise   To   Thee   I   now will   give.
That in   the   light of   life   My   walk may   be   with Thee.

129   [Selected Stanzas]

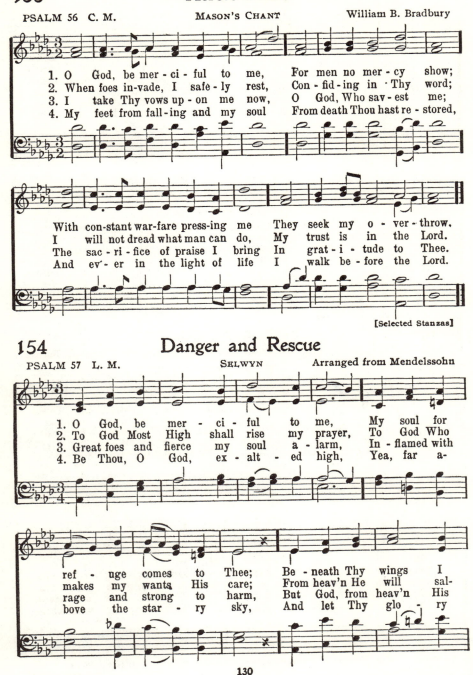

153 Heroic Faith

PSALM 56 C. M. MASON'S CHANT William B. Bradbury

1. O God, be mer - ci - ful to me, For men no mer - cy show;
2. When foes in-vade, I safe - ly rest, Con - fid-ing in Thy word;
3. I take Thy vows up - on me now, O God, Who sav - est me;
4. My feet from fall-ing and my soul From death Thou hast re - stored,

With con-stant war-fare press-ing me They seek my o - ver - throw.
I will not dread what man can do, My trust is in the Lord.
The sac - ri - fice of praise I bring In grat - i - tude to Thee.
And ev' - er in the light of life I walk be - fore the Lord.

[Selected Stanzas]

154 Danger and Rescue

PSALM 57 L. M. SELWYN Arranged from Mendelssohn

1. O God, be mer - ci - ful to me, My soul for
2. To God Most High shall rise my prayer, To God Who
3. Great foes and fierce my soul a - larm, In - flamed with
4. Be Thou, O God, ex - alt - ed high, Yea, far a -

ref - uge comes to Thee; Be - neath Thy wings I
makes my wants His care; From heav'n He will sal -
rage and strong to harm, But God, from heav'n His
bove the star - ry sky, And let Thy glo - ry

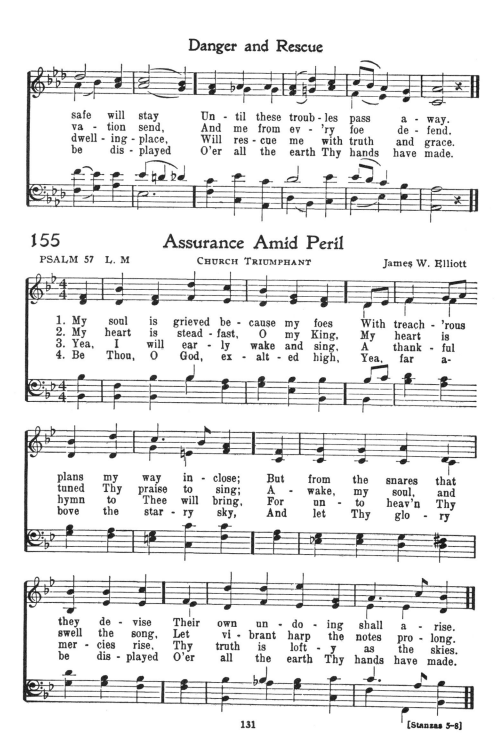

Danger and Rescue

safe will stay Un-til these troub-les pass a-way.
va-tion send, And me from ev-'ry foe de-fend.
dwell-ing-place, Will res-cue me with truth and grace.
be dis-played O'er all the earth Thy hands have made.

155   Assurance Amid Peril

PSALM 57 L. M   CHURCH TRIUMPHANT   James W. Elliott

1. My soul is grieved be-cause my foes With treach-'rous
2. My heart is stead-fast, O my King, My heart is
3. Yea, I will ear-ly wake and sing, A thank-ful
4. Be Thou, O God, ex-alt-ed high, Yea, far a-

plans my way in-close; But from the snares that
tuned Thy praise to sing; A-wake, my soul, and
hymn to Thee will bring, For un-to heav'n Thy
bove the star-ry sky, And let Thy glo-ry

they de-vise Their own un-do-ing shall a-rise.
swell the song, Let vi-brant harp the notes pro-long.
mer-cies rise, Thy truth is loft-y as the skies.
be dis-played O'er all the earth Thy hands have made.

131   [Stanzas 5-8]

Wickedness and Retribution

PSALM 58 C. M. BONE PASTOR John B. Dykes

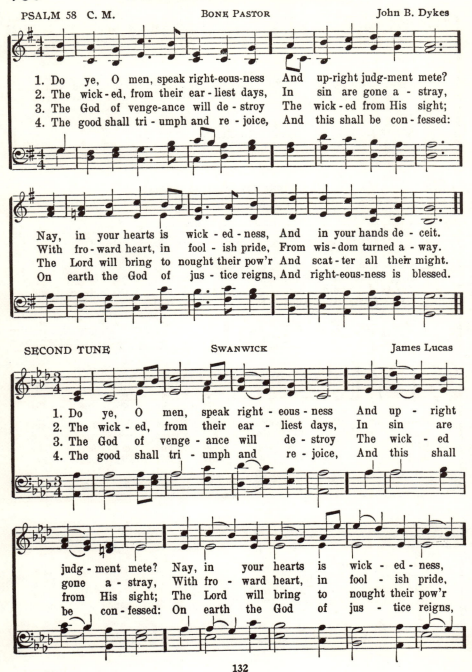

1. Do ye, O men, speak right-eous-ness And up-right judg-ment mete?
2. The wick-ed, from their ear-liest days, In sin are gone a-stray,
3. The God of venge-ance will de-stroy The wick-ed from His sight;
4. The good shall tri-umph and re-joice, And this shall be con-fessed:

Nay, in your hearts is wick-ed-ness, And in your hands de-ceit.
With fro-ward heart, in fool-ish pride, From wis-dom turned a-way.
The Lord will bring to nought their pow'r And scat-ter all their might.
On earth the God of jus-tice reigns, And right-eous-ness is blessed.

SECOND TUNE SWANWICK James Lucas

1. Do ye, O men, speak right-eous-ness And up-right
2. The wick-ed, from their ear-liest days, In sin are
3. The God of venge-ance will de-stroy The wick-ed
4. The good shall tri-umph and re-joice, And this shall

judg-ment mete? Nay, in your hearts is wick-ed-ness,
gone a-stray, With fro-ward heart, in fool-ish pride,
from His sight; The Lord will bring to nought their pow'r
be con-fessed: On earth the God of jus-tice reigns,

And in your hands de-ceit, And in your hands de-ceit.
From wis-dom turned a-way, From wis-dom turned a-way.
And scat-ter all their might, And scat-ter all their might.
And right-eous-ness is blessed, And right-eous-ness is blessed.

157 A Cry for Help

PSALM 59 C. M.   EAGLEY   James Walch

1. Pro-tect and save me, O my God, From foes that seek my life,
2. The work-ers of in-iq-ui-ty A-gainst me lie in wait;
3. Be-hold their wick-ed-ness, O Lord, To help me, O a-wake;
4. My en-e-mies with dead-ly rage Re-new their fierce at-tack;
5. O God, my strength, on Thee I wait, To Thee for ref-uge flee;

And set me high, se-cure a-bove The ris-ing tide of strife.
Tho' I am in-no-cent, O Lord, They gath-er in their hate.
Lord God of Hosts, Thou, Is-rael's God, A-rise, and venge-ance take.
They think the Lord will not re-gard, But Thou wilt turn them back.
My God with mer-cy will de-fend, Tri-um-phant I shall be.

6 O God, our shield, let wickedness
   And pride be put to shame,
Till all shall know that Thou dost rule
   And all shall fear Thy Name.

7 Let wickedness that raged in power
   Now rage in impotence;
But I will glory in Thy strength,
   My refuge and defense.

8 When all the night of woe is past
   And morning dawns at length,
Then I shall praise Thy grace, O God,
   My refuge and my strength.

9 To Thee, O God most merciful,
   My thankful song I raise;
My might, my strong, secure abode,
   I will proclaim Thy praise.

Defeat and Triumphant Hope

PSALM 60 C. M.   FARRANT   Richard Farrant

1. O God, Thou hast re - ject - ed us, And
2. Lo, Thou hast torn and rent our land, Thy
3. Through ways of tri - al and dis - tress Thy
4. A glo - rious ban - ner Thou hast giv'n To
5. That Thy be - lov - ed may be saved And
6. God in His ho - li - ness hath said: I

hast af - flict - ed sore; Thou hast been an - gry,
judg - ments dread ap - pall; O heal her shat - tered
peo - ple Thou hast led, A bit - ter cup Thou
those who fear Thy Name, A ban - ner to dis -
from their foes set free, Help with the might of
will tri - um - phant be, All hea - then lands I

but in grace O once a - gain re - store.
strength be - fore She tot - ter to her fall.
giv - est us Of mis - er - y and dread.
play a - broad, And thus the truth pro - claim.
Thy right hand, In mer - cy an - swer me.
claim as Mine, And they shall bow to Me.

7 Now, therefore, who will lead us on
   Sin's strongholds to possess?
   No longer cast us off, O God,
   But give our hosts success.

8 Give Thou Thy help against the foe,
   For help of man is vain;
   Through God we shall do valiantly,
   The victory He shall gain.

159 Communion with God

PSALM 61 C. P. M.   MERIBAH   Lowell Mason

1. O God, re-gard my hum-ble plea; I can-not be so far from Thee But Thou wilt hear my cry; When I by troub-le am dis-tressed, Then lead me on the Rock to rest That high-er is than I.

2. In Thee my soul hath shel-ter found, And Thou hast been from foes a-round The tow'r to which I flee. With-in Thy house will I a-bide; My ref-uge sure, what-e'er be-tide, Thy shel-t'ring wings shall be.

3. For Thou, O God, my vows hast heard, On me the her-it-age con-ferred Of those that fear Thy Name; A blest a-noint-ing Thou dost give, And Thou wilt make me ev-er live Thy prais-es to pro-claim.

4. Be-fore Thy face shall I a-bide; O God, Thy truth and grace pro-vide To guard me in the way; So I will make Thy prais-es known, And, hum-bly bend-ing at Thy throne, My vows will dai-ly pay.

135

160 Confidence in God

PSALM 61 C. M. HAVEN Thomas Hastings

1. O God, give ear un - to my cry, And to my voice at - tend;
2. When troub-les o - ver-whelm my heart, Then Thou wilt hear my cry,
3. A ref - uge Thou hast been for me When storms of troub-le low'r;
4. With-in Thy ho - ly tem - ple, Lord, I ev - er will a - bide;

Though far from home and from Thy house, To Thee my prayers as - cend.
For safe - ty lead me to the Rock That high-er is than I.
When foes as - sail, then Thou hast been My strong de-fense and tow'r.
Be - neath the cov - ert of Thy wings In con - fi-dence I hide.

[Selected Stanzas]

161 Dependence on God

PSALM 62 C. M. SAWLEY James Walch

1. My soul in si - lence waits for God, My Sav-iour He has proved;
2. My en - e - mies my ru - in seek, They plot with fraud and guile;
3. My soul, in si - lence wait for God; He is my help ap-proved,
4. My hon - or is se - cure with God, My Sav-iour He is known;
5. On Him, ye peo - ple, ev - er-more Re - ly with con - fi-dence;

He on - ly is my rock and tow'r; I nev - er shall be moved.
De - ceit - ful, they pre - tend to bless, But in-ward-ly re - vile.
He on - ly is my rock and tow'r, And I shall not be moved.
My ref - uge and my rock of strength Are found in God a - lone.
Be - fore Him pour ye out your heart, For God is our de - fense.

136

Dependence on God

6 For surely men are helpers vain,
　The high and the abased;
Yea, lighter than a breath are they
When in the balance placed.

7 Trust not in harsh oppression's power
　Nor in unrighteous gain;
If wealth increase, yet on your gold
Ye set your hearts in vain.

8 For God has spoken o'er and o'er,
　And unto me has shown,
That saving power and lasting strength
Belong to Him alone.

9 Yea, loving-kindness evermore
　Belongs to Thee, O Lord;
And Thou according to his work
Dost every man reward.

162　God our Strength

PSALM 62　C. M.　　　FOUNTAIN　　　Lowell Mason

1. My soul in si - lence waits for God, My Sav - iour He has proved;
2. For God has spo - ken o'er and o'er, And un - to me has shown,

He on - ly is my rock and tow'r; I nev - er shall be moved.
That sav - ing pow'r and last - ing strength Be - long to Him a - lone.

My hon - or is se - cure with God, My Sav - iour He is known;
Yea, lov - ing-kind-ness ev - er-more Be - longs to Thee, O Lord;

My ref - uge and my rock of strength Are found in God a - lone.
And Thou ac - cord - ing to his work Dost ev - 'ry man re - ward.

　　　[Selected Stanzas]

163 Satisfaction in God

PSALM 63 C. M.   THE GREEN HILL   George C. Stebbins

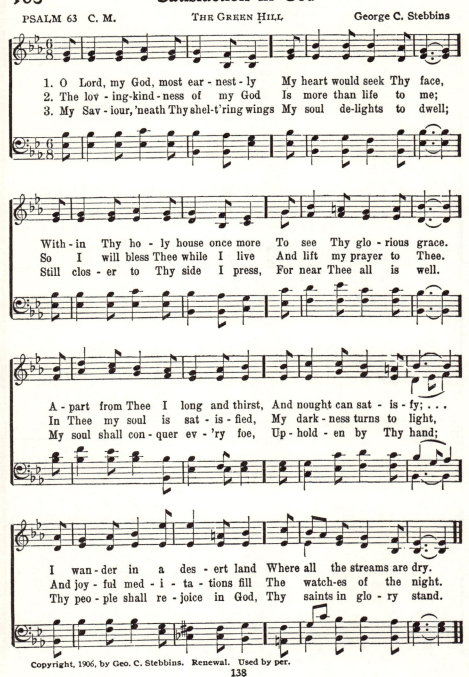

1. O Lord, my God, most ear-nest-ly My heart would seek Thy face,
2. The lov-ing-kind-ness of my God Is more than life to me;
3. My Sav-iour, 'neath Thy shel-t'ring wings My soul de-lights to dwell;

With-in Thy ho-ly house once more To see Thy glo-rious grace.
So I will bless Thee while I live And lift my prayer to Thee.
Still clos-er to Thy side I press, For near Thee all is well.

A-part from Thee I long and thirst, And nought can sat-is-fy; ...
In Thee my soul is sat-is-fied, My dark-ness turns to light,
My soul shall con-quer ev-'ry foe, Up-hold-en by Thy hand;

I wan-der in a des-ert land Where all the streams are dry.
And joy-ful med-i-ta-tions fill The watch-es of the night.
Thy peo-ple shall re-joice in God, Thy saints in glo-ry stand.

164 Spiritual Longing and Devotion

PSALM 63 C. P. M.   AMERICUS   Charles H. Gabriel

Not too fast

1. Thou art my God, O God of grace, And ear - nest-ly I seek Thy face, My heart cries out for Thee; My spir - it thirsts Thy grace to taste, An ex - ile in this des - ert waste In which no wa - ters be, In which no wa - ters be.

2. I long as in the times of old Thy pow'r and glo - ry to be - hold With - in Thy ho - ly place; Be - cause Thy ten - der love I see More pre - cious far than life to me, My lips shall praise Thy grace, My lips shall praise Thy grace.

3. Thus will I bless Thee while I live, And with up - lift - ed hands will give Praise to Thy ho - ly Name; When by Thy boun - ty well sup - plied, Then shall my soul be sat - is - fied, My mouth shall praise pro - claim, My mouth shall praise pro - claim.

4. My lips shall in Thy praise de - light When on my bed I rest at night And med - i - tate on Thee; Be - cause Thy hand as - sist - ance brings, Be - neath the shad - ow of Thy wings My heart shall joy - ful be, My heart shall joy - ful be.

165 Prayer for Protection

PSALM 64 C. M.   MONORA   William B. Bradbury

1. Hear, Lord, the voice of my com-plaint, Pre-serve my life from fear,
2. The wick-ed in their base de-signs Grow ar-ro-gant and bold;
3. The wick-ed, by their sins o'er-come, Shall soon be bro't to shame;

Hide me from plot-ting en-e-mies And e-vil crowd-ing near.
Con-spir-ing se-cret-ly they think That God will not be-hold;
The hand of God shall yet ap-pear, And all shall fear His Name.

The work-ers of in-iq-ui-ty Their dead-ly shafts pre-pare;
They search out more in-iq-ui-ty, Their tho'ts and plans are deep,
The just shall tri-umph in the Lord, Their trust shall be se-cure,

They aim at me their treach-'rous words; O save me from their snare.
But God will smite, for He is near His saints to guard and keep.
And end-less glo-ry then shall crown The up-right and the pure.

166 Divine Grace Magnified

PSALM 65 L. M   HOLBORN HILL   St. Alban's Tune Book

1. Praise waits in Zi - on, Lord, for Thee, And un - to
2. A - gainst us sin has bat - tled hard; For help we
3. How blest are they whom Thou dost choose To come and
4. By might - y deeds in right - eous - ness Prayer's an - swer

Thee shall vows be paid; O Thou that hear - est
look to Thee and pray; Thou our trans - gres - sions
in Thy courts a - bide; Com - mun - ing in Thy
sure - ly comes from Thee, O God our Sav - iour,

those who cry, To Thee by all shall prayer be made.
wilt for - give, Yea, Thou wilt take them all a - way.
ho - ly house, With good we shall be sat - is - fied.
God the' trust Of all Thy saints on land or sea.

5 Thy power has set the mountains firm,
    O God Almighty, girt with strength;
  At Thy command the waves are still,
    The nations cease from war at length.

6 The tokens of Thy mighty power
    Lead men in every clime to fear;
  From east to west through all the earth
    Thou sendest gladness far and near.

167   Harvest Thanksgiving

PSALM 65   L. M.   STIASTNY   Arranged from Johann Stiastny

1. Thou vis-it-est the earth with show'rs, Thy boundless store sup-plies its need;
2. The fur-rows where the seed is sown   Are soft-ened by Thy gen-tle rain;
3. The year with good-ness Thou dost crown, Thy ways o'er-flow with bless-ed-ness;
4. The pas-tures teem with flocks and herds, The gold-en grain waves o'er the fields;

For fields en-riched and well pre-pared Thou dost pro-vide the sow-er's seed.
Thy gra-cious care and prov-i-dence Sup-ply and bless the spring-ing grain.
The hills and valleys, clothed with green, Are joy-ful in their fruit-ful-ness.
All na-ture, sing-ing joy-ful-ly, Her trib-ute of thanks-giv-ing yields.

[Stanzas 7–10]

168   The Fatherly Goodness of God

PSALM 65   C. P. M.   MALONE   Luther O. Emerson

1. Be - fore Thee, Lord, a peo-ple waits   To praise Thy Name in Zi-on's gates,
2. How great my tres-pass-es ap-pear,   But Thou from guilt my soul wilt clear,
3. The good-ness of Thy house, O Lord,   The joys Thy ho-ly courts af-ford,
4. On Thy sus-tain-ing arm de-pend,   To earth's and sea's re-mot-est end,
5. The tribes of earth's re-mot-est lands   Be - hold the to-kens of Thy hands

To Thee shall vows be paid;   Thou hear-er of the suppliant's prayer,
And my trans-gres-sions hide.   How blest Thy cho-sen, who by grace
Our souls shall sat-is-fy;   By deeds of might, in jus-tice wrought,
All men in ev-'ry age;   Thy strength es-tab-lish-es the hills,
And bow in god-ly fear;   The east, where beams the morn-ing light,

The Fatherly Goodness of God

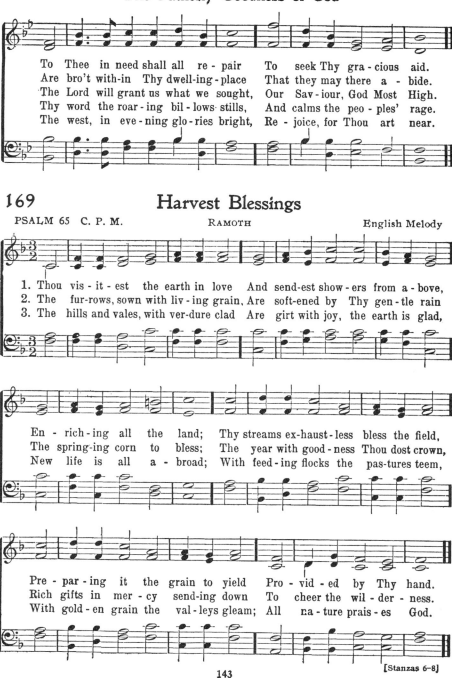

To Thee in need shall all re - pair   To seek Thy gra - cious aid.
Are bro't with-in Thy dwell-ing-place   That they may there a - bide.
The Lord will grant us what we sought,   Our Sav-iour, God Most High.
Thy word the roar-ing bil-lows stills,   And calms the peo - ples' rage.
The west, in eve-ning glo-ries bright,   Re - joice, for Thou art near.

169   Harvest Blessings

PSALM 65 C. P. M.   RAMOTH   English Melody

1. Thou vis - it - est the earth in love   And send-est show-ers from a - bove,
2. The fur-rows, sown with liv-ing grain, Are soft-ened by Thy gen-tle rain
3. The hills and vales, with ver-dure clad Are girt with joy, the earth is glad,

En - rich-ing all the land; Thy streams ex-haust-less bless the field,
The spring-ing corn to bless; The year with good-ness Thou dost crown,
New life is all a - broad; With feed-ing flocks the pas-tures teem,

Pre - par-ing it the grain to yield   Pro - vid - ed by Thy hand.
Rich gifts in mer - cy send-ing down   To cheer the wil - der - ness.
With gold - en grain the val - leys gleam; All na - ture prais - es God.

143   [Stanzas 6-8]

170 A Celebration of Divine Grace

PSALM 65 7s and 6s   MENDEBRAS   German Melody

1. Praise waits for Thee in Zi - on; All men shall wor-ship there And pay their
2. How blest the man Thou call-est And bring-est near to Thee, That in Thy
3. O God of our sal - va - tion, Since Thou dost love the right, Thou wilt an

vows be - fore Thee, O God Who hear-est prayer. Our sins rise up a - gainst us, Pre-
courts for-ev - er His dwell-ing-place may be; He shall with-in Thy tem-ple Be
an - swer send us In wondrous deeds of might. In all earth's hab-i - ta - tions, On

vail - ing day by day, But Thou wilt show us mer-cy And take their guilt a - way.
sat - is - fied with grace, And filled with all the goodness Of Thy most ho - ly place.
all the boundless sea, Man finds no sure re - li - ance, No peace, a - part from Thee.

171 God in Nature

PSALM 65 7s and 6s   WEBB   George J. Webb

1. Thy might sets fast the moun-tains; Strength girds Thee ev-er-more To calm the
2. To bless the earth Thou send-est From Thy a - bun-dant store The wa - ters
3. The year with good Thou crownest, The earth Thy mer-cy fills, The wil - der-

God in Nature

rag-ing peo-ples And still the o-cean's roar. Thy maj - es - ty and greatness Are
of the spring-time, En - rich-ing it once more. The seed by Thee pro-vid - ed Is
ness is fruit-ful, And joy-ful are the hills; With corn the vales are covered, The

thro' all lands confessed, And joy on earth Thou sendest A - far, from east to west.
sown o'er hill and plain, And Thou with gentle show-ers Dost bless the springing grain.
flocks in pas-tures graze; All na - ture joins in sing-ing A joy-ful song of praise.

[Stanzas 4–6]

172 The Blessings of Grace

PSALM 65 C. M.   St. Stephen   Isaac Smith

1. Praise waits in Zi - on, Lord, for Thee; There we will pay our vow;
2. A - gainst me my be - set - ting sins Pre - vail from day to day,
3. O blest the man whom Thou dost choose, And draw in love to Thee,
4. We sure - ly shall be sat - is - fied With Thy a - bun - dant grace,

O Thou, the God that hear - est prayer, Be - fore Thee all shall bow.
But Thou in Thy for - giv - ing grace Wilt take them all a - way.
That in Thy sa - cred courts, O Lord, He may a dwell - er be.
Yea, with the good-ness of Thy house, Of Thy most ho - ly place.

145   [Selected Stanzas]

Joyous Praise

PSALM 66 C. M.   HENRY   Sylvanus B. Pond

1. All lands, to God.... in joy-ful sounds A - loft your
2. Say ye to God,... How ter - ri - ble In all Thy
3. Yea, all the earth... shall wor - ship Thee, And un - to
4. O come, be - hold... the works of God, His might - y

voi - ces raise; Sing forth... the hon - - or
works art Thou! To Thee... Thy foes.... by
Thee shall sing; To Thy... great Name... shall
do - ings see; In deal - - ing with.... the

of.... His Name, And glo - - rious make His praise.
Thy... great pow'r Shall be.... con - strained to bow.
songs.. of joy With loud... ho - san - nas ring.
sons... of men Most won - der - ful is He.

5 He led in safety through the flood
　　The people of His choice,
He turned the sea to solid ground;
　　In Him let us rejoice.

6 He rules forever by His might,
　　His eyes the nations try;
Let not the proud rebellious ones
　　Exalt themselves on high.

174 The Obligations of Grace

PSALM 66 C. M.   ANCYRA   Benjamin C. Unseld

1. O all ye peo - ples, bless our God, A - loud pro-claim His praise,
2. Thro' pain and troub-le Thou hast led, And hum-bled all our pride;
3. Come, ye that fear the Lord, and hear What He has done for me;
4. O let the Lord, our gra - cious God, For - ev - er bless - ed be,

Who safe - ly holds our soul in life, And stead - fast makes our ways.
But, in the end, to lib - er - ty And wealth Thy hand did guide.
My cry for help is turned to praise, For He has set me free.
Who has not turned my prayer from Him, Nor yet His grace from me.

Thou, Lord, hast proved and test - ed us As sil - ver tried by fire,
Here in Thy house I give to Thee The life that Thou dost bless,
If in my heart I sin re - gard, My prayer He will not hear;
O all ye peo - ples, bless our God, A - loud pro-claim His praise,

Thy hand has made our bur - den great And thwart-ed our de - sire.
And pay the sol - emn vows I made When I was in dis - tress.
But tru - ly God has heard my voice, My prayer has reached His ear.
Who safe - ly holds our soul in life, And stead-fast makes our ways.

[Stanzas 7-13]

175 Personal Testimony

PSALM 66 C. P. M. ADOWA Charles H. Gabriel

1. Come, all ye peo - ple, bless our God And tell His
2. We come with of - f'rings to His house, And here we
3. Come, hear, all ye that fear the Lord, While I with
4. The Lord, Who turns a - way the plea Of those who

glo - rious praise a - broad, Who holds our soul in life,
pay the sol - emn vows We ut - tered in dis - tress;
grate - ful heart re - cord What God has done for me;
love in - iq - ui - ty, Has an - swered my re - quest;

Who nev - er lets our feet be moved And, though our
To Him our all we ded - i - cate, To Him we
I cried to Him in deep dis - tress, And now His
He has not turned a - way my prayer, His grace and

faith He oft has proved, Up - holds us in the strife.
whol - ly con - se - crate The lives His mer - cies bless.
won - drous grace I bless, For He has set me free.
love He makes me share; His Name be ev - er blest.

176 A Revived Church and Missions

PSALM 67 7s and 6s   AURELIA   Samuel S. Wesley

1. O God, to us show mer-cy And bless us in Thy grace;
2. O God, let all men praise Thee, Let all the na-tions sing,
3. O God, let peo-ple praise Thee, Let all the na-tions sing,

Cause Thou to shine up-on us The bright-ness of Thy face;
In ev-'ry land let prais-es And songs of glad-ness ring;
For earth in rich a-bun-dance To us her fruit shall bring.

That so Thy way most ho-ly On earth may soon be known,
For Thou shalt judge the peo-ple In truth and right-eous-ness,
The Lord our God shall bless us, Our God shall bless-ing send,

And un-to ev-'ry peo-ple Thy sav-ing grace be shown.
And through the earth the na-tions Shall Thy just rule con-fess.
And all the earth shall fear Him To its re-mot-est end.

177 The Missionary Church

PSALM 67 L. M. SIALKOT George C. Stebbins

1. O God, be mer-ci-ful and bless, And let us see Thy
2. O let the na-tions all be glad And sing to God with
3. The earth has yield-'ed her in-crease, And God, yea, our own

shin-ing face, That all the earth may know Thy way, And
joy and mirth, For Thou shalt judge with eq-ui-ty And
God, shall bless; We shall be blest, and all the earth Shall

all men taste Thy sav-ing grace. O let the na-tions
lead the na-tions of the earth. O let the na-tions
rev-'rent-ly His Name con-fess. O let the na-tions

praise Thee, Lord, Let all give thanks with glad ac-cord.
praise Thee, Lord, Let all give thanks with glad ac-cord.
praise Thee, Lord, Let all give thanks with glad ac-cord.

178   A Missionary Prayer

PSALM 67 S. M.   LABAN   Lowell Mason

1. Lord, bless and pit-y us, Shine on us with Thy face,
2. Thy praise, O gra-cious God, Let all the na-tions sing;
3. The na-tions Thou wilt judge And lead them in Thy ways;
4. The earth her fruit shall yield, For God, our God, will bless;

That all the earth Thy way may know And men may see Thy grace.
Let all men wor-ship Thee with joy And songs of glad-ness bring.
Let all men praise Thy Name, O God, Let all the peo-ple praise.
We shall be blest, and all the world His glo-ry shall con-fess.

179   Invocation and Praise

PSALM 68 L. M.   ALSTONE   Christopher E. Willing

1. Let God a-rise, and by His might Let all His foes be put to flight;
2. Je-ho-vah's prais-es sound a-broad, Re-joice be-fore the liv-ing God;
3. A fa-ther of the fa-ther-less, A judge of wid-ows in dis-tress,
4. God frees the cap-tive and He sends The bless-ed-ness of home and friends,

But, O ye right-eous, glad-ly sing, Ex-ult be-fore your God and King.
Pre-pare the way that He may come And make the des-ert pla-ces bloom.
Is God, the God of bound-less grace, Who dwells with-in His ho-ly place.
And on-ly those in dark-ness stay Who will not trust Him and o-bey.

151

180 Manifold Mercies

PSALM 68 L. M. JUNIATA David D. Wood

1. God saved His peo - ple from dis-tress And led them thro' the wil - der-ness;
2. With co-pious show'rs Thou didst assuage The thirst-ing of Thy her - it-age,
3. The Lord sent forth His might-y word, And shouts of vic - to - ry were heard;
4. When God His cho - sen peo - ple led, The kings and ar - mies turned and fled;
5. God's peo - ple rest - ed, free from care, In glo-rious peace and beau - ty fair;
6. All moun-tains un - to God be-long, But Zi - on's ho - ly mountains strong

Then mountains trem-bled in their place, The heav'ns were bowed before His face.
Thy con-gre-ga - tion dwelt se-cure; Thou, God, art gra-cious to the poor.
The wom-en came, a might-y throng, To join the glad tri - um-phant song.
The hosts of God vic - to-rious fought, And home their spoils and trophies bro't.
Their might-y King did o - ver-throw The hos - tile kings like driv - en snow.
A - bove them all the Lord loves well, And there He will for - ev - er dwell.

[Stanzas 5-12]

7 Great hosts to holy wars have trod,
  The armies of the living God;
Among them He reveals His face,
  The God of justice and of grace.

8 Thou hast ascended up on high
  And captive led captivity;
They come with gifts, who did rebel,
  That with them God the Lord might dwell.

181 God Our Deliverer

PSALM 68 L. M. WARE George Kingsley

1. Blest be the Lord! for us He cares And dai - ly all our bur - den bears;
2. God's un - re - lent - ing en - e - mies No peace shall find in earth or seas;
3. With glo-rious pomp our King and God Has en-tered in - to His a - bode,
4. As - sem-ble ye be - fore His face, All ye that spring from Is-rael's race;

God Our Deliverer

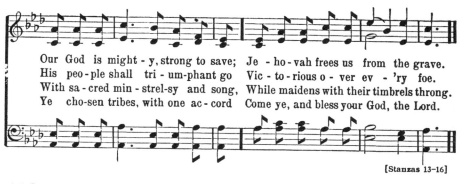

Our God is might-y, strong to save; Je-ho-vah frees us from the grave.
His peo-ple shall tri-um-phant go Vic-to-rious o-ver ev-'ry foe.
With sa-cred min-strel-sy and song, While maidens with their timbrels throng.
Ye cho-sen tribes, with one ac-cord Come ye, and bless your God, the Lord.

[Stanzas 13–16]

182 God the Conquering King

PSALM 68 L. M.   SHELTERING WING   Joseph Barnby

1. O Zi-on, 'tis thy God's com-mand That thou in strength se-cure-ly stand;
2. O Thou, Whose glo-rious tem-ple stands In Zi-on, famed thro' hea-then lands,
3. Thou wilt re-buke the fierce and strong Who hate the right and choose the wrong,
4. The heathen prin-ces yet shall flee From i-dols and re-turn to Thee;
5. Praise God and sing His matchless worth, Ye kings and kingdoms of the earth;

O God, con-firm and strengthen still, Thy pur-pos-es in us ful-fill.
Kings shall Thy pow'r and glo-ry see, And bring their pres-ents un-to Thee.
And scat-ter those who peace ab-hor, The na-tions that de-light in war.
Earth's sin-ful and be-night-ed lands To God shall soon stretch out their hands.
He dwells with-in the heav'n-ly height, And ut-ters forth His voice of might.

[Stanzas 17–23]

6 Ascribe ye strength to God on high,
His might transcendent fills the sky;
His glory and omnipotence
Remain His people's sure defense.

7 Forth from Thy dwelling-place, O God,
Thy awful glory shines a-broad;
Thy people's strength is all from Thee;
Blest be Thy Name eternally.

153

Ascension Blessings

183

PSALM 68 7s and 6s   MISSIONARY HYMN   Lowell Mason

1. O Lord, Thou hast as - cend - ed On high in might to reign;
2. Blest be the Lord Who dai - ly Our heav - y bur - den bears,
3. Sing un - to God, ye na - tions, Ye king-doms of the earth;
4. All glo - ry, might, and hon - or As - cribe to God on high;

Cap - tiv - i - ty Thou lead - est A cap - tive in Thy train.
The God of our sal - va - tion Who for His peo - ple cares.
Sing un - to God, all peo - ple, And praise His match-less worth.
His arm pro - tects His peo - ple Who on His pow'r re - ly.

Rich gifts to Thee are of - fered By men who did re - bel,
Our God is near to help us, Our God is strong to save;
He rides in roy - al tri - umph Up - on the heav'ns a - broad;
Forth from Thy ho - ly dwell - ing Thy aw - ful glo - ries shine;

Who pray that now Je - ho - vah Their God with them may dwell.
The Lord a - lone is a - ble To ran - som from the grave.
He speaks, the moun-tains trem - ble Be - fore the voice of God.
Thou strength-en - est Thy peo - ple; Un - end - ing praise be Thine.

[Selected Stanzas]

154

184

Suffering and Prayer

PSALM 69 C. M.   ELLA   Isaac B. Woodbury

1. Save me, O God, be - cause the floods Come in up - on my soul; I sink in depths where none can stand, Deep wa - ters o'er me roll.
2. My con - stant call - ing wea - ries me, My throat is parched and dried; My eyes grow dim while for my God Still wait - ing I a - bide.
3. The foes who hate me un - pro - voked Are strong and still in - crease, Tho' to dis - arm their en - mi - ty My right I yield for peace.
4. O God, my fol - ly and my sin Thy ho - ly eye can see; Yet save from shame, Lord God of Hosts, Thy saints that wait on Thee.
5. For - bid, O God, our cov - enant God, That those who seek Thy face Should see Thy serv - ant put to shame And share in my dis - grace.

6 It is for Thee I am reproached,
For Thee I suffer shame,
Until my brethren know me not,
And hated is my name.

7 It is my zeal for Thy abode
That has consumed my life;
Reproached by those reproaching Thee,
I suffer in the strife.

8 I wept, with fasting bowed my soul,
Yet that was made my shame;
When I in sackcloth clothed myself,
Their byword I became.

9 The men who sit within the gate
With slander do me wrong,
And they who linger at their cups
Make me their jest and song.

155

185 Petitions for Deliverance

PSALM 69 C. M. ST. FLAVIAN Daye's Psalter

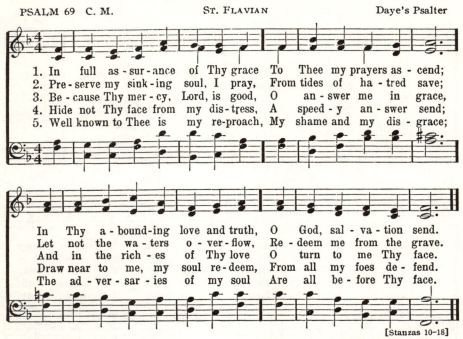

1. In full as-sur-ance of Thy grace To Thee my prayers as-cend;
2. Pre-serve my sink-ing soul, I pray, From tides of ha-tred save;
3. Be-cause Thy mer-cy, Lord, is good, O an-swer me in grace,
4. Hide not Thy face from my dis-tress, A speed-y an-swer send;
5. Well known to Thee is my re-proach, My shame and my dis-grace;

In Thy a-bound-ing love and truth, O God, sal-va-tion send.
Let not the wa-ters o-ver-flow, Re-deem me from the grave.
And in the rich-es of Thy love O turn to me Thy face.
Draw near to me, my soul re-deem, From all my foes de-fend.
The ad-ver-sar-ies of my soul Are all be-fore Thy face.

[Stanzas 10–18]

6 My heart is broken by reproach,
   My soul is full of grief;
I looked in vain for comforters,
   For pity and relief.

7 They gave me bitter gall for food,
   And taunting words they spake;
They gave me vinegar to drink,
   My burning thirst to slake.

8 Their peace and plenty be their snare,
   In blindness let them grope;
Thy indignation on them pour,
   And desolate their hope.

9 Because they proudly persecute
   Those whom Thou, Lord, dost smite,
Let them be blotted from Thy book
   And banished from Thy sight.

186 Anticipation of Answered Prayer

PSALM 69 C. M. BALERMA Arranged by Robert Simpson

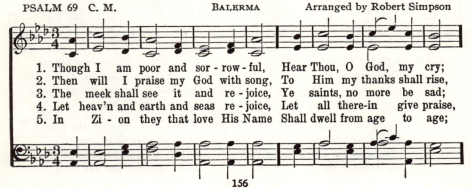

1. Though I am poor and sor-row-ful, Hear Thou, O God, my cry;
2. Then will I praise my God with song, To Him my thanks shall rise,
3. The meek shall see it and re-joice, Ye saints, no more be sad;
4. Let heav'n and earth and seas re-joice, Let all there-in give praise,
5. In Zi-on they that love His Name Shall dwell from age to age;

Anticipation of Answered Prayer

Let Thy sal - va - tion come to me And lift me up on high.
And this shall please Je - ho - vah more Than of - fered sac - ri - fice.
For lo, Je - ho - vah hears the poor And makes His pris - 'ners glad.
For Zi - on God will sure - ly save, Her bro - ken walls will raise.
Yea, there shall be their last - ing rest, Their chil-dren's her - it - age.

[Stanzas 19–23]

187 Supplication and Testimony

PSALM 69 10s   EVENTIDE   William H. Monk

1. Thy lov - ing - kind - ness, Lord, is good and free, In ten - der
2. Need - y and sor - row - ful, to Thee I cry; Let Thy sal -
3. With joy the meek shall see my soul re - stored, Your heart shall
4. Let heav'n a - bove His grace and glo - ry tell, Let earth and

mer - cy turn Thou un - to me; Hide not Thy face from me in
va - tion set my soul on high; Then I will sing and praise Thy
live, ye saints that seek the Lord; He helps the need - y and re -
sea and all that in them dwell; Sal - va - tion to His peo - ple

my dis - tress, In mer - cy hear my prayer, Thy serv - ant bless.
ho - ly Name, My thank-ful song Thy mer - cy shall pro - claim.
gards their cries, Those in dis - tress the Lord will not de - spise.
God will give, And they that love His Name with Him shall live.

157   [Selected Stanzas]

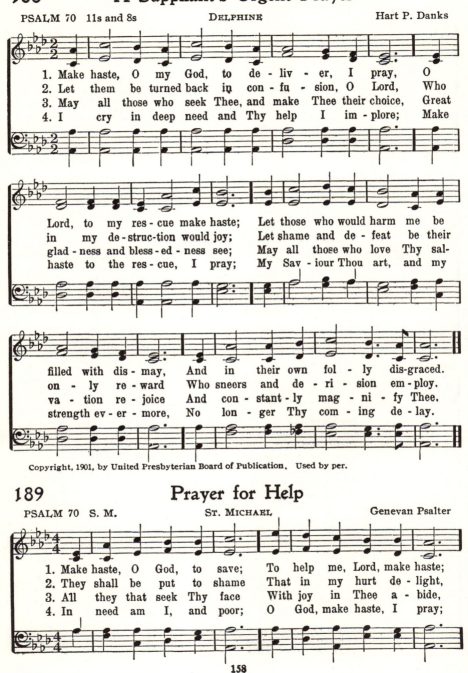

188 A Suppliant's Urgent Prayer

PSALM 70 11s and 8s   DELPHINE   Hart P. Danks

1. Make haste, O my God, to de - liv - er, I pray, O
2. Let them be turned back in con - fu - sion, O Lord, Who
3. May all those who seek Thee, and make Thee their choice, Great
4. I cry in deep need and Thy help I im - plore; Make

Lord, to my res - cue make haste; Let those who would harm me be
in my de - struc - tion would joy; Let shame and de - feat be their
glad - ness and bless - ed - ness see; May all those who love Thy sal -
haste to the res - cue, I pray; My Sav - iour Thou art, and my

filled with dis - may, And in their own fol - ly dis - graced.
on - ly re - ward Who sneers and de - ri - sion em - ploy.
va - tion re - joice And con - stant - ly mag - ni - fy Thee.
strength ev - er - more, No lon - ger Thy com - ing de - lay.

Copyright, 1901, by United Presbyterian Board of Publication. Used by per.

189 Prayer for Help

PSALM 70 S. M.   ST. MICHAEL   Genevan Psalter

1. Make haste, O God, to save; To help me, Lord, make haste;
2. They shall be put to shame That in my hurt de - light,
3. All they that seek Thy face With joy in Thee a - bide,
4. In need am I, and poor; O God, make haste, I pray;

158

Prayer for Help

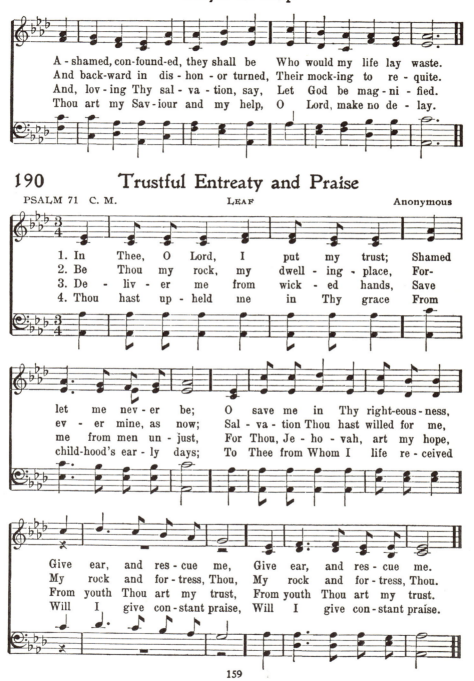

A - shamed, con-found-ed, they shall be Who would my life lay waste.
And back-ward in dis - hon - or turned, Their mock-ing to re - quite.
And, lov-ing Thy sal - va - tion, say, Let God be mag - ni - fied.
Thou art my Sav-iour and my help, O Lord, make no de - lay.

190 Trustful Entreaty and Praise

PSALM 71 C. M.   LEAF   Anonymous

1. In   Thee, O   Lord, I   put my   trust; Shamed
2. Be   Thou my   rock, my   dwell - ing - place, For-
3. De - liv - er   me   from wick - ed   hands, Save
4. Thou hast up - held me   in   Thy   grace From

let me nev - er be; O save me in Thy right-eous-ness,
ev - er mine, as now; Sal - va - tion Thou hast willed for me,
me from men un - just, For Thou, Je - ho - vah, art my hope,
child-hood's ear - ly days; To Thee from Whom I life re - ceived

Give ear, and res - cue me, Give ear, and res - cue me.
My   rock and for - tress, Thou, My   rock and for - tress, Thou.
From youth Thou art my trust, From youth Thou art my trust.
Will I   give con - stant praise, Will I   give con - stant praise.

191 Abiding Confidence and Hope

PSALM 71 C. M. SILOAM Isaac B. Woodbury

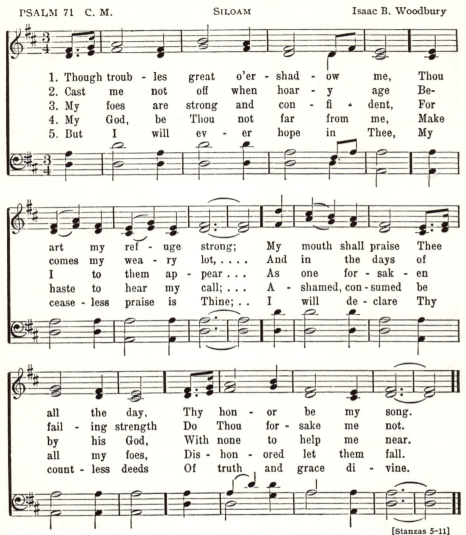

1. Though troub-les great o'er-shad-ow me, Thou art my ref-uge strong; My mouth shall praise Thee all the day, Thy hon-or be my song.

2. Cast me not off when hoar-y age Be-comes my wea-ry lot, ... And in the days of fail-ing strength Do Thou for-sake me not.

3. My foes are strong and con-fi-dent, For I to them ap-pear ... As one for-sak-en by his God, With none to help me near.

4. My God, be Thou not far from me, Make haste to hear my call; ... A-shamed, con-sumed be all my foes, Dis-hon-ored let them fall.

5. But I will ev-er hope in Thee, My cease-less praise is Thine; .. I will de-clare Thy count-less deeds Of truth and grace di-vine.

[Stanzas 5–11]

6 Yea, I will tell the mighty acts
Performed by God the Lord;
Thy righteousness, and Thine alone,
With praise I will record.

7 For from my early youth, O God,
By Thee have I been taught,
And faithfully have I declared
The wonders Thou hast wrought.

192 A Prayer of Faith

PSALM 71 C. M.   AVON   Hugh Wilson

1. O gra-cious God, for-sake me not When I am old and gray, That un-to those that fol-low me I may Thy might dis-play.

2. Thy per-fect right-eous-ness, O God, The height of heav'n ex-ceeds; O who is like to Thee, Who hast Per-formed such might-y deeds?

3. Thou Who hast sent me man-y griefs Wilt yet my soul re-store, And out of sor-row's low-est depths Wilt bring me forth once more.

4. O turn a-gain and com-fort me, My wan-ing strength in-crease, And for Thy faith-ful-ness, O God, My praise shall nev-er cease.

[Stanzas 12–17]

5 Thou Holy One of Israel,
  To Thee sweet songs I raise;
The soul Thou hast redeemed from death
  Shall give Thee joyful praise.

6 My enemies that seek my hurt
  Thy help has put to shame;
My thankful tongue will ceaselessly
  Thy righteousness proclaim.

161

193

The Reign of Christ

PSALM 72 C. M.   HYMN   John E. Gould

1. O God, to Thy A - noint-ed King   Give truth and right-eous - ness;
2. Then ev - 'ry fruit - ful moun-tain side   Shall yield its rich in - crease,
3. The poor man's cause He will main-tain,   The need - y He will   bless,
4. So men shall fear Thee while the sun   In   dai - ly splen-dor   glows,
5. Like rain up - on the new-mown grass,   That falls re - fresh-ing - ly,
6. The right-eous in His glo - rious day   Shall flour-ish and in - crease;

Thy peo - ple He will just - ly judge   And give   the poor re - dress.
And right-eous-ness in all   the land   Shall bear   the fruit of   peace.
And He will break the strength of those   Who would   the poor op - press.
And through all a - ges, while the moon   On   earth   its light be - stows.
Like gen-tle show'rs that cheer the earth,   So   shall   His com - ing   be.
The earth, un-til   the moon shall fade,   Shall have   a - bun-dant peace.

194

The Kingdom of Our Lord

PSALM 72 C. M.   HOLY CROSS   Arranged by James C. Wade

1. His wide   do - min - ion shall ex - tend   From sea   to   ut - most sea,
2. The tribes that in   the des - ert dwell   Shall bow   be - fore His throne;
3. The kings shall come from dis - tant lands   And   is - lands of   the sea;
4. Yea, all   the kings shall bow   to Him,   His   rule   all na - tions hail;
5. The poor   and need - y He shall spare,   And   save their souls from fear;
6. So   they   shall live, and bring to Him   Their gifts   of fin - est gold;

The Kingdom of Our Lord

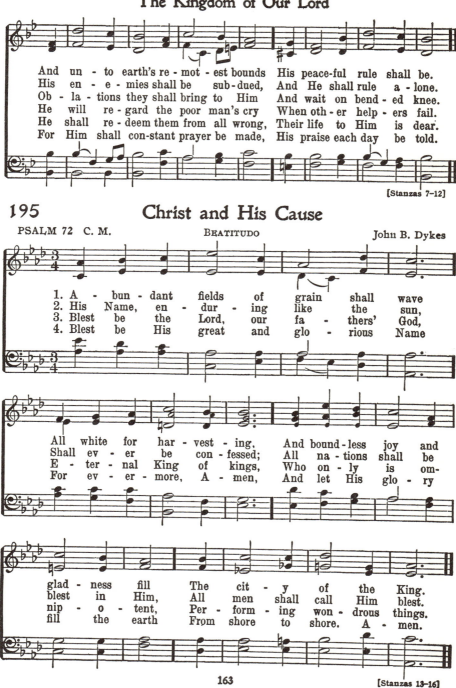

And un - to earth's re - mot - est bounds His peace-ful rule shall be.
His en - e - mies shall be sub-dued, And He shall rule a - lone.
Ob - la - tions they shall bring to Him And wait on bend - ed knee.
He will re - gard the poor man's cry When oth - er help - ers fail.
He shall re - deem them from all wrong, Their life to Him is dear.
For Him shall con-stant prayer be made, His praise each day be told.

[Stanzas 7–12]

195 ## Christ and His Cause

PSALM 72 C. M.   BEATITUDO   John B. Dykes

1. A - bun - dant fields of grain shall wave
2. His Name, en - dur - ing like the sun,
3. Blest be the Lord, our fa - thers' God,
4. Blest be His great and glo - rious Name

All white for har - vest - ing, And bound - less joy and
Shall ev - er be con - fessed; All na - tions shall be
E - ter - nal King of kings, Who on - ly is om -
For ev - er - more, A - men, And let His glo - ry

glad - ness fill The cit - y of the King.
blest in Him, All men shall call Him blest.
nip - o - tent, Per - form - ing won - drous things.
fill the earth From shore to shore. A - men.

[Stanzas 13–16]

196 Grateful Adoration

PSALM 72 C. M.　　　　TABLER　　　　E. H. Frost

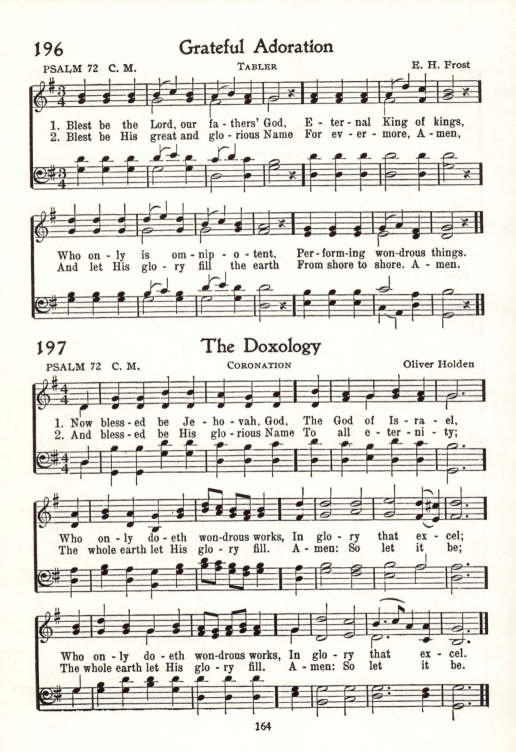

1. Blest be the Lord, our fa - thers' God, E - ter - nal King of kings,
2. Blest be His great and glo - rious Name For ev - er - more, A - men,

Who on - ly is om - nip - o - tent, Per - form-ing won-drous things.
And let His glo - ry fill the earth From shore to shore. A - men.

197 The Doxology

PSALM 72 C. M.　　　　CORONATION　　　　Oliver Holden

1. Now bless - ed be Je - ho - vah, God, The God of Is - ra - el,
2. And bless - ed be His glo - rious Name To all e - ter - ni - ty;

Who on - ly do - eth won-drous works, In glo - ry that ex - cel;
The whole earth let His glo - ry fill. A - men: So let it be;

Who on - ly do - eth won-drous works, In glo - ry that ex - cel.
The whole earth let His glo - ry fill. A - men: So let it be.

198 The Blessings of Immanuel's Reign

PSALM 72 L. M.   HURSLEY   German Melody

1. O God, be Thy A - noint - ed Son With truth and
2. Then o - ver moun - tain side and plain Shall peace spring
3. Then shall Thy fear on earth be known Long as the
4. Like co - pious rain in time of dearth, So shall His
5. The just shall flour - ish in His day, And ev - er-

right - eous - ness en - dowed, That jus - tice may on
forth from right - eous - ness; The poor man's cause will
sun and moon shall shine; While end - less gen - er-
gra - cious com - ing be; As gen - tle show'rs that
more shall peace ex - tend; From sea to sea shall

earth be done, The meek pro - tect - ed from the proud.
He main - tain, And save the weak, that none op - press.
a - tions run King-dom and glo - ry shall be Thine.
cheer the earth, So He shall bring pros - per - i - ty.
be His sway, And to the earth's re - mot - est end.

6 The desert lands to Him shall bow,
And all the islands of the sea,
And kings with gifts shall pay their vow,
His enemies shall bend the knee.

7 In great compassion for the weak
He ever will maintain their right,
Will help the poor and save the meek;
Their lives are precious in His sight.

199 The King and His Kingdom

PSALM 72 L. M. MISSIONARY CHANT Heinrich C. Zeuner

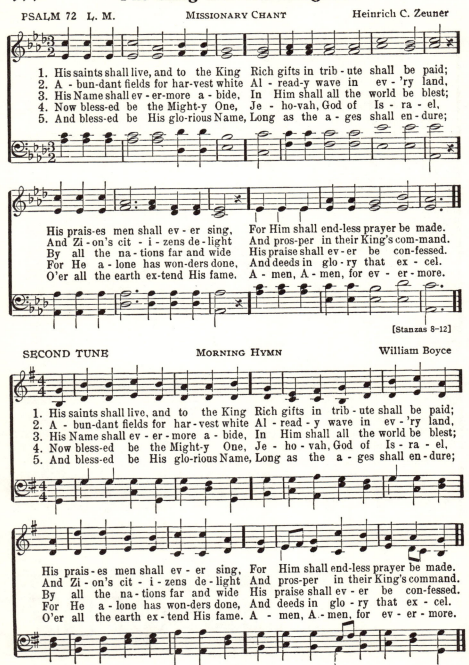

1. His saints shall live, and to the King Rich gifts in trib-ute shall be paid;
2. A-bun-dant fields for har-vest white Al-read-y wave in ev-'ry land,
3. His Name shall ev-er-more a-bide, In Him shall all the world be blest;
4. Now bless-ed be the Might-y One, Je-ho-vah, God of Is-ra-el,
5. And bless-ed be His glo-rious Name, Long as the a-ges shall en-dure;

His prais-es men shall ev-er sing, For Him shall end-less prayer be made.
And Zi-on's cit-i-zens de-light And pros-per in their King's com-mand.
By all the na-tions far and wide His praise shall ev-er be con-fessed.
For He a-lone has won-ders done, And deeds in glo-ry that ex-cel.
O'er all the earth ex-tend His fame. A-men, A-men, for ev-er-more.

[Stanzas 8–12]

SECOND TUNE MORNING HYMN William Boyce

1. His saints shall live, and to the King Rich gifts in trib-ute shall be paid;
2. A-bun-dant fields for har-vest white Al-read-y wave in ev-'ry land,
3. His Name shall ev-er-more a-bide, In Him shall all the world be blest;
4. Now bless-ed be the Might-y One, Je-ho-vah, God of Is-ra-el,
5. And bless-ed be His glo-rious Name, Long as the a-ges shall en-dure;

His prais-es men shall ev-er sing, For Him shall end-less prayer be made.
And Zi-on's cit-i-zens de-light And pros-per in their King's command.
By all the na-tions far and wide His praise shall ev-er be con-fessed.
For He a-lone has won-ders done, And deeds in glo-ry that ex-cel.
O'er all the earth ex-tend His fame. A-men, A-men, for ev-er-more.

200   The Enthroned Christ

PSALM 72   6s and 5s   ST. GERTRUDE   Arthur S. Sullivan

1. Christ shall have do-min-ion O-ver land and sea, Earth's re-mot-est
2. When the need-y seek Him, He will mer-cy show; Yea, the weak and
3. Ev-er and for-ev-er Shall His Name en-dure, Long as suns con-
4. Un-to God Al-might-y Joy-ful Zi-on sings; He a-lone is

re-gions Shall His em-pire be; They that wilds in-hab-it
help-less Shall His pit-y know; He will sure-ly save them
tin-ue It shall stand se-cure; And in Him for-ev-er
glo-rious, Do-ing won-drous things. Ev-er-more, ye peo-ple,

Shall their wor-ship bring, Kings shall ren-der trib-ute, Na-tions serve our King.
From op-pres-sion's might, For their lives are pre-cious In His ho-ly sight.
All men shall be blest, And all na-tions hail Him King of kings con-fessed.
Bless His glo-rious Name, His e-ter-nal glo-ry Thro' the earth pro-claim.

CHORUS

Christ shall have do-min-ion O-ver land and sea,

Earth's re-mot-est re-gions Shall His em-pire be.

[Selected Stanzas]

A Vindication of God's Ways

PSALM 73 11s   MOBILE   John P. Campbell

1. God lov - eth the right - eous, His good - ness is sure,
2. The wick - ed are pros - pered and firm in their strength,
3. In gar - ments of boast - ing and vi - o - lence decked,
4. De - spis - ing God's peo - ple, they cause them to drain

He nev - er for - sak - eth the good and the pure;
No pangs do they suf - fer, though death come at length;
With wealth more a - bun - dant than heart could ex - pect,
The cup of op - pres - sion, in - jus - tice, and pain;

Yet once my faith fal - tered, I en - vied the proud,
They are not in troub - le as oth - er men are,
They scoff, and the help - less they proud - ly op - press,
They ques - tion God's knowl - edge and bold - ly de - fy

In doubt and dis - qui - et my spir - it was bowed.
The plagues of their fel - lows they view from a - far.
The heav'ns and the earth they as - sume to pos - sess.
The might and the jus - tice of God the Most High.

5 The wicked, grown wealthy, have comfort and peace,
While I, daily chastened, see troubles increase,
And, wronging God's children, I cried in my pain,
That clean hands are worthless and pure hearts are vain.

A Vindication of God's Ways

6 I went to God's temple: my doubts were dispelled,
   The end of life's journey I clearly beheld;
   I saw in what peril ungodly men stand
   With sudden destruction and ruin at hand.

7 As when one awaking forgetteth his dream,
   So God will despise them, though great they may seem;
   My envy was senseless, my grief was for nought,
   Because I was faithless, and foolish my thought.

SECOND TUNE   ST. DENIO   Welsh Melody

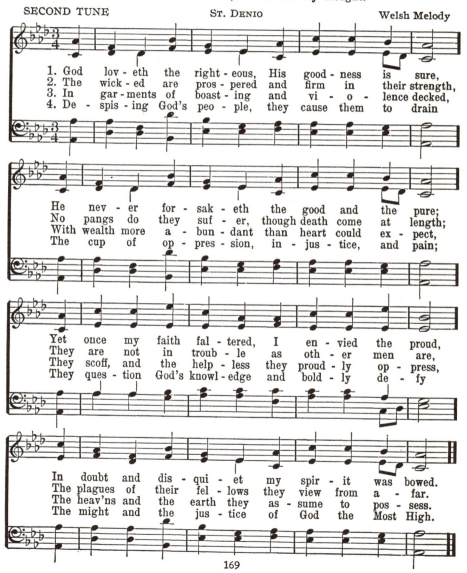

1. God lov - eth the right - eous, His good - ness is sure,
2. The wick - ed are pros - pered and firm in their strength,
3. In gar - ments of boast - ing and vi - o - lence decked,
4. De - spis - ing God's peo - ple, they cause them to drain

He nev - er for - sak - eth the good and the pure;
No pangs do they suf - er, though death come at length;
With wealth more a - bun - dant than heart could ex - pect,
The cup of op - pres - sion, in - jus - tice, and pain;

Yet once my faith fal - tered, I en - vied the proud,
They are not in trou - ble as oth - er men are,
They scoff, and the help - less they proud - ly op - press,
They ques - tion God's knowl - edge and bold - ly de - fy

In doubt and dis - qui - et my spir - it was bowed.
The plagues of their fel - lows they view from a - far.
The heav'ns and the earth they as - sume to pos - sess.
The might and the jus - tice of God the Most High.

169

202 Guidance and Glory

PSALM 73 11s
CARTER
E. Grace Updegraff

1. In doubt and temp-ta - tion I rest, Lord, in Thee;
2. In glo - ry Thou on - ly my por - tion shalt be,
3. All they that for-sake Thee must per - ish and die,

My hand is in Thy hand, Thou car - est for me;
On earth for none oth - er I long but for Thee;
But near to my Sav - iour most bless - ed am I;

My soul with Thy coun - sel through life Thou wilt guide,
My flesh and heart fal - ter, but God is my stay,
I make Thee my ref - uge, my Lord and my God;

rit.

And aft - er - ward make me in glo - ry a - bide.
The strength of my spir - it, my por - tion for aye.
Thy grace and Thy glo - ry I pub - lish a - broad.

Guidance and Glory

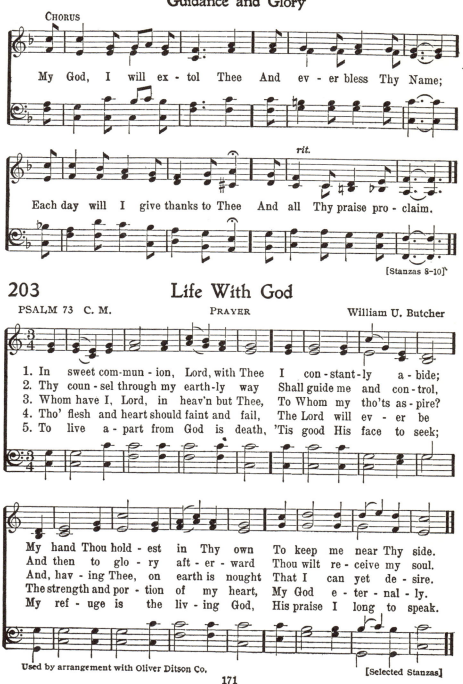

CHORUS

My God, I will ex-tol Thee And ev-er bless Thy Name;

rit.

Each day will I give thanks to Thee And all Thy praise pro-claim.

[Stanzas 8-10]

203   Life With God

PSALM 73 C. M.   PRAYER   William U. Butcher

1. In sweet com-mun-ion, Lord, with Thee   I con-stant-ly a-bide;
2. Thy coun-sel through my earth-ly way   Shall guide me and con-trol,
3. Whom have I, Lord, in heav'n but Thee,   To Whom my tho'ts as-pire?
4. Tho' flesh and heart should faint and fail,   The Lord will ev-er be
5. To live a-part from God is death,   'Tis good His face to seek;

My hand Thou hold-est in Thy own   To keep me near Thy side.
And then to glo-ry aft-er-ward   Thou wilt re-ceive my soul.
And, hav-ing Thee, on earth is nought   That I can yet de-sire.
The strength and por-tion of my heart,   My God e-ter-nal-ly.
My ref-uge is the liv-ing God,   His praise I long to speak.

Used by arrangement with Oliver Ditson Co.

[Selected Stanzas]

204 God Our Only Good

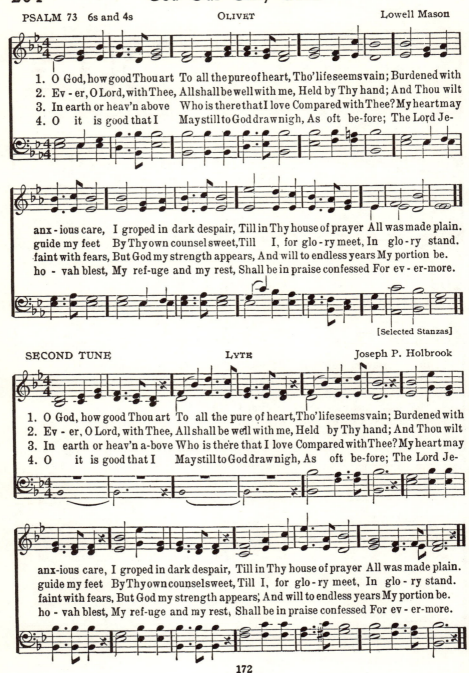

PSALM 73 6s and 4s   OLIVET   Lowell Mason

1. O God, how good Thou art To all the pure of heart, Tho' life seems vain; Burdened with
2. Ev - er, O Lord, with Thee, All shall be well with me, Held by Thy hand; And Thou wilt
3. In earth or heav'n above Who is there that I love Compared with Thee? My heart may
4. O it is good that I May still to God draw nigh, As oft be-fore; The Lord Je-

anx - ious care, I groped in dark despair, Till in Thy house of prayer All was made plain.
guide my feet By Thy own counsel sweet, Till I, for glo - ry meet, In glo - ry stand.
faint with fears, But God my strength appears, And will to endless years My portion be.
ho - vah blest, My ref-uge and my rest, Shall be in praise confessed For ev - er-more.

[Selected Stanzas]

SECOND TUNE   LYTE   Joseph P. Holbrook

1. O God, how good Thou art To all the pure of heart, Tho' life seems vain; Burdened with
2. Ev - er, O Lord, with Thee, All shall be well with me, Held by Thy hand; And Thou wilt
3. In earth or heav'n a-bove Who is there that I love Compared with Thee? My heart may
4. O it is good that I May still to God draw nigh, As oft be-fore; The Lord Je-

anx - ious care, I groped in dark despair, Till in Thy house of prayer All was made plain.
guide my feet By Thy own counsel sweet, Till I, for glo - ry meet, In glo - ry stand.
faint with fears, But God my strength appears, And will to endless years My portion be.
ho - vah blest, My ref-uge and my rest, Shall be in praise confessed For ev - er-more.

205 The Church in Trial

PSALM 74 C. M.　　　　　COWPER　　　　　Lowell Mason

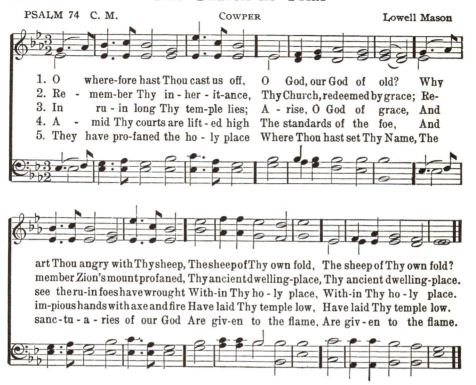

1. O where-fore hast Thou cast us off, O God, our God of old? Why
art Thou angry with Thy sheep, The sheep of Thy own fold, The sheep of Thy own fold?

2. Re - mem-ber Thy in - her - it-ance, Thy Church, redeemed by grace; Remember Zion's mount profaned, Thy ancient dwelling-place, Thy ancient dwelling-place.

3. In ru - in long Thy tem-ple lies; A - rise, O God of grace, And
see the ru-in foes have wrought With-in Thy ho - ly place, With-in Thy ho - ly place.

4. A - mid Thy courts are lift - ed high The standards of the foe, And
im-pious hands with axe and fire Have laid Thy temple low, Have laid Thy temple low.

5. They have pro-faned the ho - ly place Where Thou hast set Thy Name, The
sanc-tu - a - ries of our God Are giv-en to the flame, Are giv-en to the flame.

6 We see no signs of power divine,
　No prophet speaks for Thee,
And none can tell, and none can know,
　How long these woes shall be.

7 How long, O God, shall blasphemy
　And shame reproach our land?
Why dost Thou not destroy Thy foes
　With Thy almighty hand?

8 O God, Thou art our King of old,
　Salvation Thou hast wrought;
In safety through the mighty sea
　Our fathers Thou hast brought.

9 With mighty arm Thou didst destroy
　The pride of boastful man,
And for Thy people made a path
　Where mighty waters ran.

10 The day is Thine, and Thine the night,
　And Thine the shining sun;
At Thy command earth's bounds are set
　And changing seasons run.

11 Mark how Thy enemies, O Lord,
　Against Thee proudly speak;
Preserve Thy saints from wicked men,
　Be mindful of the meek.

12 Fulfill, O Lord, Thy covenant,
　Our strong protector be,
For in the earth are dark abodes
　Of crime and cruelty.

13 Let not Thy saints be put to shame,
　No longer in Thy sight
Permit Thy foes to vaunt themselves;
　Lord, vindicate the right.

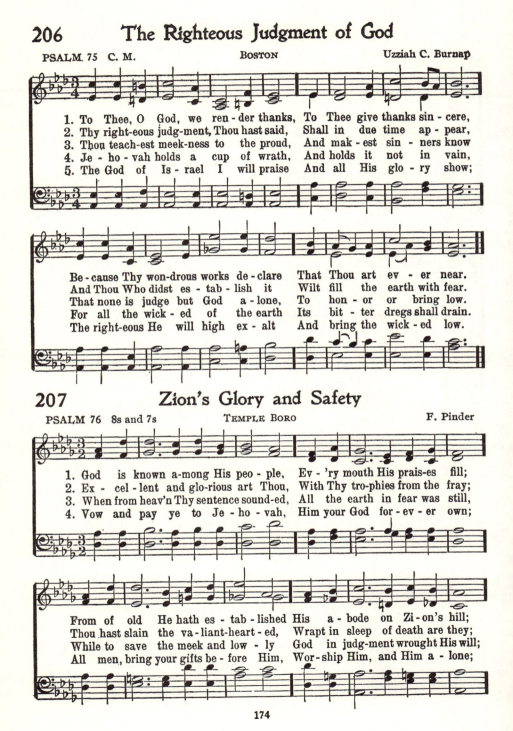

206 The Righteous Judgment of God

PSALM 75 C. M.   BOSTON   Uzziah C. Burnap

1. To Thee, O God, we ren - der thanks, To Thee give thanks sin - cere,
2. Thy right-eous judg-ment, Thou hast said, Shall in due time ap - pear,
3. Thou teach-est meek-ness to the proud, And mak - est sin - ners know
4. Je - ho - vah holds a cup of wrath, And holds it not in vain,
5. The God of Is - rael I will praise And all His glo - ry show;

Be - cause Thy won-drous works de - clare That Thou art ev - er near.
And Thou Who didst es - tab - lish it Wilt fill the earth with fear.
That none is judge but God a - lone, To hon - or or bring low.
For all the wick - ed of the earth Its bit - ter dregs shall drain.
The right-eous He will high ex - alt And bring the wick - ed low.

207 Zion's Glory and Safety

PSALM 76 8s and 7s   TEMPLE BORO   F. Pinder

1. God is known a-mong His peo - ple, Ev - 'ry mouth His prais-es fill;
2. Ex - cel - lent and glo-rious art Thou, With Thy tro-phies from the fray;
3. When from heav'n Thy sentence sound-ed, All the earth in fear was still,
4. Vow and pay ye to Je - ho - vah, Him your God for - ev - er own;

From of old He hath es - tab - lished His a - bode on Zi - on's hill;
Thou hast slain the va - liant-heart - ed, Wrapt in sleep of death are they;
While to save the meek and low - ly God in judg-ment wrought His will;
All men, bring your gifts be - fore Him, Wor - ship Him, and Him a - lone;

174

Zion's Glory and Safety

There He broke the sword and ar - row, Bade the noise of war be still.
When Thy an - ger once is ris - en, Who can stand in that dread day?
E'en the wrath of man shall praise Thee, Thy de - signs it shall ful - fill.
Might - y kings o - bey and fear Him, Prin - ces bow be - fore His throne.

208 Aspects of the Divine Character

PSALM 76 L. M.   EASTON   Arranged from Mozart

1. A - mong His peo - ple God is known, Most glo - rious
2. When God the right - eous judge ap - peared To save the
3. The wrath of man shall praise the Lord, Re - strained by
4. Let all to Him their pres - ents bring, To Him Whom

in His might and grace; He makes Je - ru - sa -
meek from wrong and shame, The earth stood still and
His al - might - y will; Your vows to God the
all the world should fear; Ye kings and prin - ces,

lem His throne, Her peace - ful hills His dwell - ing - place.
great - ly feared; Then forth from heav'n His sen - tence came.
King re - cord, Your cov - enant made with Him ful - fill.
own your King, With rev -'rence and with awe draw near.

175   [Selected Stanzas]

209 Doubts Overcome by Faith

PSALM 77 L. M. SESSIONS Luther O. Emerson

1. To God for help will I re-pair, To God will
   I di-rect my prayer, And sure-ly He will
   an-swer me, His great sal-va-tion I shall see.

2. In long-con-tin-ued grief I stand And seek the
   Lord with out-stretched hand; I find no com-fort
   for my soul, The clouds of dark-ness o'er me roll.

3. I think of God and call to mind His good-ness,
   yet no peace I find; I still pour out my
   sad com-plaints, My bur-dened spir-it al-most faints.

4. With sleep-less eyes and speech-less grief I search the
   past to find re-lief, The for-mer years when
   days were bright And songs of glad-ness cheered my night.

5. My con-stant med-i-ta-tions bring My heart to
   anx-ious ques-tion-ing: Has God cast off, and
   will He be No lon-ger mer-ci-ful to me?

6 Has God forgotten to be kind?
  Shall I His promise faithless find?
  For me shall wrath henceforth replace
  His tender mercies and His grace?

7 In weakness I was pressed with fear,
  But better hopes my spirit cheer;
  Past mercies lead me to rely
  Upon the help of God Most High.

8 Thy deeds, O Lord, will I relate
  And on Thy wonders meditate;
  Thy way, O God, is just and right,
  And none is like to Thee in might.

9 Among the nations Thou hast shown
  Thy wondrous power and made it known;
  Thou art the God that mightily
  Redeemed and set Thy people free.

10 At sight of Thee the waters fled,
   The quaking clouds their torrents shed,
   The lightnings flashed, the thunder pealed,
   The trembling earth her fear revealed.

11 Thy way, O God, was in the sea,
   But, though Thy paths mysterious be,
   Thy people Thou didst safely keep
   As shepherds lead their helpless sheep.

210 Questionings and Comfort

PSALM 77 L. M.   FILLMORE   Jeremiah Ingalls

Slowly

1. To God will I di-rect my prayer, And He will
2. The thought of God brought me no peace, But rath-er
3. Re-call-ing days when faith was bright, When songs of
4. I asked in fear and bit-ter-ness, Will God for-
5. These doubts and fears that troub-led me Were born of

make my needs His care; I trust Him still, though in my grief
made my fears in-crease; With sleep-less eyes and speech-less pain
glad-ness filled my night, I pon-dered o'er my griev-ous woes
sake me in dis-tress? Shall I His prom-ise faith-less find?
my in-firm-i-ty; Tho' I am weak, God is most high,

No an-swer yet has brought re-lief; With hands stretched
My faint-ing spir-it grieved in vain; The bless-ed-
And search-ing ques-tion-ing a-rose: Will God cast
Has God for-got-ten to be kind? Has He in
And on His good-ness I re-ly; Of all His

out through all the night, Un-com-fort-ed I sought for light.
ness of long a-go Made deep-er still my pres-ent woe.
off, and nev-er-more His fa-vor to my soul re-store?
an-ger hope-less-ly Re-moved His love and grace from me?·
won-ders I will tell, And on His deeds my tho'ts shall dwell.

177

211 The Wonderful Deeds of God

PSALM 77 L. M. YOAKLEY William Yoakley

1. { O God, most ho-ly are Thy ways, And who like Thee deserves my praise?
   { Thou on-ly do-est won-drous things, The whole wide world Thy glory sings;

2. { O God, from Thee the wa-ters fled, The depths were moved with mighty dread,
   { The swell-ing clouds their tor-rents poured, And o'er the earth the tempest roared;

3. { Thy way was in the sea, O God, Thro might-y waters, deep and broad;
   { None un-der-stood but God a-lone, To man Thy footsteps were unknown;

Thy outstretched arm Thy peo-ple saved, Tho' sore dis-tressed and long en-slaved.
'Mid lightning's flash and thun-der's sound Great trembling shook the sol-id ground.
But safe Thy peo-ple Thou didst keep, Al-might-y Shep-herd of Thy sheep.

[Stanzas 6–8]

212 Hallowed Memories

PSALM 77 C. M. SAXONY William J. Kirkpatrick

1. I thought up-on the days of old, The years de-part-ed long,
2. My heart in-quired with anx-ious care, Will God for-ev-er spurn?
3. For-ev-er shall His prom-ise fail? Has God for-got-ten grace?
4. These doubts are my in-firm-i-ty, My thoughts at once re-ply;
5. I will com-mem-o-rate, O Lord, Thy won-drous deeds of old,
6. O God, most ho-ly is Thy way, Most per-fect, good, and right;

I held com-mun-ion with my heart, By night re-called my song.
Shall we no more His fa-vor see? Will mer-cy ne'er re-turn?
Has He with-drawn His ten-der love, In an-ger hid His face?
I call back years of God's right hand, The years of God Most High.
And med-i-tate up-on Thy works Of pow'r and grace un-told.
Thou art the on-ly liv-ing God, The God of won-drous might.

Copyright, 1900, by Wm. J. Kirkpatrick. Used by per. [Selected Stanzas]

Hallowed Memories

SECOND TUNE   AULD LANG SYNE   Scotch Melody

1. I thought up - on the days of old, The years de - part - ed. long,
2. For - ev - er shall His prom - ise fail? Has God for - got - ten grace?
3. I will com-mem - o - rate, O Lord, Thy won - drous deeds of old,

I held com-mun - ion with my heart, By night re - called my song.
Has He with-drawn His ten - der love, In an - ger hid His face?
And med - i - tate up - on Thy works Of pow'r and grace un - told.

My heart in-quired with anx - ious care, Will God for - ev - er spurn?
These doubts are my in - firm - i - ty, My thoughts at once re - ply;
O God, most ho - ly is Thy way, Most per - fect, good, and right;

Shall we no more His fa - vor see? Will mer - cy ne'er re - turn?
I call back years of God's right hand, The years of God Most High.
Thou art the on - ly liv - ing God, The God of won-drous might.

213 Lessons from the Past

PSALM 78   10s and 11s   CHIOS   Charles H. Gabriel

1. My peo - ple, give ear, at - tend to my word,
2. In - struct - ing our sons we glad - ly re - cord
3. Let chil - dren thus learn from his - to - ry's light
4. The sto - ry be told, to warn and re - strain,
5. God's won - der - ful works to them He had shown,
6. He gave them to drink, re - liev - ing their thirst,

In par - a - bles new deep truths shall be heard;
The prais - es, the works, the might of the Lord,
To hope in our God and walk in His sight,
Of hearts that were hard, re - bel - lious, and vain,
His mar - vel - ous deeds their fa - thers had known;
And forth from the rock caused wa - ter to burst;

The won - der - ful sto - ry our fa - thers made known
For He hath com - mand - ed that what He hath done
The God of their fa - thers to fear and o - bey,
Of sol - diers who fal - tered when bat - tle was near,
He made for their path - way the wa - ters di - vide,
Yet faith - less they tempt - ed their God, and they said,

To chil - dren suc - ceed - ing by us must be shown.
Be passed in tra - di - tion from fa - ther to son.
And ne'er like their fa - thers to turn from His way.
Who kept not God's cov - enant nor walked in His fear.
His glo - ri - ous pil - lar of cloud was their guide.
Can He Who gave wa - ter sup - ply us with bread?

Lessons from the Past

7 Jehovah was wroth because they forgot
To hope in their God, and trusted Him not;
Yet gracious, He opened the doors of the sky
And rained down the manna in richest supply.

8 With bread from on high their need He supplied,
And more did He do when thankless they sighed;
The strong winds commanding from south and from east,
He sent them abundance of quail for their feast.

9 Though well they were filled, their folly they chose,
Till God in His wrath o'erwhelmed them with woes;
He slew of their strongest and smote their young men,
But still unbelieving they sinned even then.

10 Because of their sin He smote with His rod,
And then they returned and sought for their God;
Their Rock and Redeemer was God the Most High,
Yet false were their praises, their promise a lie.

11 Not right with their God in heart and in will,
They faithlessly broke His covenant still;
But He, in compassion, reluctant to slay,
Forgave them and oft turned His anger away.

12 His pity was great, though often they sinned,
For they were but flesh, a swift passing wind;
Yet though His compassion and grace they beheld,
They tempted and grieved Him and often rebelled.

13 They limited God, the Most Holy One,
And hindered the work His grace had begun;
The hand that was mighty to save they forgot,
The day of redemption remembering not.

14 Ungrateful and blind, no longer they thought
Of wonders and signs and mighty deeds wrought,
Of how all the rivers of Egypt ran red,
And plagues in God's anger were heaped on their head.

15 They thought not of how, their freedom to gain,
In Egypt's abodes the first-born were slain,
And how all God's people were led forth like sheep,
The flock He delighted in safety to keep.

214 Reminders from Israel's History

PSALM 78 10s and 11s   STELLA   Crown of Jesus Music

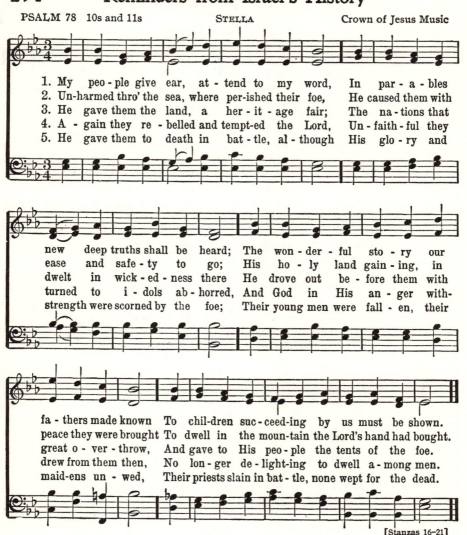

1. My peo-ple give ear, at-tend to my word, In par-a-bles new deep truths shall be heard; The won-der-ful sto-ry our fa-thers made known To chil-dren suc-ceed-ing by us must be shown.
2. Un-harmed thro' the sea, where per-ished their foe, He caused them with ease and safe-ty to go; His ho-ly land gain-ing, in peace they were brought To dwell in the moun-tain the Lord's hand had bought.
3. He gave them the land, a her-it-age fair; The na-tions that dwelt in wick-ed-ness there He drove out be-fore them with great o-ver-throw, And gave to His peo-ple the tents of the foe.
4. A-gain they re-belled and tempt-ed the Lord, Un-faith-ful they turned to i-dols ab-horred, And God in His an-ger with-drew from them then, No lon-ger de-light-ing to dwell a-mong men.
5. He gave them to death in bat-tle, al-though His glo-ry and strength were scorned by the foe; Their young men were fall-en, their maid-ens un-wed, Their priests slain in bat-tle, none wept for the dead.

[Stanzas 16–21]

6 Then mercy awoke, the Lord in His might
   Returned, and the foes were scattered in flight;
   Again to His people His favor He showed,
   And chose in Mount Zion to fix His abode.

7 His servant He called, a shepherd of sheep,
   From tending his flock, the people to keep;
   So David, their shepherd, with wisdom and might
   Protected and fed them and led them aright.

Religious Training

PSALM 78 C. M.   HEBER   George Kingsley

1. O come, my peo - ple, to my law At-
2. My mouth shall speak in par - a - bles Of
3. We will not from their chil - dren hide Je-
4. A tes - ti - mo - ny and a law The

ten - tive - ly give ear; With will - ing heart and
hid - den truths of old, Which, hand - ed down from
ho - vah's wor - thy praise, But tell the great - ness
Lord our God de - creed, And bade our fa - thers

teach - a - ble The words of wis - dom hear.
age to age, To us our fa - thers told.
of His strength, His won - drous works and ways.
teach their sons, That they His ways might heed.

[Selected Stanzas]

5 He willed that each succeeding race
  His deeds might learn and know,
That children's children to their sons
  Might all these wonders show.

6 Let children learn God's righteous ways
  And on Him stay their heart,
That they may not forget His works
  Nor from His ways depart.

The Church Under Discipline

PSALM 79   8s and 7s   SALONICA   Charles E. Pollock

Slowly

1. In Thy her - it - age the hea - then Now, O
2. O how long a - gainst Thy peo - ple Shall Thy
3. O re - mem - ber not a - gainst us E - vil
4. Let Thy foes no lon - ger scorn Thee, Now a -

God, tri - um - phant stand; They de - file Thy ho - ly
an - ger burn, O Lord? On Thy en - e - mies, the
by our fa - thers wrought; Haste to help us in Thy
venge Thy serv - ants slain; Loose the pris - 'ner, save the

tem - ple, They de - stroy Thy cho - sen land;
hea - then, Be Thy in - dig - na - tion poured;
mer - cy, Near to ru - in we are brought;
dy - ing, All Thy en - e - mies re - strain;

Ruth - less, they have slain Thy serv - ants, They have
Smite the king - doms that de - fy Thee, Call - ing
Help - us, God of our sal - va - tion, For the
Then Thy flock, Thy cho - sen peo - ple, Un - to

The Church Under Discipline

caused Thy saints to mourn, In the sight of all a-
not up-on Thy Name; They have long de-voured Thy
glo-ry of Thy Name; For Thy Name's sake come and
Thee their thanks shall raise, And to ev-'ry gen-er-

bout us We en-dure re-proach and scorn.
peo-ple And have swept Thy land with flame.
save us, Take a-way our sin and shame.
a-tion We will sing Thy glo-rious praise.

217 Forgiving Mercy Besought

PSALM 79 S. M.   GORTON   Arranged from Beethoven

1. Re-mem-ber not, O God, The sins of long a-go;
2. O Lord, our Sav-iour, help, And glo-ri-fy Thy Name;
3. In Thy com-pas-sion hear Thy pris-'ner's plain-tive sigh,
4. Then, safe with-in Thy fold, We will ex-alt Thy Name;

In ten-der mer-cy vis-it us, Dis-tressed and hum-bled low.
De-liv-er us from all our sins And take a-way our shame.
And in the great-ness of Thy pow'r Save those a-bout to die.
Our thank-ful hearts with songs of joy Thy good-ness will pro-claim.

185   [Selected Stanzas]

A Suppliant Church

PSALM 80 10s   LANGRAN   James Langran

1. O Thou great Shep-herd of Thy cho-sen race, Who lead-est like a
2. How long, O Lord, wilt Thou dis-dain our prayer? For Thou hast fed us
3. A vine Thou broughtest forth from E-gypt's land; The na-tions were thrust
4. Why hast Thou bro-ken down its cir-cling wall That they may pluck who
5. Look down, be-hold and vis-it this Thy vine Which Thou hast plant-ed
6. O let Thy hand Thy cho-sen one sus-tain, The son of man Thou

flock Thy Is-rael dear, From out the cher-u-bim re-veal Thy face,
with the bread of tears, And bit-ter sor-row Thou hast made us share;
out to give it room; It took deep root, it spread on ev-'ry hand,
pass a-long the way? Wild beasts from out the wood de-stroy it all
with Thy own right hand, The branch Thou mad-est strong and owned it Thine,
mad-est strong to be; So we shall faith-ful to Thy cause re-main;

Be-fore our host now let Thy might ap-pear. Come Thou, O God, to
The na-tions round us mock with scorn-ful jeers. O God of Hosts, Thy
The hills were cov-ered with its shade and bloom; Its boughs were like great
And feed up-on Thy vine by night and day. O God of Hosts, we
For it is burned with fire, no more to stand; Thy peo-ple per-ish
Re-vive Thou us, and we will call on Thee. Je-ho-vah, God of

save us and re-store; We shall be saved when shines Thy face once more.
peo-ple now re-store; We shall be saved when shines Thy face once more.
ce-dars spread-ing wide; They reached the sea, its roots the riv-er-side.
pray Thee now, re-store; We shall be saved when shines Thy face once more.
in Thy an-ger sore Be-cause Thy face now shines on them no more.
Hosts, a-gain re-store; We shall be saved when shines Thy face once more.

Restoration and Revival

PSALM 80 10s   SUNDOWN   John H. Gower

Voices in Unison

1. O Thou great Shep-herd of Thy cho-sen race, Who lead-est
2. O let Thy hand Thy cho-sen one sus-tain, The son of

Voices in Harmony

like a flock Thy Is-rael dear, From out the cher-u-
man Thou mad-est strong to be; So we shall faith-ful

bim re-veal Thy face, Be-fore our host now let Thy
to Thy cause re-main; Re-vive Thou us, and we will

Unison

might ap-pear. Come Thou, O God, to save us and re-store;
call on Thee. Je-ho-vah, God of Hosts, a-gain re-store;

Harmony

We shall be saved when shines Thy face once more.
We shall be saved when shines Thy face once more.

Copyright by John H. Gower. Used by per.   [Selected Stanzas]

220 Prayer for Restoring Grace

PSALM 80 11s   SANKEY   Ira D. Sankey

1. Great Shep - herd Who lead - est Thy peo - ple in love,
2. O haste, Lord, to hear us and pit - y our woes,
3. A place for Thy peo - ple Thou, Lord, didst pre - pare,
4. Thy vine - yard no lon - ger Thy ten - der care knows,
5. The branch of Thy plant - ing is burned and cut down,
6. When Thou shalt re - vive us Thy Name we will praise,

'Mid cher - u - bim dwell - ing, shine Thou from a - bove;
Af - flic - tion our por - tion, de - spised by our foes;
Thy vine deep - ly root - ed re - ward - ed Thy care;
De - fense - less, the vic - tim and spoil of her foes;
Brought nigh to de - struc - tion be - cause of Thy frown;
And nev - er - more, turn - ing, de - part from Thy ways;

In might come and save us, Thy peo - ple re - store,
O Lord God Al - might - y, in mer - cy re - store,
Its branch - es like ce - dars, ma - jes - tic and free,
O turn, we be - seech Thee, all glo - ry is Thine,
The man of Thy right hand with wis - dom en - due,
O Lord God al - might - y, in mer - cy re - store,

ritard

And we shall be saved when Thy face shines once more.
And we shall be saved when Thy face shines once more.
Spread o - ver the moun - tains from riv - er to sea.
Look down in Thy mer - cy and vis - it Thy vine.
The son of man strength - en Thy pleas - ure to do.
And we shall be saved when Thy face shines once more.

Longing for Revival

PSALM 80 11s   CARITAS   Adoniram J. Gordon

1. Great Shep - herd Who lead - est Thy peo - ple in love,
2. O haste, Lord, to hear us and pit - y our woes,
3. When Thou shalt re - vive us Thy Name we will praise,

'Mid cher - u - bim dwell - ing, shine Thou from a - bove;
Af - flic - tion our por - tion, de - spised by our foes;
And nev - er - more, turn - ing, de - part from Thy ways;

In might come and save us, Thy peo - ple re - store,
O Lord God Al - might - y, in mer - cy re - store,
O Lord God Al - might - y, in mer - cy re - store,

And we shall be saved when Thy face shines once more.
And we shall be saved when Thy face shines once more.
And we shall be saved when Thy face shines once more.

[Selected Stanzas]

189

222 A Summons to Joyful Worship

PSALM 81 8s and 7s   STOCKWELL   Darius E. Jones

1. Now to God, our Strength and Sav-iour, Ren-der
2. Let the trump-et, far re-sound-ing, This our
3. I, thy God, re-moved thy bur-dens, When thou
4. O My peo-ple, hear My plead-ings; O that
5. I am God the Lord Who saved thee, And from

praise and loud-ly sing; In our fa-thers' God re-
fes-tal day pro-claim, By our fa-thers' God ap-
call-edst, set thee free, Proved thee in the thirst-y
thou wouldst heark-en now; No strange wor-ship shalt thou
cru-el bond-age freed; O-pen wide thy mouth of

joic-ing, All your no-blest mu-sic bring.
point-ed, When from bond-age Is-rael came.
des-ert, In the thun-der an-swered thee.
of-fer, Nor to i-dols shalt thou bow.
long-ing; I will sat-is-fy thy need.

6 But My people would not hearken,
   Yea, they would not yield to Me;
So I left them in their blindness,
   Their own counselors to be.

7 If My people would obey Me,
   Gladly walking in My ways,
Soon would I, their foes subduing,
   Fill their lips with songs of praise.

8 All the haters of Jehovah
   Shall His clemency implore,
And the days of those that love Him
   Shall endure for evermore.

9 Yea, with wheat the very finest
   I their hunger will supply,
Bid the very rocks yield honey
   That shall fully satisfy.

190

Responsibility of Civil Officers

PSALM 82 7s and 6s   ALGIERS   John B. Herbert

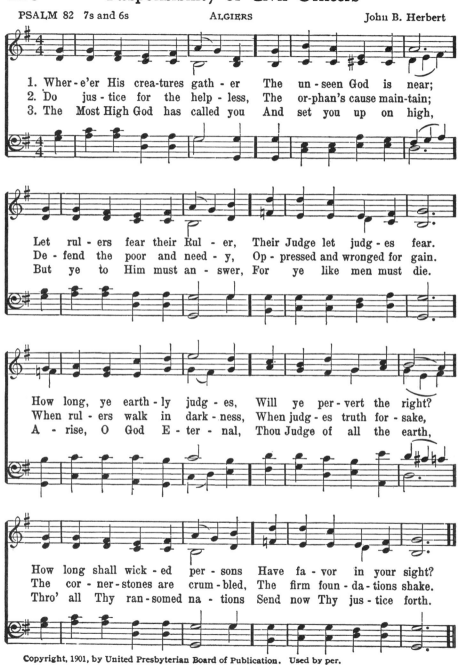

1. Wher-e'er His crea-tures gath-er The un-seen God is near;
2. Do jus-tice for the help-less, The or-phan's cause main-tain;
3. The Most High God has called you And set you up on high,

Let rul-ers fear their Rul-er, Their Judge let judg-es fear.
De-fend the poor and need-y, Op-pressed and wronged for gain.
But ye to Him must an-swer, For ye like men must die.

How long, ye earth-ly judg-es, Will ye per-vert the right?
When rul-ers walk in dark-ness, When judg-es truth for-sake,
A-rise, O God E-ter-nal, Thou Judge of all the earth,

How long shall wick-ed per-sons Have fa-vor in your sight?
The cor-ner-stones are crum-bled, The firm foun-da-tions shake.
Thro' all Thy ran-somed na-tions Send now Thy jus-tice forth.

224 The Foes of the Church

PSALM 83 C. M.　　　GREEN HILL　　　Albert L. Peace

1. O God, no lon-ger hold Thy peace, No lon-ger si-lent be;
2. A-gainst Thy own, whom Thou dost love, Their craft Thy foes em-ploy;
3. Thy an-cient foes, con-spir-ing still, With one con-sent a-gree,
4. O God, Who in our fa-thers' time Didst smite our foes and Thine,
5. Make them like dust and stub-ble blown Be-fore the whirl-wind dire,
6. Con-found them in their sin till they To Thee for par-don fly,

Thy en-e-mies lift up their head To fight Thy saints and Thee.
They think to cut Thy peo-ple off, Thy Church they would de-stroy.
And they who with Thy peo-ple strive Make war, O God, with Thee.
So smite Thy en-e-mies to-day Who in their pride com-bine.
In ter-ror driv'n be-fore the storm Of Thy con-sum-ing fire.
Till in dis-may they trem-bling own That Thou art God Most High.

225 Delight in the House of God

PSALM 84 C. M.　　　ERSKINE　　　Charles H. Gabriel

Slowly

1. How dear to me, O Lord of Hosts, The place where Thou dost dwell;
2. Be-neath Thy care the spar-row finds A place of peace-ful rest;
3. Blest they who dwell with-in Thy house, Their per-fect strength Thou art;

The tab-er-na-cles of Thy grace In pleas-ant-ness ex-cel.
Where she may safe-ly lay her young The swal-low finds a nest;
Their joy-ful praise shall nev-er cease, Thy ways are in their heart.

Delight in the House of God

My spir - it longs, yea, e - ven faints, Thy sa - cred courts to see;
Then, Lord of Hosts, my King, my God, Thy love will shel - ter me;
Their tears of grief, like ear - ly rain, Sweet springs of joy shall fill;

My thirst - ing heart and flesh cry out, O liv - ing God, for Thee.
Be - neath Thy al - tar's peace - ful shade My dwell - ing-place shall be.
With strength renewed they jour - ney safe To Zi - on's ho - ly hill.

226 Longings for Sanctuary Fellowship

PSALM 84 C. M. AUDITE AUDIENTES ME Arthur S. Sullivan

Voices in Unison

Organ

1. O Lord of Hosts, to Thee I cry, Our fa - thers' God, to Thee; Let my pe - ti - tion
2. A sin-gle day with-in Thy courts, Where I Thy beau-ty see, Is bet-ter than a
3. A sun and shield is God, the Lord, To light-en and de-fend; The Lord to such as

Voices in Harmony

reach Thy ear, My prayer accept-ed be; O God our shield, look Thou on us, Re-
thousand days, My God, a-part from Thee. A low - ly sta - tion in Thy house Were
look to Him Will grace and glory send; To those that walk in righteousness No

veal Thy-self in grace, And let Thy own a-noint-ed one Be-hold Thee face to face.
dear-er to my heart Than in the tents of wick-ed-ness To claim the chiefest part.
good will He de - ny; O Lord of Hosts, how blest are they Who on Thy grace re-ly.

193 [Stanzas 4-6]

Delight in Church Ordinances

PSALM 84   7s and 6s   St. Edith   Justin H. Knecht and
                                                     Edward Husband

1. O Lord of Hosts, how love-ly Thy tab-er-na-cles are;
2. Be-neath Thy care the spar-row Finds place for peace-ful rest;
3. Blest they who dwell in Zi-on, Whose joy and strength Thou art;

For them my heart is yearn-ing In ban-ish-ment a-far.
To keep her young in safe-ty The swal-low finds a nest;
For-ev-er they will praise Thee, Thy ways are in their heart.

My soul is long-ing, faint-ing, Thy sa-cred courts to see;
Then, Lord, my King Al-might-y, Thy love will shel-ter me;
Tho' tried, their tears like show-ers Shall fill the springs of peace,

My heart and flesh are cry-ing, O liv-ing God, for Thee.
Be-side Thy ho-ly al-tar My dwell-ing-place shall be.
And all the way to Zi-on Their strength shall still in-crease.

228 True Blessedness

PSALM 84 7s and 6s   CRUX CHRISTI   Arthur H. Mann

1. Lord God of Hosts, in mer - cy My sup - pli - ca - tion hear;
2. In Thy blest courts to wor - ship, My God, a sin - gle day
3. A sun and shield for - ev - er Is God, the Lord Most High;

Al - might - y and all - faith - ful, Our fa - thers' God, give ear;
Is bet - ter than a thou - sand While far from Thee I stray;
To those who walk up - right - ly No good will He de - ny;

Our shield and great de - fend - er, No lon - ger hide Thy face,
Tho' in a low - ly sta - tion, The serv - ice of my Lord
His saints, His grace re - ceiv - ing, Shall soon His glo - ry see;

But look up - on Thy serv - ant, A - noint - ed by Thy grace.
I choose a - bove all pleas - ures That sin - ful ways af - ford.
O Lord of Hosts, most bless - ed Are they that trust in Thee.

[Stanzas 4-6]

Days in the Sanctuary

229

PSALM 84 L. M.   ELLERTON   Joseph Barnby

1. How love - ly, Lord of Hosts, to me The tab - er -
2. The spar - row has her place of rest; The swal - low,
3. Blest they who in Thy house a - bide, They still to
4. Ad - vanc - ing still from strength to strength, They on - ward
5. Up - on us look, O God, our shield, The face of
6. Je - ho - vah, God our Shield and Sun, Will grace and

na - cles of Thy grace; O how I long, yea, faint to see
thro' Thy kind - ly care, Has found where she may build her nest
Thee shall ren - der praise; Blest they who in Thy strength con-fide,
go where saints have trod, Till ev - 'ry one ap - pears at length
Thy a - noint - ed see; A thou-sand oth - er days can yield
glo - ry sure - ly give; No good will He with-hold from one

Thy hal - lowed courts, Thy dwell - ing - place; For Thee my
And brood her young in safe - ty there; Thy al - tars
And in whose hearts are Zi - on's ways; Tho' pass - ing
In Zi - on's courts be - fore his God; Je - ho - vah,
No glad - ness like one day with Thee; Tho' on - ly
Who in His sight shall right - ly live; O Lord of

heart and spir - it sigh, For Thee, O liv - ing God, I cry.
as my rest I sing, O Lord of Hosts, my God, my King.
thro' the vale of tears, Like springs of joy Thy grace ap - pears.
God of Hosts, give ear, Our fa - thers' God, in mer - cy hear.
at Thy door I wait, No tents of sin give joy so great.
Hosts, most blest is he Who puts his stead - fast trust in Thee.

196

230 Assurance of Blessing

PSALM 85 L. M. ROCKINGHAM OLD Arranged by Edward Miller

1. Lord, Thou hast great - ly blessed our land, Thou hast brought
2. O Thou, Who in a for - mer day Didst turn Thy
3. O will Thy an - ger nev - er cease, For - ev - er
4. To us Thy mer - cy now af - ford And show us
5. The Lord's sal - va - tion will ap - pear To men of

back our cap - tive band, Thy par - d'ning grace has
dread - ful wrath a - way, In grace Thy peo - ple,
shall Thy wrath in - crease? Re - vive and quick - en
Thy sal - va - tion, Lord; Yea, Thou wilt an - swer
faith and god - ly fear, And glo - ry in our

made us free And cov - ered our in - iq - ui - ty.
Lord, re - turn, And let Thy wrath no lon - ger burn.
us once more, And Thy sal - va - tion's joy re - store.
us in peace, If from our fol - ly we will cease.
land shall dwell When we shall heed God's pre - cepts well.

6 Now truth agrees with mercy mild,
Now law and peace are reconciled;
Behold the truth from earth arise,
With justice shining from the skies.

7 The Lord will send His blessing down,
And harvests all our land shall crown;
Before Him righteousness abides,
And in His steps our feet He guides.

Encouragement in Prayer

PSALM 85 L. P. M.   REDAL   William B. Bradbury

1. Lord, Thou hast fa - vor shown Thy land, Re - stored a -
2. In grace Thy peo - ple, Lord, re - turn, Nor lon - ger
3. O Lord, to us Thy mer - cy show, And Thy sal -

gain Thy cap - tive band; Thy peo - ple's sins Thou par - doned hast,
let Thy an - ger burn; Wilt Thou for - ev - er an - gry be?
va - tion now be - stow; We wait to hear what God will say;

And all their guilt hast cov - ered o'er, Re - moved from
Thro' a - ges shall Thy wrath sur - vive? Wilt Thou not
Peace to His peo - ple He will speak, And to His

them Thy an - ger sore, All Thy fierce wrath be - hind Thee cast.
us a - gain re - vive, That so we may re - joice in Thee?
saints, but let them seek No more in fol - ly's path to stray.

Expectancy of Grace

PSALM 85 L. P. M.　　　　MELITA　　　　John B. Dykes

1. O Lord, to us Thy mer - cy show, And Thy sal - va - tion
2. His sav - ing help is sure - ly near To those His ho - ly
3. Truth spring-ing forth the earth shall crown, And right - eous - ness from

now be - stow; We wait to hear what God will say;
Name that fear; Thus glo - ry dwells in all our land.
heav'n look down, And God on us His good - ness shed;

Peace to His peo - ple He will speak, And to His saints, but
Now heav'n - ly truth u - nites with grace, And right - eous - ness and
Our land shall then with plen - ty flow, Be - fore Him right - eous-

let them seek No more in fol - ly's path to stray.
peace em - brace, In full ac - cord they ev - er stand.
ness shall go, And cause us in His steps to tread.

[Stanzas 3-5]

233 Confident Pleading

PSALM 86 L. M. ROLLAND William B. Bradbury

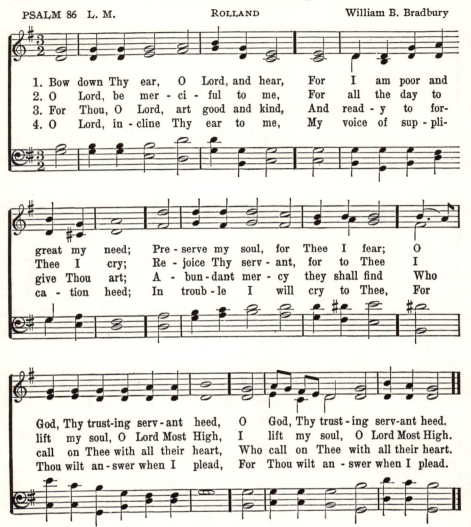

1. Bow down Thy ear, O Lord, and hear, For I am poor and
2. O Lord, be mer - ci - ful to me, For all the day to
3. For Thou, O Lord, art good and kind, And read - y to for-
4. O Lord, in - cline Thy ear to me, My voice of sup - pli-

great my need; Pre - serve my soul, for Thee I fear; O
Thee I cry; Re - joice Thy serv - ant, for to Thee I
give Thou art; A - bun - dant mer - cy they shall find Who
ca - tion heed; In troub - le I will cry to Thee, For

God, Thy trust - ing serv - ant heed, O God, Thy trust - ing serv - ant heed.
lift my soul, O Lord Most High, I lift my soul, O Lord Most High.
call on Thee with all their heart, Who call on Thee with all their heart.
Thou wilt an - swer when I plead, For Thou wilt an - swer when I plead.

5 There is no God but Thee alone,
　　Nor works like Thine, O Lord Most High;
　All nations shall surround Thy throne
　　And their Creator glorify.

6 In all Thy deeds how great Thou art!
　　Thou one true God, Thy way make clear;
　Teach me with undivided heart
　　To trust Thy truth, Thy Name to fear.

234 Devout Prayers and Pleas

PSALM 86 L. M.   Calm   John B. Dykes

1. O Lord, my God, my joy - ful heart Will give Thee praise for ev - er - more,
2. O God, the proud a-gainst me rise, The wick-ed who de-light in strife;
3. In Thee, O Lord, all grace is found, Thy peo-ple shall Thy mer - cy know;
4. In mer - cy turn and look on me, Thy serv-ant true, Thy cho-sen one;
5. Some to-ken of Thy love be - stow, Which they who hate me now may see;

For rich in grace to me Thou art, My soul from death Thou didst re - store.
They set not Thee be - fore their eyes, They seek to take a - way my life.
Thy truth and good-ness still a - bound, To wrath and an - ger Thou art slow.
Let me Thy great sal - va - tion see, And strengthen me my course to run.
Let all, O Lord, be brought to know That Thou dost help and com - fort me.

[Stanzas 7–11]

SECOND TUNE   Angelus   Altered from Georg Joseph

1. O Lord, my God, my joy - ful heart Will give Thee praise for ev - er - more,
2. O God, the proud a-gainst me rise, The wick-ed who de-light in strife;
3. In Thee, O Lord, all grace is found, Thy peo-ple shall Thy mer - cy know;
4. In mer - cy turn and look on me, Thy serv-ant true, Thy cho - sen one;
5. Some to-ken of Thy love be - stow, Which they who hate me now may see;

For rich in grace to me Thou art, My soul from death Thou didst re-store.
They set not Thee be - fore their eyes, They seek to take a - way my life.
Thy truth and good-ness still a - bound, To wrath and an - ger Thou art slow.
Let me Thy great sal - va - tion see, And strengthen me my course to run.
Let all, O Lord, be brought to know That Thou dost help and com-fort me.

235 Confiding Prayer

PSALM 86 6s and 4s   MASON   William F. Sherwin

1. Lord, my pe-ti-tion heed, Now help me in my need,
2. Com-fort Thy serv-ant now, While at Thy throne I bow,
3. Lord, hear me while I pray, While now in troub-le's day

My Sav-iour be; I am Thy serv-ant, Lord, My trust is
For Thou art love. Thy par-d'ning grace is free; Sin-ners who
I seek Thy face. To an-swer, Lord, is Thine; Thou on-ly

in Thy word, Mer-cy to me af-ford, I cry to Thee.
call on Thee Thy ten-der mer-cy see, O God a-bove.
art di-vine, Most bright Thy glo-ries shine, O God of grace.

236 Desires and Aspirations

PSALM 86 6s and 4s   DONORA   William H. Doane

1. By all whom Thou hast made Be praise and wor-ship paid
2. Help me Thy will to do, Thy truth I will pur-sue,
3. How great Thy love ap-pears That bade death's gloom-y fears
4. Show me Thy mer-cy true, Thy serv-ant's strength re-new,

Desires and Aspirations

Thro' earth a - broad; Thy Name be glo - ri - fied, There is none
Teach me to fear; Give me the sin - gle eye Thy Name to
No more dis - may; O God, to an - ger slow, Save me from
De - liv-'rance send; To me Thy good - ness show, Thy com - fort,

great be - side, Match-less Thy works a - bide, For Thou art God.
glo - ri - fy, O Lord, my God Most High, With heart sin - cere.
ev - 'ry foe, Thy lov - ing - kind-ness show, Thy truth dis - play
Lord, be-stow; Let those that hate me know Thou art my friend.

[Stanzas 4-7]

237 The Church of God

PSALM 87 8s, 7s, 4   ZION   Thomas Hastings

1. Zi - on, found-ed on the mountains, God, thy Mak-er, loves thee well; He has
2. Hea-then lands and hos-tile peo-ples Soon shall come the Lord to know; Na - tions
3. When the Lord shall count the na-tions, Sons and daughters He shall see, Born to

cho-sen thee, most pre-cious, He de-lights in thee to dwell; God's own cit - y,
born a - gain in Zi - on Shall the Lord's sal-va-tion show; God Al-might-y
end-less life in Zi - on, And their joy-ful song shall be, "Bless - ed Zi - on,

Who can all thy glo-ry tell? God's own cit - y, Who can all thy glo-ry tell?
Shall on Zi-on strength bestow, God Al-might-y Shall on Zi - on strength be-stow.
All our fountains are in thee, Bless-ed Zi - on, All our fountains are in thee."

The Church Universal

PSALM 87 8s, 7s, 4   REGENT SQUARE   Henry Smart

1. Zi - on, found - ed on the moun-tains, God, thy Mak - er,
2. Hea - then lands and hos - tile peo - ples Soon shall come the
3. When the Lord shall count the na - tions, Sons and daugh - ters

loves thee well; He has cho - sen thee, most pre - cious,
Lord to know; Na - tions born a - gain in Zi - on
He shall see, Born to end - less life in Zi - on,

He de - lights in thee to dwell; God's own cit - y,
Shall the Lord's sal - va - tion show, God Al - might - y,
And their joy - ful song shall be, "Bless - ed Zi - on,

God's own cit - y, Who can all thy glo - ry tell?
God Al - might - y Shall on Zi - on strength be - stow.
Bless - ed Zi - on, All our foun - tains are in thee."

The Church of Christ

PSALM 87 7s   GUERNSEY   William O. Perkins

1. Zi - on, on the ho - ly hills, God, thy Mak - er, loves thee well;
2. When the Lord the names shall write Of thy sons, a count-less throng,

All thy courts His pres - ence fills, He de - lights in thee to dwell.
God Most High will thee re - quite, He Him-self will make thee strong.

Won-drous shall thy glo - ry be, Cit - y blest of God, the Lord;
Then in song and joy - ful mirth Shall Thy ran-somed sons a - gree,

Na-tions shall be born in thee, Un - to life from death re - stored.
Sing-ing forth through-out the earth, "All my foun-tains are in thee."

240 An Outpouring of Sorrow

PSALM 88 8s and 7s IRVING W. Irving Hartshorn

1. Lord, the God of my sal - va - tion, Day and night I cry to Thee;
2. Thou hast bro't me down to dark-ness, 'Neath Thy wrath I am op - pressed;
3. Un - to Thee with hands up-lift-ed Dai - ly I di - rect my cry;
4. Still, O Lord, re-newed each morn-ing Un - to Thee my prayer shall be;
5. Friend and lov - er are de-part-ed, Dark and lone - ly is my way;

Let my prayer now find ac-cept-ance, In Thy mer - cy an-swer me.
All the bil - lows of af - flic - tion O - ver-whelm my soul dis - tressed.
Hear, O Lord, my sup - pli - ca - tion, Hear and save me ere I die.
Cast me not a - way for-ev - er, Let me now Thy fa - vor see.
Lord, be Thou my friend and help-er, Still to Thee, O Lord, I pray.

Full of troub - les and af - flic - tion, Nigh to death my soul is brought
Thou hast made my friends de-spise me, And com - pan - ion - less I go,
Wilt Thou wait to show Thy won-ders And Thy mer - cy to the dead?
All my life is spent in sor - row, Grief and ter - ror al - ways nigh,
Lord, the God of my sal-va - tion, Day and night I cry to Thee;

Help - less, like one cast for - ev - er From Thy care and from Thy thought.
Bound, and help - less in my bond-age, Pin - ing in my bit - ter woe.
Let me live to tell Thy prais-es, By Thy lov - ing-kind-ness led.
Waves of wrath have surged a-bout me; Show Thy mer - cy ere I die.
Let my prayer now find ac-cept-ance, In Thy mer - cy an-swer me.

241 The Mercies and Faithfulness of God

PSALM 89 L. M. MARYTON H. Percy Smith

1. My song for - ev - er shall re - cord The ten - der
2. I sing of mer - cies that en - dure, For - ev - er
3. Be - hold God's truth and grace dis - played, For He has
4. The heav'ns shall join in glad ac - cord To praise Thy
5. Who in the heav'n - ly dwell - ings fair Can with the

mer - cies of the Lord; Thy faith - ful - ness will
build - ed firm and sure, Of faith - ful - ness that
faith - ful cov - enant made, And He has sworn that
won - drous works, O Lord; Thy faith - ful - ness shall
Lord Him - self com - pare? Or who a - mong the

I pro - claim, And ev - 'ry age shall know Thy Name.
nev - er dies, Es - tab - lished change-less in the skies.
Da - vid's son Shall ev - er sit up - on his throne.
praise com - mand Where ho - ly ones as - sem - bled stand.
might - y shares The like - ness that Je - ho - vah bears.

6 With fear and reverence at His feet
   God's holy ones in council meet;
   Yea, more than all about His throne
   Must He be feared, and He alone.

7 O Thou Jehovah, God of Hosts,
   What mighty one Thy likeness boasts?
   In all Thy works and vast designs
   Thy faithfulness forever shines.

8 The swelling sea obeys Thy will,
   Its angry waves Thy voice can still;
   Thy mighty enemies are slain,
   Thy foes resist Thy power in vain.

9 The heavens and earth, by right divine,
   The world and all therein, are Thine;
   The whole creation's wondrous frame
   Proclaims its Maker's glorious Name.

242
God the Source of Joy

PSALM 89 L. M. LUX CŒLESTIS Henry Basford

Slowly

1. Al - might - y God, Thy loft - y throne Has jus - tice
2. With bless - ing is the na - tion crowned Whose peo - ple
3. Thy Name with glad - ness they con - fess, Ex - alt - ed
4. All glo - ry un - to God we yield, Je - ho - vah

for its cor - ner - stone, And shin - ing bright be -
know the joy - ful sound; They in the light, O
in Thy right - eous - ness; Their fame and might to
is our help and shield; All praise and hon - or

fore Thy face Are truth and love and bound - less grace.
Lord, shall live, The light Thy face and fa - vor give.
Thee be - long, For in Thy fa - vor they are strong.
we will bring To Is - rael's Ho - ly One, our King.

By permission of C. W. Thompson and Co. [Stanzas 10–13]

243
Covenant Faithfulness

PSALM 89 L. M. ROTHWELL William Tans'ur

1. In vi - sion to His saints God spake: From out the peo - ple
2. My cho - sen serv - ant I ap - point, With ho - ly oil his
3. No en - e - my shall him af - fright, His ad - ver - sar - ies
4. Yea, he shall tri - umph in My Name, And great shall be his
5. Thou art my Fa - ther, he shall cry, My God, my rock of

208

Covenant Faithfulness

one I take, A might-y lead-er, true and brave, Or-dained, ex-
head a-noint; My hand with him shall still re-main, My arm his
I will smite, My faith-ful-ness to him will prove, And nev-er-
pow'r and fame, From sea to sea his might-y hand Shall hold do-
ref-uge high; My first-born son shall he be owned, A-bove the

alt-ed, strong to save, Or-dained, ex-alt-ed, strong to save.
strength shall well sus-tain, My arm his strength shall well sus-tain.
more My grace re-move, And nev-er-more My grace re-move.
min-ion o'er the land, Shall hold do-min-ion o'er the land.
kings of earth en-throned, A-bove the kings of earth en-throned.

[Stanzas 14–28]

6 For him My mercy shall endure,
My covenant made with him is sure,
His throne and race I will maintain
Forever, while the heavens remain.

7 Should sons of his My laws forsake,
My just commands and statutes break,
Then, though My rod their sins reprove,
My mercy I will not remove.

8 Though they be chastened sore and tried,
My faithfulness shall yet abide;
My plighted word I will not break,
Nor change the promise that I spake.

9 My oath is steadfast, ever sure,
My servant's race shall still endure;
His throne forever firm shall stay
When sun and moon have passed away.

10 On Thy anointed wrath is poured
As if Thy covenant were abhorred;
Thou hast profaned his kingly crown,
His matchless strength is broken down.

11 He is reproached and spoiled of all,
His enemies upon him fall;
His beauty is consumed away,
Forgotten is his kingly sway.

12 Cut off in youth, his sacred name
Is covered now with deepest shame;
How long, O Lord, shall wrath abide?
Thy face forever wilt Thou hide?

13 Think on my life; O Lord, take thought;
Hast Thou created man for nought?
What man that lives has power to save
His soul from death, and from the grave?

14 Where are Thy mercies which of old
Were in Thy promises foretold?
Remember, Lord, the bitter shame
Heaped on Thy own anointed's name.

15 Blest be the Lord for evermore,
Whose promise stands from days of yore.
His word is faithful now as then;
Blest be His Name. Amen, Amen.

209

244 The Cry of the Mortal

PSALM 90 8s and 7s   ARMSTRONG   Arranged from Brinley Richards

1. Lord, thro' all the gen-er-a-tions Of the chil-dren of our race,
2. Each suc-ceed-ing gen-er-a-tion At Thy might-y word ap-pears;
3. In Thy wrath our spir-its lan-guish, Sin-ful 'neath Thy search-ing eye;
4. Who can weigh Thy just dis-pleas-ure, Who can fear Thee as he ought?
5. Long the clouds of e-vil low-er; Bless us now with glad-some days;

In our fears and trib-u-la-tions, Thou hast been our dwell-ing-place.
Thou dost count in time's du-ra-tion One day as a thou-sand years.
All our days are passed in an-guish, In Thy wrath we pine and die.
Teach us now our days to meas-ure And to wis-dom turn our thought.
Let Thy serv-ants see Thy pow-er, Let their chil-dren learn Thy praise.

Ere the vast and wide cre-a-tion By Thy word was caused to be,
Death, with swift and sud-den warn-ing, Calls us from life's dream a-way,
Three-score years and ten we tar-ry, Four-score years the strong may stay,
Lord, re-turn, re-gard our sad-ness; With Thy serv-ants now a-bide;
On us let the grace and beau-ty Of the Lord our God re-main,

Or the moun-tains held their sta-tion, Thou art God e-ter-nal-ly.
Like the grass, green in the morn-ing, With-ered ere the close of day.
Long the load of grief to car-ry, Till at last we fly a-way.
Fill our days with joy and glad-ness, With Thy mer-cy sat-is-fied.
Strength-en us for no-ble du-ty That our work be not in vain.

245 The Lord Our Dwelling-Place

PSALM 90 L. M.   ST CATHERINE   Arranged by J. G. Walton

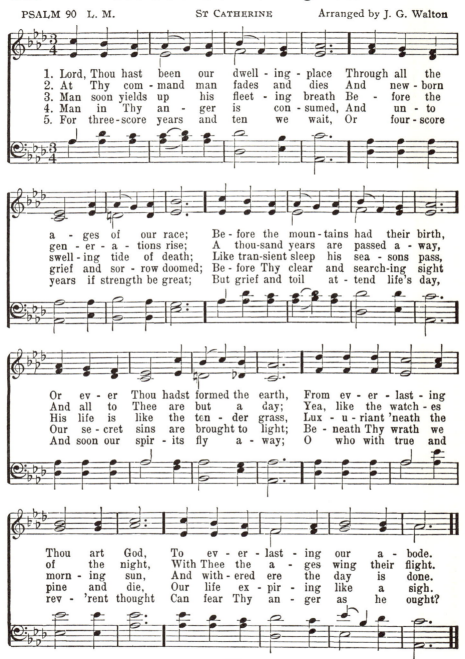

1. Lord, Thou hast been our dwell - ing - place Through all the
2. At Thy com - mand man fades and dies And new - born
3. Man soon yields up his fleet - ing breath Be - fore the
4. Man in Thy an - ger is con - sumed, And un - to
5. For three-score years and ten we wait, Or four-score

a - ges of our race; Be - fore the moun - tains had their birth,
gen - er - a - tions rise; A thou-sand years are passed a - way,
swell - ing tide of death; Like tran-sient sleep his sea - sons pass,
grief and sor - row doomed; Be - fore Thy clear and search-ing sight
years if strength be great; But grief and toil at - tend life's day,

Or ev - er Thou hadst formed the earth, From ev - er - last - ing
And all to Thee are but a day; Yea, like the watch - es
His life is like the ten - der grass, Lux - u - riant 'neath the
Our se - cret sins are brought to light; Be - neath Thy wrath we
And soon our spir - its fly a - way; O who with true and

Thou art God, To ev - er - last - ing our a - bode.
of the night, With Thee the a - ges wing their flight.
morn - ing sun, And with - ered ere the day is done.
pine and die, Our life ex - pir - ing like a sigh.
rev - 'rent thought Can fear Thy an - ger as he ought?

246 A Pilgrim's Prayers

PSALM 90 L. M.   SANDS   William J. Kirkpatrick

1. O teach Thou us   to count our days   And set our hearts on wis-dom's
2. O send the day   of   joy and light,   For long has been our sor-row's
3. So let there be   on   us be-stowed   The beau-ty   of   the Lord our

ways;   Turn, Lord, to   us   in   our dis-tress,   In   pit-y
night;   Af-flict-ed through the wea-ry years,   We wait un-
God;   The work ac-com-plished by   our hand   Es-tab-lish

now Thy serv-ants bless;   Let mer-cy's dawn   dis-pel our night,
til   Thy help ap-pears;   With us   and with   our sons a-bide,
Thou, and make it stand;   Yea, let   our hope-ful la-bor be

And all our day with joy be bright,   And all our day with joy be bright.
In   us   let God   be glo-ri-fied,   In   us   let God   be glo-ri-fied.
Es-tab-lished ev-er-more by Thee,   Es-tab-lished ev-er-more by Thee.

[Stanzas 6-8]

247 God Our Help and Hope

PSALM 90 C. M. LAFAYETTE John B. Herbert

1. O God, our help in a - ges past, Our hope for years to come,
2. Un - der the shad-ow of Thy throne Thy saints have dwelt se - cure;
3. Be - fore the hills in or - der stood, Or earth re-ceived her frame,
4. A thou - sand a - ges in Thy sight Are like an eve - ning gone,
5. Time, like an ev - er - roll - ing stream, Bears all its sons a - way;
6. O God, our help in a - ges past, Our hope for years to come,

Our shel - ter from the storm - y blast, And our e - ter - nal home.
Suf - fi - cient is Thine arm a - lone, And our de - fense is sure.
From ev - er - last - ing Thou art God, To end - less years the same.
Short as the watch that ends the night Be - fore the ris - ing sun.
They fly for - got - ten, as a dream Dies at the ope - ning day.
Be Thou our guard while troub - les last, And our e - ter - nal home.

SECOND TUNE DUNDEE Scotch Psalter

1. O God, our help in a - ges past, Our hope for years to come,
2. Un - der the shad-ow of Thy throne Thy saints have dwelt se - cure;
3. Be - fore the hills in or - der stood, Or earth re-ceived her frame,
4. A thou-sand a - ges in Thy sight Are like an eve-ning gone,
5. Time, like an ev - er - roll-ing stream, Bears all its sons a - way;
6. O God, our help in a - ges past, Our hope for years to come,

Our shel - ter from the storm - y blast, And our e - ter - nal home.
Suf - fi - cient is Thine arm a - lone, And our de - fense is sure.
From ev - er - last - ing Thou art God, To end - less years the same.
Short as the watch that ends the night Be - fore the ris - ing sun.
They fly for - got - ten, as a dream Dies at the ope - ning day.
Be Thou our guard while troub - les last, And our e - ter - nal home.

213

248 Overshadowing Protection

PSALM 91 L. M.   ZEPHYR   William B. Bradbury

1. The man who once has found a - bode With - in the
2. I of the Lord my God will say, He is my
3. The Lord with His pro - tect - ing care Shall keep thee
4. Thou shalt be - neath His wings a - bide, And safe with-

se - cret place of God Shall with Al - might - y
ref - uge and my stay; To Him for safe - ty
from the hid - den snare; When fear - ful plagues a -
in His care con - fide; His faith - ful - ness shall

God a - bide, And in His shad - ow safe - ly hide.
I will flee, In Him my con - stant trust shall be.
round pre - vail Thy life the scourge shall not as - sail.
ev - er be A sure pro - tec - tion un - to thee.

5 No nightly terrors shall alarm,
No deadly shaft by day shall harm,
Nor pestilence that walks by night,
Nor plagues that waste in noonday light.

6 At thy right hand, though thousands die,
No harm shall unto thee come nigh;
But thou secure, unharmed, shalt see
What wicked men's reward shall be.

The Reward of Perfect Trust

PSALM 91 L. M.   MARTHINA   J. Christopher Marks

1. Be - cause thy trust is God a - lone, Thy ref - uge
2. An - gel - ic guards at His com - mands Will bear thee
3. Though fierce and treach-'rous foes as - sail, Their pow'r and
4. Be - cause on Me he set his love, I will his

is the High - est One, No e - vil shall up-
safe - ly in their hands, Will keep thee, lest, if
wrath shall not pre - vail; Their cru - el strength, their
con - stant Sav - iour prove, And since to him My

on thee come, Nor plague ap - proach thy guard - ed home.
left a - lone, Thou dash thy foot a - gainst a stone.
ven - omed spite, Thou shalt o'er - come with con - qu'ring might.
Name is known, I will ex - alt him as My own.

5 As oft as he shall call on Me,
   Most gracious shall My answer be;
   I will be with him in distress,
   And in his trouble I will bless.

6 Complete deliverance I will give,
   And honor him while he shall live;
   Abundant life I will bestow,
   To him My full salvation show.

250 The Duty of Praise

PSALM 92 L. M. CHRISTINE Ernest R. Kroeger

1. How good it is to thank the Lord, And praise to Thee, Most
2. O Lord, with joy my heart ex-pands Be - fore the won - ders
3. When as the grass the wick - ed grow, When sin - ners flour - ish
4. Thou, Lord, hast high ex - alt - ed me With roy - al strength and
5. The right-eous man shall flour - ish well, And in the house of

High, ac - cord, To show Thy love with morn - ing light,
of Thy hands; Great works, Je - ho - vah, Thou hast wrought,
here be - low, Then is there end - less ru - in nigh,
dig - ni - ty; With Thy a - noint - ing I am blest,
God shall dwell; He shall be like a good - ly tree,

And tell Thy faith - ful - ness each night; Yea, good it is Thy
Ex - ceed - ing deep Thy ev - 'ry thought; A fool - ish man knows
But Thou, O Lord, art throned on high; Thy foes shall fall be -
Thy grace and fa - vor on me rest; I thus ex - ult o'er
And all his life shall fruit - ful be; For right - eous is the

praise to sing, And all our sweet - est mu - sic bring.
not their worth, Nor he whose mind is of the earth.
fore Thy might, The wick - ed shall be put to flight.
all my foes, O'er all that would my cause op - pose.
Lord and just, He is my Rock, in Him I trust.

251 Joyful Worship

PSALM 92   8s and 7s   ELLESDIE   Arranged from Mozart

1. It is good to sing Thy prais-es And to thank Thee, O Most High,
2. Thou hast filled my heart with glad-ness Thro' the works Thy hands have wrought;
3. But the good shall live be-fore Thee, Plant-ed in Thy dwell-ing-place,

Show-ing forth Thy lov-ing-kind-ness When the morn-ing lights the sky.
Thou hast made my life vic-to-rious, Great Thy works and deep Thy thought.
Fruit-ful trees and ev-er ver-dant, Nour-ished by Thy bound-less grace.

It is good when night is fall-ing Of Thy faith-ful-ness to tell,
Thou, O Lord, on high ex-alt-ed, Reign-est ev-er-more in might;
In His good-ness to the right-eous God His right-eous-ness dis-plays;

While with sweet, me-lo-dious prais-es Songs of ad-o-ra-tion swell.
All Thy en-e-mies shall per-ish, Sin be ban-ished from Thy sight.
God my rock, my strength and ref-uge, Just and true are all His ways.

[Selected Stanzas]

252   The Divine Rule and Power

PSALM 93 S. M.   RIALTO   George F. Root

1. Je-ho-vah sits en-throned In maj-es-ty most bright,
2. The world es-tab-lished stands On its foun-da-tions broad;
3. The floods have lift-ed up Their voice in maj-es-ty,
4. Thy tes-ti-mo-nies, Lord, In faith-ful-ness ex-cel,

Ap-par-eled in om-nip-o-tence, And gird-ed round with might.
His throne is fixed, He reigns su-preme, The ev-er-last-ing God.
But might-y is the Lord our God A-bove the rag-ing sea.
And ho-ly must Thy serv-ants be Who in Thy tem-ple dwell.

253   God the Righteous Judge

PSALM 94 L. M.   LYTHAM   James Malley

1. O Lord, Thou Judge of all the earth, To Whom all
2. How long, O Lord, in boast-ful pride Shall wick-ed
3. The wid-ow and the fa-ther-less They slay, and
4. Be wise, ye fools and brut-ish men; Shall not He
5. The Lord will judge in right-eous-ness, From Him all

venge-ance doth be-long, A-rise and show Thy
men tri-um-phant stand? How long shall they af-
help-less stran-gers smite; The faith-ful God they
see Who formed the eye? Shall not He hear Who
truth and knowl-edge flow; The fool-ish thoughts of

218

God the Righteous Judge

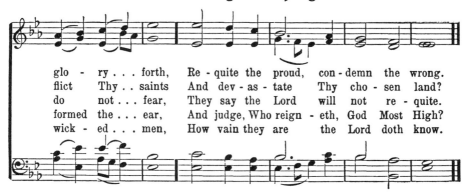

glo - ry . . . forth,	Re - quite the proud,	con - demn the wrong.
flict	Thy . . saints	And dev - as - tate	Thy cho - sen land?
do	not . . . fear,	They say the Lord	will not re - quite.
formed	the . . . ear,	And judge, Who reign - eth, God Most High?
wick - ed . . . men,	How vain they are	the Lord doth know.

6 That man is blest whom Thou, O Lord,
   With chastening hand dost teach Thy will,
   For in the day when sinners fall
   That man in peace abideth still.

7 The Lord will not cast off His own,
   Nor His inheritance forsake;
   Just judgment shall at length prevail,
   And upright hearts shall courage take.

8 Who will arise for my defense
   Against the wicked in the land?
   Against iniquity and wrong
   What man for me will valiant stand?

9 Unless the Lord had been my help,
   My life had quickly passed away;
   But when my foot had almost slipped,
   O Lord, Thy mercy was my stay.

10 Amid the doubts that fill my mind
   Thy comforts, Lord, bring joy to me;
   Can wickedness, though throned in might,
   Have fellowship, O Lord, with Thee?

11 The wicked, in their might arrayed,
   Against the righteous join their power,
   But to the Lord I flee for help,
   He is my refuge and my tower.

12 Our God, the refuge of His saints,
   Will fight against iniquity;
   Avenger of the innocent
   The Lord omnipotent will be.

254 An Invitation to Worship

PSALM 95 L. M.   SALOME   William B. Bradbury

1. O come be-fore the Lord, our King, And in His pres-ence let us sing;
2. Al-might-y pow'r the Lord main-tains, Ex-alt-ed o-ver all He reigns;
3. O come and let us wor-ship now, Be-fore our Mak-er let us bow;
4. Take heed and hard-en not your heart As did your fa-thers, nor de-part
5. Take heed that ye pro-voke Him not As did your fa-thers, who for-got,

1. O come be-fore the Lord, our King, And in His pres-ence let us sing;

Let us in glad and joy-ful lays The Rock of our sal-va-tion praise;
He holds the val-leys in His hand, He makes the mighty moun-tains stand;
We are His sheep and He our God, He feeds our souls in pas-tures broad;
From God to fol-low in their ways; For with com-plaints in-stead of praise,
With err-ing heart, God's ho-ly ways And grieved Him all their sin-ful days;

Let us in glad and joy-ful lays The Rock of our sal-va-tion praise;

Be-fore . . . . . Him come . . . with thank - - - ful
To Him . . . . . be-long . . . . both land . . . . . and
He safe- - - - ly leads . . . us in . . . . . . the
With doubt . . in-stead . . . of faith . . . . con-
To whom . . . . . in wrath . . Je - ho - - - vah

Be-fore Him come with thank-ful song, Be-fore Him come with

song, In joy-ful psalms His praise pro-long.
sea, Cre-a-tor of the world is He.
way; O come and heed His voice to-day.
fessed, They put His mer - - - cy to the test.
sware, My prom-ised rest they shall not share.

thank-ful song, In joy-ful psalms His praise pro-long.

255 Adoration and Submission

PSALM 95   8s and 7s   LOVE DIVINE   John Zundel

1. Now with joy-ful ex-ul-ta-tion Let us sing Je-ho-vah's praise,
2. For, how great a God, and glo-rious, Is Je-ho-vah Whom we sing;
3. To the Lord, such might re-veal-ing, Let us come with rev-'rence meet,
4. While He prof-fers peace and par-don Let us hear His voice to-day,

To the Rock of our sal-va-tion Loud ho-san-nas let us raise;
O-ver i-dol-gods vic-to-rious, Great is He, our God and King.
And, be-fore our Mak-er kneel-ing, Let us wor-ship at His feet.
Lest, if we our hearts should hard-en, We should per-ish in the way;

Thank-ful trib-ute glad-ly bring-ing, Let us come be-fore Him now,
In His hand are earth's deep pla-ces, His the strength of all the hills,
He is our own God and leads us, We the peo-ple of His care;
Lest to us, so un-be-liev-ing, He in judg-ment shall de-clare:

And, with psalms His prais-es sing-ing, Joy-ful in His pres-ence bow.
His the sea whose bounds He tra-ces, His the land His boun-ty fills.
With a shep-herd's hand He feeds us As His flock in pas-tures fair.
Ye, so long My Spir-it griev-ing, Nev-er in My rest can share.

256 Worship and Its Motives

PSALM 95 C. M. CHOPIN Isaac B. Woodbury

1. O come and to Je - ho - vah sing,
2. Be - fore His pres - ence let us come
3. Je - ho - vah is a might - y King,
4. To Him the spa - cious sea be - longs,
5. O come, and bow - ing down to Him

To Him our voi - ces raise; Let us in
With praise and thank - ful voice; Let us sing
A - bove all gods His throne; The depths of
He made its waves and tides; And by His
Our wor - ship let us bring; Yea, let us

our most joy - ful songs, The Lord our Sav - iour
psalms to Him with grace, With grate - ful hearts re-
earth are in His hand, The moun - tains are His
hand the ris - ing land Was formed, and still a-
kneel be - fore the Lord, Our Mak - er and our

praise, The Lord our Sav - - iour praise.
joice, With grate - ful hearts re - joice.
own, The moun - tains are His own.
bides, Was formed, and still a - bides.
King, Our Mak - er and our King.

222   [Selected Stanzas]

The Evangel of the Kingdom

PSALM 96 C. M. ST. LEONARD Henry Hiles

1. O sing a new song to the Lord, Sing all the earth to God;
2. The Lord is great a - bove all gods, Let glad ho - san - nas rise;
3. Let all the peo - ples of the earth Give glo - ry to the Lord,
4. To all the na - tions of the earth The bless - ed ti - dings bring;
5. Let heav'n and earth and sound-ing sea To Him glad trib - ute bring;

In dai - ly prais - es bless His Name And tell His grace a - broad.
The hea-then gods are i - dols vain; Je - ho - vah made the skies.
Give Him the glo - ry due His Name And strength to Him ac - cord;
Tell all the world Je - ho - vah reigns, The u - ni - ver - sal King.
Let field and wood and all there - in Be - fore Je - ho - vah sing;

A - mong the na - tions far and wide His glo - ry cel - e - brate;
Great hon - or is be - fore His face, And maj - es - ty di - vine;
With of - f'rings come ye to His courts, In ho - ly beau - ty bow,
The world shall there-fore stand un - moved, Es - tab-lished by His might;
For, lo, He comes to judge the earth, And all the world shall see

To all the peo - ples of the earth His won-drous works re - late.
With - in His ho - ly dwell-ing-place Both strength and beau - ty shine.
Let all the earth with rev - 'rence come And serve Je - ho - vah now.
And just is He to judge the wrong And vin - di - cate the right.
His ev - er - last - ing faith-ful - ness, His truth and eq - ui - ty.

258 The Message of Redemption

PSALM 96 L. M.　　　　　　LUCILE　　　　　　Charles H. Gabriel

1. O sing a new song to the Lord, Sing all the
2. Tell all the world His won-drous ways, Tell hea-then
3. The hea-then gods are i-dols vain; The shin-ing
4. Let ev-'ry tongue and ev-'ry tribe Give to the
5. O fear and bow, a-dorned with grace, And tell each

earth and bless His Name; From day to day His
na-tions far and near; Great is the Lord, and
heav'ns the Lord sup-ports; Both light and hon-or
Lord due praise and sing; All glo-ry un-to
land that God is King; The earth He found-ed

praise re-cord, The Lord's re-deem-ing grace pro-claim.
great His praise, And Him a-lone let na-tions fear.
lead His train, While strength and beau-ty fill His courts.
Him as-cribe, Come, throng His courts, and of-f'rings bring.
in its place, And jus-tice to the world will bring.

6 Let heaven be glad, let earth rejoice,
　　The teeming sea resound with praise;
Let waving fields lift high their voice,
　　And all the trees their anthem raise.

7 So let them shout before our God,
　　For, lo, He comes, He comes with might,
To wield the scepter and the rod,
　　To judge the world with truth and right.

259. The Universal King

PSALM 96 11s, 10, 9   WESLEY   Lowell Mason

1. Sing to the Lord, sing His praise, all ye peo - ples,
2. Tell of His won - drous works, tell of His glo - ry,
3. Vain are the hea - then gods, i - dols and help - less;
4. Give un - to God Most High glo - ry and hon - or,
5. Make all the na - tions know God reigns for - ev - er;
6. Let heav'n and earth be glad; waves of the o - cean,

New be your song as new hon - ors ye pay;
Till through the na - tions His Name is re - vered;
God made the heav'ns, and His glo - ry they tell;
Come with your of - f'rings and hum - bly draw near;
Earth is es - tab - lished as He did de - cree;
For - est and field, ex - ul - ta - tion ex - press;

Sing of His maj - es - ty, bless Him for - ev - er,
Praise and ex - alt Him, for He is al - might - y,
Hon - or and maj - es - ty shine out be - fore Him,
In ho - ly beau - ty now wor - ship Je - ho - vah,
Right - eous and just is the King of the na - tions,
For God is com - ing, the Judge of the na - tions,

Show His sal - va - tion from day to day.
God o - ver all let the Lord be feared.
Beau - ty and strength in His tem - ple dwell.
Trem - ble be - fore Him with god - ly fear.
Judg - ing the peo - ple with eq - ui - ty.
Com - ing to judge in His right - eous - ness.

260 Divine Sovereignty

PSALM 97 L. M.
NOCTURN
Frederick H. Burstall

1. Je - ho - vah reigns; let earth be glad And all the isles their joy make known;
2. Con-sum-ing fire de-stroys His foes, A - round the world His lightnings blaze;
3. The heav'ns His righteousness pro-claim, Thro' earth His glo - ry shines a - broad;
4. Thy Church re-joi - ces to be - hold Thy judgments in the earth, O Lord;
5. All ye that tru - ly love the Lord, Hate sin, for He is just and pure;
6. For good men light and joy are sown To bless them in the har - vest-time;

With clouds and dark-ness He is clad, On truth and jus - tice rests His throne.
The trem-bling earth His pres-ence knows, The moun-tains melt be-fore His gaze.
From i - dol-wor-ship turn with shame And bow be - fore the liv - ing God.
Thy glo - ry to the world un - fold, Su-preme o'er all be Thou a - dored.
To saints His help He will ac - cord And keep them in His love se - cure.
Ye saints, your joy in God make known And ev - er praise His Name sub-lime.

SECOND TUNE
ELY
Thomas Turton

1. Je - ho - vah reigns; let earth be glad And all the isles their joy make known;
2. Con-sum-ing fire de-stroys His foes, A - round the world His lightnings blaze;
3. The heav'ns His righteousness proclaim, Thro' earth His glo - ry shines a - broad;
4. Thy Church re-joi - ces to be - hold Thy judg-ments in the earth, O Lord;
5. All ye that tru - ly love the Lord, Hate sin, for He is just and pure;
6. For good men light and joy are sown To bless them in the har - vest-time;

With clouds and dark-ness He is clad, On truth and jus - tice rests His throne.
The trem-bling earth His presence knows, The mountains melt be-fore His gaze.
From i - dol-wor-ship turn with shame And bow be - fore the liv - ing God.
Thy glo - ry to the world un - fold, Su-preme o'er all be Thou a - dored.
To saints His help He will ac - cord And keep them in His love se - cure.
Ye saints, your joy in God make known And ev - er praise His Name sub-lime.

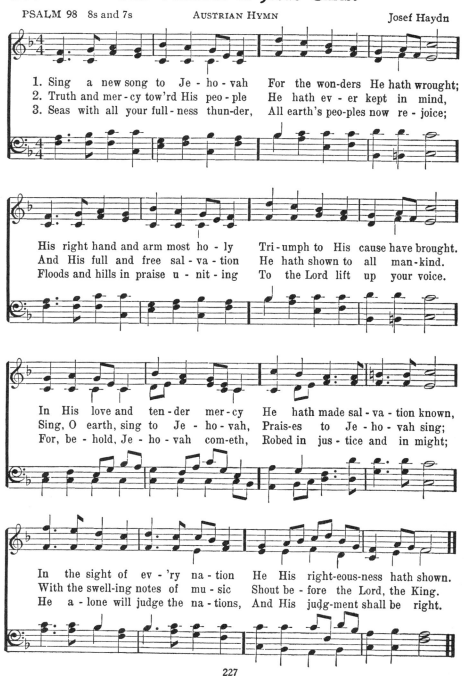

261   The Victories of Jesus Christ

PSALM 98   8s and 7s   AUSTRIAN HYMN   Josef Haydn

1. Sing a new song to Je - ho - vah   For the won-ders He hath wrought;
2. Truth and mer - cy tow'rd His peo - ple   He hath ev - er kept in mind,
3. Seas with all your full - ness thun-der,   All earth's peo-ples now re - joice;

His right hand and arm most ho - ly   Tri - umph to His cause have brought.
And His full and free sal - va - tion   He hath shown to all man-kind.
Floods and hills in praise u - nit - ing   To the Lord lift up your voice.

In His love and ten - der mer - cy   He hath made sal - va - tion known,
Sing, O earth, sing to Je - ho - vah,   Prais-es to Je - ho - vah sing;
For, be - hold, Je - ho - vah com-eth,   Robed in jus - tice and in might;

In the sight of ev - 'ry na - tion   He His right-eous-ness hath shown.
With the swell-ing notes of mu - sic   Shout be - fore the Lord, the King.
He a - lone will judge the na - tions,   And His judg-ment shall be right.

A Salvation for the World

PSALM 98   6s and 5s   REPOSE   Anonymous

1. Un - to God our Sav - iour   Sing a joy - ful song;
2. Joy - ful, all ye peo - ple,   Sing be - fore the Lord;
3. Waves of might - y o - cean,   Earth with full - ness stored,

Won - drous are His do - ings,   For His arm is strong.
Shout and sing His prais - es   Now in glad ac - cord;
Floods and fields and moun - tains,   Sing be - fore the Lord;

He has wrought sal - va - tion,   He has made it known,
With the harp and trump - et   Joy - ful prais - es bring;
For He comes with jus - tice,   E - vil to re - dress,

And be - fore the na - tions   Is His jus - tice shown.
Come, re - joice be - fore Him,   God, the Lord, your King.
And to judge the na - tions   In His right - eous - ness.

The Glad Tidings

263

PSALM 98 6s and 5s ST. MARY MAGDALENE John B. Dykes

1. Un - to God our Sav - iour Sing a joy - ful song;
2. He re - mem - bers mer - cy, Faith - ful to His own,
3. Waves of might - y o - cean, Earth with full - ness stored

Won - drous are His do - ings, For His arm is strong.
And our God's sal - va - tion All the earth has known.
Floods and fields and moun - tains, Sing be - fore the Lord;

He has brought sal - va - tion, He has made it known,
Joy - ful, all ye peo - ple, Sing be - fore the Lord;
For He comes with jus - tice, E - vil to re - dress,

And be - fore the na - tions Is His jus - tice shown.
Shout and sing His prais - es Now in glad ac - cord.
And to judge the na - tions In His right-eous - ness.

229

[Selected Stanzas]

Missionary Triumphs

PSALM 98 L. M.   GILEAD   Arranged from Mehul

1. Come, let us sing be-fore the Lord New songs of
2. The great sal-va-tion of our God Is seen through
3. He called to mind the truth and grace Be-stowed up-
4. All lands, to God lift up your voice, Sing praise to
5. Praise ye the Lord with harp and song, With voice of

praise with sweet ac-cord, For won-ders great by
all the earth a-broad; Be-fore the na-tions'
on His cho-sen race, And un-to earth's re-
Him, with shouts re-joice; With voice of joy and
psalms His praise pro-long; In swell-ing cho-rus

Him are done, His might-y arm has vic-t'ry won.
won-d'ring sight He has re-vealed His truth and right.
mot-est bound Glad ti-dings of sal-va-tion sound.
loud ac-claim Let all u-nite and praise His Name.
glad-ly sing And shout be-fore the Lord the King.

6 Let earth be glad, let ocean roar,
   And praises sound from shore to shore;
Let floods and hills with glad accord
   Show forth their joy before the Lord.

7 For, lo, He comes; at His command
   All nations shall in judgment stand;
In justice robed, and throned in light,
   The Lord shall judge, dispensing right.

265   The Majesty and Holiness of God

PSALM 99   C. M.   ELLACOMBE   German Melody

1. Je - ho - vah reigns in maj - es - ty;   Let all the na - tions quake.
2. The might-y King loves jus - tice well,   And eq - ui - ty or - dains;
3. When priests and proph-ets called on God,   He their pe - ti - tions heard;

He dwells be - tween the cher - u - bim;   Let earth's foun - da - tions shake.
He rules His peo - ple right - eous-ly   And faith-ful - ness main-tains.
His cloud-y pil - lar led them on,   And they o - beyed His word.

Su - preme in Zi - on is the Lord,   Ex - alt - ed glo - rious - ly;
O mag - ni - fy the Lord our God,   Let Him ex - alt - ed be;
Tho' send-ing judg-ments for their sins,   He par-doned gra-cious - ly;

Ye na - tions, praise His name with awe,   The Ho - ly One is He.
In wor - ship at His foot-stool bow,   The Ho - ly One is He.
Ex - alt the Lord and wor - ship Him,   The Ho - ly One is He.

266

The Holiness of God

PSALM 99 12s, 13, 10 NICÆA John B. Dykes

1. God is King for - ev - er: let the na - tions trem - ble;
2. Mer - ci - ful as might - y, He de - lights in jus - tice,
3. Ho - ly men of old in Him a - lone con - fid - ed;

Throned a - bove the cher - u - bim, by all the earth a - dored;
For He reigns in right-eous-ness and rules in eq - ui - ty;
He for - gave their sins, al - though they felt His chas-t'ning rod;

He is great in Zi - on, high a - bove all peo - ples;
Wor-ship and ex - alt Him, bow-ing down be - fore Him,
In His ho - ly tem - ple wor - ship and a - dore Him,

Praise Him with fear, for ho - ly is the Lord.
Per - fect in pow'r and ho - li - ness is He.
Faith - ful and ho - ly is the Lord our God.

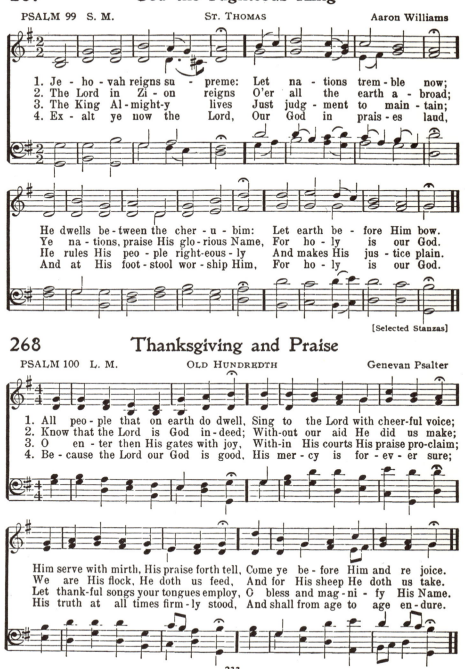

267 God the Righteous King

PSALM 99 S. M. ST. THOMAS Aaron Williams

1. Je - ho - vah reigns su - preme: Let na - tions trem - ble now;
2. The Lord in Zi - on reigns O'er all the earth a - broad;
3. The King Al - might - y lives Just judg - ment to main - tain;
4. Ex - alt ye now the Lord, Our God in prais - es laud,

He dwells be - tween the cher - u - bim: Let earth be - fore Him bow.
Ye na - tions, praise His glo - rious Name, For ho - ly is our God.
He rules His peo - ple right - eous - ly And makes His jus - tice plain.
And at His foot - stool wor - ship Him, For ho - ly is our God.

[Selected Stanzas]

268 Thanksgiving and Praise

PSALM 100 L. M. OLD HUNDREDTH Genevan Psalter

1. All peo - ple that on earth do dwell, Sing to the Lord with cheer - ful voice;
2. Know that the Lord is God in - deed; With - out our aid He did us make;
3. O en - ter then His gates with joy, With - in His courts His praise pro - claim;
4. Be - cause the Lord our God is good, His mer - cy is for - ev - er sure;

Him serve with mirth, His praise forth tell, Come ye be - fore Him and re joice.
We are His flock, He doth us feed, And for His sheep He doth us take.
Let thank - ful songs your tongues employ, O bless and mag - ni - fy His Name.
His truth at all times firm - ly stood, And shall from age to age en - dure.

269

Universal Praise

PSALM 100 8s   BEN AVON   George C. Stebbins

1. All peo-ple that dwell on the earth,   Your songs to Je-ho-vah now raise;
2. Know ye that Je-ho-vah is God,   Our Sov-'reign and Mak-er is He;
3. With thank-ful-ness en-ter His gates,   His praise in His tem-ple pro-claim;
4. For gra-cious and good is the Lord,   His mer-cy to us nev-er ends;

Come, serve Him with gladness and joy,   Ap-proach Him with anthems of praise.
His peo-ple, for-ev-er His own,   The sheep of His pas-ture are we.
Your voi-ces in thanks-giv-ing raise,   And bless ye His glo-ri-ous Name.
His faith-ful-ness, true to His word,   Thro' a-ges un-end-ing ex-tends.

Copyright, 1912, by United Presbyterian Board of Publication. Used by per.

270

Gladness in Worship

PSALM 100 C. M.   ASPURG   Johann G. Frech

1. O make a joy-ful noise, ye lands, And serve the Lord with fear;
2. Know that the Lord is God a-lone; He made us and will keep,
3. With glad thanks-giv-ing throng His gates, His good-ness to pro-claim;
4. For He is good, and time shall prove His mer-cies ev-er sure,

With glad-ness wait His high com-mands, And with a song draw near.
For His we are, and not our own, His peo-ple and His sheep.
With-in His courts, where mer-cy waits, Give thanks and bless His Name.
And while the a-ges on-ward move His truth shall still en-dure.

271   Godly Resolves

PSALM 101   7s and 6s   SOJOURNER   R. DeWitt Mallary

1. Of mer - cy and of jus - tice My thank-ful song shall be;
2. On what is base and e - vil I will not set my heart;
3. The faith - ful and the up - right Shall min - is - ter to me;

O Lord, in joy - ful prais - es My song shall rise to Thee.
Trans-gress-ors' ways ab - hor - ring, With them I take no part.
The ly - ing and de - ceit - ful My fa - vor shall not see.

With - in my house I pur - pose To walk in wis - dom's way;
No fro - ward man or e - vil Shall my com - pan - ion be;
I will in dai - ly judg - ment All wick - ed - ness re - ward,

O Lord, I need Thy pres - ence; How long wilt Thou de - lay?
I will not suf - fer slan - der Or pride or treach - er - y.
And cleanse from e - vil - do - ers The cit - y of the Lord.

235

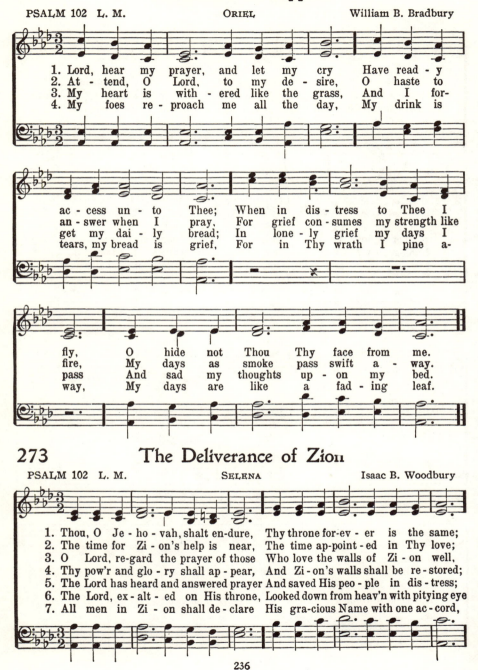

272 Affliction and Appeal

PSALM 102 L. M.   ORIEL   William B. Bradbury

1. Lord, hear my prayer, and let my cry Have read - y
2. At - tend, O Lord, to my de - sire, O haste to
3. My heart is with - ered like the grass, And I for -
4. My foes re - proach me all the day, My drink is

ac - cess un - to Thee; When in dis - tress to Thee I
an - swer when I pray, For grief con - sumes my strength like
get my dai - ly bread; In lone - ly grief my days I
tears, my bread is grief, For in Thy wrath I pine a -

fly, O hide not Thou Thy face from me.
fire, My days as smoke pass swift a - way.
pass And sad my thoughts up - on my bed.
way, My days are like a fad - ing leaf.

273 The Deliverance of Zion

PSALM 102 L. M.   SELENA   Isaac B. Woodbury

1. Thou, O Je - ho - vah, shalt en - dure, Thy throne for-ev - er is the same;
2. The time for Zi - on's help is near, The time ap-point - ed in Thy love;
3. O Lord, re-gard the prayer of those Who love the walls of Zi - on well,
4. Thy pow'r and glo - ry shall ap - pear, And Zi - on's walls shall be re - stored;
5. The Lord has heard and answered prayer And saved His peo - ple in dis - tress;
6. The Lord, ex - alt - ed on His throne, Looked down from heav'n with pitying eye
7. All men in Zi - on shall de - clare His gra - cious Name with one ac - cord,

236

The Deliverance of Zion

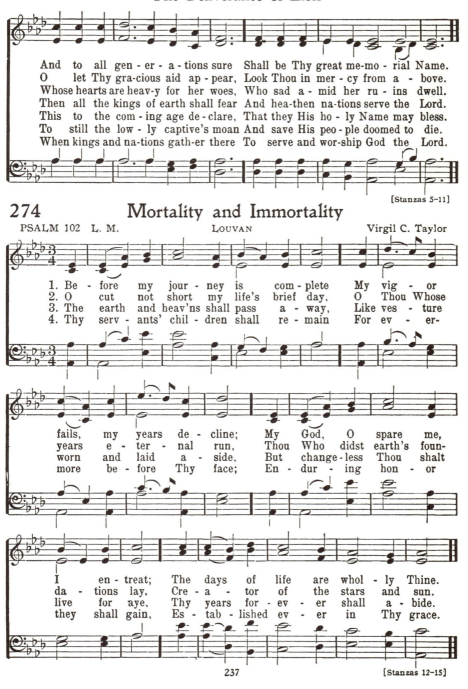

And to all gen - er - a - tions sure Shall be Thy great me-mo - rial Name.
O let Thy gra-cious aid ap - pear, Look Thou in mer - cy from a - bove.
Whose hearts are heav-y for her woes, Who sad a - mid her ru - ins dwell.
Then all the kings of earth shall fear And hea-then na-tions serve the Lord.
This to the com - ing age de - clare, That they His ho - ly Name may bless.
To still the low - ly captive's moan And save His peo - ple doomed to die.
When kings and na-tions gath-er there To serve and wor-ship God the Lord.

[Stanzas 5–11]

274   Mortality and Immortality

PSALM 102 L. M.   LOUVAN   Virgil C. Taylor

1. Be - fore my jour - ney is com - plete My vig - or
2. O cut not short my life's brief day, O Thou Whose
3. The earth and heav'ns shall pass a - way, Like ves - ture
4. Thy serv - ants' chil - dren shall re - main For ev - er-

fails, my years de - cline; My God, O spare me,
years e - ter - nal run, Thou Who didst earth's foun-
worn and laid a - side, But change-less Thou shalt
more be - fore Thy face; En - dur - ing hon - or

I en - treat; The days of life are whol - ly Thine.
da - tions lay, Cre - a - tor of the stars and sun.
live for aye, Thy years for - ev - er shall a - bide.
they shall gain, Es - tab - lished ev - er in Thy grace.

237   [Stanzas 12–15]

PSALM 102 7s   BLUMENTHAL   Arranged from Blumenthal

1. Thou, O Lord, art God a-lone;   Ev-er-last-ing is Thy throne;
2. If   with love com-pas-sion-ate   We, Thy serv-ants, mourn her state,
3. This all a-ges shall re-cord   For the glo-ry of the Lord;
4. As one lays a gar-ment by,   Thou wilt change the star-ry sky

Through the a-ges men shall sing   Praise to heav'n's e-ter-nal King.
Wilt   not Thou, O gra-cious Lord, Help in Zi-on's need af-ford?
Thou   dost hear the hum-ble prayer, For the help-less Thou dost care.
Like   a ves-ture worn and old,   But Thy years shall ne'er be told.

Thou, en-throned a-bove the skies,   Wilt for Zi-on's help a-rise;
Lord, Thy glo-ry shall ap-pear,   Kings and na-tions then shall fear;
Thou e-ter-nal art, and great,   Heav'n and earth Thou didst cre-ate,
Thou wilt make Thy serv-ants' race   Ev-er live be-fore Thy face,

Let Thy grace to her ap-pear,   For the prom-ised time is near.
And Thy Name shall be a-dored   When Thy Zi-on is re-stored.
Heav'n and earth shall pass a-way,   Change-less Thou shalt live for aye.
And for-ev-er at Thy side   Chil-dren's chil-dren shall a-bide.

[Selected Stanzas]

276 The Church and Her Head

PSALM 102 7s MERCY Arranged from Gottschalk

1. Thou, O Lord, art God a - lone;
2. Thou, en throned a - bove the skies,
3. If with love com - pas - sion - ate
4. Lord, Thy glo - ry shall ap - pear,

Ev - er - last - ing is Thy throne;
Wilt for Zi - on's help a - rise;
We, Thy serv - ants, mourn her state,
Kings and na - tions then shall fear;

Through the a - ges men shall sing
Let Thy grace to her ap - pear,
Wilt not Thou, O gra - cious Lord,
And Thy Name shall be a - dored

Praise to heav'n's e - ter - nal King.
For the prom - ised time is near.
Help in Zi - on's need af - ford?
When Thy Zi - on is re - stored.

[Selected Stanzas]

239

277 Thankful Joy and Praise

PSALM 103 C. M. HOWARD Elizabeth H. Cuthbert

1. O praise and bless the Lord, my soul, His won - drous love pro - claim; Join heart and voice and all my pow'rs To bless His ho - ly Name.
2. O praise and bless the Lord, my soul, And ev - er thank - ful be; For - get not all the ben - e - fits He has be - stowed on thee.
3. He free - ly par - dons all thy sins, And He is strong to save; He heals thy sick - ness, soothes thy pain, And ran - soms from the grave.
4. He crowns thee with His grace and love, And with His strength en - dued, Thou mount - est up with ea - gle's wings, Thy joy - ous youth re - newed.
5. The Lord will judge in right - eous - ness For all that are op - pressed; To all His saints His gra - cious acts And ways are man - i - fest.
6. The Lord is ev - er mer - ci - ful, And un - to an - ger slow; His lov - ing - kind - ness and His grace In rich a - bun - dance flow.

7 He will not chide for evermore,
   He turns His wrath away;
   He has not strictly marked our sins,
   Our evil to repay.

8 As heaven is high above the earth,
   So great His mercy proves;
   As far from us as east from west
   He all our sin removes.

240

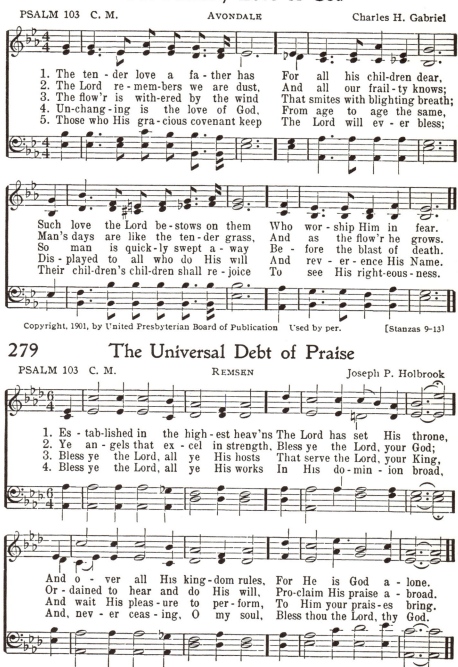

278 The Fatherly Love of God

PSALM 103 C. M. AVONDALE Charles H. Gabriel

1. The ten - der love a fa - ther has For all his chil-dren dear,
2. The Lord re - mem-bers we are dust, And all our frail - ty knows;
3. The flow'r is with-ered by the wind That smites with blighting breath;
4. Un-chang-ing is the love of God, From age to age the same,
5. Those who His gra - cious covenant keep The Lord will ev - er bless;

Such love the Lord be - stows on them Who wor - ship Him in fear.
Man's days are like the ten - der grass, And as the flow'r he grows.
So man is quick - ly swept a - way Be - fore the blast of death.
Dis - played to all who do His will And rev - er - ence His Name.
Their chil-dren's chil-dren shall re - joice To see His right-eous - ness.

Copyright, 1901, by United Presbyterian Board of Publication Used by per. [Stanzas 9-13]

279 The Universal Debt of Praise

PSALM 103 C. M. REMSEN Joseph P. Holbrook

1. Es - tab-lished in the high - est heav'ns The Lord has set His throne,
2. Ye an - gels that ex - cel in strength, Bless ye the Lord, your God;
3. Bless ye the Lord, all ye His hosts That serve the Lord, your King,
4. Bless ye the Lord, all ye His works In His do - min - ion broad,

And o - ver all His king-dom rules, For He is God a - lone.
Or - dained to hear and do His will, Pro-claim His praise a - broad.
And wait His pleas - ure to per - form, To Him your prais - es bring.
And, nev - er ceas - ing, O my soul, Bless thou the Lord, thy God.

[Stanzas 14-17]

280 The Tender Mercies of God

PSALM 103   8s and 7s   AUTUMN   Louis von Esch

1. O my soul, bless thou Je - ho - vah, All with-
2. He with ten - der mer - cies crowns thee, Sat - is-
3. Yea, the Lord is full of mer - cy And com-
4. As the heav'ns are high a - bove us, Great His

in me bless His Name; Bless Je - ho - vah and for - get not
fies thy full re - quest, So that like the tire - less ea - gle
pas - sion for dis - tress, Slow to an - ger and a - bun - dant
love to us has proved; Far as east from west is dis - tant,

All His mer - cies to pro - claim. He for - gives all thy trans-
Thou with youth re - newed art blessed. Right - eous is the Lord in
In His grace and ten - der - ness. He will not be an - gry
He has all our sins re - moved. As a fa - ther loves his

gres - sions, Heals thy sick - ness - es and pains; He re-
judg - ment Un - to all that are op - pressed; To His
al - way, Nor will He for - ev - er chide; Tho' we
chil - dren, Feel - ing pit - y for their woes, So the

The Tender Mercies of God

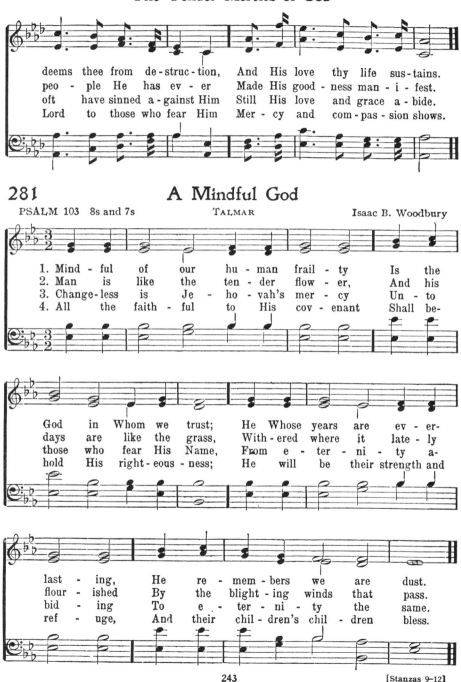

deems thee from de-struc-tion, And His love thy life sus-tains.
peo - ple He has ev - er Made His good - ness man - i - fest.
oft have sinned a-gainst Him Still His love and grace a - bide.
Lord to those who fear Him Mer - cy and com-pas-sion shows.

281 A Mindful God

PSALM 103   8s and 7s   TALMAR   Isaac B. Woodbury

1. Mind - ful of our hu - man frail - ty Is the
2. Man is like the ten - der flow - er, And his
3. Change-less is Je - ho - vah's mer - cy Un - to
4. All the faith - ful to His cov - enant Shall be-

God in Whom we trust; He Whose years are ev - er-
days are like the grass, With - ered where it late - ly
those who fear His Name, From e - ter - ni - ty a-
hold His right - eous - ness; He will be their strength and

last - ing, He re - mem - bers we are dust.
flour - ished By the blight - ing winds that pass.
bid - ing To e - ter - ni - ty the same.
ref - uge, And their chil - dren's chil - dren bless.

[Stanzas 9–12]

282 — The Blessed and Only Potentate

PSALM 103 3s and 7s   RATHBUN   Ithamar Conkey

1. In the heav'ns the Lord Al-might-y Fixed His
2. Bless the Lord, ye might-y an-gels, Ye that
3. Bless the Lord, all ye His serv-ants, Min-is-
4. Bless the Lord, all things cre-a-ted; Be His

ev-er-last-ing throne; O-ver all is His do-
heark-en to His voice, All His gra-cious word ful-
ters of God Most High; Ye His hosts, that do His
ho-ly Name a-dored All through-out His wide do-

min-ion, He is God, and He a-lone.
fill-ing; Ev-er bless Him and re-joice.
pleas-ure, God your Mak-er glo-ri-fy.
min-ion; O my soul, bless thou the Lord.

[Stanzas 13-16]

283 — Motives to Gratitude

PSALM 103 11s and 10s   TUNBRIDGE   James Walch

1. O come, my soul, bless thou the Lord thy Mak-er,
2. Good is the Lord and full of kind com-pas-sion,
3. His love is like a fa-ther's to his chil-dren,
4. We fade and die like flow'rs that grow in beau-ty,
5. High in the heav'ns His throne is fixed for-ev-er,

244

Motives to Gratitude

And all with-in me bless His ho-ly Name; Bless thou the
Most slow to an - ger, plen-te-ous in love; Rich is His
Ten - der and kind to all who fear His Name, For well He
Like ten - der grass that soon will dis-ap-pear; But ev-er-
His king-dom rules o'er all from pole to pole; Bless ye the

Lord, for - get not all His mer - cies, His par-d'ning grace and
grace to all that hum-bly seek Him, Bound-less and end - less
knows our weak-ness and our frail - ty, He knows that we are
more the love of God is change-less, Still shown to those who
Lord through all His wide do - min - ion, Bless His most ho - ly

CHORUS

sav - ing love pro - claim.
as the heav'ns a - bove.
dust, He knows our frame. Bless Him, ye an - gels, won-drous in
look to Him in fear.
Name, O thou my soul.

might, Bless Him, His serv - ants that in His will de - light.

[Selected Stanzas]

284 The Wonders of Divine Grace

PSALM 103 11s and 10s   PILGRIMS   Henry Smart

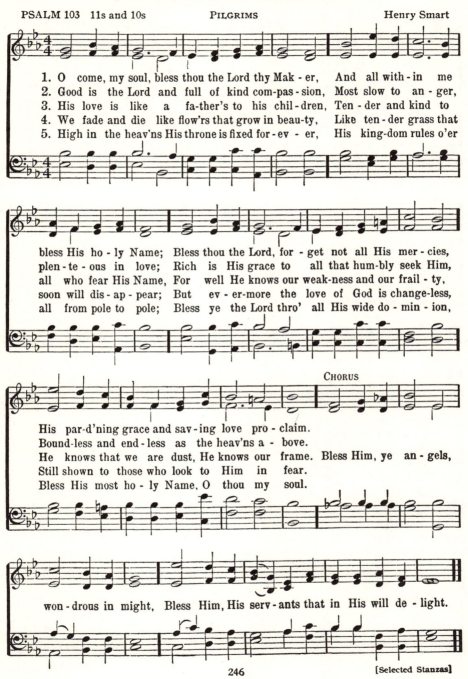

1. O come, my soul, bless thou the Lord thy Mak - er, And all with-in me
2. Good is the Lord and full of kind com-pas-sion, Most slow to an - ger,
3. His love is like a fa-ther's to his chil-dren, Ten - der and kind to
4. We fade and die like flow'rs that grow in beau-ty, Like ten - der grass that
5. High in the heav'ns His throne is fixed for-ev - er, His king-dom rules o'er

bless His ho - ly Name; Bless thou the Lord, for - get not all His mer - cies,
plen - te - ous in love; Rich is His grace to all that hum-bly seek Him,
all who fear His Name, For well He knows our weak-ness and our frail - ty,
soon will dis - ap - pear; But ev - er-more the love of God is change-less,
all from pole to pole; Bless ye the Lord thro' all His wide do - min - ion,

CHORUS

His par-d'ning grace and sav-ing love pro - claim.
Bound-less and end-less as the heav'ns a - bove.
He knows that we are dust, He knows our frame. Bless Him, ye an - gels,
Still shown to those who look to Him in fear.
Bless His most ho - ly Name, O thou my soul.

won - drous in might, Bless Him, His serv - ants that in His will de - light.

246   [Selected Stanzas]

285 The Greatness of God in Nature

PSALM 104 10s and 11s LYONS Arranged from Michael Haydn

1. My soul, bless the Lord! the Lord is most great;
2. He rides on the clouds, the wings of the storm,
3. O'er moun-tain and plain the dark wa-ters raged;
4. He caus-es the springs of wa-ter to flow

With glo-ry ar-rayed, ma-jes-tic His state;
The light-ning and wind His mis-sion per-form;
His voice they o-beyed, the floods were as-suaged;
In streams 'mid the hills and val-leys be-low;

The light is His gar-ment, the skies are His shade,
The earth He has found-ed her sta-tion to keep,
Up-lift-ing the moun-tains He or-dered a bound,
Be-side them with sing-ing the birds greet the day,

And o-ver the wa-ters His courts He has laid.
And wrapped as a ves-ture a-bout her the deep.
For-bid-ding the wa-ters to cov-er the ground
And there the beasts gath-er their thirst to al-lay.

286 A Faithful Creator

PSALM 104 10s and 11s STANLEY John Stanley

1. He wa - ters the hills with rain from the skies,
2. The trees which the Lord has plant - ed are fed,
3. The sea - sons are fixed by wis - dom di - vine,
4. The Lord makes the night, when, leav - ing their lair,
5. How man - y and wise Thy works are, O Lord!
6. Thy crea - tures all look to Thee for their food;

And plen - ti - ful grass and herbs He sup - plies,
And o - ver the earth their branch - es are spread;
The slow chang - ing moon shows forth God's de - sign;
The li - ons creep forth, God's boun - ty to share;
The earth with the wealth of wis - dom is stored,
Thy hand o - pens wide they gath - er the good;

Sup - ply - ing the cat - tle, and bless - ing man's toil
They keep in their shel - ter the birds of the air,
The sun in his cir - cuit his Mak - er o - beys,
The Lord makes the morn - ing, when beasts steal a - way
The sea bears in safe - ty the ships to and fro,
Thy face Thou con - ceal - est, in an - guish they yearn;

With bread in a - bun - dance, with wine and with oil.
The life of each crea - ture the Lord makes His care.
And run - ning his jour - ney hastes not nor de - lays.
And men are be - gin - ning the work of the day.
And crea - tures un - num - bered it shel - ters be - low.
Their breath Thou with - hold - est, to dust they re - turn.

[Stanzas 5–10]

A Meditation on Providence

PSALM 104   10s and 11s   ASPINWALL   Charles H. Gabriel

1. Thy Spir-it, O Lord, makes life to a-bound;
2. Be-fore the Lord's might earth trem-bles and quakes,
3. Re-joic-ing in God, my thought shall be sweet,

The earth is re-newed, and fruit-ful the ground;
The moun-tains are rent, and smoke from them breaks;
While sin-ners de-part in ru-in com-plete;

To God as-cribe glo-ry and wis-dom and might,
The Lord I will wor-ship through all of my days,
My soul, bless Je-ho-vah, His Name be a-dored,

Let God in His crea-tures for-ev-er de-light.
Yea, while I have be-ing my God I will praise.
Come, praise Him, ye peo-ple, and wor-ship the Lord.

288   The Creator Glorified

PSALM 104   C. M.   MOLINE   William J. Kirkpatrick

1. O Lord, how man-i-fold the works In wis-dom wrought by Thee;
2. Let God re-joice in all His works, And let His works pro-claim
3. While life shall last, my thank-ful lips A song to God will raise,
4. My heart shall think up-on His grace In med-i-ta-tion sweet;

The wealth of Thy cre-a-tion fills The earth and might-y sea.
For ev-er-more their Mak-er's praise And glo-ri-fy His Name.
And while my be-ing I pos-sess, My Mak-er I will praise.
My soul, re-joic-ing in the Lord, His prais-es shall re-peat.

Copyright, 1901, by Wm. J. Kirkpatrick. Used by per.   [Selected Stanzas]

289   The Unfailing Faithfulness of God

PSALM 105   C. M.   BOARDMAN   Arranged from L. Devereux

1. O praise the Lord, His deeds make known, And call up-on His Name;
2. Let hearts re-joice that seek the Lord, His ho-ly Name a-dore;
3. Ye chil-dren of God's cov-e-nant, Who of His grace have heard,
4. The Lord our God is God a-lone, All lands His judg-ments know;
5. While yet our fa-thers were but few, So-journ-ers in the land,

Sing ye to Him, His prais-es sing, His won-drous works pro-claim.
Seek ye Je-ho-vah and His strength, Seek Him for ev-er-more.
For-get not all His won-drous deeds And judg-ments of His word.
His prom-ise He re-mem-bers still, While gen-er-a-tions go.
He sware that Ca-naan should be theirs, And made His cov-enant stand.

250

The Unfailing Faithfulness of God

6 He suffered none to do them wrong
   In all their pilgrim way;
   Yea, for their sake were kings reproved
   And covered with dismay.

7 His stern command restrained their foes
   And filled them with alarm:
   Touch not My own anointed ones,
   Nor do My prophets harm.

8 He wholly broke the staff of bread
   And called for famine sore,
   And He prepared His people's way
   By sending one before.

9 Then Joseph, sold to slavery,
   With cruel chains was bound;
   Till his prediction came to pass,
   Distress and grief he found.

10 The king released him from his bonds
   And made him rule the land,
   Subjecting chiefs and senators
   To his controlling hand.

11 To Egypt Israel followed then,
   And there grew great and strong,
   Until their friends became their foes
   And did them grievous wrong.

12 God sent His servant Moses then,
   And Aaron, whom He chose;
   Great signs and wonders they displayed
   To terrify their foes.

13 In darkness they were taught to fear
   God's great and holy Name;
   On man and beast, on vine and field,
   His awful judgment came.

14 He smote the first-born in the land,
   The chief of all their strength,
   Enriched His people with the spoil
   And brought them forth at length.

15 He led them forth in health and strength,
   None weak in all their band,
   And Egypt, filled with fear, rejoiced
   To see them leave the land.

16 He spread a cloud to cover them,
   Most glorious and bright,
   And made a fiery pillar shine
   To give them light by night.

17 At their request He sent them quails,
   And bread of heaven bestowed;
   And from the rock, to quench their thirst,
   The living waters flowed.

18 His sacred word to Abraham
   He kept, though waiting long,
   And brought His chosen people forth
   With joy and thankful song.

19 The lands and toil of wicked men
   He gave them to possess,
   That they might keep His holy laws;
   Jehovah praise and bless.

SECOND TUNE WOODSTOCK Deodatus Dutton, Jr.

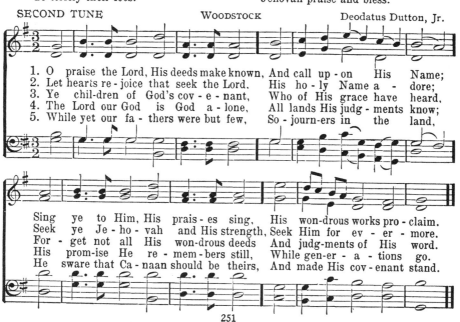

1. O praise the Lord, His deeds make known, And call up-on His Name;
2. Let hearts re-joice that seek the Lord. His ho-ly Name a-dore;
3. Ye chil-dren of God's cov-e-nant, Who of His grace have heard.
4. The Lord our God is God a-lone, All lands His judg-ments know;
5. While yet our fa-thers were but few, So-journ-ers in the land,

Sing ye to Him, His prais-es sing, His won-drous works pro-claim.
Seek ye Je-ho-vah and His strength, Seek Him for ev-er-more.
For-get not all His won-drous deeds And judg-ments of His word.
His prom-ise He re-mem-bers still, While gen-er-a-tions go.
He sware that Ca-naan should be theirs, And made His cov-enant stand.

251

Praise and Confession

PSALM 106 C. M. BARRE Edward Clark

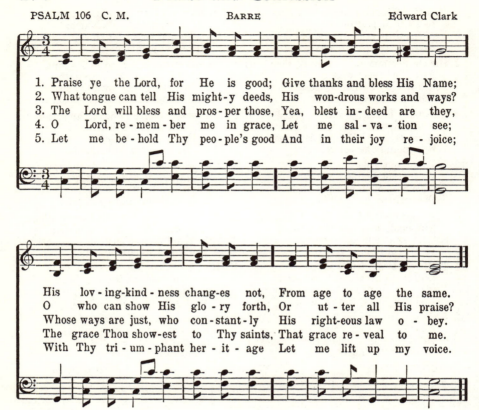

1. Praise ye the Lord, for He is good; Give thanks and bless His Name;
2. What tongue can tell His might-y deeds, His won-drous works and ways?
3. The Lord will bless and pros-per those, Yea, blest in-deed are they,
4. O Lord, re-mem-ber me in grace, Let me sal-va-tion see;
5. Let me be-hold Thy peo-ple's good And in their joy re-joice;

His lov-ing-kind-ness chang-es not, From age to age the same.
O who can show His glo-ry forth, Or ut-ter all His praise?
Whose ways are just, who con-stant-ly His right-eous law o-bey.
The grace Thou show-est to Thy saints, That grace re-veal to me.
With Thy tri-um-phant her-it-age Let me lift up my voice.

6 In evil we have gone astray,
   And sinful is our race;
Rebelliously our fathers walked,
   Forgetful of Thy grace

7 Though they rebelled, yet for their help
   In saving strength He came
To make His power almighty known
   And glorify His Name.

8 He brought them safely through the sea
   And overwhelmed their foes;
Their faith was stirred, and for the time
   Their songs of praise arose.

9 Forgetful soon, they tempted God,
   Nor for His counsel cared;
He sent them leanness in their souls,
   Whilst they earth's bounties shared.

10 With envy they regarded those
   Whom God to them had sent;
The opening earth, the kindling flame,
   Brought awful punishment.

11 A golden image they adored,
   And worshiped at its shrine;
Thus they despised the living God
   And scorned His love divine.

291 Sin and Divine Patience

PSALM 106 C. M.   NOTTINGHAM   Jeremiah Clark

1. Their God and Sav-iour they for-got, Their help-er and their stay,
2. Yea, they de-spised the pleas-ant land, The prom-ised land of God,
3. They sac-ri-ficed to hea-then gods, And God their sin re-paid,
4. The Lord ap-proved the right-eous act Of him who sin ab-horred,
5. By wick-ed strife they an-gered God, His wrath they did pro-voke;
6. En-snared, they served the hea-then gods, And by them were be-guiled;

But Mo-ses plead the prom-ised grace And turned God's wrath a-way.
And tempt-ed Him to make them fall And scat-ter them a-broad.
Then ho-ly wrath a-venged the wrong, And so the plague was stayed.
And hon-ored him for ev-er-more With just and great re-ward.
And, stirred by their re-bel-lious cries, Their lead-er rash-ly spoke.
The blood of chil-dren sac-ri-ficed The ver-y land de-filed.

[Stanzas 12–23]

7 Against His own inheritance
   Jehovah's wrath arose,
His chosen people He condemned
   To serve their heathen foes.

8 Though from their harsh oppressors' hand
   Ofttimes He set them free,
Rebellious still, they were brought low
   In their iniquity.

9 When unto God they cried, He heard
   And turned again His face,
In boundless love remembering
   The covenant of His grace.

10 He even touched their captors' hearts,
   And made their very foes
Compassionate and pitiful
   To feel his people's woes.

11 Save us, O Lord, our gracious God,
   From alien lands reclaim,
That we may triumph in Thy praise
   And bless Thy holy Name.

12 Blessed be the Lord our covenant God,
   All praise to Him accord;
Let all the people say, Amen.
   Praise ye, praise ye, the Lord.

292 Redeeming Love

PSALM 107 7s   HALLE   Arranged from Haydn

1. Praise the Lord, for He is good, For His mer - cies
2. From cap - tiv - i - ty re - leased, From the south and
3. Wan - d'ring in the wil - der - ness, Far they roamed the
4. To Je - ho - vah then they cried In their troub - le,
5. Sons of men, a - wake to praise God the Lord Who

ev - er sure From e - ter - ni - ty have stood,
from the north, From the west and from the east,
des - ert way, Found no set - tled dwell - ing - place
and He saved; He Him - self be - came their guide,
reigns a - bove, Gra - cious in His works and ways,

To e - ter - ni - ty en - dure; Let His ran - somed
In His love He brought them forth, Ran - somed out of
Where in peace se - cure to stay, Till with thirst and
Led them to the rest they craved By a path - way
Won - drous in re - deem - ing love; Long - ing souls He

peo - ple raise Songs to their Re - deem - er's praise.
ev - 'ry land From the ad - ver - sa - ry's hand.
hun - ger pressed Cour - age sank with - in their breast.
straight and sure, To a cit - y strong, se - cure.
sat - is - fies, Hun - gry hearts with good sup - plies.

254

293   Emancipation from Spiritual Slavery

PSALM 107   7s   DIX   Arranged from Conrad Kocher

1. Rebels, who had dared to show Proud contempt of
God Most High, Bound in iron and in woe,
Shades of death and darkness nigh, Humbled low with
toil and pain, Fell, and looked for help in vain.

2. To Jehovah then they cried In their trouble,
and He saved, Threw the prison open wide
Where they lay to death enslaved, Bade the gloomy
shadows flee, Broke their bonds and set them free.

3. Sons of men, awake to praise God the Lord Who
reigns above, Gracious in His works and ways,
Wondrous in redeeming love; Iron bars He
breaks like clay, And the brazen gates give way.

255   [Stanzas 6-8]

Praise for Gracious Deliverances

PSALM 107 7s   SACRED MORN   William H. Squires

1. Men who walk in fol-ly's way, And to e-vil
2. To Je-ho-vah then they cry In their troub-le,
3. Sons of men, a-wake to praise God the Lord Who

turn a-side, Find that sor-row will re-pay
and He saves, Sends com-pas-sion-ate re-ply,
reigns a-bove, Gra-cious in His works and ways,

Those who wis-dom's laws de-fied; Down to death's dark
Gives the health their spir-it craves, Res-cues them with
Won-drous in re-deem-ing love; Let them all thank-

por-tals led, They ab-hor their dai-ly bread.
gra-cious aid From the snares their fol-ly laid.
of-f'rings bring, Cel-e-brate His deeds, and sing.

[Stanzas 9-11]

295 The Sovereign of the Sea

PSALM 107 7s   ROSEFIELD   H. A. César Malan

1. They that traf-fic on the sea, While un-ceas-ing
2. By the bil-lows heav'n-ward tossed, Down to dread-ful
3. To Je-ho-vah then they cry In their troub-le,
4. Sons of men, a-wake to praise God the Lord Who

watch they keep, See Je-ho-vah's maj-es-ty
depths a-gain, Troub-led much, their cour-age lost,
and He saves, Drives the dark-ness from the sky,
reigns a-bove, Gra-cious in His works and ways,

And His won-ders in the deep; For He bids the
Reel-ing, they like drunk-en men Find their skill and
Calms the storm and stills the waves, Makes their sad fore-
Won-drous in re-deem-ing love; Praise Him where the

storm-wind fly, Lift-ing o-cean's waves on high
pow'r o'er-thrown; None can save but God a-lone.
bod-ings cease, To their hav-en guides in peace.
peo-ple meet, Praise Him in the eld-ers' seat.

[Stanzas 12-15]

296 Providential Visitations

PSALM 107 7s   GREATOREX   Chester G. Allen

1. Springs and streams no lon - ger bless, All the
2. Once a - gain the wa - ters well, All the
3. Now He bless - es them in - deed, They are
4. His con - tempt the princ - es taste; Driv - en
5. When His right - eous judg - ments come, Strong to

dry and thirst - y land; Fer - tile fields in ver - dant dress
des - ert blos - soms fair; There He makes the hun - gry dwell,
great - ly mul - ti - plied; On the hills their cat - tle feed,
out they help - less fly, Wan-d'ring in the track-less waste;
bless and to de - stroy, All in - iq - ui - ty is dumb,

God con - verts to des - ert sand; For that they who
There a cit - y they pre - pare, Plant their vines and
Fast in - creas - ing, spread-ing wide; Then a - gain they
But He lifts the need - y high, Where no e - vil
All the right - eous sing for joy; Who Je - ho - vah

dwell there - in Turn to wick - ed - ness and sin.
sow their fields, And the earth her in - crease yields.
are brought low Through op - pres - sion, grief, and woe.
shall an - noy, And with chil - dren gives him joy.
wise - ly heed, In His works His mer - cy read.

258   [Stanzas 16-20]

297 The Praise of the Redeemed

PSALM 107 C. M.   OSTEND   Lowell Mason

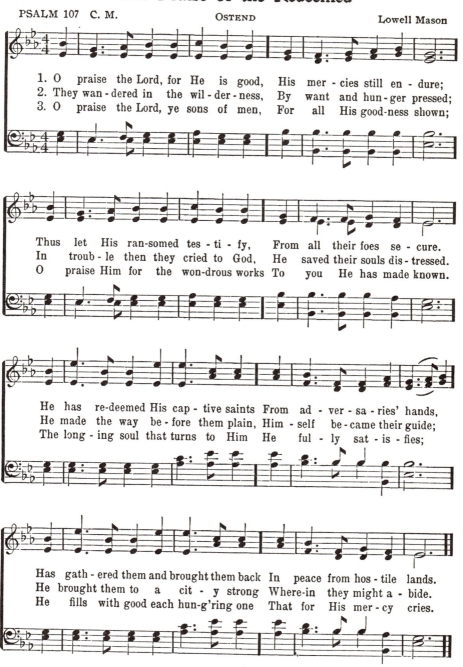

1. O praise the Lord, for He is good, His mer - cies still en - dure;
2. They wan - dered in the wil - der - ness, By want and hun - ger pressed;
3. O praise the Lord, ye sons of men, For all His good - ness shown;

Thus let His ran - somed tes - ti - fy, From all their foes se - cure.
In troub - le then they cried to God, He saved their souls dis - tressed.
O praise Him for the won - drous works To you He has made known.

He has re - deemed His cap - tive saints From ad - ver - sa - ries' hands,
He made the way be - fore them plain, Him - self be - came their guide;
The long - ing soul that turns to Him He ful - ly sat - is - fies;

Has gath - ered them and brought them back In peace from hos - tile lands.
He brought them to a cit - y strong Where - in they might a - bide.
He fills with good each hun - g'ring one That for His mer - cy cries.

[Selected Stanzas]

298 Gratitude and Confidence

PSALM 108   6s and 4s   CUTTING   William F. Sherwin

1. My stead-fast heart, O God, Will sound Thy praise a-broad With tune-ful string; The dawn shall hear my song, Thy praise I will pro-long, And where Thy peo-ple throng Thanks-giv-ing bring.

2. Thy truth and ten-der love Are high as heav'n a-bove; Thy help we crave. Be Thou ex-alt-ed high A-bove the loft-y sky; Lest Thy be-lov-ed die, O hear and save.

3. God's word shall sure-ly stand; His Name through ev-'ry land Shall be a-dored; Lord, who shall lead our host? Thy aid we cov-et most, In Thee is all our boast, Strong in the Lord.

260

Exultant Confidence

PSALM 108 S. M.   FERGUSON   George Kingsley

1. My heart is fixed, O God, A grate - ful song I raise; A - wake, O harp, in joy - ful strains, A - wake, my soul, to praise.
2. A - mong the na - tions, Lord, To Thee my song shall rise; Thy truth is great a - bove the heav'ns, Thy mer - cies reach the skies.
3. A - bove the heav'ns, O God, And o - ver all the earth, Let men ex - alt Thy glo - rious Name And tell Thy match - less worth.
4. Stretch forth Thy might - y hand In an - swer to our prayer, And let Thy own be - lov - ed ones Thy great sal - va - tion share.
5. The ho - ly God hath said, All lands shall own My sway; My peo - ple shall My glo - ry share, The hea - then shall o - bey.

6 O who will lead our hosts
  To triumph o'er the foe,
If Thou shalt cast us off, O God,
  Nor with our armies go?

7 The help of man is vain,
  Be Thou our helper, Lord;
Through Thee we shall do valiantly
  If Thou Thy aid afford.

300 Divine Retribution for Evil

PSALM 109 L. M.   MEROE   William B. Bradbury

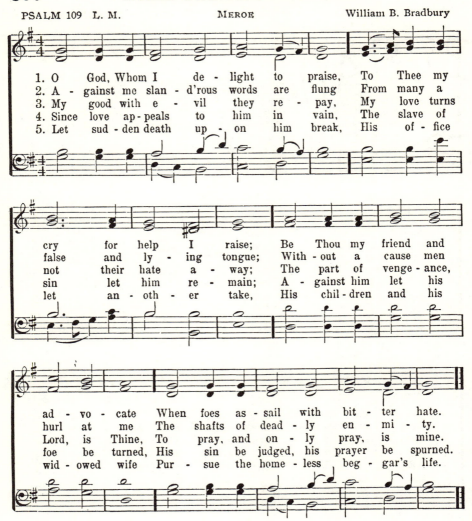

1. O God, Whom I de - light to praise, To Thee my
2. A - gainst me slan - d'rous words are flung From many a
3. My good with e - vil they re - pay, My love turns
4. Since love ap - peals to him in vain, The slave of
5. Let sud - den death up - on him break, His of - fice

cry for help I raise; Be Thou my friend and
false and ly - ing tongue; With - out a cause men
not their hate a - way; The part of venge - ance,
sin let him re - main; A - gainst him let his
let an - oth - er take, His chil - dren and his

ad - vo - cate When foes as - sail with bit - ter hate.
hurl at me The shafts of dead - ly en - mi - ty.
Lord, is Thine, To pray, and on - ly pray, is mine.
foe be turned, His sin be judged, his prayer be spurned.
wid - owed wife Pur - sue the home - less beg - gar's life.

6 Let creditors consume his toil
And strangers make his wealth their spoil;
Let none in pity heed his claim,
Cut off his race, blot out his name.

7 His parents' sins be not forgot
Till Thou from earth his memory blot
Since he remembered not to show
Compassion to the sons of woe.

8 He cursing loved and blessing loathed;
Unblest, with cursing he is clothed;
For thus the justice of the Lord
My adversaries will reward.

9 O God, the Lord, for Thy Name's sake
Let me of Thy good grace partake;
My need is great, and great Thou art
To heal my wounded, stricken heart.

Divine Retribution for Evil

10 With failing strength I fast and pine,
Like shadows swift my days decline,
And when my foes my weakness see
They shake the head in scorn at me.

11 O Lord my God, Thy help I crave,
In Thy great loving-kindness save;
Before my foes Thy mercy show;
That Thou dost help me make them know.

12 What though they curse, if Thou wilt bless?
Then joy shall banish my distress,
And shame shall overwhelm the foes
Who would Thy servant's way oppose.

13 Thanksgiving to the Lord I raise,
The multitude shall hear my praise,
For by the needy God will stand
To save them from oppression's hand.

301   Supplication and Trust

PSALM 109 C. M.   FINGAL   James S. Anderson

1. O Lord, my God, for Thy Name's sake In mer-cy deal with me; Be-cause Thy kind-ness is so great, From troub-le set me free.

2. O Thou Who art my Lord and God, Thy gra-cious help ex-tend, And for Thy lov-ing-kind-ness' sake O save me and de-fend.

3. My voice shall great-ly bless the Lord And sing His wor-thy praise, And I a-mid the mul-ti-tude My thank-ful song will raise.

4. The Lord be praised, for ev-er near The help-less poor He stands, Pro-tect-ing them with won-drous pow'r From their op-press-ors' hands.

[Selected Stanzas]

Our Lord Jesus

PSALM 110   8s and 7s   BIRDSTOWN   Charles H. Gabriel

1. The Lord un-to His Christ hath said, In glo-ry I en-
2. Thy peo-ple will be glad-ly Thine When Thou shalt come vic-
3. The Lord at Thy right hand shall smite Earth's kings in in-dig-

throne Thee Till all Thy foes, in tri-umph led, Their
to-rious, In ho-ly beau-ty Thou shalt shine, Like
na-tion, And He shall judge with sov-'reign right Thro'-

sov-'reign King shall own Thee; From Zi-on shall Je-ho-vah send Thy
morn-ing fair and glo-rious; The word of God shall not de-part: The
out His wide cre-a-tion; While liv-ing streams His strength sustain, The

scep-ter, till be-fore Thee bend The knees of proud re-bel - lion.
King of Right-eous-ness Thou art, A Roy-al Priest for-ev - er.
Christ the vic-to-ry shall gain, Head o-ver all ex-alt - ed.

Christ Our Priest-King

PSALM 110 C. M.　　　　ALL SAINTS NEW　　　　Henry S. Cutler

1. The Lord un-to His Christ hath said, Sit Thou at My right hand
2. Thy peo-ple will be glad-ly Thine When Thou shalt come in might
3. Thou shalt sub-due the kings of earth With God at Thy right hand;

Un-til I make Thy en-e-mies Sub-mit to Thy com-mand.
Like dawn-ing day, like hope-ful youth, With ho-ly beau-ty bright.
The na-tions Thou shalt rule in might And judge in ev-'ry land.

A scep-ter pros-pered by the Lord Thy might-y hand shall wield;
A priest-hood that shall nev-er end The Lord hath giv-en Thee;
The Christ, re-freshed by liv-ing streams, Shall nei-ther faint nor fall,

From Zi-on Thou shalt rule the world, And all Thy foes shall yield.
This He hath sworn, and ev-er-more Ful-filled His word shall be.
And He shall be the glo-rious Head, Ex-alt-ed o-ver all.

The Marvelous Works of God

PSALM 111 L. M.   GERMANY   Gardiner's Sacred Melodies

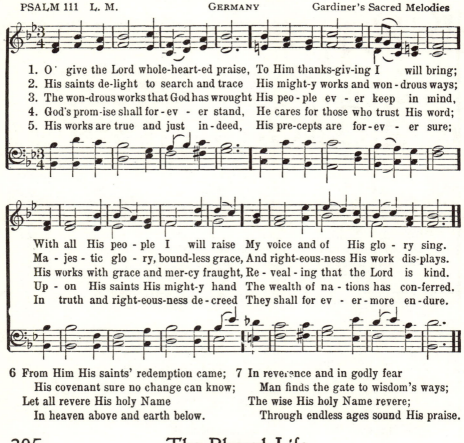

1. O give the Lord whole-heart-ed praise, To Him thanks-giv-ing I will bring;
2. His saints de-light to search and trace His might-y works and won-drous ways;
3. The won-drous works that God has wrought His peo-ple ev - er keep in mind,
4. God's prom-ise shall for - ev - er stand, He cares for those who trust His word;
5. His works are true and just in-deed, His pre-cepts are for-ev - er sure;

With all His peo-ple I will raise My voice and of His glo - ry sing.
Ma - jes - tic glo - ry, bound-less grace, And right-eous-ness His work dis-plays.
His works with grace and mer-cy fraught, Re - veal - ing that the Lord is kind.
Up - on His saints His might-y hand The wealth of na - tions has con-ferred.
In truth and right-eous-ness de-creed They shall for ev - er-more en-dure.

6 From Him His saints' redemption came;
His covenant sure no change can know;
Let all revere His holy Name
In heaven above and earth below.

7 In reverence and in godly fear
Man finds the gate to wisdom's ways;
The wise His holy Name revere;
Through endless ages sound His praise.

The Blessed Life

PSALM 112 L. M.   WELTON   H. A. César Malan

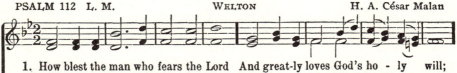

1. How blest the man who fears the Lord And great-ly loves God's ho - ly will;
2. A-bound-ing wealth shall bless his home, His right-eous-ness shall still en - dure,
3. The man whose hand the weak befriends In judg-ment shall his cause main-tain;
4. Of e - vil ti - dings not a - fraid, His trust is in the Lord a - lone;
5. With kind re-mem-brance of the poor, For their dis-tress his gifts pro - vide;
6. To shame the wick-ed shall be brought, While righteous men shall fa - vor gain;

The Blessed Life

His chil-dren share his great re - ward, And bless-ings all their days shall fill.
To him shall light a - rise in gloom, For he is mer - ci - ful and pure.
A peace un-moved his life at - tends, And long his mem-'ry shall re - main.
His heart is stead-fast, un - dis - mayed, For he shall see his foes o'er-thrown.
His right-eous-ness shall thus en - dure, His name in hon - or shall a - bide.
Un-right-eous hopes shall come to naught, Its due re-ward shall sin ob - tain.

306 The Glory and Condescension of God

PSALM 113 L. M.   ANDRE   William B. Bradbury

1. Praise God, ye serv - ants of the Lord, Praise, praise His Name with
2. From ris - ing un - to set - ting sun Praised be the Lord, the
3. On whom but God can we re - ly, The Lord our God Who
4. He lifts the poor and makes them great, With joy He fills the

one ac - cord; Bless ye the Lord, His Name a - dore From
Might - y One; He reigns o'er all, su - preme in might, A-
reigns on high, Who con - de - scends to see and know The
des - o - late; Praise ye the Lord and bless His Name, His

this time forth for ev - er - more, From this time forth for ev - er - more.
bove the heav'ns in glo - ry bright, A - bove the heav'ns in glo - ry bright.
things of heav'n and earth be - low, The things of heav'n and earth be - low?
mer - cy and His might pro-claim, His mer - cy and His might pro-claim.

307 Bondage and Deliverance

PSALM 114 L. M.   BLOOMFIELD CHANT   William B. Bradbury

1. When Is-rael out of E-gypt went,
2. The sea be-held and fled a-way,
3. What ail-eth thee, O troub-led sea?
4. O trem-ble, earth, be-fore the Lord,

From peo-ple of a speech un-known,
The Jor-dan's wa-ters back-ward turned,
Thou Jor-dan, why thy riv-en tide?
In pres-ence of Je-ho-vah fear,

The Lord a-mong His peo-ple dwelt,
The loft-y moun-tains and the hills
Ye moun-tains and ye lit-tle hills,
Be-neath Whose touch the flint-y rock

And there He set His roy-al throne.
With trem-bling awe our God dis-cerned.
Why thus dis-mayed on ev-'ry side?
Be-came a fount of wa-ters clear.

308 The Living and True God

PSALM 115 L. M.　　　　　GAIRNEY BRIDGE　　　　　Ernest R. Kroeger

1. Not un-to us, O Lord of heav'n, But un-to
2. The i-dol gods of hea-then lands Are but the
3. Let Is-rael trust in God a-lone, The Lord Whose
4. All ye that fear Him and a-dore, The Lord in-
5. The heav'ns are God's since time be-gan, But He hath

Thee be glo-ry giv'n; In love and truth Thou dost ful-fill
work of hu-man hands; They can-not see, they can-not speak,
grace and pow'r are known; To Him your full al-le-giance yield,
crease you more and more; Both great and small who Him con-fess,
giv'n the earth to man; The dead praise not the liv-ing God,

The coun-sels of Thy sov-'reign will; Though na-tions
Their ears are deaf, their hands are weak; Like them shall
And He will be your help and shield; All those who
You and your chil-dren He will bless; Yea, blest are
But we will sound His praise a-broad, Yea, we will

fail Thy pow'r to own, Yet Thou dost reign, and Thou a-lone.
be all those who hold To gods of sil-ver and of gold.
fear Him God will bless, His saints have proved His faith-ful-ness.
ye of Him Who made The heav'ns, and earth's found-da-tions laid.
ev-er bless His Name; Praise ye the Lord, His praise pro-claim.

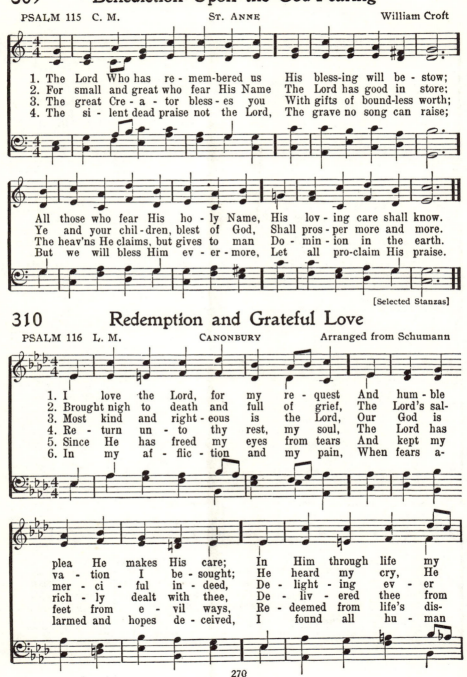

309 Benediction Upon the God-Fearing

PSALM 115 C. M. ST. ANNE William Croft

1. The Lord Who has re-mem-bered us His bless-ing will be - stow;
2. For small and great who fear His Name The Lord has good in store;
3. The great Cre - a - tor bless - es you With gifts of bound-less worth;
4. The si - lent dead praise not the Lord, The grave no song can raise;

All those who fear His ho - ly Name, His lov - ing care shall know.
Ye and your chil - dren, blest of God, Shall pros - per more and more.
The heav'ns He claims, but gives to man Do - min - ion in the earth.
But we will bless Him ev - er - more, Let all pro-claim His praise.

[Selected Stanzas]

310 Redemption and Grateful Love

PSALM 116 L. M. CANONBURY Arranged from Schumann

1. I love the Lord, for my re - quest And hum - ble
2. Brought nigh to death and full of grief, The Lord's sal -
3. Most kind and right - eous is the Lord, Our God is
4. Re - turn un - to thy rest, my soul, The Lord has
5. Since He has freed my eyes from tears And kept my
6. In my af - flic - tion and my pain, When fears a -

plea He makes His care; In Him through life my
va - tion I be - sought; He heard my cry, He
mer - ci - ful in - deed, De - light - ing ev - er
rich - ly dealt with thee, De - liv - ered thee from
feet from e - vil ways, Re - deemed from life's dis -
larmed and hopes de - ceived, I found all hu - man

270

Redemption and Grateful Love

faith shall rest, For He both hears and an - swers prayer.
sent re - lief, My soul from depths of woe He brought.
to af - ford His help to me in time of need.
death's con - trol, From sin and sor - row set thee free.
tress - ing fears, With Him I walk, and Him I praise.
help - ers vain, But in the Lord my soul be - lieved.

311 The Living Sacrifice

PSALM 116 L. M. WALLACE Benjamin F. Baker

1. What shall I ren - der to the Lord For all His
2. Sal - va - tion's cup of bless - ing now I take, and
3. His saints the Lord de - lights to save, Their death is
4. With thank - ful heart I of - fer now My gift, and
5. With - in His house, the house of prayer, I ded - i -

ben - e - fits to me? How shall my soul by
call up - on God's Name; Be - fore His saints I
pre - cious in His sight; He has re - deemed me
call up - on God's Name; Be - fore His saints I
cate my - self to God; Let all His saints His

grace re - stored Give wor - thy thanks, O Lord, to Thee?
pay my vow And here my grat - i - tude pro - claim.
from the grave, And in His serv - ice I de - light.
pay my vow And here my grat - i - tude pro - claim.
grace de - clare And join to sound His praise a - broad.

[Stanzas 7-11]

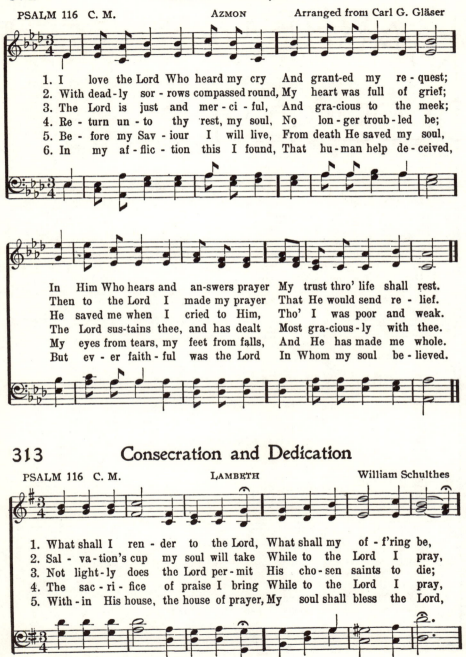

312 Granted Prayers

PSALM 116 C. M. AZMON Arranged from Carl G. Gläser

1. I love the Lord Who heard my cry And grant-ed my re-quest;
2. With dead-ly sor-rows compassed round, My heart was full of grief;
3. The Lord is just and mer-ci-ful, And gra-cious to the meek;
4. Re-turn un-to thy rest, my soul, No lon-ger troub-led be;
5. Be-fore my Sav-iour I will live, From death He saved my soul,
6. In my af-flic-tion this I found, That hu-man help de-ceived,

In Him Who hears and an-swers prayer My trust thro' life shall rest.
Then to the Lord I made my prayer That He would send re-lief.
He saved me when I cried to Him, Tho' I was poor and weak.
The Lord sus-tains thee, and has dealt Most gra-cious-ly with thee.
My eyes from tears, my feet from falls, And He has made me whole.
But ev-er faith-ful was the Lord In Whom my soul be-lieved.

313 Consecration and Dedication

PSALM 116 C. M. LAMBETH William Schulthes

1. What shall I ren-der to the Lord, What shall my of-f'ring be,
2. Sal-va-tion's cup my soul will take While to the Lord I pray,
3. Not light-ly does the Lord per-mit His cho-sen saints to die;
4. The sac-ri-fice of praise I bring While to the Lord I pray,
5. With-in His house, the house of prayer, My soul shall bless the Lord,

For all the gra-cious ben-e-fits He has be-stowed on me?
And with His peo-ple I will meet, My thank-ful vows to pay.
From death Thou hast de-liv-ered me, Thy serv-ant, Lord, am I.
And with His peo-ple I will meet, My thank-ful vows to pay.
And prais-es to His ho-ly Name Let all His saints ac-cord.

[Stanzas 7–11]

314   World-Wide Worship

PSALM 117 L. M.   SABBATH BELL   John H. Tenney

1. With thank-ful voice praise ye the Lord, Je-ho-vah's
2. For lov-ing-kind-ness ev-er great Tow'rd us and

praise in song re-cord; Yea, all ye peo-ple ev-'ry-
all who on Him wait, For truth to end-less years the

where, Je-ho-vah's wor-thy praise de-clare.
same, Praise ye Je-ho-vah's ho-ly Name.

The Universal Fellowship of Worship

PSALM 117   8s and 7s   KINROSS   George C. Stebbins

1. Praise Je-ho-vah, all ye na-tions, All ye peo-ple, praise proclaim; For His grace and lov-ing-kind-ness O sing prais-es to His Name. For the greatness of His mer-cy Constant praise to Him accord; Evermore His truth endureth; Hallelujah, praise the Lord.

Copyright, 1901, by Geo. C. Stebbins. Used by per.

316   The World-Wide Praise of God

PSALM 117   6s and 4s   BRAUN   Johann G. Braun

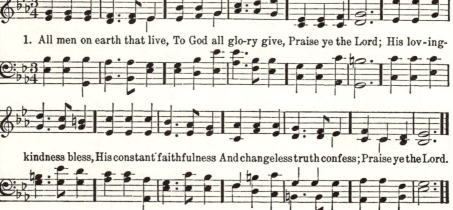

1. All men on earth that live, To God all glo-ry give, Praise ye the Lord; His lov-ing-kindness bless, His constant faithfulness And changeless truth confess; Praise ye the Lord.

317 God an All-Sufficient Helper

PSALM 118 C. M.   HEAVENLY FOLD   William F. Sherwin

1. O praise the Lord, for He is good; Let all in heav'n a - bove
2. The Lord with me, I will not fear Tho' hu - man might op - pose;
3. Tho' na - tions com-pass me a - bout, The swarm-ing hosts of sin,
4. Sal - va-tion's joy - ful song is heard Wher-e'er the right-eous dwell;

And all His saints on earth pro-claim His ev - er - last - ing love.
The Lord my help - er, I shall be Tri - um-phant o'er my foes.
Yet in the Name of God the Lord I shall the vic - t'ry win.
For them God's hand is strong to save And do - eth all things well.

In my dis - tress I called on God; In grace He an - swered me,
No trust in men, or kings of men, Can con - fi - dence af - ford,
The Lord hath helped and kept me safe When foes were fierce and strong;
I shall not die, but live and tell The won-ders of the Lord;

Re - moved my bonds, en - larged my place, From troub - le set me free.
But they are strong, and sure their trust, Whose hope is in the Lord.
The Lord my Sav - iour is be - come, He is my strength and song.
He hath not giv'n my soul to death, But chas-tened and re - stored.

Thoughts for the Sanctuary

PSALM 118 C. M. ZERAH Lowell Mason

1. The glo-rious gates of right-eous-ness Throw o-pen un-to me,
2. This is Thy tem-ple-gate, O Lord, The just shall en-ter there;
3. The stone re-ject-ed and de-spised Is now the cor-ner-stone;
4. In this the day that Thou hast made Tri-um-phant-ly we sing;
5. Ho-san-na! Ev-er blest be He That com-eth in God's Name,

And I will en-ter them with praise, O Lord, my God, to Thee,
My Sav-iour, I will give Thee thanks, O Thou that hear-est prayer,
How won-drous are the ways of God, Un-fath-omed and un-known!
Send now pros-per-i-ty, O Lord, O Lord, sal-va-tion bring,
The bless-ing of Je-ho-vah's house Up-on you we pro-claim,

And I will en-ter them with praise, O Lord, my God, to Thee.
My Sav-iour, I will give Thee thanks, O Thou that hear-est prayer.
How won-drous are the ways of God, Un-fath-omed and un-known!
Send now pros-per-i-ty, O Lord, O Lord, sal-va-tion bring.
The bless-ing of Je-ho-vah's house Up-on you we pro-claim.

[Stanzas 9–15]

6 The light of joy to shine on us
   The Lord our God hath made;
Now be the precious sacrifice
   Upon His altar laid.

7 O Lord, my God, I praise Thy Name,
   All other names above;
O give Him thanks, for He is good
   And boundless is His love.

319 Deliverance and Victory

PSALM 118 L. M.   STONEFIELD   Samuel Stanley

1. Give thanks and praise to God a - bove,
2. Let all His serv - ants tell a - broad
3. In bond - age of dis - tress and grief
4. Though foes as - sail I will not fear,
5. Who put their trust in God Most High

For ev - er - last - ing is His love;
The nev - er - fail - ing grace of God;
To God I cried, and sought re - lief;
For at my side the Lord is near;
On ev - er - last - ing strength re - ly;

Praise Him, ye saints, your Sav - iour praise,
Let all who fear Je - ho - - vah's Name
In won - drous love He heard my plea
The Lord my help - er, I shall win
Their con - - fi - dence shall pass a - way

For - ev - - er good in all His ways.
His ev - - er - last - ing love pro - claim.
And set my soul at lib - - er - ty.
The vic - - t'ry o'er the hosts of sin.
Who make the arm of flesh their stay.

277

320   Thankfulness and Triumphant Joy

PSALM 118   L. M.   APPLETON   William Boyce

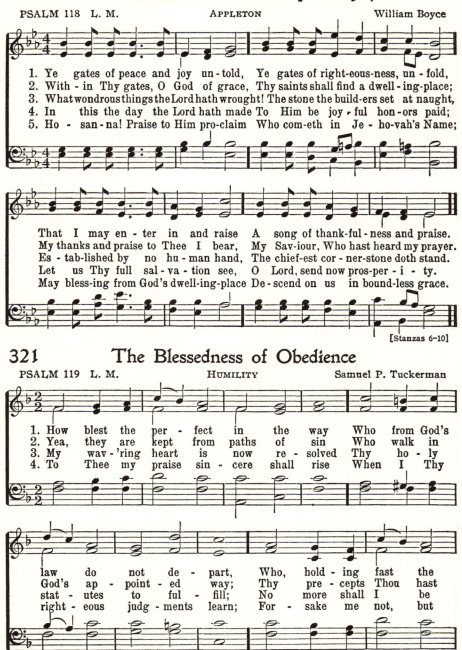

1. Ye gates of peace and joy un-told, Ye gates of right-eous-ness, un-fold,
2. With-in Thy gates, O God of grace, Thy saints shall find a dwell-ing-place;
3. What wondrous things the Lord hath wrought! The stone the build-ers set at naught,
4. In this the day the Lord hath made To Him be joy-ful hon-ors paid;
5. Ho-san-na! Praise to Him pro-claim Who com-eth in Je-ho-vah's Name;

That I may en-ter in and raise A song of thank-ful-ness and praise.
My thanks and praise to Thee I bear, My Sav-iour, Who hast heard my prayer.
Es-tab-lished by no hu-man hand, The chief-est cor-ner-stone doth stand.
Let us Thy full sal-va-tion see, O Lord, send now pros-per-i-ty.
May bless-ing from God's dwell-ing-place De-scend on us in bound-less grace.

[Stanzas 6–10]

321   The Blessedness of Obedience

PSALM 119   L. M.   HUMILITY   Samuel P. Tuckerman

1. How blest the per-fect in the way Who from God's
2. Yea, they are kept from paths of sin Who walk in
3. My wav-'ring heart is now re-solved Thy ho-ly
4. To Thee my praise sin-cere shall rise When I Thy

law do not de-part, Who, hold-ing fast the
God's ap-point-ed way; Thy pre-cepts Thou hast
stat-utes to ful-fill; No more shall I be
right-eous judg-ments learn; For-sake me not, but

278

The Blessedness of Obedience

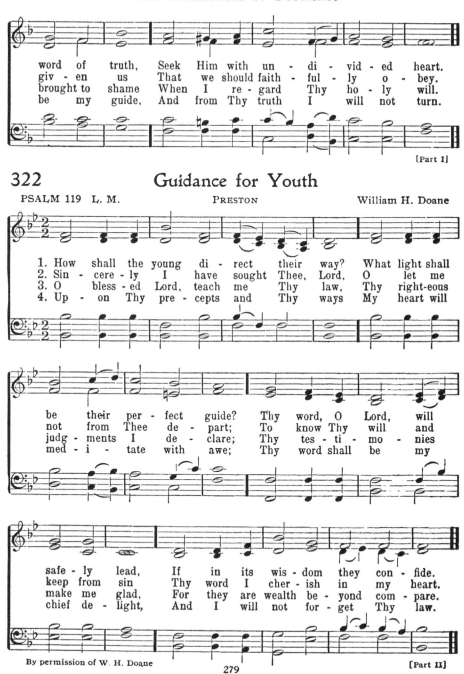

word of truth, Seek Him with un - di - vid - ed heart.
giv - en us That we should faith - ful - ly o - bey.
brought to shame When I re - gard Thy ho - ly will.
be my guide, And from Thy truth I will not turn.

[Part I]

322   Guidance for Youth

PSALM 119 L. M.   PRESTON   William H. Doane

1. How shall the young di - rect their way? What light shall
2. Sin - cere - ly I have sought Thee, Lord, O let me
3. O bless - ed Lord, teach me Thy law, Thy right-eous
4. Up - on Thy pre - cepts and Thy ways My heart will

be their per - fect guide? Thy word, O Lord, will
not from Thee de - part; To know Thy will and
judg - ments I de - clare; Thy tes - ti - mo - nies
med - i - tate with awe; Thy word shall be my

safe - ly lead, If in its wis - dom they con - fide.
keep from sin, Thy word I cher - ish in my heart.
make me glad, For they are wealth be - yond com - pare.
chief de - light, And I will not for - get Thy law.

By permission of W. H. Doane   279   [Part II]

323 Our Pilgrimage Guide

PSALM 119 C. M. ST. MARTIN'S William Tans'ur

1. Thy serv-ant, blest by Thee, shall live And keep Thy word with awe; Lord, o-pen Thou my eyes to see The won-ders of Thy law.
2. A pil-grim in the earth am I, Thy will to me re-veal; To know Thy truth my spir-it yearns, Con-sumed with ar-dent zeal.
3. Thou dost re-buke the proud, O Lord, Who hate Thy ho-ly Name; But since I keep Thy right-eous law, De-liv-er me from shame.
4. I on Thy stat-utes med-i-tate, Tho' e-vil men de-ride; Thy faith-ful word is my de-light, My coun-sel-or and guide.

[Part III]

324 Our Only Source of Help

PSALM 119 C. M. NORTHREPPS Josiah Booth

1. My griev-ing soul re-vive, O Lord, Ac-cord-ing to Thy word;
2. Teach me to know Thy ho-ly way And think up-on Thy deeds;
3. Keep me from false-hood, let Thy law With me in grace a-bide;
4. I cleave un-to Thy truth, O Lord; From shame de-liv-er me;

280

Our Only Source of Help

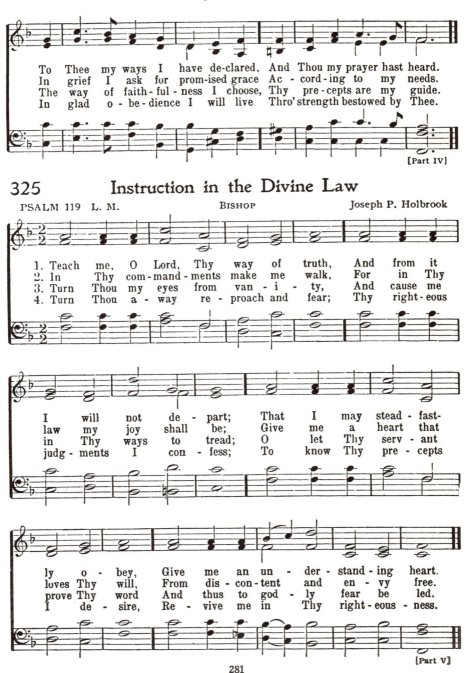

To Thee my ways I have de-clared, And Thou my prayer hast heard.
In grief I ask for prom-ised grace Ac - cord-ing to my needs.
The way of faith-ful - ness I choose, Thy pre-cepts are my guide.
In glad o - be-dience I will live Thro' strength bestowed by Thee.

[Part IV]

325   Instruction in the Divine Law

PSALM 119 L. M.   BISHOP   Joseph P. Holbrook

1. Teach me, O Lord, Thy way of truth, And from it
2. In Thy com-mand-ments make me walk, For in Thy
3. Turn Thou my eyes from van - i - ty, And cause me
4. Turn Thou a - way re - proach and fear; Thy right-eous

I will not de - part; That I may stead - fast-
law my joy shall be; Give me a heart that
in Thy ways to tread; O let Thy serv - ant
judg - ments I con - fess; To know Thy pre - cepts

ly o - bey, Give me an un - der - stand-ing heart.
loves Thy will, From dis - con-tent and en - vy free.
prove Thy word And thus to god - ly fear be led.
I de - sire, Re - vive me in Thy right-eous - ness.

[Part V]

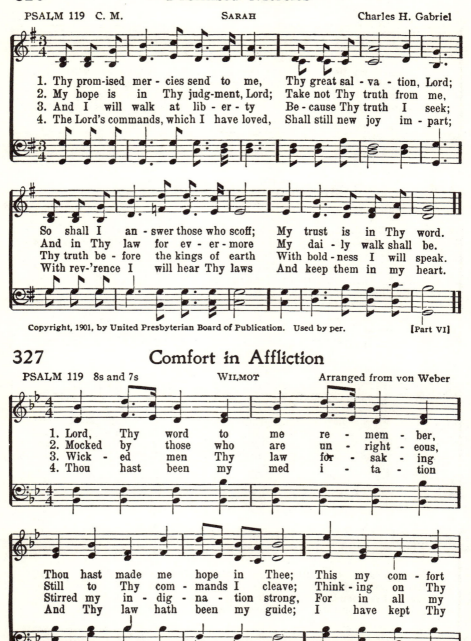

326 Promised Mercies

PSALM 119 C. M. SARAH Charles H. Gabriel

1. Thy prom-ised mer - cies send to me, Thy great sal - va - tion, Lord;
2. My hope is in Thy judg-ment, Lord; Take not Thy truth from me,
3. And I will walk at lib - er - ty Be - cause Thy truth I seek;
4. The Lord's commands, which I have loved, Shall still new joy im - part;

So shall I an - swer those who scoff; My trust is in Thy word.
And in Thy law for ev - er - more My dai - ly walk shall be.
Thy truth be - fore the kings of earth With bold - ness I will speak.
With rev-'rence I will hear Thy laws And keep them in my heart.

Copyright, 1901, by United Presbyterian Board of Publication. Used by per. [Part VI]

327 Comfort in Affliction

PSALM 119 8s and 7s WILMOT Arranged from von Weber

1. Lord, Thy word to me re - mem - ber,
2. Mocked by those who are un - right - eous,
3. Wick - ed men Thy law for - sak - ing
4. Thou hast been my med i - ta - tion

Thou hast made me hope in Thee; This my com - fort
Still to Thy com - mands I cleave; Think - ing on Thy
Stirred my in - dig - na - tion strong, For in all my
And Thy law hath been my guide; I have kept Thy

Comfort in Affliction

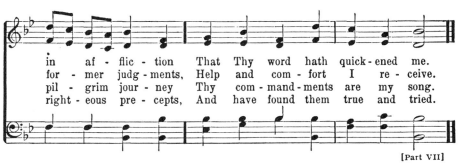

in af - flic - tion That Thy word hath quick - ened me.
for - mer judg - ments, Help and com - fort I re - ceive.
pil - grim jour - ney Thy com - mand - ments are my song.
right - eous pre - cepts, And have found them true and tried.

[Part VII]

328 God the Portion of the Soul

PSALM 119 S. M.   HOBART   Henry Tucker

1. Thou art my por - tion, Lord; Thy
2. I thought up - on my ways, Thy
3. While snares be - set my path, Thy
4. All those who fear Thy Name Shall

words I ev - er heed; With all my heart Thy
tes - ti - mo - nies learned; With ear - nest haste, and
law I keep in view; At mid - night I will
my com - pan - ions be; Thy mer - cy fills the

grace I seek, Thy prom - is - es I plead.
wait - ing not, To Thy com - mands I turned.
give Thee praise For all Thy judg - ments true.
earth, O Lord; Thy stat - utes teach Thou me.

329

The Divine Goodness

PSALM 119   9s and 8s   NILUS   Charles H. Gabriel

1. Thou, Lord, hast dealt well with Thy serv - ant, Thy prom - ise is
2. Be - fore my af - flic - tion I wan - dered, But now Thy good
3. The proud have as - sailed me with slan - der; Thy pre-cepts shall
4. Af - flic - tion has been for my prof - it, That I to Thy

faith - ful and just; In - struct me in judg - ment and
word I o - bey; O Thou, Who art ho - ly and
still be my guide; Thy law is my joy and my
stat - utes might hold; Thy law to my soul is more

knowl - edge, For in Thy com - mand - ments I trust.
gra - cious, Now teach me Thy stat - utes, I pray.
treas - ure, Though sin - ners may boast in their pride.
pre - cious Than thou - sands of sil - ver and gold.

Copyright, 1912, by United Presbyterian Board of Publication. Used by per.   [Part IX]

330

Illumination and Testimony

PSALM 119   L. M.   MARCHFIELD   Edward A. Collier

1. Thou, Who didst make and fash - ion me, O make me
2. Thou, Lord, art just in all Thy ways, And faith - ful
3. Show mer - cy, Lord, that I may live, For in Thy
4. Let those that fear Thee turn to me, Thy truth to

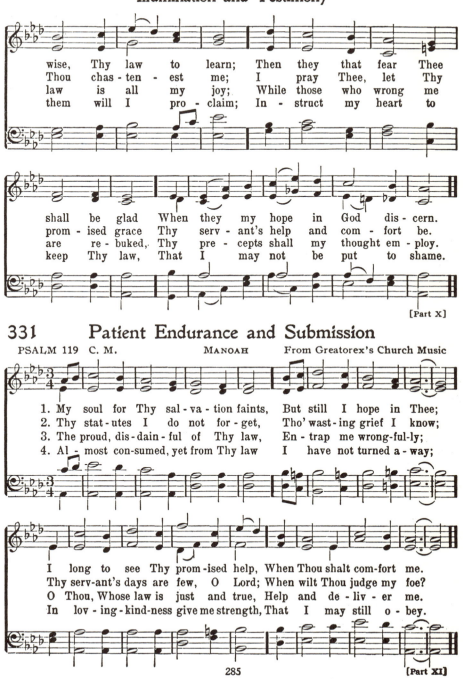

wise, Thy law to learn; Then they that fear Thee
Thou chas-ten-est me; I pray Thee, let Thy
law is all my joy; While those who wrong me
them will I pro-claim; In-struct my heart to

shall be glad When they my hope in God dis-cern.
prom-ised grace Thy serv-ant's help and com-fort be.
are re-buked, Thy pre-cepts shall my thought em-ploy.
keep Thy law, That I may not be put to shame.

[Part X]

331 Patient Endurance and Submission

PSALM 119 C. M.　　　　MANOAH　　From Greatorex's Church Music

1. My soul for Thy sal-va-tion faints, But still I hope in Thee;
2. Thy stat-utes I do not for-get, Tho' wast-ing grief I know;
3. The proud, dis-dain-ful of Thy law, En-trap me wrong-ful-ly;
4. Al-most con-sumed, yet from Thy law I have not turned a-way;

I long to see Thy prom-ised help, When Thou shalt com-fort me.
Thy serv-ant's days are few, O Lord; When wilt Thou judge my foe?
O Thou, Whose law is just and true, Help and de-liv-er me.
In lov-ing-kind-ness give me strength, That I may still o-bey.

285

[Part XI]

332 The Immutable Word

PSALM 119 L. M. ROCKINGHAM NEW Lowell Mason

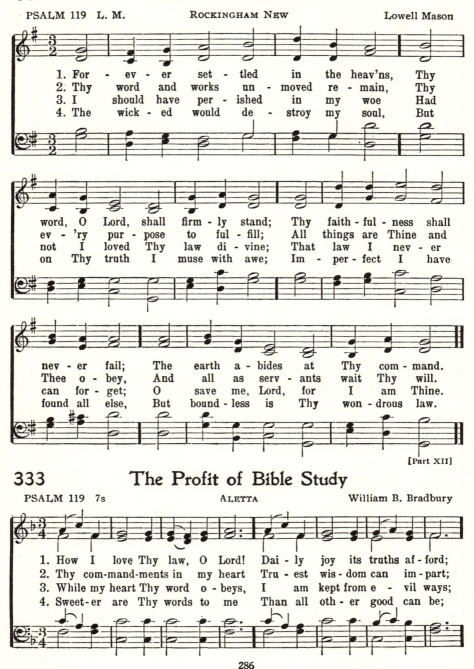

1. For - ev - er set - tled in the heav'ns, Thy
2. Thy word and works un - moved re - main, Thy
3. I should have per - ished in my woe Had
4. The wick - ed would de - stroy my soul, But

word, O Lord, shall firm - ly stand; Thy faith - ful - ness shall
ev - 'ry pur - pose to ful - fill; All things are Thine and
not I loved Thy law di - vine; That law I nev - er
on Thy truth I muse with awe; Im - per - fect I have

nev - er fail; The earth a - bides at Thy com - mand.
Thee o - bey, And all as serv - ants wait Thy will.
can for - get; O save me, Lord, for I am Thine.
found all else, But bound - less is Thy won - drous law.

[Part XII]

333 The Profit of Bible Study

PSALM 119 7s ALETTA William B. Bradbury

1. How I love Thy law, O Lord! Dai - ly joy its truths af - ford;
2. Thy com - mand - ments in my heart Tru - est wis - dom can im - part;
3. While my heart Thy word o - beys, I am kept from e - vil ways;
4. Sweet - er are Thy words to me Than all oth - er good can be;

The Profit of Bible Study

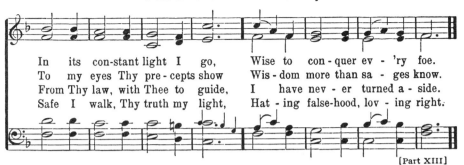

In its con-stant light I go, Wise to con-quer ev-'ry foe.
To my eyes Thy pre-cepts show Wis-dom more than sa-ges know.
From Thy law, with Thee to guide, I have nev-er turned a-side.
Safe I walk, Thy truth my light, Hat-ing false-hood, lov-ing right.

[Part XIII]

334 The Enlightening Power of the Word

PSALM 119 L. M. REPENTANCE Theodore E. Perkins

1. Thy word sheds light up-on my path; A shin-ing
2. In my dis-tress I plead with Thee, Send help ac-
3. In dan-ger oft and nigh to death, Thy law re-
4. Thy pre-cepts are my her-it-age, For dai-ly

light, it guides my feet; Thy right-eous judg-ments
cord-ing to Thy word; Ac-cept my sac-ri-
mem-bered is my aid; The wick-ed seek my
they my heart re-joice; To keep Thy stat-utes

to ob-serve My sol-emn vow I now re-peat.
fice of praise And make me know Thy judg-ments, Lord.
o-ver-throw, Yet from Thy truth I have not strayed.
faith-ful-ly Shall ev-er be my will-ing choice.

[Part XIV]

335 Devotion to the Divine Law

PSALM 119 L. M.   HANDY   Joseph P. Holbrook

1. De - ceit and false - hood I ab - hor, But love Thy law, Thy
2. Ac - cord - ing to Thy gra - cious word Up - hold me, Lord, de -
3. The fro - ward Thou hast set at nought Who vain - ly wan - der

truth re - vealed; My stead - fast hope is in Thy word;
liv - er me; O do not let me be a - shamed
from the right; The wick - ed Thou dost count as dross;

Thou art my ref - uge and my shield; The paths of sin I
Of pa - tient hope and trust in Thee; O hold Thou me, and
Thy just de - crees are my de - light; For fear of Thee I

have not trod, But kept the pre - cepts of my God.
I shall stand And ev - er fol - low Thy com - mand.
stand in awe And rev - 'rence Thy most ho - ly law.

[Part XV]

336 Watching and Eager Longing

PSALM 119 8s and 7s   ROBINSON   Thomas Hastings

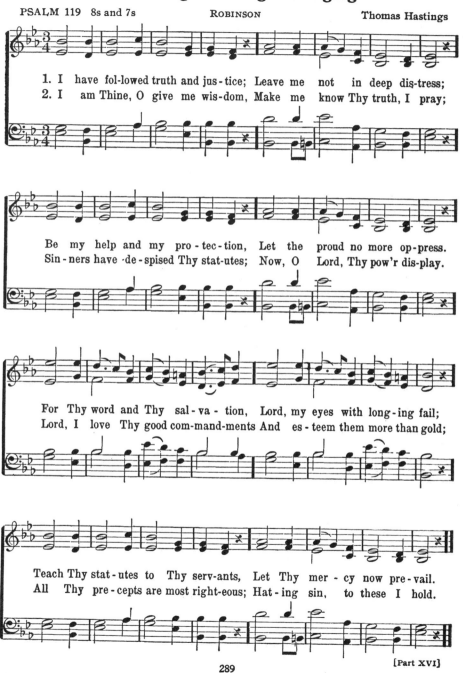

1. I have fol-lowed truth and jus-tice; Leave me not in deep dis-tress;
2. I am Thine, O give me wis-dom, Make me know Thy truth, I pray;

Be my help and my pro-tec-tion, Let the proud no more op-press.
Sin-ners have de-spised Thy stat-utes; Now, O Lord, Thy pow'r dis-play.

For Thy word and Thy sal-va-tion, Lord, my eyes with long-ing fail;
Lord, I love Thy good com-mand-ments And es-teem them more than gold;

Teach Thy stat-utes to Thy serv-ants, Let Thy mer-cy now pre-vail.
All Thy pre-cepts are most right-eous; Hat-ing sin, to these I hold.

[Part XVI]

The Wondrous Testimonies of God

PSALM 119 L. M.   BROOKFIELD   Thomas B. Southgate

1. Thy won-drous tes - ti - mo - nies, Lord, My soul will
2. I thirst for Thy com - mand - ments, Lord, And for Thy
3. Di - rect my foot - steps in Thy word, From sin's do -
4. O make Thy face to shine on me, And teach me

keep and great - ly praise; Thy word, by faith - ful
mer - cy press my claim; O look on me, and
min - ion save my soul, From man's op - pres - sion
all Thy laws to keep; Be - cause Thy stat - utes

lips pro - claimed, To sim - plest minds the truth con - veys.
show the grace Dis - played to all who love Thy Name.
set me free. That I may yield to Thy con - trol.
are de - spised, With o - ver - whelm - ing grief I weep.

[Part XVII]

338

True Love for the Word

PSALM 119 C. M.   CHURCH   Joseph P. Holbrook

1. O Lord, Thy per - fect right-eous-ness Is in Thy judg-ments shown;
2. Be - cause Thy foes for - get Thy law My soul is great-ly stirred;
3. Tho' I am hum - ble and de - spised, I strive Thy will to do;
4. De - light a - mid dis - tress and pain Do Thy com-mand-ments give;

290

True Love for the Word

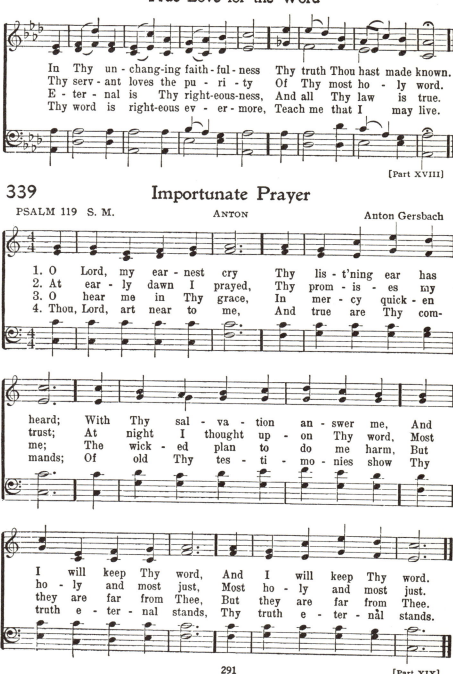

In Thy un-chang-ing faith-ful-ness Thy truth Thou hast made known.
Thy serv-ant loves the pu-ri-ty Of Thy most ho-ly word.
E-ter-nal is Thy right-eous-ness, And all Thy law is true.
Thy word is right-eous ev-er-more, Teach me that I may live.

[Part XVIII]

339   Importunate Prayer

PSALM 119 S. M.   ANTON   Anton Gersbach

1. O Lord, my ear-nest cry Thy lis-t'ning ear has
2. At ear-ly dawn I prayed, Thy prom-is-es my
3. O hear me in Thy grace, In mer-cy quick-en
4. Thou, Lord, art near to me, And true are Thy com-

heard; With Thy sal-va-tion an-swer me, And
trust; At night I thought up-on Thy word, Most
me; The wick-ed plan to do me harm, But
mands; Of old Thy tes-ti-mo-nies show Thy

I will keep Thy word, And I will keep Thy word.
ho-ly and most just, Most ho-ly and most just.
they are far from Thee, But they are far from Thee.
truth e-ter-nal stands, Thy truth e-ter-nal stands.

[Part XIX]

340 Divine Help Invoked

PSALM 119 L. M. EUCHARIST Isaac B. Woodbury

1. Re - gard my grief and res - cue me, For I do
2. Far is sal - va - tion from the men Who do not
3. I bear the spite of man - y foes, Yet from Thy
4. Be - hold how I Thy pre - cepts love! In kind - ness,

not for - get Thy laws; As Thou hast prom - ised,
seek Thy stat - utes, Lord; Great are Thy mer - cies,
law I do not swerve; I saw the faith - less
Lord, re - vive Thou me; The sum of all Thy

save me, Lord; Re - deem my soul, and plead my cause.
quick - en me Ac - cord - ing to Thy ho - ly word.
and was grieved, For they Thy word do not ob - serve.
word is truth, Thy word a - bides e - ter - nal - ly.

[Part XX]

341 Praise and Perfect Peace

PSALM 119 C. M. ST. JAMES Raphael Courteville

1. Though might-y foes as - sail me, Lord, I fear not them, but Thee;
2. De - ceit and false-hood I ab - hor, But in Thy law de - light;
3. Great peace has he who loves Thy law, Un - moved, he safe - ly stands;
4. Thy tes - ti - mo - nies I have kept, They are my chief de - light;

Praise and Perfect Peace

As bound-less wealth and price-less spoil, Thy word re-joic-es me.
Through-out the day I praise Thy Name, For all Thy ways are right.
For Thy sal-va-tion I have hoped And fol-lowed Thy com-mands.
Ob-serv-ant of Thy law and truth, I walk be-fore Thy sight.

[Part XXI]

342   Longing and Confession

PSALM 119 L. M.   ERNAN   Lowell Mason

1. O let my sup-pli-cat-ing cry By Thee, my
2. In-struct-ed in Thy ho-ly law, To praise Thy
3. For Thy sal-va-tion I have longed, And in Thy
4. Thy serv-ant like a wan-d'ring sheep Has lost the

gra-cious Lord, be heard; Give wis-dom and de-
word I lift my voice; O Lord, be Thou my
law is my de-light; En-rich my soul with
path and gone a-stray; Re-store my soul and

liv-er me Ac-cord-ing to Thy faith-ful word.
pres-ent help, For Thy com-mand-ments are my choice.
life di-vine, And help me by Thy judg-ments right.
lead me home, For Thy com-mands I would o-bey.

343 The False Tongue

PSALM 120 L. M.   RETREAT   Thomas Hastings

1. I cried to God in my dis-tress, And by the
2. What woe for false-hood can a-tone, Or pun-ish
3. A-las for me, whose lot is cast With those who
4. In thought and act I am for peace, Peace I pur-

Lord my prayer was heard; O save me, Lord, from
the de-ceit-ful tongue, The tongue whose speech con-
find their joy in strife! With those who hate the
sue and ev-er seek; But those a-bout me

ly-ing lips And from the false, de-ceit-ful word.
sumes like fire, Whose words like dead-ly shafts are flung?
paths of peace I long have dwelt and spent my life.
are for strife, Though I in love and kind-ness speak.

344 Quiet Trust

PSALM 121 C. M.   ST. AGNES   John B. Dykes

1. I to the hills will lift my eyes; O whence shall come my aid?
2. He will not let thy foot be moved, Thy guard-ian nev-er sleeps;
3. Thy faith-ful keep-er is the Lord, Thy shel-ter and thy shade;
4. From e-vil He will keep thee safe, For thee He will pro-vide;

Quiet Trust

My help is from the Lord a-lone. Who heav'n and earth has made.
With watch-ful and un-slum-b'ring care His own He safe-ly keeps.
'Neath sun or moon, by day or night, Thou shalt not be a-fraid.
Thy go-ing out, thy com-ing in, For-ev-er He will guide.

345   Our Unsleeping Guardian

PSALM 121   7s   GUIDE   Marcus M. Wells

1. {To the hills I lift my eyes; Whence shall help for me a-rise?
   From the Lord shall come my aid, Who the heav'n and earth has made.}
2. {Thy pro-tect-or is the Lord, Shade for thee He will af-ford;
   Nei-ther sun nor moon shall smite, God shall guard by day and night.}

He will guide thro' dan-gers all, Will not suf-fer thee to fall;
He will ev-er keep thy soul, What would harm He will con-trol;

He Who safe His peo-ple keeps Slum-bers not and nev-er sleeps.
In the home and by the way He will keep thee day by day.

Unwavering Trust in God

PSALM 121 7s   PILOT   John E. Gould

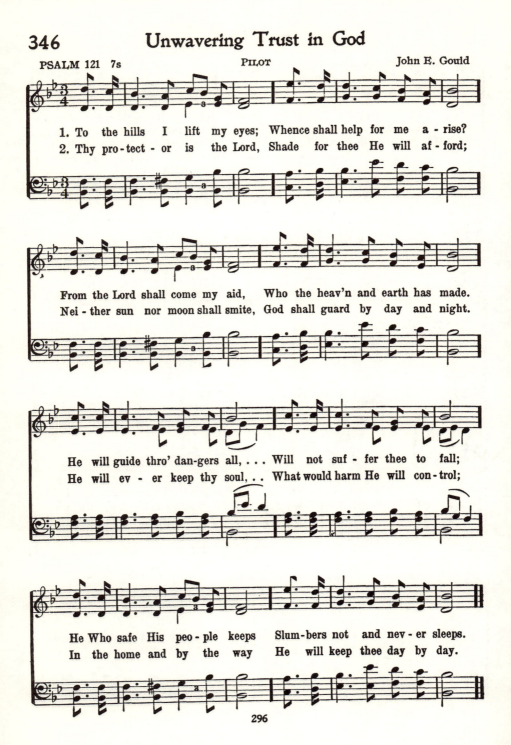

1. To the hills I lift my eyes; Whence shall help for me a - rise?
2. Thy pro-tect-or is the Lord, Shade for thee He will af-ford;

From the Lord shall come my aid, Who the heav'n and earth has made.
Nei-ther sun nor moon shall smite, God shall guard by day and night.

He will guide thro' dan-gers all, . . . Will not suf-fer thee to fall;
He will ev - er keep thy soul, . . What would harm He will con-trol;

He Who safe His peo-ple keeps Slum-bers not and nev-er sleeps.
In the home and by the way He will keep thee day by day.

347 The Watchful Care of God

PSALM 121   10s and 4s   LUX BEATA   Albert L. Peace

1. Un - to the hills a - round do I lift up My long-ing
2. He will not suf - fer that thy foot be moved, Safe shalt thou
3. Je - ho - vah is Him - self thy keep-er true; Thy change-less
4. From ev - 'ry e - vil shall He keep thy soul, From ev - 'ry

eyes; O whence for me shall my sal - va - tion come,
be; No care - less slum - ber shall His eye - lids close
shade Je - ho - vah, ev - er - more on thy right hand,
sin; Je - ho - vah shall pre - serve thy go - ing out,

From whence a - rise? From God the Lord doth come my cer - tain
Who keep - eth thee; Be - hold He sleep - eth not, He slumb'reth
Him - self hath made; And thee no sun by day shall ev - er
Thy com - ing in; A - bove thee watch - ing, He Whom we a -

aid, From God the Lord Who heav'n and earth hath made.
ne'er, Who keep - eth Is - rael in His ho - ly care.
smite, No moon shall harm thee in the si - lent night.
dore Shall keep thee hence-forth, yea, for ev - er - more.

297

348 Attachment to the Church

PSALM 122 C. M. HARVEY'S CHANT William B. Bradbury

1. With joy and glad-ness in my soul I hear the call to
2. We stand with-in thy sa-cred walls, O Zi-on, blest for
3. They come to learn Je-ho-vah's will, His might-y deeds to
4. O pray that Zi-on may be blest And have a-bun-dant

prayer; Let us go up to God's own house And
aye, Where-in the peo-ple of the Lord U-
own, For there is judg-ment's roy-al seat, Mes-
peace, For all that love thee in their hearts Shall

bow be-fore Him there, And bow be-fore Him there.
nit-ed hom-age pay, U-nit-ed hom-age pay.
si-ah's king-ly throne, Mes-si-ah's king-ly throne.
pros-per and in-crease, Shall pros-per and in-crease.

5 I pray the Lord that peace may still
   Within thy walls abound,
And ever in thy palaces
   Prosperity be found.

6 Yea, for the sake of friends and kin,
   My heart desires thy peace,
And for the house of God the Lord
   My care shall never cease.

349 Love for the Lord's House

PSALM 122 10s   MORECAMBE   Frederick C. Atkinson

1. My heart was glad to hear the wel-come sound,
2. God's peo-ple to Je-ru-sa-lem re-pair
3. Let ear-nest prayer be made for Zi-on's peace;
4. For all my breth-ren and com-pan-ions' sakes

The call to seek Je-ho-vah's house of prayer;
To hear His word and wor-ship Him with praise;
Thy sons who hold thee dear shall pros-per well;
My prayer shall be, Let peace in thee a-bide;

Our feet are stand-ing here on ho-ly ground,
The throne of jus-tice stands e-ter-nal there,
May bless-ing in thy pal-a-ces in-crease
Since God the Lord in thee His dwell-ing makes,

With-in thy gates, thou cit-y grand and fair.
Mes-si-ah's throne through end-less length of days.
And peace with-in thy walls for-ev-er dwell.
To thee my love shall nev-er be de-nied.

350 Devotion to the Church

PSALM 122 L. M. ILLA Lowell Mason

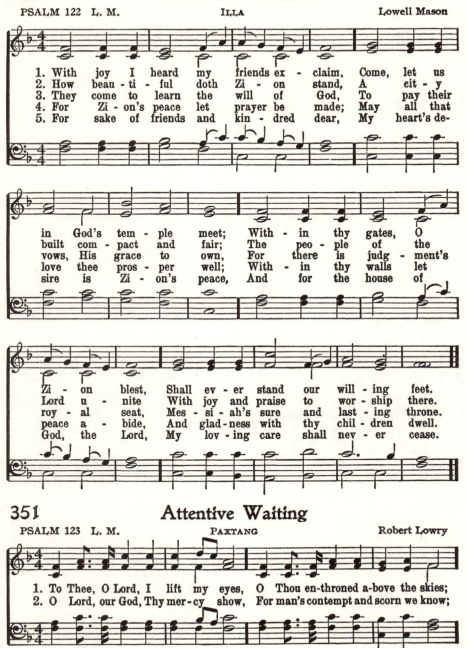

1. With joy I heard my friends ex - claim, Come, let us
2. How beau - ti - ful doth Zi - on stand, A cit - y
3. They come to learn the will of God, To pay their
4. For Zi - on's peace let prayer be made; May all that
5. For sake of friends and kin - dred dear, My heart's de-

in God's tem - ple meet; With - in thy gates, O
built com - pact and fair; The peo - ple of the
vows, His grace to own, For there is judg - ment's
love thee pros - per well; With - in thy walls let
sire is Zi - on's peace, And for the house of

Zi - on blest, Shall ev - er stand our will - ing feet.
Lord u - nite With joy and praise to wor - ship there.
roy - al seat, Mes - si - ah's sure and last - ing throne.
peace a - bide, And glad - ness with thy chil - dren dwell.
God, the Lord, My lov - ing care shall nev - er cease.

351 Attentive Waiting

PSALM 123 L. M. PAXTANG Robert Lowry

1. To Thee, O Lord, I lift my eyes, O Thou en-throned a-bove the skies;
2. O Lord, our God, Thy mer-cy show, For man's contempt and scorn we know;

300

Attentive Waiting

As serv-ants watch their mas-ter's hand, Or maid-ens by their mis-tress stand,
Reproach and shame Thy saints en-dure From wick-ed men who dwell se-cure;

So to the Lord our eyes we raise, Un-til His mer-cy He dis-plays.
Man's proud contempt and scorn we know; O Lord, our God, Thy mer-cy show.

REFRAIN

To Thee, O Lord, I lift my eyes, O Thou en-throned a-bove the skies.

352 Escape from Enemies

PSALM 124 C. M.   BOYNTON   H. A. César Malan

1. Had not the Lord been Is-rael's help When an-gry foes as-sailed,
2. With-out His help the wa-ters proud Had o-ver-whelmed our soul,
3. We are es-caped, as from the snare A bird in safe-ty flies;
4. Our help is in the glo-rious Name, The Name of match-less worth,

Had not the Lord been on our side, Our right-eous cause had failed.
But, praised be God, the waves of wrath Are un-der His con-trol.
The snare is bro-ken and our souls In lib-er-ty a-rise.
Of Him to Whom all pow'r be-longs, The Lord of heav'n and earth.

353 Divine Deliverance

PSALM 124 10s   OLD 124TH   Genevan Psalter

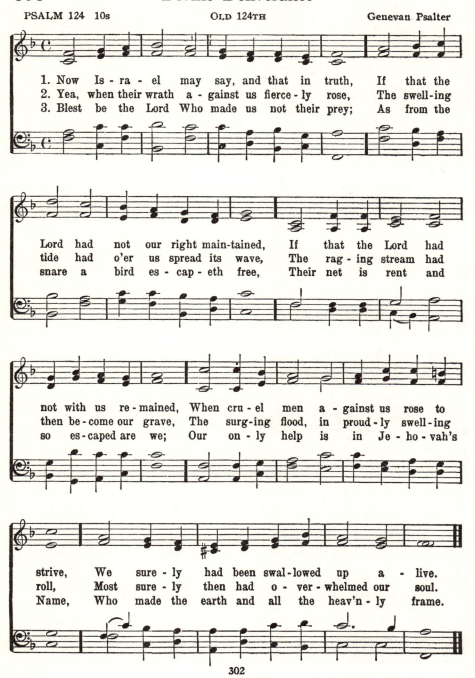

1. Now Is-ra-el may say, and that in truth, If that the
2. Yea, when their wrath a-gainst us fierce-ly rose, The swell-ing
3. Blest be the Lord Who made us not their prey; As from the

Lord had not our right main-tained, If that the Lord had
tide had o'er us spread its wave, The rag-ing stream had
snare a bird es-cap-eth free, Their net is rent and

not with us re-mained, When cru-el men a-gainst us rose to
then be-come our grave, The surg-ing flood, in proud-ly swell-ing
so es-caped are we; Our on-ly help is in Je-ho-vah's

strive, We sure-ly had been swal-lowed up a-live.
roll, Most sure-ly then had o-ver-whelmed our soul.
Name, Who made the earth and all the heav'n-ly frame.

354 Our Sure Defense

PSALM 125 C. M.   BRADFORD   Arranged from Handel

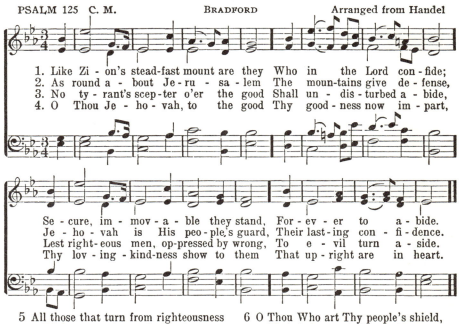

1. Like Zi - on's stead-fast mount are they Who in the Lord con - fide;
2. As round a - bout Je - ru - sa - lem The moun-tains give de - fense,
3. No ty - rant's scep-ter o'er the good Shall un - dis-turbed a - bide,
4. O Thou Je - ho - vah, to the good Thy good-ness now im - part,

Se - cure, im - mov - a - ble they stand, For - ev - er to a - bide.
Je - ho - vah is His peo-ple's guard, Their last-ing con - fi - dence.
Lest right-eous men, op-pressed by wrong, To e - vil turn a - side.
Thy lov - ing - kind-ness show to them That up - right are in heart.

5 All those that turn from righteousness
  With wayward, wandering feet,
  With sinners God will lead them forth,
  The sinner's doom to meet.

6 O Thou Who art Thy people's shield,
  Their helper and their guide,
  Upon them let Thy grace and peace
  For evermore abide.

SECOND TUNE   ALBANO   Vincent Novello

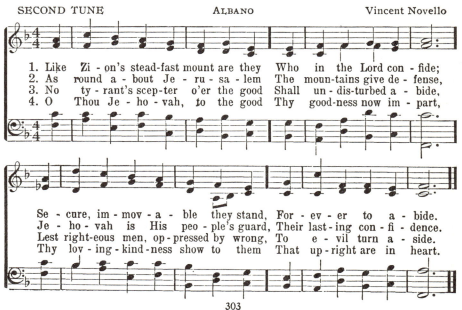

1. Like Zi - on's stead-fast mount are they Who in the Lord con - fide;
2. As round a - bout Je - ru - sa - lem The moun-tains give de - fense,
3. No ty - rant's scep-ter o'er the good Shall un - dis-turbed a - bide,
4. O Thou Je - ho - vah, to the good Thy good-ness now im - part,

Se - cure, im - mov - a - ble they stand, For - ev - er to a - bide.
Je - ho - vah is His peo-ple's guard, Their last-ing con - fi - dence.
Lest right-eous men, op-pressed by wrong, To e - vil turn a - side.
Thy lov - ing - kind-ness show to them That up - right are in heart.

355 Protecting Grace

PSALM 125 7s and 6s   MIRIAM   Joseph P. Holbrook

1. All who with heart con-fid-ing   De-pend on God a-lone,
2. No scep-ter of op-pres-sion   Shall hold un-bro-ken sway,
3. The men who false-hood cher-ish,   For-sak-ing truth and right,

Like Zi-on's mount a-bid-ing,   Shall ne'er be o-ver-thrown.
Lest un-to base trans-gres-sion   The right-eous turn a-way.
With wick-ed men shall per-ish,   God will their sin re-quite.

Like Zi-on's cit-y bound-ed   By guard-ing moun-tains broad,
Thy fa-vor be im-part-ed   To god-ly men, O Lord;
From sin Thy saints de-fend-ing,   Their joy, O Lord, in-crease

His peo-ple are sur-round-ed   For-ev-er by their God.
Bless all that are pure-heart-ed,   The good with good re-ward.
With mer-cy nev-er end-ing   And ev-er-last-ing peace.

The Divine Protection

356

PSALM 125   7s and 6s   KNOWHEAD   Charles H. Gabriel

1. All who with heart con - fid - ing De - pend on God a - lone,
2. No scep - ter of op - pres - sion   Shall hold un - bro - ken sway,
3. The men who false - hood cher - ish, For - sak - ing truth and right,

Like Zi - on's mount a - bid - ing, Shall ne'er be o - ver - thrown.
Lest un - to base trans - gres - sion The right - eous turn a - way.
With wick - ed men shall per - ish, God will their sin re - quite.

Like Zi - on's cit - y bound - ed By guard - ing moun - tains broad,
Thy fa - vor be im - part - ed   To god - ly men, O Lord;
From sin Thy saints de - fend - ing, Their joy, O Lord, in - crease

His peo - ple are sur - round - ed For - ev - er by their God.
Bless all that are pure - heart - ed, The good with good re - ward.
With mer - cy nev - er end - ing And ev - er - last - ing peace.

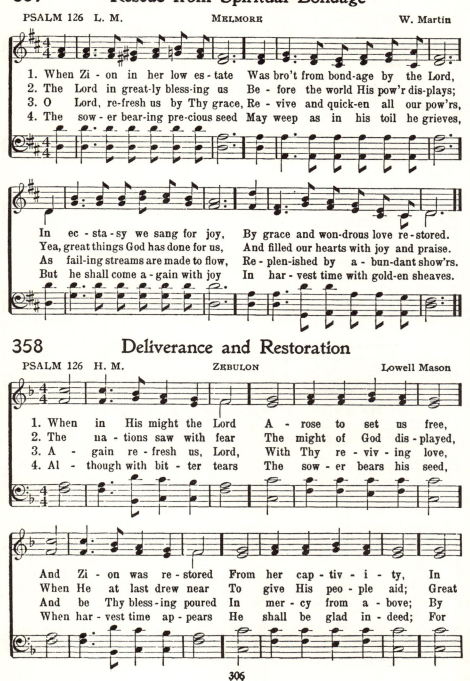

357   Rescue from Spiritual Bondage

PSALM 126 L. M.   MELMORE   W. Martin

1. When Zi - on in her low es - tate   Was bro't from bond-age by the Lord,
2. The Lord in great-ly bless-ing us   Be - fore the world His pow'r dis-plays;
3. O Lord, re-fresh us by Thy grace,   Re - vive and quick-en all our pow'rs,
4. The sow - er bear-ing pre-cious seed   May weep as in his toil he grieves,

In ec - sta - sy we sang for joy,   By grace and won-drous love re - stored.
Yea, great things God has done for us,   And filled our hearts with joy and praise.
As fail-ing streams are made to flow,   Re - plen-ished by a - bun-dant show'rs.
But he shall come a - gain with joy   In har - vest time with gold-en sheaves.

358   Deliverance and Restoration

PSALM 126 H. M.   ZEBULON   Lowell Mason

1. When in His might the Lord   A - rose to set us free,
2. The na - tions saw with fear   The might of God dis - played,
3. A - gain re - fresh us, Lord,   With Thy re - viv - ing love,
4. Al - though with bit - ter tears   The sow - er bears his seed,

And Zi - on was re - stored   From her cap - tiv - i - ty,   In
When He at last drew near   To give His peo - ple aid;   Great
And be Thy bless-ing poured   In mer - cy from a - bove;   By
When har - vest time ap - pears   He shall be glad in - deed;   For

trans-ports then of joy and mirth We praised the Lord of all the earth.
things for us the Lord has wrought, And glad-ness to our hearts has brought.
grace re - vive our hearts a - gain, As streams refreshed by co - pious rain.
they that in the sow-ing weep Shall yet in joy and glad-ness reap.

359 Conscious Dependence on God

PSALM 127 L. M.   ROSE HILL   Joseph E. Sweetser

1. Un - less the Lord the house shall build, The wea - ry
2. In vain you rise ere morn - ing - break, And late your
3. Lo, chil - dren are a great re - ward, A gift from
4. And blest the man whose age is cheered By stal - wart

build - ers toil in vain; Un - less the Lord the
night - ly vig - ils keep, And of the bread of
God in ver - y truth; With ar - rows is his
sons and daugh - ters fair; No en - e - mies by

cit - y shield, The guards a use - less watch main - tain.
toil par - take; God gives to His be - lov - ed sleep.
quiv - er stored Who joys in chil - dren of his youth.
him are feared, No lack of love, no want of care.

307

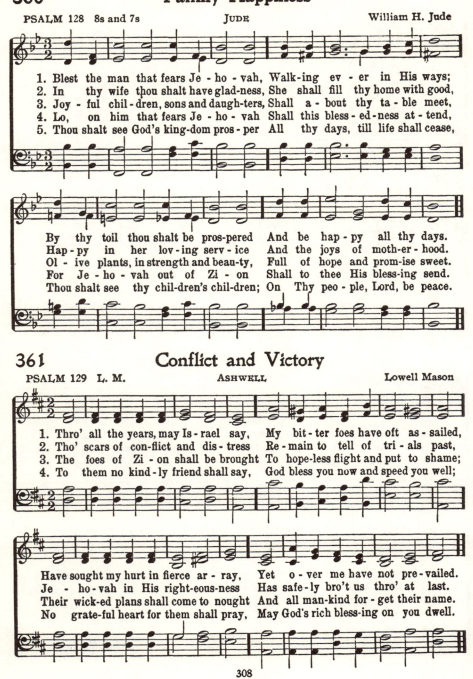

360
Family Happiness

PSALM 128   8s and 7s   JUDE   William H. Jude

1. Blest the man that fears Je - ho - vah, Walk-ing ev - er in His ways;
2. In   thy wife thou shalt have glad-ness, She shall fill thy home with good,
3. Joy - ful chil - dren, sons and daugh-ters, Shall a - bout thy ta - ble meet,
4. Lo, on him that fears Je - ho - vah Shall this bless - ed - ness at - tend,
5. Thou shalt see God's king-dom pros - per All   thy days, till life shall cease,

By   thy toil thou shalt be pros-pered And be hap - py all thy days.
Hap - py in   her lov - ing serv - ice And the joys of moth-er - hood.
Ol - ive plants, in strength and beau-ty, Full of hope and prom-ise sweet.
For Je - ho - vah out of Zi - on Shall to thee His bless-ing send.
Thou shalt see thy chil-dren's chil-dren; On Thy peo - ple, Lord, be peace.

361
Conflict and Victory

PSALM 129   L. M.   ASHWELL   Lowell Mason

1. Thro' all the years, may Is - rael say, My bit - ter foes have oft as - sailed,
2. Tho' scars of con-flict and dis - tress Re - main to tell of tri - als past,
3. The foes of Zi - on shall be brought To hope-less flight and put to shame;
4. To them no kind - ly friend shall say, God bless you now and speed you well;

Have sought my hurt in fierce ar - ray, Yet o - ver me have not pre - vailed.
Je - ho - vah in His right-eous-ness Has safe - ly bro't us thro' at last.
Their wick-ed plans shall come to nought And all man-kind for - get their name.
No grate-ful heart for them shall pray, May God's rich bless-ing on you dwell.

Redemption and Forgiveness

PSALM 130 10s and 4s   SANDON   Charles H. Purday

1. From out the depths I cry, O Lord, to Thee; Lord,
2. I wait for God, the Lord, and on His word My
3. Hope in the Lord, ye wait-ing saints, and He Will

hear my call; I love Thee, Lord, for Thou dost heed my plea,
hope re - lies; My soul still waits and looks un - to the Lord
well pro - vide, For mer - cy and re - demp-tion full and free

For - giv - ing all; If Thou shouldst mark our sins, who then could
Till light a - rise; I look for Him to drive a - way my
With Him a - bide; From sin and e - vil, might-y though they

stand? But grace and mer - cy dwell at Thy right hand.
night, Yea, more than watch - men look for morn - ing light.
seem, His arm al - might - y will His saints re - deem.

363

Waiting Upon God

PSALM 130   8s and 7s   EVENING PRAYER   George C. Stebbins

1. From the depths do I in-voke Thee, Lord, to me in-cline Thy ear;
2. Lord, if Thou shouldst mark transgressions, In Thy pres-ence who shall stand?
3. For Je-ho-vah I am wait-ing, And my hope is in His word,
4. For the Lord my soul is wait-ing More than watch-ers in the night,
5. Hope in God, ye wait-ing peo-ple; Mer-cies great with Him a-bound;

To my voice be Thou at-ten-tive, And my sup-pli-ca-tion hear.
But with Thee there is for-give-ness, That Thy Name may fear com-mand.
In His word of prom-ise giv-en; Yea, my soul waits for the Lord.
More than they for morn-ing watch-ing, Watch-ing for the morn-ing light.
With the Lord a full re-demp-tion From the guilt of sin is found.

364

Penitence and Hope

PSALM 130   8s and 4   HANFORD   Arthur S. Sullivan

1. From out the depths I cry to Thee; O let Thy ear at-ten-tive be,
2. If marked by Thee our sin ap-peared, Who, Lord, could stand in judgment cleared?
3. I wait for Thee, my soul doth wait, Thy word my hope in ev-'ry strait;
4. O Is-rael, hope thou in the Lord, His mer-cy will thy faith re-ward,

Hear Thou my sup-pli-cat-ing plea, Have mer-cy, Lord.
For-give-ness, that Thou mayst be feared, There is with Thee.
None watch, O Lord, at morn-ing's gate As I for Thee.
He full re-demp-tion will ac-cord From all thy sin.

365 Pardoning Mercy

PSALM 130 8s, 5, 3   BULLINGER   Ethelbert W. Bullinger

1. From the depths my prayer as-cend-eth Un - to God on high;
2. None can stand un-scathed and blame-less In Thy judg-ment just,
3. Lord, my hope is in Thy prom-ise, And I wait for Thee
4. With the Lord is ten - der mer - cy, And re-deem-ing love;

Hear, O Lord, my sup - pli-ca - tion And my cry.
But the con - trite in Thy mer - cy Hum - bly trust.
More then they who watch for morn - ing, Light to see.
Is - rael, look for full sal-va - tion From a - bove.

SECOND TUNE   STEPHANOS   Henry W. Baker

1. From the depths my prayer as - cend-eth Un - to God on high;
2. None can stand un-scathed and blame-less In Thy judg-ment just,
3. Lord, my hope is in Thy prom-ise, And I wait for Thee
4. With the Lord is ten - der mer - cy, And re-deem-ing love;

Hear, O Lord, my sup - pli - ca - tion And my cry.
But the con - trite in Thy mer - cy Hum - bly trust.
More than they who watch for morn - ing, Light to see.
Is - rael, look for full sal - va - tion From a - bove.

366 Humility and Meekness

PSALM 131 S. M. OLMUTZ Arranged by Lowell Mason

1. Not haugh-ty is my heart, Not loft-y is my pride;
2. With child-like trust, O Lord, In Thee I calm-ly rest,
3. Ye peo-ple of the Lord, In Him a-lone con-fide;

I do not seek to know the things God's wis-dom hath de-nied.
Con-tent-ed as a lit-tle child Up-on its moth-er's breast.
From this time forth and ev-er-more His wis-dom be your guide.

367 God and His Church

PSALM 132 8s and 7s ULSTER Robert Lowry

1. Gra-cious Lord, re-mem-ber Da-vid, How he
2. Far a-way God's ark was rest-ing; It is
3. Let the king be-hold Thy fa-vor For Thy
4. Thou, the Lord, hast cho-sen Zi-on, Thou hast
5. I will cause the might of Da-vid Ev-er

made Thy house his care, How he vowed to seek no pleas-ure
with His peo-ple now; We will go in-to His tem-ple,
serv-ant Da-vid's sake, Un-to whom a sa-cred prom-ise
ev-er loved her well; This My rest-ing-place for-ev-er,
more and more to grow, On the path of My A-noint-ed

God and His Church

Till Thy house he should pre-pare. Lord, re-mem-ber his de-
At His foot-stool we will bow. With the ark Thy might re-
Sure and faith-ful, Thou didst make. If his chil-dren keep Thy
Here, Thou sayst, I choose to dwell. Sure-ly I will bless and
I will make a lamp to glow; All His en-e-mies shall

vo-tion; Rest-less in his courts he trod Till he
veal-ing, En-ter, Lord, in-to Thy rest; Let Thy
cov-enant And Thy tes-ti-mo-ny own, Then, as
help her, Feed her poor, her saints make glad, And her
per-ish, I will cov-er them with shame, But His

found a hab-i-ta-tion Fit for Is-rael's might-y God,
priests be clothed with jus-tice, Let Thy joy-ful saints be blest,
Thou, O Lord, hast prom-ised, They shall sit up-on his throne,
priests shall stand be-fore Me In sal-va-tion's gar-ments clad,
crown shall ev-er flour-ish, Bless-ed be His ho-ly Name,

Till he found a hab-i-ta-tion Fit for Is-rael's might-y God.
Let Thy priests be clothed with jus-tice, Let Thy joy-ful saints be blest.
Then, as Thou, O Lord, hast prom-ised, They shall sit up-on his throne.
And her priests shall stand be-fore Me In sal-va-tion's gar-ments clad.
But His crown shall ev-er flour-ish, Bless-ed be His ho-ly Name.

368 The House of God

PSALM 132 L. M. FEDERAL STREET Henry K. Oliver

1. A - rise, O Lord, our God, a - rise And en - ter
2. Thy gra - cious cov - 'nant, Lord, ful - fill, Turn not a -
3. Thy Zi - on Thou hast cho - sen, Lord, And Thou hast
4. I will a - bun - dant - ly pro - vide For Zi - on's
5. Sal - va - tion shall a - dorn her priests, Her saints shall

now in - to Thy rest; O let this house be
way from us Thy face; Es - tab - lish Thou Mes -
said, I love her well, This is my con - stant
good, the Lord hath said; I will sup - ply her
shout with joy di - vine, Mes - si - ah's pow'r shall

Thy a - bode, For - ev - er with Thy pres - ence blest.
si - ah's throne And let Him reign with - in this place.
rest - ing - place, And here will I de - light to dwell.
dai - ly need And sat - is - fy her poor with bread.
be re - vealed, His glo - ry in His Church shall shine.

[Selected Stanzas]

369 Brotherly Love

PSALM 133 C. M. INVITATION Arranged from Wallace

1. How pleas - ant and how good it is When breth - ren in the Lord
2. Such love is like a - noint - ing oil In con - se - cra - tion poured;
3. To those who dwell in broth - er - hood The Lord His bless - ing sends,

314

Brotherly Love

In one an-oth-er's joy de-light And dwell in sweet ac-cord.
Such love is like the morn-ing dew, With sweet re-fresh-ment stored.
He crowns them with the crown of life, Of life that nev-er ends.

370   The Communion of Saints

PSALM 133 C. P. M.   PRESSLY   Charles H. Gabriel

1. How good and pleas-ant is the sight When breth-ren make it their de-
2. Such love in peace and joy dis-tils, As o'er the slopes of Her-mon's

light   To dwell in blest ac-cord; Such love is like a-noint-ing oil
hills   Re-fresh-ing dew de-scends; The Lord commands His bless-ing there,

That con-se-crates for ho-ly toil The serv-ants of the Lord.
And they that walk in love shall share In life that nev-er ends.

The Unity of Brotherhood

PSALM 133   8s and 7s   JUBILEE   Arthur S. Sullivan

1. Be - hold, how pleas-ant and how good That we, one Lord con - fess - ing,
2. Be - hold, how pleas-ant and how good That we, one Lord con - fess - ing,

To - geth - er dwell in broth - er - hood, Our u - ni - ty ex - press - ing;
To - geth - er dwell in broth - er - hood, Our u - ni - ty ex - press - ing;

'Tis like the oil on Aar - on's head, The seal of or - di - na - tion,
'Tis like the dew from Her - mon fair On Zi - on's hill de - scend - ing;

That o'er his robes the sweet-ness shed Of per - fect con - se - cra - tion.
The Lord commands His bless - ing there In life that is un - end - ing.

Doxology and Benediction

PSALM 134 C. P. M.   WYOMING   Theodore E. Perkins

1. Come, all ye serv-ants of..... the Lord, Lift
2. Yea, in His place of ho - - li - ness Lift

up your voice with one ac - cord Je - ho-vah's Name to bless;
up your hands the Lord to bless; And un - to you be giv'n,

Ye that are stand-ing night by night With-
The joys that Zi - on doth af - ford, The

Ye that
The joys

in the house of His de - light, His glo-rious Name con-fess.
rich - est bless-ing of the Lord Who made the earth and heav'n.

With in the
The rich-est

Incentives to Praise

PSALM 135   9s and 8s   HARVEST-TIDE   A. Croil Falconer

1. O praise ye the Name of Je - ho - vah, Pro-
2. O praise ye the Lord for His good - ness; 'Tis
3. I know that the Lord is al - might - y, Su-
4. His hand guides the clouds in their cours - es, The
5. To ran - som His peo - ple from bond - age Great
6. Great na - tions and kings that op - posed Him Were

claim ye His glo - ry a - broad; O praise Him, ye
pleas - ant His prais - es to sing; His peo - ple, His
preme in do - min - ion is He, Per - form - ing His
light - ning flames forth at His will, The wind and the
won - ders and signs He dis - played; He smote all the
smit - ten by God's might - y hand; Their rich - es He

serv - ants ap - point - ed To stand in the house of our God.
cho - sen and pre - cious, Your prais - es with grat - i - tude bring.
will and good pleas - ure In heav'n and in earth and the sea.
rain He re - leas - es His sov - 'reign de - signs to ful - fill.
first - born of E - gypt, Till Pha - raoh made haste and o - beyed.
gave to His peo - ple, And made them in - her - it the land.

7 Thy Name shall abide, O Jehovah,
　　Through all generations renowned;
　　The Lord is the judge of His people,
　　His mercies forever abound.

8 Men's idols of gold and of silver
　　Can speak not, nor hearken, nor see;
　　Like them shall their makers be helpless,
　　Unblest shall their worshipers be.

9 Ye people who worship Jehovah,
　　His praises with gladness proclaim;
　　His servants, and all ye that fear Him,
　　Sing praise to His glorious Name.

10 O Church of our God, sing His praises,
　　For with you and in you He dwells;
　　O sing Hallelujahs before Him,
　　Whose glory all praises excels.

374   Adoration of God

PSALM 135   9s and 8s   JANET   George C. Stebbins

1. O praise ye the Name of Je - ho - vah,
2. O praise ye the Lord for His good - ness;
3. I know that the Lord is al - might - y,
4. Ye peo - ple who wor - ship Je - ho - vah,
5. O Church of our God, sing His prais - es,

Pro - claim ye His glo - ry a - broad;
'Tis pleas - ant His prais - es to sing;
Su - preme in do - min - ion is He,
His prais - es with glad - ness pro - claim;
For with you and in you He dwells;

O praise Him, ye serv - ants ap - point - ed
His peo - ple, His cho - sen and pre - cious,
Per - form - ing His will and good pleas - ure
His serv - ants, and all ye that fear Him,
O sing Hal - le - lu - jahs be - fore Him,

To stand in the house of our God.
Your prais - es with grat - i - tude bring.
In heav'n and in earth and the sea.
Sing praise to His glo - ri - ous Name.
Whose glo - ry all prais - es ex - cels.

375 Invitations to Praise

PSALM 135 L. M. CREATION Arranged from Haydn

1. Ex - alt the Lord, His praise pro - claim;
2. The Lord is good, His praise pro - claim;
3. I know the Lord is high in state,
4. He makes the va - pors to as - cend
5. For - ev - er praise and bless His Name,

All ye His serv - ants, praise His Name,
Since it is pleas - ant, praise His Name;
A - bove all gods our Lord is great;
In clouds from earth's re - mot - est end;
And in the Church His praise pro - claim;

Who in the Lord's house ev - er stand
His peo - ple for His own He takes
The Lord per - forms what He de - crees,
The light - nings flash at His com - mand,
In Zi - on is His dwell - ing - place;

And hum - bly serve at His com - mand.
And His.... pe - cul - iar treas - ure makes.
In heav'n... and earth, in depths and seas.
He holds.... the tem - pest in His hand.
Praise ye.... the Lord, show forth His grace.

320

[Selected Stanzas]

376 Enduring Mercy

PSALM 136 7s   BETTER LAND   William F. Sherwin

1. Praise Je - ho - vah for His love, God of gods, en-throned a - bove;
2. God by wis - dom framed the skies, Made the earth from o - cean rise,
3. He made E-gypt's great-ness vain, Caused their first-born to be slain,
4. God the sea a - sun-der clave, Bro't His peo - ple thro' the wave,

Praise the might-y King of kings, Who a - lone doth won-drous things;
Gave the sun by day for light, Moon and stars to rule the night;
Bro't forth Is - rael from their land, Stretch-ing out His might - y hand;
Drowned their foes be-neath the deep, Thro' the des - ert led His sheep;

For His mer - cy doth en - dure, Ev - er faith - ful, ev - er sure.
For His mer - cy doth en - dure, Ev - er faith - ful, ev - er sure.
For His mer - cy doth en - dure, Ev - er faith - ful, ev - er sure.
For His mer - cy doth en - dure, Ev - er faith - ful, ev - er sure.

5 Mighty kings of mighty name
He destroyed and put to shame,
Made their land a heritage
For His saints from age to age;
    For His mercy doth endure,
    Ever faithful, ever sure.

6 God remembered all our woe,
Rescued us from every foe,
Food to all doth He supply,
Praise the Lord enthroned on high;
    For His mercy doth endure,
    Ever faithful, ever sure.

321

377 Divine Love

PSALM 136 L. M.   BELOIT   Carl G. Reissiger

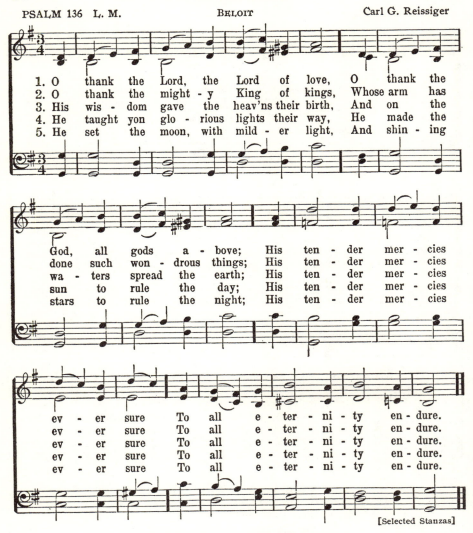

1. O thank the Lord, the Lord of love, O thank the
2. O thank the might - y King of kings, Whose arm has
3. His wis - dom gave the heav'ns their birth, And on the
4. He taught yon glo - rious lights their way, He made the
5. He set the moon, with mild - er light, And shin - ing

God, all gods a - bove; His ten - der mer - cies
done such won - drous things; His ten - der mer - cies
wa - ters spread the earth; His ten - der mer - cies
sun to rule the day; His ten - der mer - cies
stars to rule the night; His ten - der mer - cies

ev - er sure To all e - ter - ni - ty en - dure.
ev - er sure To all e - ter - ni - ty en - dure.
ev - er sure To all e - ter - ni - ty en - dure.
ev - er sure To all e - ter - ni - ty en - dure.
ev - er sure To all e - ter - ni - ty en - dure.

[Selected Stanzas]

6 He thought on us amid our woes,
And rescued us from all our foes;
His tender mercies ever sure
To all eternity endure

7 Give thanks to heaven's Almighty King,
Who daily feeds each living thing;
His tender mercies ever sure
To all eternity endure.

322

378 The Unfailing Mercy of God

PSALM 136 8s and 7s   CONSTANCE   Arthur S. Sullivan

1. Give thanks to God, for good is He, His grace a-bid-eth ev-er;
2. His wis-dom made the heav'ns to be, His grace a-bid-eth ev-er;
3. He helped us in our deep-est woes, His grace a-bid-eth ev-er;

To Him all praise and glo-ry be, His mer-cy fail-eth nev-er.
He spread the earth a-bove the sea, His mer-cy fail-eth nev-er.
He ran-somed us from all our foes, His mer-cy fail-eth nev-er.

His won-drous works with praise re-cord, His grace a-bid-eth ev-er,
Praise Him Whose sun doth bring the day, His grace a-bid-eth ev-er;
Each crea-ture's need He doth sup-ply, His grace a-bid-eth ev-er;

The on-ly God, the sov-'reign Lord, Whose mer-cy fail-eth nev-er.
The moon and stars His might dis-play, Whose mer-cy fail-eth nev-er.
Give thanks to God, en-throned on high, Whose mer-cy fail-eth nev-er.

[Selected Stanzas]

379 Memories of Zion

PSALM 137 L. M. OLIVE'S BROW William B. Bradbury

1. By Babel's streams we sat and wept, For mem-'ry
2. There our rude cap-tors, flushed with pride, A song re-
3. Not songs but sighs to us be-long When Zi-on's
4. O Zi-on fair, God's ho-ly hill, Where-in our

still to Zi-on clung; The winds a-lone our
quired to mock our wrongs; Our spoil-ers called for
walls in ru-in lie; How shall we sing Je-
God de-lights to dwell, Let my right hand for-

harp-strings swept, That on the droop-ing wil-lows hung.
mirth, and cried, Come, sing us one of Zi-on's songs.
ho-vah's song While in an al-ien land we die?
get her skill If I for-get to love thee well.

5 If I do not remember thee,
    Then let my tongue from utterance cease,
  If any earthly joy to me
    Be dear as Zion's joy and peace.

6 Remember, Lord, the dreadful day
    Of Zion's cruel overthrow;
  How happy he who shall repay
    The bitter hatred of her foe.

380 Remembrance of Church Privileges

PSALM 137 10s   BENEDICTION   Edward J. Hopkins

1. By Ba - bel's riv - er - side we sat in tears,
2. For they who led us there a cap - tive throng
3. O how shall we thus sing at their com - mand
4. Yea, let my tongue, I pray, all si - lent be,

Re - mem - b'ring Zi - on's pride in for - mer years,
Re - quired that we pre - pare for them a song;
Songs of the Lord, our King, in this strange land?
If I do not al - way re - mem - ber thee;

While on the weep - ing wil - lows there were hung
Yea, there our cap - tors asked for mirth and praise,
O Zi - on, if I e'er for - get thy woe,
If I pre - fer not thee, though in thy grief,

The harps our grief had si - lenced and un - strung.
Re - quired a song of Zi - on's hap - py days.
Let my right hand its skill no lon - ger know.
A - bove all oth - er joys my ver - y chief.

[Selected Stanzas]

381 Exultation in God

PSALM 138 L. M.   THE SOLID ROCK   William B. Bradbury

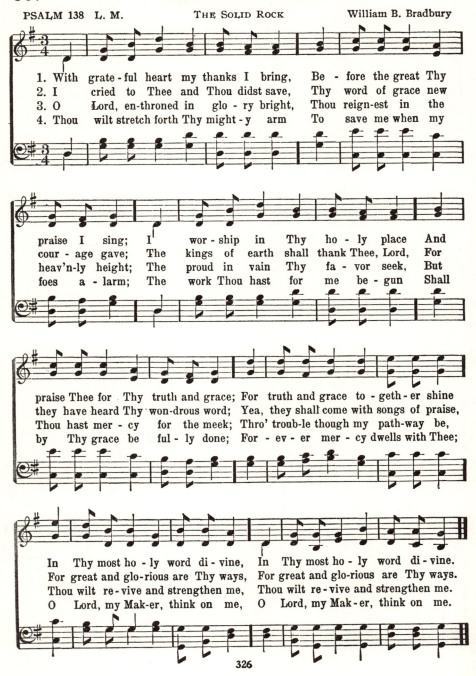

1. With grate-ful heart my thanks I bring, Be - fore the great Thy
2. I cried to Thee and Thou didst save, Thy word of grace new
3. O Lord, en-throned in glo - ry bright, Thou reign-est in the
4. Thou wilt stretch forth Thy might - y arm To save me when my

praise I sing; I wor - ship in Thy ho - ly place And
cour - age gave; The kings of earth shall thank Thee, Lord, For
heav'n-ly height; The proud in vain Thy fa - vor seek, But
foes a - larm; The work Thou hast for me be - gun Shall

praise Thee for Thy truth and grace; For truth and grace to - geth - er shine
they have heard Thy won-drous word; Yea, they shall come with songs of praise,
Thou hast mer - cy for the meek; Thro' troub-le though my path-way be,
by Thy grace be ful - ly done; For - ev - er mer - cy dwells with Thee;

In Thy most ho - ly word di - vine, In Thy most ho - ly word di - vine.
For great and glo-rious are Thy ways, For great and glo-rious are Thy ways.
Thou wilt re - vive and strengthen me, Thou wilt re - vive and strengthen me.
O Lord, my Mak - er, think on me, O Lord, my Mak - er, think on me.

382

A Vision of God

PSALM 139 L. M. WOODWORTH William B. Bradbury

1. Lord, Thou hast searched me, and dost know Wher-e'er I rest, wher-e'er I go;
2. My words from Thee I can - not hide, I feel Thy pow'r on ev - 'ry side;
3. Where can I go a - part from Thee, Or whith-er from Thy presence flee?
4. If I the wings of morn-ing take, And far a - way my dwelling make,
5. If deep-est dark-ness cov - er me, The dark-ness hid -eth not from Thee;

Thou know-est all that I have planned, And all my ways are in Thy hand.
O won-drous knowl-edge, aw-ful might, Un-fathomed depth, un-measured height!
In heav'n? it is Thy dwell-ing fair; In death's a-bode? lo, Thou art there.
The hand that lead-eth me is Thine, And my sup-port Thy pow'r di - vine.
To Thee both night and day are bright, The dark-ness shin-eth as the light.

383

The Lord Our Maker

PSALM 139 L. M. ST. CRISPIN George J. Elvey

1. All that I am I owe to Thee, Thy wis-dom, Lord, hath fash-ioned me;
2. Ere in - to be - ing I was bro't, Thy eye did see, and in Thy tho't
3. Thy tho'ts, O God, how man - i - fold, More pre-cious un - to me than gold!
4. The wick-ed Thou wilt sure-ly slay, From me let sin - ners turn a - way;
5. Search me, O God, my heart dis-cern, Try me, my in - most tho't to learn;

I give my Mak - er thank-ful praise, Whose wondrous works my soul a-maze.
My life in all its per - fect plan Was or-dered ere my days be-gan.
I muse on their in - fin - i - ty, A - wak-ing I am still with Thee.
They speak a-gainst the Name di - vine, I count God's en - e - mies as mine.
And lead me, if in sin I stray, To choose the ev - er - last - ing way.

[Stanzas 6–10]

384 The Searcher of Hearts

PSALM 139 C. M.   BINGHAM   Anonymous

1. O Lord, my in-most heart and thought Thy search-ing eye doth see;
2. Each spo-ken word, each si-lent tho't, Thou, Lord, dost un-der-stand;
3. If I the wings of morn-ing take To some re-mot-est land,
4. From Thee, O Lord, I can-not hide, Tho' dark-ness cov-er me;
5. Search me, O God, and know my heart, Try me, my tho'ts to know;

Wher-e'er I rest, wher-e'er I go, My ways are known to Thee.
Be-fore me and be-hind art Thou, Re-strain-ing by Thy hand.
Still I shall be up-held by Thee And guid-ed by Thy hand.
The dark-ness and the light of day Are both a-like to Thee.
O lead me, if in sin I stray, In paths of life to go.

[Selected Stanzas]

SECOND TUNE   HORSLEY   William Horsley

1. O Lord, my in-most heart and tho't Thy search-ing eye doth see;
2. Each spo-ken word, each si-lent tho't, Thou, Lord, dost un-der-stand;
3. If I the wings of morn-ing take To some re-mot-est land,
4. From Thee, O Lord, I can-not hide, Tho' dark-ness cov-er me;
5. Search me, O God, and know my heart, Try me, my tho'ts to know;

Wher-e'er I rest, wher-e'er I go, My ways are known to Thee.
Be-fore me and be-hind art Thou, Re-strain-ing by Thy hand.
Still I shall be up-held by Thee And guid-ed by Thy hand.
The dark-ness and the light of day Are both a-like to Thee.
O lead me, if in sin I stray, In paths of life to go.

385 Peril and Prayer

PSALM 140   7s and 6s   PETITION   Arranged from Haydn

1. De - liv - er me from e - vil,   Pre - serve me, Lord, from wrong;
2. O Lord, I have con - fessed Thee   To be my God a - lone;
3. Let e - vil smite the e - vil   And cause their o - ver - throw;

A - gainst the foes that gath - er   Be Thou my help - er strong.
O hear my sup - pli - ca - tion   And be Thy mer - cy shown;
The need - y and af - flict - ed   The Lord will help, I know;

From those who plot to hurt me   And spread their treach'rous snare
O God the Lord, my Sav - iour,   My shield a - mid the strife,
Thy saints, redeemed from e - vil,   Their thanks to Thee shall give;

Pre - serve me, Lord, and keep me   Safe - guard - ed in Thy care.
Let not the wick - ed tri - umph   Who plot a - gainst my life.
The right - eous and the up - right   Shall in Thy pres - ence live.

386 Prayerful Desire

PSALM 141 L. M.   HESPERUS   Henry Baker

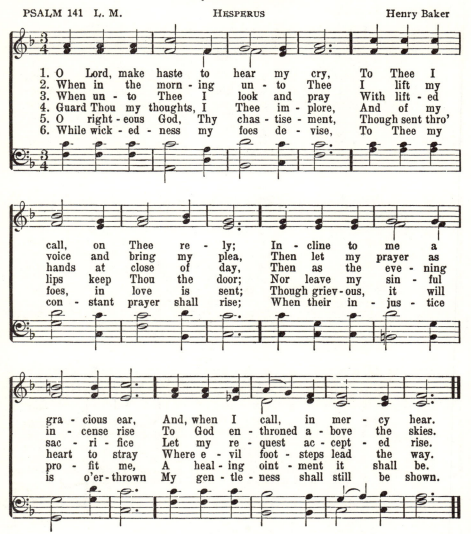

1. O Lord, make haste to hear my cry, To Thee I call, on Thee re - ly; In - cline to me a gra - cious ear, And, when I call, in mer - cy hear.

2. When in the morn - ing un - to Thee I lift my voice and bring my plea, Then let my prayer as in - cense rise To God en - throned a - bove the skies.

3. When un - to Thee I look and pray With lift - ed hands at close of day, Then as the eve - ning sac - ri - fice Let my re - quest ac - cept - ed rise.

4. Guard Thou my thoughts, I Thee im - plore, And of my lips keep Thou the door; Nor leave my sin - ful heart to stray Where e - vil foot - steps lead the way.

5. O right - eous God, Thy chas - tise - ment, Though sent thro' foes, in love is sent; Though griev - ous, it will pro - fit me, A heal - ing oint - ment it shall be.

6. While wick - ed - ness my foes de - vise, To Thee my con - stant prayer shall rise; When their in - jus - tice is o'er - thrown My gen - tle - ness shall still be shown.

7 Brought nigh to death and sore distressed,
O Lord, my God, in Thee I rest;
Forsake me not, I look to Thee,
Let me Thy great salvation see.

8 Themselves entangled in their snare,
Their own defeat my foes prepare;
O keep me, Lord, nor let me fall,
Protect and lead me safe through all.

387 **Our Only Saviour**

PSALM 142 L. M. HAMBURG Arranged by Lowell Mason

1. To God my ear-nest voice I raise, To God my voice im-plor-ing prays;
2. When gloom and sor-row com-pass me, The path I take is known to Thee,
3. All un-pro-tect-ed, lo, I stand, No friend-ly guard-ian at my hand,
4. O Lord, my Sav-iour, now to Thee, With-out a hope be-sides, I flee,
5. Be Thou my help when troub-les throng, For I am weak and foes are strong;
6. The righteous then shall gath-er round To share the bless-ing I have found,

Be-fore His face my grief I show And tell my troub-le and my woe.
And all the toils that foes do lay To snare Thy serv-ant in his way.
No place of flight or ref-uge near, And none to whom my soul is dear.
To Thee, my shel-ter from the strife, My por-tion in the land of life.
My cap-tive soul from pris-on bring, And thank-ful prais-es I will sing.
Their hearts made glad because they see How rich-ly God has dealt with me.

388 **Christ Our Refuge and Portion**

PSALM 142 L. M. SAXBY Timothy R. Matthews

1. To Thee, O Lord, I hum-bly cry, To Thee my sup-pli-ca-tion make,
2. Thou knowest, Lord, my deep dis-tress, The lone-ly path, the hid-den snare,
3. My prayer is un-to Thee, O Lord, No ref-uge but in Thee I know,
4. Be Thou my Sav-iour, O my Lord, For I am weak and foes are strong;
5. A-round me shall the righteous throng, And crowned with joy Thy saints shall be,

To Thee I bring my sad com-plaint, To Thee my bit-ter grief I take.
How ref-uge fail-eth, friends for-sake, And no man for my soul doth care.
No por-tion but in Thee I find; Lord, in my need Thy mer-cy show.
My cap-tive soul from pris-on bring, And glad shall be my thank-ful song.
Their hearts made glad because the Lord In rich-est grace hath dealt with me.

389 Contrite Trust

PSALM 143 6s   INVITATION   Frederick C. Maker

1. Lord, hear me in dis - tress, Re - gard my
2. The en - e - my has sought My soul in
3. Re - call - ing for - mer days And all Thy
4. My fail - ing spir - it see, O Lord, to

sup - pliant cry, And in Thy faith - ful - ness And
dust to tread; To dark - ness I am brought, For -
won - drous deeds, The mem - 'ry of Thy ways To
me make haste; Hide not Thy face from me, Lest

right - eous - ness re - ply. In judg - ment do not cause
got - ten as the dead. My spir - it, crushed with grief,
hope and com - fort leads. To Thee I stretch my hands,
bit - ter death I taste. O let the morn re - turn,

Thy serv - ant to be tried; Be - fore Thy
Is sad and o - ver - borne; My heart finds
Let me not plead in vain; I wait as
Let mer - cy light my day; For Thee in

Contrite Trust

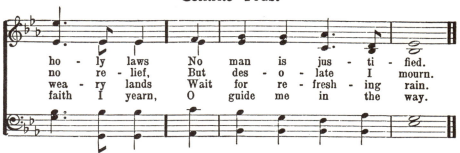

ho -	ly	laws	No	man	is	jus -	ti -	fied.
no	re -	lief,	But	des -	o -	late	I	mourn.
wea -	ry	lands	Wait	for	re -	fresh -	ing	rain.
faith	I	yearn,	O	guide	me	in	the	way.

5 Lord, save me from my foe,
   To Thee for help I flee;
Teach me Thy way to know,
   I have no God but Thee.
By Thy good Spirit led
   From trouble and distress,
My erring feet shall tread
   The path of uprightness.

6 O Lord, for Thy Name's sake
   Revive my fainting heart;
My soul from trouble take,
   For just and true Thou art.
Remove my enemy,
   My cruel foe reward;
In mercy rescue me
   Who am Thy servant, Lord.

SECOND TUNE   BRADBURY   Anonymous

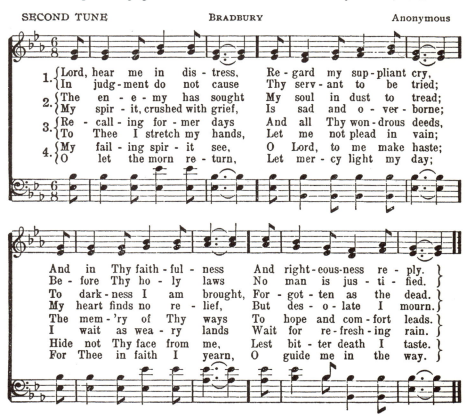

1. {Lord, hear me in dis - tress,   Re - gard my sup - pliant cry,
   {In judg - ment do not cause   Thy serv - ant to be tried;
2. {The en - e - my has sought   My soul in dust to tread;
   {My spir - it, crushed with grief,   Is sad and o - ver - borne;
3. {Re - call - ing for - mer days   And all Thy won - drous deeds,
   {To Thee I stretch my hands,   Let me not plead in vain;
4. {My fail - ing spir - it see,   O Lord, to me make haste;
   {O let the morn re - turn,   Let mer - cy light my day;

And in Thy faith - ful - ness   And right - eous - ness re - ply.
Be - fore Thy ho - ly laws   No man is jus - ti - fied.
To dark - ness I am brought,   For - got - ten as the dead.
My heart finds no re - lief,   But des - o - late I mourn.
The mem - 'ry of Thy ways   To hope and com - fort leads.
I wait as wea - ry lands   Wait for re - fresh - ing rain.
Hide not Thy face from me,   Lest bit - ter death I taste.
For Thee in faith I yearn,   O guide me in the way.

390 **Earnest Desire and Supplication**

PSALM 143 6s   JEWETT   Arranged from von Weber

1. Lord, hear me in distress, Regard my suppliant cry,
2. To Thee I stretch my hands, Let me not plead in vain;
3. By Thy good Spirit led From trouble and distress,

And in Thy faithfulness And righteousness reply.
I wait as weary lands Wait for refreshing rain.
My erring feet shall tread The path of uprightness.

In judgment do not cause Thy servant to be tried;
O let the morn return, Let mercy light my day;
O Lord, for Thy Name's sake Revive my fainting heart;

Before Thy holy laws No man is justified.
For Thee in faith I yearn, O guide me in the way.
My soul from trouble take, For just and true Thou art.

334   [Selected Stanzas]

391 Reliance and Supplication

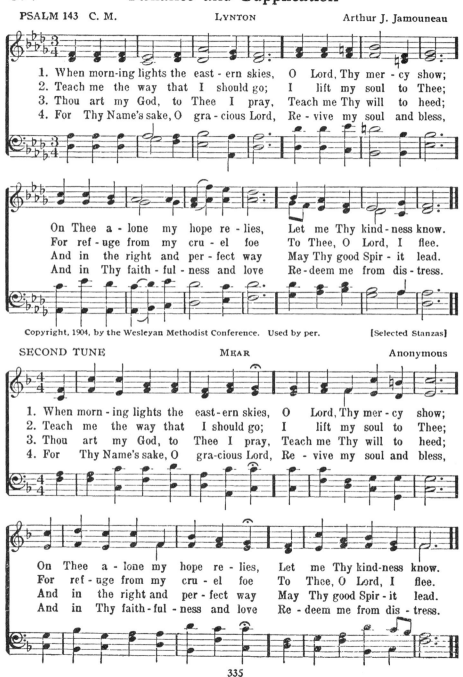

PSALM 143 C. M. LYNTON Arthur J. Jamouneau

1. When morn-ing lights the east-ern skies, O Lord, Thy mer-cy show;
2. Teach me the way that I should go; I lift my soul to Thee;
3. Thou art my God, to Thee I pray, Teach me Thy will to heed;
4. For Thy Name's sake, O gra-cious Lord, Re-vive my soul and bless,

On Thee a-lone my hope re-lies, Let me Thy kind-ness know.
For ref-uge from my cru-el foe To Thee, O Lord, I flee.
And in the right and per-fect way May Thy good Spir-it lead.
And in Thy faith-ful-ness and love Re-deem me from dis-tress.

Copyright, 1904, by the Wesleyan Methodist Conference. Used by per.   [Selected Stanzas]

SECOND TUNE   MEAR   Anonymous

1. When morn-ing lights the east-ern skies, O Lord, Thy mer-cy show;
2. Teach me the way that I should go; I lift my soul to Thee;
3. Thou art my God, to Thee I pray, Teach me Thy will to heed;
4. For Thy Name's sake, O gra-cious Lord, Re-vive my soul and bless,

On Thee a-lone my hope re-lies, Let me Thy kind-ness know.
For ref-uge from my cru-el foe To Thee, O Lord, I flee.
And in the right and per-fect way May Thy good Spir-it lead.
And in Thy faith-ful-ness and love Re-deem me from dis-tress.

335

392
Trustful Praise and Prayer

PSALM 144 C. P. M.   EXMOUTH   A. Browns

1. Blest be the Lord, my rock, my might, My con-stant
2. Lord, what is man, what hath he wrought, The son of
3. Lord, bow Thy heav'ns, in might de-scend, Touch Thou the
4. Stretch forth Thy hand and res-cue me From troub-le's
5. Now will I sing a glad new song, Thy praise, O
6. O Thou to Whom in trust I flee, Stretch forth Thy

help-er in the fight, My shield, my right-eous-ness,
man, that in Thy thought To hold him Thou shouldst deign?
hills, the moun-tains rend, And they shall smoke and flame;
dark and rag-ing sea, And from the al-ien throng,
God, I will pro-long, For Thou hast heard my prayer;
hand and res-cue me From all the al-ien throng,

My strong high tower, my Sav-iour true, Who doth my
For man is like a breath, a sigh, His days on
As ar-rows send Thy light-nings out To put Thy
Whose mouth but van-i-ty doth speak, Whose hand of
Sal-va-tion Thou dost give to kings, Thy own dost
Whose mouth but van-i-ty doth speak, Whose hand of

en-e-mies sub-due, My shel-ter in dis-tress.
earth as quick-ly fly As shad-ows o'er the plain.
en-e-mies to rout, And fill Thy foes with shame.
strength a-gainst the weak Is filled with craft and wrong.
keep, with shel-t'ring wings, From hurt-ful sword and snare.
strength a-gainst the weak Is filled with craft and wrong.

393 National Prosperity

PSALM 144 C. P. M.   SHORTLE   Charles G. Goodrich

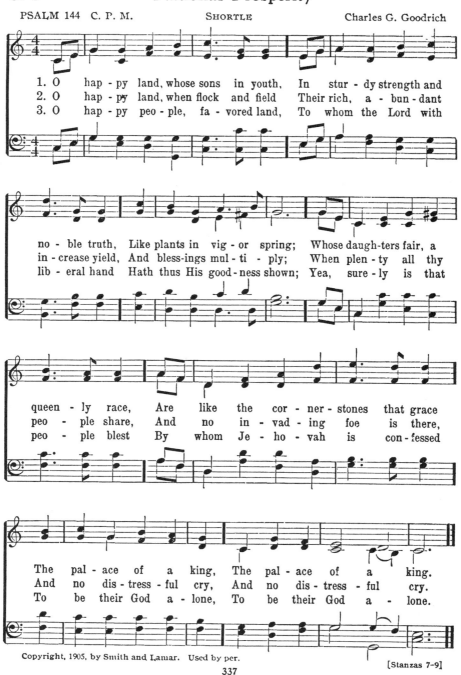

1. O hap-py land, whose sons in youth, In stur-dy strength and
2. O hap-py land, when flock and field Their rich, a-bun-dant
3. O hap-py peo-ple, fa-vored land, To whom the Lord with

no-ble truth, Like plants in vig-or spring; Whose daugh-ters fair, a
in-crease yield, And bless-ings mul-ti-ply; When plen-ty all thy
lib-eral hand Hath thus His good-ness shown; Yea, sure-ly is that

queen-ly race, Are like the cor-ner-stones that grace
peo-ple share, And no in-vad-ing foe is there,
peo-ple blest By whom Je-ho-vah is con-fessed

The pal-ace of a king, The pal-ace of a king.
And no dis-tress-ful cry, And no dis-tress-ful cry.
To be their God a-lone, To be their God a-lone.

[Stanzas 7-9]

Our Glorious King

PSALM 145 C. M.   GERARD   Arranged by Arthur S. Sullivan

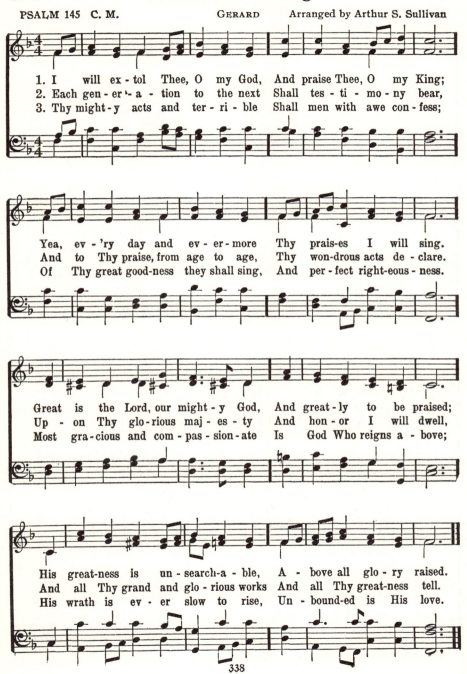

1. I will ex-tol Thee, O my God, And praise Thee, O my King;
2. Each gen-er-a-tion to the next Shall tes-ti-mo-ny bear,
3. Thy might-y acts and ter-ri-ble Shall men with awe con-fess;

Yea, ev-'ry day and ev-er-more Thy prais-es I will sing.
And to Thy praise, from age to age, Thy won-drous acts de-clare.
Of Thy great good-ness they shall sing, And per-fect right-eous-ness.

Great is the Lord, our might-y God, And great-ly to be praised;
Up-on Thy glo-rious maj-es-ty And hon-or I will dwell,
Most gra-cious and com-pas-sion-ate Is God Who reigns a-bove;

His great-ness is un-search-a-ble, A-bove all glo-ry raised.
And all Thy grand and glo-rious works And all Thy great-ness tell.
His wrath is ev-er slow to rise, Un-bound-ed is His love.

338

395 The Kingdom of Grace

PSALM 145 C. M.   SILVERTON   William B. Bradbury

1. The Lord, our God, is good to all, From Him all bless-ing flows;
2. By all Thy works Thou shalt be praised, And by Thy saints be blest;
3. The prais-es of Thy might-y deeds Thro' all the earth shall ring,
4. E - ter - nal is Thy king-dom, Lord, Thy throne shall ev - er stand;

On all His works His ten - der love And mer - cy He be - stows.
Thy glo-rious king-dom and Thy pow'r Shall ev - er be con - fessed.
To show the glo-rious maj - es - ty Of heav'n's e - ter - nal King.
All gen - er - a - tions to the end Shall bow to Thy com - mand.

[Stanzas 7-10]

396 The Goodness of God

PSALM 145 C. M.   FULTON   Ernest R. Kroeger

1. The Lord is strong to help the weak, Up-hold-ing those that fall,
2. Thy crea-tures look to Thee for food, From day to day sup - plied,
3. The Lord is right in all His ways, His works His love de - clare,
4. The hope of those that fear His Name The Lord will sat - is - fy;
5. All those that set their love on Him Shall full sal - va - tion know,
6. My mouth shall bless the Lord my God And all His praise pro - claim;

Re - stor - ing those bowed down with grief, And do - ing good to all.
And Thou dost for their sus - te - nance With o - pen hand pro - vide.
And He is nigh to ev - 'ry one That breathes the trust-ful prayer.
Their might-y Sav - iour He will be When un - to Him they cry.
But wick - ed men and wick - ed ways The Lord will o - ver-throw.
Let all u - nite for ev - er-more To bless His ho - ly Name.

[Stanzas 11-16]

397 The Greatness and Grace of God

PSALM 145 L. M.   DUKE STREET   John Hatton

1. O Lord, Thou art my God and King, And I will ever bless Thy Name; I will extol Thee ev'ry day, And evermore Thy praise proclaim.
2. The Lord is greatly to be praised, His greatness is beyond our thought; From age to age the sons of men Shall tell the wonders God has wrought.
3. Upon Thy glorious majesty And wondrous works my mind shall dwell; Thy deeds shall fill the world with awe, And of Thy greatness I will tell.
4. Thy matchless goodness and Thy grace Thy people shall commemorate, And all Thy truth and righteousness My joyful song shall celebrate.
5. The Lord our God is rich in grace, Most tender and compassionate; His anger is most slow to rise, His lovingkindness is most great.
6. The Lord is good in all His ways, His creatures know His constant care; To all His works His love extends, All men His tender mercies share.

7 Thy works shall give Thee thanks, O Lord,
   Thy saints Thy mighty acts shall show,
   Till o'er the earth the sons of men
   Thy kingdom, power, and glory know.

8 Eternal is Thy kingdom, Lord,
   Forever strong and ever sure;
   While generations rise and die
   Shall Thy dominion still endure.

398 Divine Grace and Compassion

PSALM 145 L. M.   NAZARETH   Theodore E. Perkins

1. The Lord up-holds the fal-t'ring feet And makes the weak se - cure - ly stand;
2. The Lord is just in all His ways, In all His works the Lord is kind,
3. His great sal-va - tion they shall know Who love the Lord's most ho - ly Name;

The bur-dened ones, bowed down with grief, Are helped by His most gra-cious hand.
And all that call on Him in truth In Him a pres - ent help - er find.
The wick - ed He will o - ver-throw And put His en - e - mies to shame.

The eyes of all up - on Thee wait; By Thee their wants are all sup-plied;
He will ful - fill the heart's de - sire Of those that fear Him and o - bey;
My mouth shall speak the glo-rious praise Of Him Whom heav'n and earth a-dore;

Thy o - pen hand is boun - ti - ful, And ev - 'ry soul is sat - is - fied.
Their cry the Lord will sure - ly hear, And He will save them when they pray.
Let all ex - alt His ho - ly Name For - ev - er and for ev - er-more.

399 The Excellency of God

PSALM 145 7, 6s, 8   ST. LOUIS   Lewis H. Redner

1. My God, I will ex-tol Thee And ev-er bless Thy Name;
2. To ev-'ry gen-er-a-tion Thy glo-ry shall be told,
3. The Lord is ver-y gra-cious And most com-pas-sion-ate;
4. The glo-ry of His king-dom Pro-claimed a-broad shall be,

Each day will I give thanks to Thee And all Thy praise pro-claim.
Thy hon-or and Thy maj-es-ty In mem-'ry I will hold;
His an-ger is most slow to rise, His mer-cy is most great;
That all may know His might-y deeds And glo-rious maj-es-ty;

Great is the Lord and might-y, And high-ly to be praised;
Thy might-y pow'r and great-ness Shall all man-kind con-fess,
On all His help-less crea-tures His ten-der mer-cies rest;
His king-dom is e-ter-nal, His throne shall stand se-cure,

His great-ness is un-search-a-ble, A-bove our knowl-edge raised.
And tell the sto-ry of Thy love, And sing Thy right-eous-ness.
By all His works He shall be praised, By all His saints be blest.
And His do-min-ion with-out end Thro' a-ges shall en-dure.

[Selected Stanzas]

400 Trust and Praise

PSALM 146 8s and 7s   BROCKLESBURY   Charlotte A. Barnard

1. Hal - le - lu - jah, praise Je - ho - vah, O my
2. Put no con - fi - dence in princ - es, Nor for
3. Hap - py is the man that choos - es Is - rael's
4. Heav'n and earth the Lord cre - a - ted, Seas and
5. Food He dai - ly gives the hun - gry, Sets the

soul, Je - ho - vah praise; I will sing the
help on man de - pend; He shall die, to
God to be his aid; He is blest whose
all that they con - tain; He de - liv - ers
mourn - ing pris - 'ner free, Rais - es those bowed

glo - rious prais - es Of my God through all my days.
dust re - turn - ing, And his pur - pos - es shall end.
hope of bless - ing On the Lord his God is stayed.
from op - pres - sion, Right-eous - ness He will main - tain.
down with an - guish, Makes the sight - less eyes to see.

6 Well Jehovah loves the righteous,
  And the stranger He befriends,
Helps the fatherless and widow,
  Judgment on the wicked sends.

7 Over all God reigns forever,
  Through all ages He is King;
Unto Him, thy God, O Zion,
  Joyful hallelujahs sing.

343

The One True Helper

PSALM 146 L. M. MIGDOL Lowell Mason

1. Praise ye the Lord, His praise pro-claim,
2. Trust not in man who soon must die,
3. His truth un-changed shall ev-er stand,
4. Thy God shall reign for ev-er-more,

And, O my soul, bless thou His Name;
But on the liv-ing God re-ly;
He saves from strong op-pres-sion's hand,
Praise Him, O Zi-on, and a-dore;

Yea, I will sound His praise a-broad
Most blest the man whose help is He
In Him the sad a help-er find,
The Lord is heav'n's e-ter-nal King,

And ev-er bless the Lord, my God.
That made the heav'n and earth and sea.
He feeds the poor and heals the blind.
To Him all praise and hon-or bring.

[Selected Stanzas]

Reasons for Praise

PSALM 147   7s and 6s   HARTFORD   John B. Dykes

1. O sing ye Hal - le - lu - jah! 'Tis good our God to praise;
2. The star - ry hosts He num - bers, He calls them all by name;
3. The heav'ns with clouds He cov - ers, He sends the cheer-ing rain;
4. No hu - man pow'r de - lights Him, No earth - ly pomp or pride;
5. He sends His swift com - mand-ment, And snow and ice en - fold
6. His stat - utes and His judg-ments He makes His peo - ple know;

'Tis pleas - ant and be - com - ing To Him our songs to raise;
His great - ness and His wis - dom His won-drous works pro - claim;
The slopes of all the moun - tains He fills with grass and grain;
He loves the meek who fear Him And in His love con - fide;
The world, and none are a - ble To stand be - fore His cold.
To them as to no oth - ers His grace He loves to show:

He builds the walls of Zi - on, He seeks her wan - d'ring sons,
The meek He lifts to hon - or, He hum - bles sin - ful pride;
To beast and bird His good - ness Their dai - ly food sup - plies;
Then praise thy God, O Zi - on, His gra - cious aid con - fess;
A - gain He gives com - mand-ment; The winds of sum - mer blow,
For match - less grace and mer - cy Your grate - ful prais - es bring;

He binds their wounds and com - forts The bro - ken-heart-ed ones.
Give thanks to Him and ut - ter His prais - es far and wide.
He cares for all His crea - tures, At - ten - tive to their cries.
He gives thee peace and plen - ty, His gifts thy chil-dren bless.
The snow and ice are melt - ed, A - gain the wa - ters flow.
To Him give thanks for - ev - er, And Hal - le - lu - jah sing.

403 Thankful Commemoration

PSALM 147 C. M.　　　　MINERVA　　　　John H. Stockton

1. Praise ye the Lord, for it is good To sing un-to our God;
2. Our Lord is great, He calls by name And counts the stars of night;
3. No hu-man might, no earth-ly pride, De-lights the Lord a-bove;

'Tis right and pleas-ant for His saints To tell His praise a-broad.
His wis-dom is un-search-a-ble, And won-drous is His might.
In them that fear Him He de-lights, In them that trust His love.

The Lord our God builds up His Church, He seeks her wan-d'ring sons;
The Lord up-holds the poor and meek, He brings the wick-ed low;
O Zi-on, praise the Lord thy God, His won-drous love con-fess;

He binds their wounds and gen-tly heals The bro-ken-heart-ed ones.
Sing praise to Him and give Him thanks And all His good-ness show.
He is thy glo-ry and thy strength, He will thy chil-dren bless.

[Selected Stanzas]

404 Universal Adoration

PSALM 148 H. M.   AMELIA   William B. Bradbury

1. Praise ye, praise ye the Lord In yon - der heav'n - ly
2. Praise Him, ye high - est heav'ns, Praise Him, ye clouds that
3. Ye crea - tures in the sea And crea - tures on the
4. Ye hills and moun - tains, praise, Each tree and beast and
5. By all let God be praised, For He a - lone is

height; Ye an - gels, all His hosts, In joy - ful praise u -
roll, Cre - a - ted by His pow'r And un - der His con -
earth, Your might - y Mak - er praise And tell His match - less
bird; Ye kings and realms of earth, Now let your praise be
great; A - bove the earth and heav'n He reigns in glo - rious

nite; O sun and moon, de - clare His might,
trol, Ye heav'ns that stand e - ter - nal - ly,
worth; Praise Him, ye storm - y winds that blow,
heard; By high and low, by young and old,
state; Praise Him, ye saints, who know His grace

Show forth His praise, ye stars of light.
Es - tab - lished by His firm de - cree.
Ye fire and hail, ye rain and snow.
Be all His praise and glo - ry told.
And ev - er dwell be - fore His face.

405

Praise-Voices

PSALM 148   8s and 7s   LYDIA   George C. Stebbins

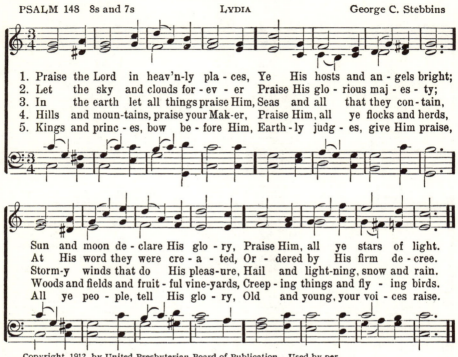

1. Praise the Lord in heav'n-ly pla - ces, Ye   His hosts and an - gels bright;
2. Let   the sky   and clouds for - ev - er   Praise His glo - rious maj - es - ty;
3. In   the earth let all things praise Him, Seas and all   that they con - tain,
4. Hills   and moun-tains, praise your Mak-er, Praise Him, all   ye flocks and herds,
5. Kings   and princ - es, bow be - fore Him, Earth - ly judg - es, give Him praise,

Sun   and moon de - clare His glo - ry, Praise Him, all   ye stars of light.
At   His word they were cre - a - ted, Or - dered by   His firm   de - cree.
Storm-y winds that do   His pleas-ure, Hail   and light-ning, snow and rain.
Woods and fields and fruit - ful vine-yards, Creep - ing things and fly - ing birds.
All   ye peo - ple, tell His glo - ry, Old   and young, your voi - ces raise.

Copyright, 1912, by United Presbyterian Board of Publication. Used by per.

6 Praise His Name with praise unending,
   For His Name alone is great;
  Over heaven and earth exalted,
   Reigns the Lord in kingly state.

7 He has greatly blessed His people,
   Therefore, all ye saints, give praise;
  Chosen of the Lord and precious,
   Thankful hallelujahs raise.

406

Exultant Praise

PSALM 149   C. M.   CHRISTMAS   Arranged from Handel

1. Praise ye the Lord a-mong His saints, New songs of glad-ness sing; Let Zi - on's
2. Yea, let them praise His blessed Name With all a - bound-ing joy,   The sound-ing
3. The Lord takes pleas-ure in His saints, He is His peo-ple's strength, And He will
4. Ye saints, by day and night re-joice, Ex - ult and joy - ful stand, Je - ho - vah's
5. This is the glo-rious judgment giv'n: His saints shall rule the earth; Then bless the

348

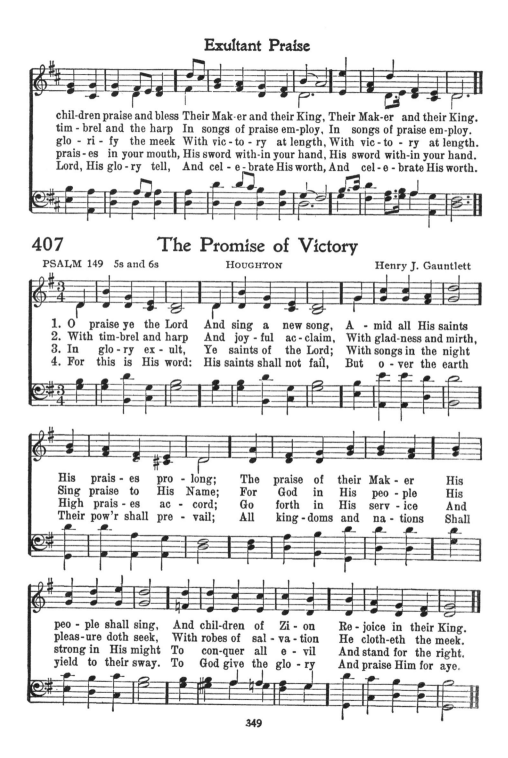

Exultant Praise

chil-dren praise and bless Their Mak-er and their King, Their Mak-er and their King.
tim - brel and the harp In songs of praise em-ploy, In songs of praise em-ploy.
glo - ri - fy the meek With vic-to-ry at length, With vic-to-ry at length.
prais-es in your mouth, His sword with-in your hand, His sword with-in your hand.
Lord, His glo-ry tell, And cel-e-brate His worth, And cel-e-brate His worth.

407 The Promise of Victory

PSALM 149 5s and 6s HOUGHTON Henry J. Gauntlett

1. O praise ye the Lord And sing a new song, A - mid all His saints
2. With tim-brel and harp And joy-ful ac-claim, With glad-ness and mirth,
3. In glo-ry ex-ult, Ye saints of the Lord; With songs in the night
4. For this is His word: His saints shall not fail, But o-ver the earth

His prais-es pro-long; The praise of their Mak-er His
Sing praise to His Name; For God in His peo-ple His
High prais-es ac-cord; Go forth in His serv-ice And
Their pow'r shall pre-vail; All king-doms and na-tions Shall

peo-ple shall sing, And chil-dren of Zi-on Re-joice in their King.
pleas-ure doth seek, With robes of sal-va-tion He cloth-eth the meek.
strong in His might To con-quer all e-vil And stand for the right.
yield to their sway. To God give the glo-ry And praise Him for aye.

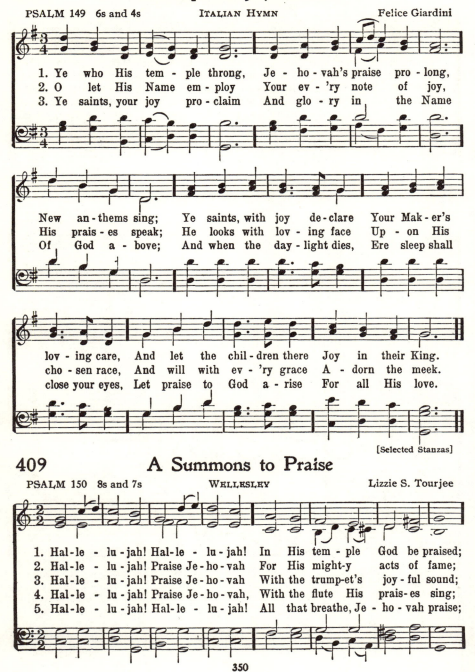

408 Triumphant Joy in God

PSALM 149   6s and 4s   ITALIAN HYMN   Felice Giardini

1. Ye who His tem - ple throng, Je - ho - vah's praise pro - long,
New an - thems sing; Ye saints, with joy de - clare Your Mak - er's
lov - ing care, And let the chil - dren there Joy in their King.

2. O let His Name em - ploy Your ev - 'ry note of joy,
His prais - es speak; He looks with lov - ing face Up - on His
cho - sen race, And will with ev - 'ry grace A - dorn the meek.

3. Ye saints, your joy pro - claim And glo - ry in the Name
Of God a - bove; And when the day - light dies, Ere sleep shall
close your eyes, Let praise to God a - rise For all His love.

[Selected Stanzas]

409 A Summons to Praise

PSALM 150   8s and 7s   WELLESLEY   Lizzie S. Tourjee

1. Hal - le - lu - jah! Hal - le - lu - jah! In His tem - ple God be praised;
2. Hal - le - lu - jah! Praise Je - ho - vah For His might - y acts of fame;
3. Hal - le - lu - jah! Praise Je - ho - vah With the trump - et's joy - ful sound;
4. Hal - le - lu - jah! Praise Je - ho - vah, With the flute His prais - es sing;
5. Hal - le - lu - jah! Hal - le - lu - jah! All that breathe, Je - ho - vah praise;

A Summons to Praise

In the high and heav'n-ly pla - ces / Be the sound-ing an - them raised.
Ex - cel - lent His might and great-ness; / Fit - ting prais - es then pro - claim.
Praise with harp and praise with vi - ol, / Let His glo - rious praise a - bound.
Praise Him with the clang-ing cym-bals, / Let them with His prais - es ring.
Let the voi - ces God hath giv - en / Joy - ful an - thems to Him raise.

410   A Universal Doxology

PSALM 150 L. M.   SOTO   Lowell Mason

1. Praise ye the Lord, ye saints be - low, And in His courts His good-ness
2. Praise ye the Lord; all crea-tures, sing The prais - es of your God and

show; Praise ye the Lord, ye hosts a - bove, In heav'n a -
King; Let all that breathe, His praise pro - claim And glo - ri -

dore His bound-less love, In heav'n a - dore His bound-less love.
fy His ho - ly Name, And glo - ri - fy His ho - ly Name.

[Selected Stanzas]

411

The Offering of Praise

PSALM 150 C. M. SABBATH EVENING Theodore E. Perkins

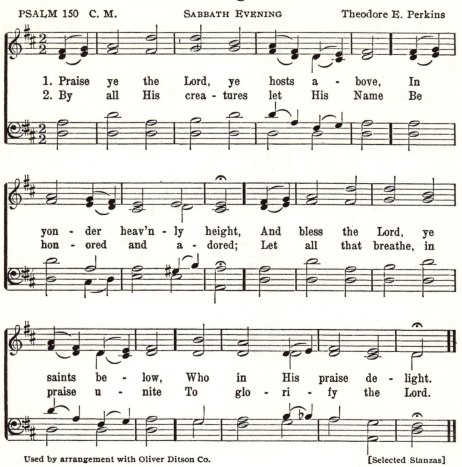

1. Praise ye the Lord, ye hosts a - bove, In
2. By all His crea - tures let His Name Be

yon - der heav'n - ly height, And bless the Lord, ye
hon - ored and a - dored; Let all that breathe, in

saints be - low, Who in His praise de - light.
praise u - nite To glo - ri - fy the Lord.

Used by arrangement with Oliver Ditson Co. [Selected Stanzas]

412

The Exaltation of God

PSALM 150 S. M. LOUISVILLE John Zundel

1. Praise ye the Lord, His saints Who throng His courts be-
2. Let all His crea - tures join To praise His ho - ly

The Exaltation of God

low, And ye, His hosts in heav'n a - bove, His
Name; Let all that breathe, their Mak - er bless And

glo - rious prais - es show, . His glo - rious prais - es show.
cel - e - brate His fame, And cel - e - brate His fame.

[Selected Stanzas]

413 The Hallelujah Chorus

PSALM 150 8s and 7s SICILIAN HYMN Sicilian Melody

1. Hal - le - lu - jah! Hal - le - lu - jah! Earth and
2. Hal - le - lu - jah! Hal - le - lu - jah! Mag - ni -

heav'n in sweet ac - cord Join to sound Je -
fy Je - ho - vah's Name; Praise the liv - ing

ho - vah's prais - es, Tell the glo - ry of the Lord.
God, your Mak - er, All that breathe, His praise pro - claim.

[Selected Stanzas]

CHORALE SECTION

414   O Lord, How Swiftly Grows

PSALM 3   MORNING PRAISE   6 6 7 5 6 7 D.   L. Bourgeois, 1551
Version of Dewey Westra, 1931

1 O Lord, how swift-ly grows The num-ber of my foes,
2 But Thou, Je-ho-vah, art A shield a-bout my heart,

Who wan-ton-ly op-press me! Yea, mul-ti-plied are they
My hope and sure re-li - ance. Thou, in the hour of dread,

That rise to my dis-may, And day by day dis-tress me.
Dost lift my wea-ry head, And bid-dest them de-fi - ance

Though heav-y my de-spair, They scorn-ful-ly de-clare,
When-e'er to God I cried, He has-tened to my side

O Lord, How Swiftly Grows

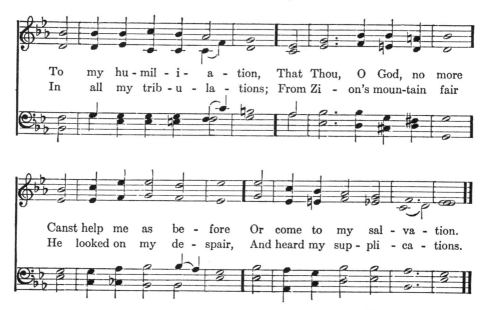

To my hu-mil-i-a-tion, That Thou, O God, no more
In all my trib-u-la-tions; From Zi-on's moun-tain fair

Canst help me as be-fore Or come to my sal-va-tion.
He looked on my de-spair, And heard my sup-pli-ca-tions.

Dutch Psalter, Psalm 3

NOTE: This selection can also be played and sung as a plain chorale, with all the notes of equal length.

3 I laid me down and slept;
I waked, for I was kept
In His divine protection;
The Lord was at my side,
My succor He supplied,
Whatever my affliction.
Defended by His hand,
I shall undaunted stand,
While thousands surge about me;
Though furious foemen wage
Their war with mighty rage,
I know they shall not rout me.

4 Arise and save me, Lord,
For Thou hast smitten hard
The jaws of them that hate me;
Yea, Thou didst fiercely break
For me Thy servant's sake
The teeth of the ungodly
I shall not suffer long,
For my salvation strong
Belongeth to Jehovah;
Thou, Lord, wilt freely pour
A blessing from Thy store
Upon us; Hallelujah!

415 Unto Thee, O Lord Jehovah

PSALM 25
Version of Rev. S. G. Brondsema, 1931

PATHWAY 8 7 8 7 7 8 7 8

L. Bourgeois, 1551

1 Un-to Thee, O Lord Je-ho-vah, Do I lift my wait-ing soul.
2 Un-to me, O Lord Je-ho-vah, Show Thy ways and teach Thou me;

O my God, in Thee I trust-ed; Let no shame now o'er me roll.
So that, by Thy Spir-it guid-ed, Clear-ly I Thy paths may see.

On my en-e-my be shame, Oft with-out a cause trans-gress-ing;
In Thy truth wilt Thou me guide, Teach me, God of my sal-va-tion;

But all those who trust Thy Name Hon-or with a-bun-dant bless-ing.
All the day for Thee I bide, Lord, with ea-ger ex-pec-ta-tion

Dutch Psalter, Psalm 25

Words and music copyrighted by the Publication Committee of the Christian Reformed Church, 1934.
NOTE: This selection can also be played and sung as a plain chorale, with all the notes of equal length.

358

Unto Thee, O Lord Jehovah

3 Call to mind, O Lord Jehovah,
    Tender mercies manifold,
And Thy store of lovingkindness
    Which has ever been of old.
Sins of youth remember not,
    Nor recall my hid' transgression;
For Thy goodness' sake, O God,
    Think of me in Thy compassion.

4 Good and upright is Jehovah
    In His dealings evermore.
Sinners are by Him instructed
    In the way untrod before.
He will ever guide the meek
    In His judgments true and holy;
Teach His ways to those who seek
    With a contrite heart and lowly.

5 All the pathways of Jehovah
    Speak of truth and mercies pure
Unto such as keep His covenant
    And His testimony sure.
For the glory of Thy Name,
    Pardon, Lord, my evil-doing;
Grievous though my sin and shame,
    Hear my cry, Thy love renewing.

6 Who is he that fears Jehovah,
    Walking with Him day by day?
God will lead him safely onward,
    Guide him in the chosen way.
Then at ease his soul shall rest,
    In Jehovah still confiding;
E'en his children shall be blest,
    Safely in the land abiding.

7 Yea, the secret of Jehovah
    Is with those who fear His Name;
With His friends in tender mercy
    He His covenant will maintain.
With a confidence complete,
    Toward the Lord my eyes are turning;
From the net He'll pluck my feet;
    He will not despise my yearning.

8 Turn Thou unto me in mercy;
    Have compassion on my soul.
I am sore distressed and lonely;
    Waves of trouble o'er me roll.
Myriad woes beset my heart,
    Myriad doubts and bitternesses;
Thou who my Deliverer art,
    Bring me out of my distresses.

9 O consider my affliction,
    All my travail, Lord, behold;
Grant me full and free remission
    Of my trespasses untold.
See mine enemies; for great
    Is the number that upbraid me;
Who, in their consuming hate,
    With their cruel scorn have flayed me.

10 Keep my soul, O gracious Savior;
    Come, I pray, deliver me,
Lest my head with shame be covered,
    For my refuge is in Thee.
Trusting in Thy power supreme,
    Lord, I wait for Thy salvation;
Come, Jehovah, and redeem
    Israel from tribulation.

416 As the Hart, About to Falter

PSALM 42
Version of Dewey Westra, 1931

THIRSTING 8 7 8 7 7 7 8 8

L. Bourgeois, 1551

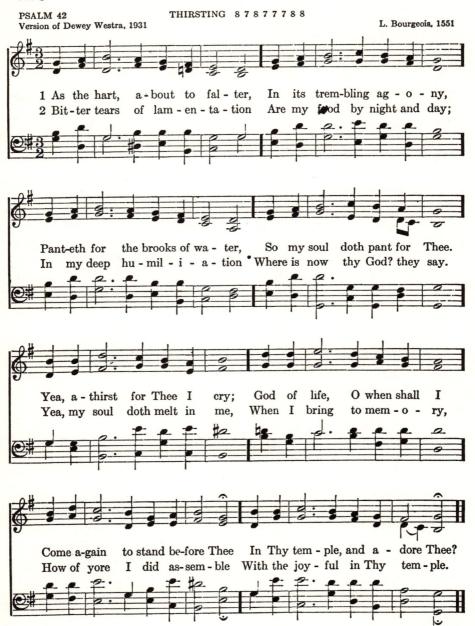

1 As the hart, a-bout to fal-ter, In its trem-bling ag-o-ny,
2 Bit-ter tears of lam-en-ta-tion Are my food by night and day;

Pant-eth for the brooks of wa-ter, So my soul doth pant for Thee.
In my deep hu-mil-i-a-tion Where is now thy God? they say.

Yea, a-thirst for Thee I cry; God of life, O when shall I
Yea, my soul doth melt in me, When I bring to mem-o-ry,

Come a-gain to stand be-fore Thee In Thy tem-ple, and a-dore Thee?
How of yore I did as-sem-ble With the joy-ful in Thy tem-ple.

Dutch Psalter, Psalm 42

NOTE: This selection can also be played and sung as a plain chorale, with all the notes of equal length.

As the Hart, About to Falter

3 O my soul, why art thou grieving,
   Why disquieted in me?
   Hope in God, thy faith retrieving;
   Let Him still thy refuge be.
   I shall yet extol His grace
   For the comfort of His face;
   He has ever turned my sorrow
   Into gladness on the morrow.

4 From the land beyond the Jordan
   I bewail my misery;
   From the foothills of Mount Hermon,
   O my God, I think of Thee.
   As the waters plunge and leap,
   Deep re-echoes unto deep;
   All Thy waves and billows roaring
   O'er my troubled soul are pouring.

5 But the Lord will send salvation,
   And by day His love provide;
   He shall be my exultation,
   And my song at eventide.
   On His praise e'en in the night
   I will ponder with delight,
   And in prayer, transcending distance,
   Seek the God of my existence.

6 I will say to God, my fortress:
   Why hast Thou forsaken me?
   Why go I about in sadness
   For my foes' dread tyranny?
   Their rebukes and scoffing words
   Pierce my bones as pointed swords,
   As they say with proud defiance:
   Where is God, thy soul's reliance?

7 O my soul, why art thou grieving;
   Why disquieted in me?
   Hope in God, thy faith retrieving;
   He will still thy refuge be.
   I shall yet through all my days
   Give to Him my thankful praise;
   God, who will from shame deliver,
   Is my God, my rock, forever.

417 Send Forth, O Lord of My Salvation

PSALM 43
Version of Rev. William Kuipers, 1931

HOLY HILL 9 8 9 9 8 6

L. Bourgeois, 1543

1 Send forth, O Lord of my sal - va - tion, Thy light and
2 Then, at Thy sa - cred al - tar bend - ing, My heart to
3 My soul, why art thou sad and griev - ing? Why so op-

truth to be my guide, O let their rays, in my pri -
God in prayer I'll raise With harp and voice, in wor - ship
pressed with anx - ious care? Hope thou in God! His Word be -

va - tion, Lead me un - to Thy hab - i - ta - tion,
blend - ing, Thy courts re - sound, while psalms, as - cend - ing
liev - ing, Thou shalt be - hold His face, re - ceiv - ing

Where 'neath Thy wing I'll be sup - plied With grace Thou wilt pro - vide.
To God, my high - est joy, bring praise For all His won - drous ways
The bless - ings of His coun - tenance fair—What bliss be - yond com - pare!

Dutch Psalter, Psalm 43

NOTE: This selection can also be played and sung as a plain chorale, with all the notes of equal length.

362

418 Praise the Lord, Ye Lands

PSALM 47
Version of Dewey Westra, 1931

ASCENDING KING 5 5 5 5 5 5 D.

L. Bourgeois, 1551

1 Praise the Lord, ye lands; Na - tions, clap your hands;
2 God has gone on high With a joy - ful ,cry;
3 Praise His maj - es - ty Un - der - stand - ing - ly;

Shout a - loud to God, Spread His fame a - broad; Praise Him
Hosts with trum - pet sound Make His praise a - bound; Sing ye
God is King a - lone On His ho - ly throne, Is - sues

loud and long With a tri - umph song; Bow as ye draw nigh,
praise to God, Tell his fame a - broad, Take a psalm and shout,
His com-mands To all hea - then lands. Lo, the prin - ces all

For the Lord Most High, Ter - ri - ble is He In His
Let His praise ring out, Lift your voice and sing Glo - ry
Gath - er at His call; His the shields of earth, His the

dig - ni - ty; And His king-dom's girth Cir - cles all the earth.
to our King; He is Lord of earth, Mag - ni - fy His worth.
power, the worth; He, the God on high, Is our Help - er nigh.

[Selected Stanzas]

Dutch Psalter, Psalm 47

Words and music copyrighted by the Publication Committee of the Christian Reformed Church, 1934.
NOTE: This selection can also be played and sung as a plain chorale, with all the notes of equal length.

419   Forth from Thy Courts, Thy Sacred Dwelling

PSALM 65   ZION'S PRAISE   9 6 9 6 D.
Version of Rev. William Kuipers, 1931   L. Bourgeois, 1543

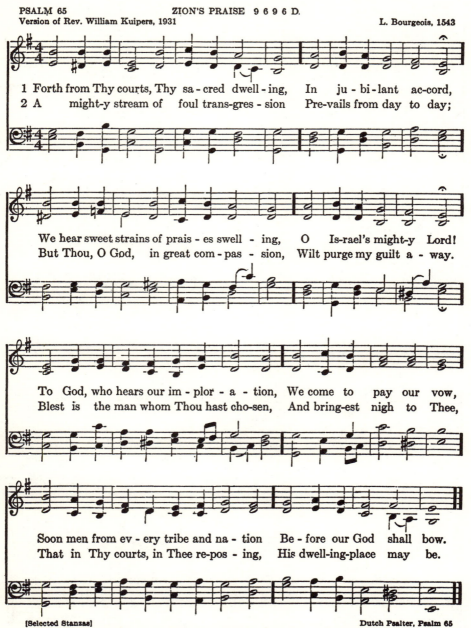

1 Forth from Thy courts, Thy sa - cred dwell - ing,   In   ju - bi - lant   ac-cord,
2 A   might-y stream of   foul trans-gres - sion   Pre-vails from day   to   day;

We hear sweet strains of prais - es swell - ing,   O   Is-rael's might-y   Lord!
But Thou, O God,   in great com - pas - sion,   Wilt purge my guilt a - way.

To God, who hears our im - plor - a - tion, We come to   pay   our   vow,
Blest is   the man whom Thou hast cho-sen,   And bring-est   nigh   to   Thee,

Soon men from ev - ery tribe and na - tion   Be - fore our God   shall   bow.
That in Thy courts, in Thee re-pos - ing,   His dwell-ing-place   may   be.

[Selected Stanzas]   Dutch Psalter, Psalm 65
Words and music copyrighted by the Publication Committee of the Christian Reformed Church, 1934.
NOTE. This selection can also be played and sung as a plain chorale, with all the notes of equal length.

Forth from Thy Courts, Thy Sacred Dwelling

3 There, in Thy holy habitation,
    Thou wilt Thy saints provide
With every blessing of salvation,
    Till all are satisfied.
By awful deeds, so just and mighty,
    God saves us from our foe;
To all who walk with Him uprightly
    He will salvation show.

4 From stores on high Thy streams flow over
    The hard and arid land;
The fields are sown with corn and clover,
    Provided by Thy hand;
The furrows, softened by Thy showers,
    Are blest with springing grain.
How great, O God, Thy love and power
    Throughout Thy vast domain!

5 The year is crowned, O Fount of blessing,
    With gifts to cheer the land;
Thy goodness fills the earth, expressing
    ˙The wonders of Thy hand.
The hills rejoice; the pastures, teeming
    With flocks that skip and spring,
The golden grain, in valleys gleaming—
    All sing to God the King.

420
God Shall Arise and by His Might

PSALM 68
Version of Rev. B. Essenburg, 1931

GREITER 8 8 7, 12 lines

Matthaeus Greiter, 1539

1 God shall a - rise and by His might Put all His en - e - mies to flight
2 But let the righteous, blessed of yore, Joy in their God as ne'er be-fore,

With shame and con-ster - na - tion. His hat-ers, haugh-ty though they be,
Faith's vic-to - ry a - chiev - ing. Their joy shall then un - bound - ed be

Shall at His au - gust pres-ence flee In ut - ter des - o - la - tion;
Who see God's face e - ter - nal - ly, Their heart's de-sire re - ceiv - ing.

For when Je - ho - vah shall ap-pear, He shall con-sume, a - far and near,
Ex - alt, ex - alt the Name of God; Sing ye His roy - al fame a-broad

God Shall Arise and by His Might

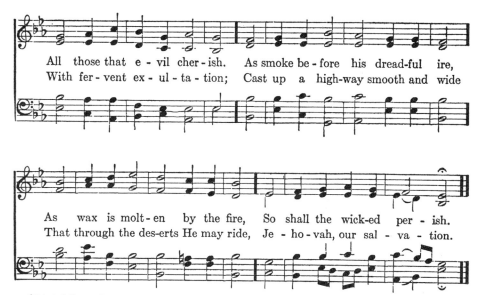

All those that e - vil cher - ish. As smoke be - fore his dread-ful ire,
With fer - vent ex - ul - ta - tion; Cast up a high-way smooth and wide

As wax is molt - en by the fire, So shall the wick-ed per - ish.
That through the des-erts He may ride, Je - ho-vah, our sal - va - tion.

[Selected Stanzas]   Dutch Psalter, Psalm 68

NOTE: This selection can also be played and sung as a plain chorale, with all the notes of equal length.

3 Sing praise, thou chosen Israel,
  Who with the folds of sheep dost dwell;
    Thou art God's joy and treasure.
  Like doves on golden-feathered wing,
  In holy beauty thou shalt bring
    Thy praise to God with pleasure.
  Jehovah scattered kings and foes,
  Redeeming thee from grievous woes;
    Praise is thy holy duty.
  For God did choose a mount so fair
  That Bashan's height cannot compare
    With Zion's fame and beauty.

4 The Lord is great, His might untold,
  His chariots thousand thousand fold,
    His armies ne'er confounded.
  Among them God with joy displays
  The glory that in Moses' days
    Mount Sinai surrounded.
  When Thou, O Lord, in glory bright,
  Ascendedst in the heavenly height
    Our captive-bonds to sever,
  Rich gifts from those who did rebel
  Thou didst receive, that men might dwell
    With Thee, O Lord, forever.

5 Let God be praised with reverence deep;
  He daily comes our lives to steep
    In bounties freely given.
  God cares for us, our God is He;
  Who would not fear His majesty
    In earth as well as heaven?
  Our God upholds us in the strife;
  To us He grants eternal life,
    And saves from desolation.
  He hears the needy when they cry,
  He saves their souls when death draws   [nigh,
    This God is our salvation.

6 Ye kings and kingdoms of the earth,
  Extol Jehovah's matchless worth
    With psalms of adoration.
  Praise Him whose glory rides on high,
  Whose thunders roll through clouded sky
    With mighty intonation.
  Ascribe ye strength to God alone,
  Whose worth in Israel is known,
    For whom the heavens tremble.
  O Lord, our strength, to Thee we bow,
  For great and terrible art Thou
    Out of Thy holy temple.

367

421 O God of Hosts, O God of Grace

PSALM 84   TABERNACLES   8 8 9 8 9 8 8
Version of Rev. William Kuipers, 1931

Maitre Pierre, 1562

1 O God of hosts, O God of grace, How love-ly is Thy
2 The spar-row finds a house to rest, ·The swal-low deft-ly

ho - ly place, How good and pleas-ant is Thy dwell - ing!
builds her nest, And broods her young hard by Thine al - tar.

My thirst-y soul longs ear-nest-ly, Yea, faints Thy ho - ly courts to see
O Lord of hosts, my God, my King, With all my soul to Thee I cling!

'Mid fes - tal throngs and mu - sic swell - ing. My heart and flesh
Hold Thou my hand, lest I should fal - ter. How blest are they

O God of Hosts, O God of Grace

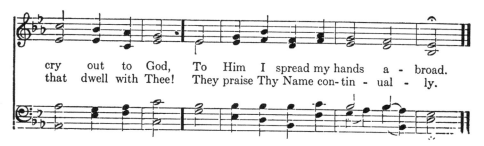

cry   out   to   God,   To   Him   I   spread my hands   a - broad.
that   dwell   with   Thee!   They   praise   Thy   Name con-tin - ual - ly.

Dutch Psalter, Psalm 84

NOTE: This selection can also be played and sung as a plain chorale, with all the notes of equal length.

3 Blest is the man whose strength Thou art,
Thy ways are hidden in his heart,
He treads the highway to Thy dwelling.
Though passing through a vale of tears,
Thy grace, O God, to him appears
With winged hope and power impelling.
The wilderness, by showers blest,
Is now a pilgrim's vale of rest.

4 From strength to strength Thy children dear
Go forward, till they all appear
In Zion's courts, God's holy mountain.
O how delightful, God of grace,
The paths of those that seek Thy face,
And yearn for waters from Thy fountain!
Jehovah, God of hosts, give ear,
O Jacob's God, in mercy hear.

5 O God, our shield, with face benign
Look on Thy servant, wholly Thine,
And keep him, Lord, Thou great Defender!
One day, passed in Thy house of praise,
Is better than a thousand days
Spent in the realm of earthly splendor.
Though only at Thy door I wait,
No tents of sin give joy so great.

6 O God Jehovah, good and kind,
On Zion's mount in clouds enshrined,
Thou art our sun and shield forever.
To upright souls that seek Thy face
Thou givest glory, truth, and grace;
E'en in death's vale Thou failest never.
O Lord of hosts, how blest is he
Who puts his stedfast trust in Thee!

422 My Mouth Shall Sing for Aye

PSALM 89
Version of Rev. William Kuipers, 1931

SOVEREIGN GRACE 12 12 13 13 13 13

Maitre Pierre, 1562

1 My mouth shall sing for aye Thy ten-der mer-cies, Lord;
2 "With My own cho-sen one, e'en Da-vid," God af-firmed,

To ev-ery age will I Thy faith-ful-ness re-cord;
"I've made a cov-e-nant, with sa-cred oath con-firmed;

I know how firm and sure Thy won-drous grace is found-ed,
I've sworn in truth to him, My serv-ant: 'I will sure-ly

Es-tab-lished in the skies by love that is un-bound-ed;
Build up thy lus-trous throne through ev-ery age se-cure-ly;

As Thy ce-les-tial throne shall nev-er sway, no nev-er,
For-ev-er will thy seed, in spite of deg-ra-da-tion,

My Mouth Shall Sing for Aye

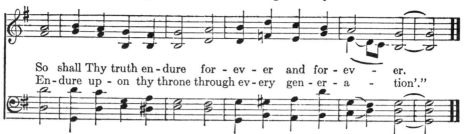

So shall Thy truth en-dure for-ev-er and for-ev - er.
En-dure up-on thy throne through ev-ery gen-er-a - tion'."

[Selected Stanzas]   Dutch Psalter, Psalm 89

NOTE: This selection can also be played and sung as a plain chorale, with all the notes of equal length.

3 The heavens praise, O Lord, Thy wonders day and night;
Thy saints on earth extol Thy faithfulness and might;
Exultingly they ask: "Who, Lord, within Thy dwelling,
Who of the kings of earth, in carnal strength excelling,
Can be compared with Thee, Jehovah great and glorious,
In all Thy wise designs triumphant and victorious?"

4 The hosts of heaven, O God, acclaim Thee Lord alone,
And greatly fear Thy Name 'bove all around Thy throne.
Who is there like to Thee, throughout this vast creation,
Jehovah, Lord of hosts, the God of our salvation,
Arrayed like Thee with power and faithfulness astounding,
Constraining saints to praise Thy wondrous grace abounding?

5 How blessed, Lord, are they who know the joyful sound,
Who, when they hear Thy voice, in happiness abound!
With stedfast step they walk, their countenances beaming
With brightness of the light that from Thy face is streaming;
Exalted by Thy might from depths of desolation,
They praise fore'er Thy Name, Thy justice and salvation.

6 Thou art, O God, our boast, the glory of our power;
Thy sovereign grace is e'er our fortress and our tower.
We lift our heads aloft, for God, our shield, is o'er us;
Through Him, through Him alone, whose presence goes before us,
We'll wear the victor's crown, no more by foes assaulted,
We'll triumph through our King, by Israel's God exalted.

7 As long as heaven stands on pillars firm and sure,
So long shall David's seed through endless years endure.
But if his children e'er forsake My law appointed,
And walk not in the ways decreed by Mine Anointed,
Then truly will I come in holy indignation,
And chastise them with rods for all their provocation.

8 Remember, Lord, how frail I am, how few my years;
My life is like a cloud that comes and disappears;
Has man, then, lived in vain? Who can, in death's dark hour,
Escape the dismal grave with all its ruinous power?
O Lord, recall Thy love, Thy words to David spoken,
Sustain us as of yore by covenant-oaths unbroken.

371

423 Jehovah Reigns As King

PSALM 97
Version of Dewey Westra, 1931

RIGHTEOUS JUDGE 6 6 7 7 6 6 6 6 6

Maitre Pierre, 1562

1 Je - ho - vah reigns as King, To Him all hom - age bring;
2 Con - sum - ing flames de - ploy Be - fore Him, to de - stroy
3 The hills, as wax by fire, Are mol - ten at His ire,

Ye is - lands, earth, and o - cean, Break forth in
His foe - men round a - bout Him, Who vain - ly
When God on His cre - a - tion Pours flam - ing

glad de - vo - tion. Dark clouds of se - cre - cy
seek to flout Him. His light - ning - bolts, when hurled,
in - dig - na - tion. The heavens in awe ex - press

En - shroud His maj - es - ty. The pil - lars of His throne
En - light - ened all the world; Earth saw and quaked with fear,
His per - fect right - eous - ness. Let all the na - tions see

Jehovah Reigns As King

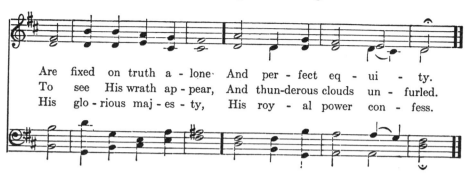

Are   fixed   on   truth   a - lone   And   per - fect   eq - ui - ty.
To   see   His   wrath   ap - pear,   And   thun-derous   clouds   un - furled.
His   glo - rious   maj - es - ty,   His   roy - al   power   con - fess.

Dutch Psalter. Psalm 97

NOTE: This selection can also be played and sung as a plain chorale, with all the notes of equal length.

4 Confounded be all they
  Who in their folly pray
  To gods of man's creation
  And boast of vain salvation.
  Jehovah, Him we laud,
  For He alone is God.
  Come, all ye gods, draw near,
  And worship Him with fear,
  By His dominion awed.

5 All Zion then rejoiced,
  When in her gates were voiced
  The judgments, O Jehovah,
  Which Thou hast wrought for Judah.
  Her daughters sang with mirth,
  For high above the earth,
  Thou, who art God alone,
  Hast made Thyself a throne
  And magnified Thy worth.

6 Ye lovers of the Lord,
  To Him all praise accord;
  Rejoice in your confession
  And hate all base transgression.
  Jehovah keepeth well
  The saints in Israel;
  He frees them from the snare
  That wicked men prepare,
  And makes them safely dwell.

7 Jehovah's kindly face
  Gives happiness and grace
  To all that are pure-hearted;
  To them is life imparted.
  Rejoice in God, ye just,
  He raised you from the dust;
  Give thanks, ye people all,
  His holy Name recall,
  Repose in Him your trust.

424 Sing, Sing a New Song to Jehovah

PSALM 98
Version of Dewey Westra, 1931

CORNERSTONE 9 8 9 8 D.

L. Bourgeois, 1551

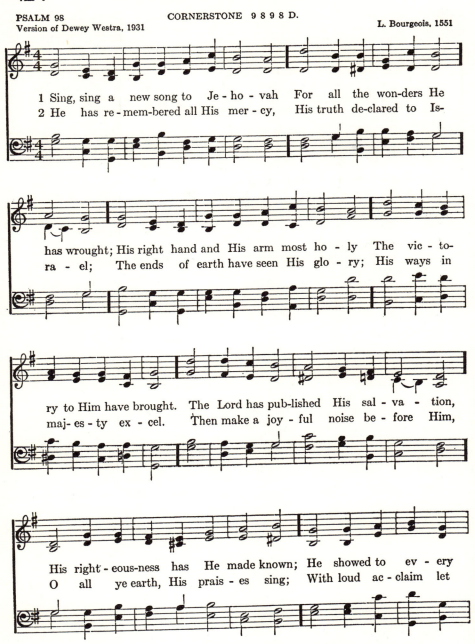

1 Sing, sing a new song to Je - ho - vah For all the won-ders He
2 He has re - mem-bered all His mer - cy, His truth de-clared to Is-

has wrought; His right hand and His arm most ho - ly The vic - to-
ra - el; The ends of earth have seen His glo - ry; His ways in

ry to Him have brought. The Lord has pub-lished His sal - va - tion,
maj - es - ty ex - cel. Then make a joy - ful noise be - fore Him,

His right - eous-ness has He made known; He showed to ev - ery
O all ye earth, His prais - es sing; With loud ac - claim let

Sing, Sing a New Song to Jehovah

hea-then   na - tion   That   judg-ment   is - sues   from   His   throne.
all   a - dore   Him   And   let the   joy - ful   an - thems   ring.

Dutch Psalter, Psalm 98
NOTE: This selection can also be played and sung as a plain chorale, with all the notes of equal length.

3 Join to the harp your glad rejoicing,
　A psalm of adoration bring,
With trumpet and the cornet voicing
　A joyful noise to God, the King.
Let oceans roar with all their fulness,
　The world and they that dwell therein;
Proclaim Jehovah's power with boldness,
　Exalt Him ever and again.

4 Let all the streams in joyous union
　Now clap their hands and praise accord,
The hills rejoice in glad communion,
　And skip for joy before the Lord.
He comes, He comes to judge the people,
　Arrayed in truth and equity;
The world shall He redeem from evil,
　And righteous shall His judgment be.

Unto the Lord Lift Thankful Voices

PSALM 105
Version of Rev. S. G. Brondsema, 1931

PIERRE 9 9 8 8 8 8

Maitre Pierre, 1562

1 Un - to the Lord lift thank-ful voic - es, Come, wor-ship
2 In joy - ful song your hearts u - nit - ing, His works most

while your soul re - joic - es; Make known His do-ings far and near
mar - vel - ous re - cit - ing, Now glo - ry in His ho - ly Name;

That peo - ples all His Name may fear, And tell, in man - y
Let those that seek Him spread His fame, In - cline their hearts to

joy - ful lay, Of all His won - ders day by day.
sing His praise, And un - to Him their an - thems raise.

Unto the Lord Lift Thankful Voices

3 Seek ye Jehovah and His power,
  Seek ye His presence every hour.
  His works, so marvelous and great,
  Remember still, and meditate
  Upon the wonders of His hands,
  The judgments which His mouth commands.

4 Ye seed from Abraham descended,
  To whom His favors were extended,
  And Jacob's children, whom the Lord
  Has chosen, hearken to His word.
  He is the Lord, our Judge divine;
  In all the earth His glories shine.

5 Jehovah's truth will stand forever,
  His covenant-bonds He will not sever;
  The word of grace which He commands
  To thousand generations stands;
  The covenant made in days of old
  With Abraham He doth uphold.

6 The Lord His covenant people planted
  In lands of nations which He granted,
  That they His statutes might observe,
  Nor from His laws might ever swerve.
  Let songs of praise to Him ascend,
  And hallelujahs without end.

I Love the Lord

426

PSALM 116
Version of Rev. William Kuipers, 1931

SACRIFICE OF PRAISE 10 11 11 10

Maitre Pierre, 1562

1 I love the Lord, the fount of life and grace; He hears my voice, my
2 The cords of death held me in deep de-spair; The pangs of hell, like

cry and sup-pli-ca-tion, In-clines His ear, gives strength and
waves by tem-pest driv-en, Rolled o'er my soul; by grief and

con-so-la-tion; In life, in death, my heart will seek His face.
sor-row riv-en, I turned in my dis-tress to God in prayer.

Dutch Psalter, Psalm 116

3 I cried, Deliver Thou my soul, O Lord!
Jehovah heard. I pledge Him my devotion.
The Lord is just, His grace wide as the ocean;
In boundless mercy He fulfils His word.

4 The Lord preserves the meek most tenderly;
Brought nigh to death, in Him I found salvation.
Come, thou my soul, relieved from agitation,
Turn to thy rest; the Lord has favored thee.

I Love the Lord

5 Thou, O Jehovah, in Thy sovereign grace,
  Hast saved my soul from death and woe appalling,
  Dried all my tears, secured my feet from falling.
  Lo, I shall live and walk before Thy face.

6 I have believed, and therefore did I speak
  When I was made to suffer tribulation;
  I said in haste and bitter desperation:
  All men are false, 'tis nought but lies they speak.

7 What shall I render to Jehovah now
  For all the riches of His consolation?
  With joy I'll take the cup of His salvation,
  And call upon His Name with thankful vow.

8 Before His saints I'll pay my vows to God;
  E'en in death's vale He keepeth me from evil;
  How dear to God the dying of His people!
  Praise Him, ye saints, and sound His Name abroad.

9 I am, O Lord, Thy servant, bound yet free,
  Thy handmaid's son, whose shackles Thou hast broken;
  Redeemed by grace, I'll render as a token
  Of gratitude my constant praise to Thee.

10 Jerusalem! Within thy courts I'll praise
  Jehovah's Name; and with a spirit lowly
  Pay àll my vows. O Zion, fair and holy,
  Come join with me and bless Him all thy days!

427
Let All Exalt Jehovah's Goodness

PSALM 118
Version of Dewey Westra, 1931

CORNERSTONE 9 8 9 8 D.

L. Bourgeois, 1551

1 Let all ex - alt Je - ho - vah's good - ness, For most com -
2 Je - ho - vah is my strength and tow - er, He is my

pas - sion - ate is He; His mer - cy, ex - cel - lent in ful - ness,
hap - pi - ness and song; He saved me in the try - ing hour, ...

En - dur - eth to e - ter - ni - ty. Let Is - rael, praise Je - ho - vah's
Hence shall my mouth His praise pro-long. The voice of glad-ness and sal -

good - ness, And say, Ex - alt His maj - es - ty; His mer - cy,
va - tion Is in the tents of right - eous - ness; There do they

Let All Exalt Jehovah's Goodness

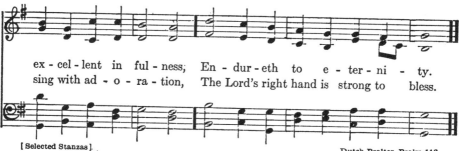

ex - cel - lent in ful - ness; En - dur - eth to e - ter - ni - ty.
sing with ad - o - ra - tion, The Lord's right hand is strong to bless.

[Selected Stanzas]

Dutch Psalter, Psalm 118

NOTE: This selection can also be played and sung as a plain chorale, with all the notes of equal length.

3 The Lord's right hand is high exalted,
　Jehovah's strong and mighty hand;
The vaunting enemy He halted,
　And made His chosen ones to stand.
I shall not die but live before Him,
　And all His mighty works declare,
That all may joyfully adore Him
　Who in His lovingkindness share.

4 In truth, the Lord has sorely chastened,
　But not to death delivered me;
In His paternal love He hastened
　To mitigate my misery.
Now open at my salutation
　The gates of truth and righteousness,
And I will enter with elation,
　There to proclaim my thankfulness.

5 The stone the builders had rejected,
　And in contempt refused to own,
To their dismay has been selected
　To be the foremost cornerstone.
This thing is from the Lord Almighty,
　It is a marvel in our eyes;
Man cannot understand it rightly
　Nor fathom it in any wise.

6 This is the day of full salvation
　That God has made and sanctified;
Come, let us voice our jubilation,
　And triumph in the grace supplied.
Save, O Jehovah, we implore Thee,
　Save now Thy people, e'en today;
Prosperity send Thou in mercy,
　And favor us upon our way.

Now blessed be the King of Glory,
　That cometh in Jehovah's Name;
Out of His temple we adore Thee,
　And all Thy blessedness proclaim.
The Lord is mighty; He provideth
　A light for us when sore afraid;
Then be our thankful sacrifices
　Upon the sacred altar laid.

8 Thou art my God, I will extol Thee,
　And magnify Thy majesty;
My God, in glory none excel Thee,
　Thy praise be to eternity.
Let all exalt Jehovah's goodness,
　For most compassionate is He;
His mercy, excellent in fulness,
　Endureth to eternity.

381

How Blessed Are the Perfect in the Way

428

PSALM 119
Version of Dewey Westra, 1931

ROYAL LAW   10 11 10 11 10 11

L. Bourgeois, 1551

1 How bless-ed are the per-fect in the way Who, walk-ing in Je-
2 O let Thy Spir-it be my con-stant aid, That all my ways may

ho-vah's law with pleas-ure, Pre-serve their pi - e - ty from day to day.
ev - er be di-rect-ed To keep Thy stat-utes, so to be o-beyed,

How blest are they who make His Word their trea-sure, Who keep His tes - ti-
That from all er - ror I may be pro - tect - ed. I · shall not be a-

mo - nies and dis - play Their love for Him whose good-ness none can mea-sure.
shamed then or a-fraid, When Thy com-mand-ments I have e'er re-spect - ed.

[Selected Stanzas]

Dutch Psalter, Psalm 119

Words and music copyrighted by the Publication Committee of the Christian Reformed Church, 1934.
NOTE: This selection can also be played and sung as a plain chorale, with all the notes of equal length.

3 O Lord, how shall a youth preserve his way,
   At every turn by vanity surrounded?
In truth, if he Thy statutes will obey,
   If on Thy Word his attitudes are founded.
Thou whom I've sought, O let me never stray
   From Thy commandments, lest I be confounded.

382

How Blessed Are the Perfect in the Way

4 Thy precepts have I hid within my heart,
  Lest I should stray and fall into transgression;
  O teach Thou me and unto me impart
  Thy statutes for a permanent possession.
  In all Thy judgments Thou most righteous art;
  Thy truth I praise in rapturous confession.

5 O teach me, Lord, the way that I should go;
  Then shall Thy servant walk therein forever.
  Give understanding all Thy paths to know;
  Then shall I keep Thy law with zealous fervor.
  Instruct me in Thy perfect will and, lo,
  I shall observe it with my whole endeavor.

6 O Lord, Thou art my portion and my lot;
  I said that I would keep Thy Word forever,
  Though to my sorrow I have oft forgot.
  With all my heart I now entreat Thy favor:
  Be merciful to me and chasten not;
  According to Thy Word be Thou my Savior.

7 O how I love Thy law! Yea, Thou canst see
  Through all the day it is my meditation;
  By Thy commandments, Lord, Thou madest me
  More wise than all who seek my ruination.
  Thy testimonies evermore shall be
  The perfect source of all my inspiration.

8 Thy Word is as a lamp unto my feet,
  A light upon my pathway unto heaven;
  I've sworn an oath, which gladly I repeat,
  That I shall keep, as always I have striven,
  Thy righteous judgments, holy and complete,
  When unto me Thy helping grace is given.

9 Great peace have they who love Thy perfect law;
  They shall not swerve from paths of consecration;
  Their happiness shall be without a flaw.
  Lord, I have ever hoped for Thy salvation;
  All Thy commandments I have kept with awe;
  Thy precepts are my daily meditation.

10 Grant life unto my soul, O Lord, I pray;
  Shed still the brightness of Thy presence o'er me;
  Then shall I praise Thee in a perfect way,
  Yea, let Thy judgments quicken and restore me.
  Thy servant like a sheep has gone astray,
  Yet Thy commandments I will keep before me.

With All My Heart Will I Record

429

PSALM 138
Version of Dewey Westra, 1931

JUBILATION 8 4 5 8 4 5 D.

L. Bourgeois, 1543

1 With all my heart will I re-cord Thy praise, O Lord,
2 O God, when-e'er I cried to Thee Thou heard-est me

And ex-al-ta-tion; Be-fore the gods with joy-ful
And didst de-liv-er; For by Thy strength, when sore a-

song Will I pro-long My ad-o-ra-tion.
fraid, My soul was stayed, O gra-cious Giv-er.

I'll wor-ship toward Thy ho-ly place And for Thy grace
The kings of earth in one ac-cord Shall thank Thee, Lord,

With All My Heart Will I Record

And truth ex - tol   Thee;   A - bove Thy Name, Thou, Lord
With praise un - bro - ken;   When o - ver all the earth

Most High, Didst mag - ni - fy Thy Word so ho - ly.
is heard The won - drous Word Which Thou hast spo - ken.

Dutch Psalter. Psalm 138

NOTE: This selection can also be played and sung as a plain chorale, with all the notes of equal length

3 They all shall sing in joyful lays
   And laud His ways
   With jubilation;
For great is God in majesty,
   The Lord is He
   Of all creation.
Jehovah looketh from on high
   With kindly eye
   Upon the lowly,
But knoweth those from far who hide,
   In sinful pride,
   Their ways unholy.

4 Lord, though I walk 'mid troubles sore,
   Thou wilt restore
   My faltering spirit;
Though angry foes my soul alarm,
   Thy mighty arm
   Will save and cheer it.
Yea, Thou wilt finish perfectly
   What Thou for me
   Hast undertaken;
May not Thy works, in mercy wrought,
   E'er come to naught,
   Or be forsaken.

Hallelujah! Praise Ye God!

PSALM 150
Version of Dewey Westra, 1931

GLORIA 7 7 7 7 8 7 7 8

Maître Pierre, 1562

1 Hal - le - lu - jah! Praise ye God! In His tem - ple shout His laud,
2 Praise Him with the trum-pet-sound, Let Je - ho - vah's praise a - bound,
3 Let the clash - ing cym-bals ring To the praise of God, the King,

Praise Him in the wide ex - tent Of His spa - cious fir - ma - ment,
Praise Him with the psal - ter - y, Harp un - to His maj - es - ty,
Praise Him with a might - y sound, Let your voic - es shake the ground

Sing Je - ho-vah's praise up-right - ly; Praise Him for the plen - i - tude
Praise Him with the pipe and tim - brel; Praise Him with stringed in-stru-ments,
With the prais - es of Je - ho - vah; All that breathe, ex-alt the Lord,

Of His bound-less mag - ni - tude, Praise Him for His deeds so might - y.
Or-gan forth His ex - cel - lence, Praise Him with the sound-ing cym - bal.
All ye men, His fame re - cord; Great is God! Sing: HAL-LE-LU-JAH!

Dutch Psalter, Psalm 150

NOTE: This selection can also be played and sung as a plain chorale, with all the notes of equal length.

Unto God, Our King

PSALM 81   TRUMPET 5 6 5 5 5 6
Version of Rev. B. Essenburg, 1931   Maitre Pierre, 1562

431

1 Un - to God, our King, Joy and strength of Is - rael,
2 This our fes - tal day Ja - cob's. God has giv - en;

Loft - y an - thems sing; Glo - rious are His ways,
Sol - emn joy dis - play Through-out all the land;

To His Name give praise With the harp and tim - brel.
This is the com - mand Of the God of heav - en.

[Selected Stanzas]   Dutch Psalter, Psalm 81

NOTE: This selection can also be played and sung as a plain chorale, with all the notes of equal length.

3 "Hear, my children, hear,"
Saith the Lord who bore thee;
"Never serve nor fear
Gods of wood or. stone;
I am God alone,
Worship and adore Me."

4 "Open," saith the Lord,
"Wide thy mouth, believing
This My covenant-word:
'I will, if thou plead,
Fill thine every need,
All thy wants relieving.'"

5 "O that to My voice
Israel would hearken!
Then they would rejoice,
Walking in My ways,
Bright and joyous days
Ne'er a foe would darken."

6 "Most abundant good,
—If thou wouldst but prove Me—
E'en the choicest food,
Honey from the comb,
Wheat the finest known,
I would pour upon thee."

432   God Jehovah Reigns

PSALM 99
Version of Rev. S. G. Brondsema, 1931

DOMINUS SANCTUS   5 5 5 5 5 5 6 6

Maître Pierre, 1562

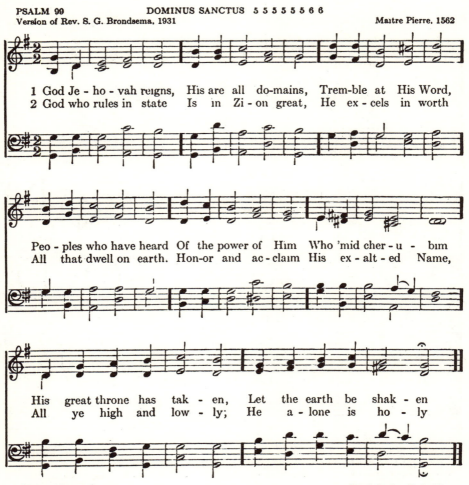

1 God Je - ho - vah reigns, His are all do-mains, Trem-ble at His Word,
2 God who rules in state Is in Zi - on great, He ex - cels in worth

Peo - ples who have heard Of the power of Him Who 'mid cher - u - bim
All that dwell on earth. Hon-or and ac - claim His ex - alt - ed Name,

His great throne has tak - en, Let the earth be shak - en
All ye high and low - ly; He a - lone is ho - ly

[Selected Stanzas]

Dutch Psalter Psalm 99

NOTE: This selection can also be played and sung as a plain chorale, with all the notes of equal length.

3 For God's royal might
  Serves His truth and right,
  Justice He maintains,
  Righteously He reigns.
  Manifesting grace
  To His chosen race,
  Jacob's seed He'll never
  From His covenant sever

4 Then let all accord
  Honor to the Lord,
  At His footstool bow,
  Seek His favor now
  Worship and acclaim
  His exalted Name,
  All ye high and lowly;
  God alone is holy.

The Lord's Prayer

Rev. John A. Heys

389

434 Our Father Which In Heaven Art

Rev. John A. Heys

Our Fa - ther which in heav-en art, hal - low-ed be Thy name.

Thy king-dom come. Thy will be done, on earth as it is in heav'n.

Give us this day our dai - ly bread. For-give, O Lord, for-give our debts,

rit. *a tempo*

as we for-give our debt - ors. In - to temp-ta - tion lead us not,

but de - liv - er us from e - vil. For Thine is the king-dom, the

pow'r and the glo - ry both now and for-ev - er-more. A - MEN.

DOXOLOGIES

AND

SPIRITUAL SONGS

DOXOLOGIES

(Psalter, No. 197)

··◁▦▷··

1.   L. M. (268)

Praise God, from whom all blessings flow,
Praise him all creatures here below,
Praise him above, ye heav'nly host,
Praise Father, Son, and Holy Ghost.

2.   C. M. (197)

To Father, Son, and Holy Ghost,
    The God whom we adore;
Be glory, as it was, is now,
    And shall be evermore.

3.   S. M. (130)

To the Eternal Three,
    In will and essence One;
To Father, Son, and Spirit be
    Co-equal honors done.

4.   L. P. M. (231)

Now to the great and sacred Three
The Father, Son, and Spirit, be
    Eternal pow'r and glory giv'n,
Thru all the worlds, where God is known,
By all the angels near the throne,
    And all the saints in earth and heav'n.

5.   C. P. M. (164)

To Father, Son, and Holy Ghost,
The God, whom heav'n's triumphant host,
    And saints on earth adore;
Be glory as in ages past,
And now it is, and so shall last,
    When time shall be no more.

6.   H. M. (245)

To God the Father's throne,
    Perpetual honors raise;·
Glory to God the Son,
    And to the Spirit praise:
With all our pow'rs, Eternal King,
Thy name we sing, while faith adores,

7.   P. M. 7s. (396)

Sing we to our God above,
Praise eternal as his love,
Praise him, all ye heav'nly host,
Father, Son, and Holy Ghost.

8.   P. M. 8s, 7s. (222)

1 May the grace of Christ the Savior,
    And the Father's boundless love,
With the Holy Spirit's favor
    Rest upon us from above.

2 Thus may we abide in union,
    With each other, and the Lord,
And possess in sweet communion,
    Joys which earth cannot afford.

───────────

AMERICA.
(National Song.)

1 My country! 'tis of thee,
    Sweet land of liberty,
        Of thee I sing;
    Land where my fathers died!
    Land of the Pilgrims' pride!
        From every mountain side
        Let freedom ring!

2 My native country, thee—
    Land of the noble, free—
        Thy name I love;
    I love thy rocks and rills,
    Thy woods and templed hills;
    My heart with rapture thrills
        Like that above.

3 Our fathers' God! to thee,
    Author of liberty,
        To thee we sing;
    Long may our land be bright
    With freedom's holy light;
    Protect us by thy might,
        Great God, our King!

SPIRITUAL SONGS

L. M. (48)

THE SONG OF MARY.

1 Our souls shall magnify the Lord,
   In God the Savior we rejoice;
   While we repeat the Virgin's song,
   May the same Spirit tune our voice!

2 The Highest saw her low estate,
   And mighty things his hand hath
      done;
   His overshadowing pow'r and grace
   Makes her the mother of his Son.

3 Let ev'ry nation call her blessed,
   And endless years prolong her fame:
   But God alone must be ador'd;
   Holy and rev'rend is his name.

4 To those that fear and trust the Lord,
   His mercy stands for ever sure;
   From age to age his promise lives,
   And the performance is secure.

5 He spake to Abra'm and his seed,
   "In thee shall all the earth be
      bless'd;"
   The mem'ry of that ancient word
   Lay long in his eternal breast.

6 But now, no more shall Israel wait,
   No more the Gentiles lie forlorn:
   Lo, the desire of nations comes!
   Behold, the promis'd Seed is born!

C. M. (312)

THE SONG OF ZACHARIAS.

1 Now be the God of Israel bless'd,
   Who makes his truth appear;
   His mighty hand fulfills his word,
   And all the oaths he sware.

2 Now he bedews king David's root
   With blessings from the skies;
   He makes the branch of promise grow
   The promis'd horn arise.

3 John was the prophet of the Lord,
   To go before his face;
   The herald which our Savior God
   Sent to prepare his ways.

4 "Behold the Lamb of God," he cries,
   That takes our guilt away;
   I saw the Spirit o'er his head,
   On his baptizing day.

5 "Be ev'ry vale exalted high,
   Sink ev'ry mountain low: [souls
   The proud must stoop, and humble
   Shall his salvation know.

6 "The heathen realms, with Israel's
      land,
   Shall join in sweet accord;
   And all, that's born of man, shall see
   The glory of the Lord.

7 "Behold the morning Star arise,
   Ye that in darkness sit!
   He marks the path that leads to peace,
   And guides our doubtful feet."

C. M. (163)

THE SONG OF SIMEON.

1 Lord, in thy temple we appear,
   As happy Simeon came,
   And hope to meet our Savior here;
   Oh! make our joys the same!

2 With what divine and vast delight
   The good old man was fill'd,
   When fondly in his wither'd arms
   He clasp'd the holy child!

3 "Now I can leave this world," he cried
   "Behold, thy servant dies!
   I've seen thy great salvation, Lord,
   And close my peaceful eyes.

4 "This is the light prepar'd to shine
   Upon the Gentile lands;
   Thine Israel's glory and their hope,
   To break their slavish bands."

5 Jesus! the vision of thy face
   Hath overpow'ring charms!
   Scarce shall I feel death's cold embrace,
   If Christ be in my arms.

6 When flesh shall fail, and heart-strings
      break,
   Sweet will the minutes roll;
   A mortal paleness on my cheek,
   But glory in my soul.

INDEXES

Index of First and Special Lines

The figures refer to the number of the sections

Index of First and Special Lines

Index of First and Special Lines

Index of First and Special Lines

Index of First and Special Lines

Index of First and Special Lines

Alphabetical Index of Tunes

The figures refer to the number of the sections

Alphabetical Index of Tunes

Metrical Index of Tunes

The figures refer to the number of the sections

Metrical Index of Tunes

Metrical Index of Tunes

Index of Composers and Sources

The figures refer to the number of the sections

Index of Composers and Sources

Index of Subjects

The figures refer to the number of the sections

Index of Subjects

Index of Subjects

Index of Subjects

Index of Subjects

289-297, 304, 310-313, 373-378, 394-403.
See also *Mercy of God.*

Majesty of........See *God, Kingly Character of.*

Omnipotence of...57-59, 76, 130, 161, 162, 241, 242, 252, 402, 403. See also *God, Creator of All.*

Omnipresence of...28-30, 166, 168, 170, 382, 384

Omniscience of.....69, 70, 87, 123, 253, 382-384

Patience of....... See *Anger of God, Restrained.*

Pity of...............See *God, Compassion of.*

Providence of..........See *Providence of God.*

Refuge, Our...16-19, 34, 36, 71, 73, 126-128, 151-154, 159-162, 190-192, 225, 227, 248, 249, 344-347, 387, 388, 392

Righteousness of...20, 31-33, 35, 94, 190-192, 230, 232, 250, 251, 260-264, 281, 304, 338, 394, 397, 399, 400

Searcher of Hearts.....See *God, Omniscience of.*

Source of All Good...6-8, 27-30, 45, 71-74, 81, 85, 88-91, 94, 121, 161, 162, 176-178, 268-270, 359, 373-378, 394-403. See also *God, Goodness of.*

Sovereignty of....3, 4, 126-128, 195, 196, 233, 236, 241, 242, 254-260, 265-270, 298, 299, 308, 309, 373-375, 404, 405. See also *Decrees, Divine;* and *God, Kingly Character of.*

Teacher, Our...60, 61, 64, 67, 72, 84, 233, 236, 253, 325, 329, 334, 389, 391

Works of...14, 15, 34, 36, 37, 39, 76, 85, 86, 166-175, 206, 209-215, 250, 251, 285-288, 304, 376-378, 402, 403. See also *God, Creator of All;* and *Providence of God.*

Wrath of ....See *Anger of God.*

Good Works...See *Activity, Christian; Consecration and Dedication;* and *Zeal.*

Gospel: See also *Christians, Church, Missions, Salvation,* and *Worship.*

Acceptance of 72-74, 242, 328, 339

Freeness of...35, 45, 46, 50-56, 60, 62, 65, 67, 68, 81, 94, 110-112, 135, 137, 140-144, 186, 187, 261-264, 268-270, 277-284, 376-378, 394-399

Fulness of...37-42, 77-79, 88, 90, 91, 125, 132-134, 190-192, 225-232, 241, 277-284, 290-294, 310-313, 317-342, 362-365, 376-378, 381, 394-403

Gracious Fruit of...36, 48, 50, 51, 69, 70, 77-79, 88-90, 109, 111, 112, 151-153, 176-178, 183, 191, 192, 213, 215, 243, 257-259, 268-270, 394-413

Invitations of...58, 59, 72-74, 76, 81, 83, 95, 125, 137, 139, 173-175, 213-215, 222, 254-259, 261-264, 268-270, 289-297, 306, 314-316, 373-378, 402-413

Preaching of...48-51, 69, 70, 89, 90, 108, 109, 112, 141-144, 174-178, 191, 192

Prevalence and Power of...37-42, 49-51, 141-144, 193-200, 261-264, 304, 381, 394-399, 402, 403

Privileges of...38, 40-42, 60-74, 81, 83, 87-91, 125-128, 145, 159, 160, 163, 164, 166, 168, 170, 172, 202, 203, 225-229, 237-239, 248, 249, 292, 310-313, 317-320, 367, 368, 394-403

Sanctifying and Saving...21, 38, 40-42, 60, 61, 64, 65, 67, 68, 89, 90, 108, 111, 112, 119, 120, 140-144, 203, 225-229, 233-236, 241, 321, 322, 332, 334, 389-391

Time of Acceptance of...............254, 255

Grace: See also *Aspirations, For Grace.*

Abiding...........................376-378

Abounding...10, 65, 132, 140, 170, 172, 179, 191, 212, 229, 234, 251, 277, 280, 292-295, 304, 348, 388, 394

Free...See *Gospel, Freeness of; Gospel, Fulness of;* and *Salvation, God's Gift.*

Growth in....38, 40-42, 145, 174, 175, 191, 225, 227, 229, 232, 234, 236, 241, 244, 246, 250, 251, 260, 322, 328, 332-334, 337, 341, 389-391

Justifying...70, 88, 140, 142, 168, 172, 175, 212, 230, 231, 235, 258, 264, 265, 277, 283, 284, 289, 290, 292-295, 304, 308, 311, 315, 320, 350, 362, 375, 388, 394, 397, 404

Quickening...16, 73, 112, 143, 163, 225, 226, 228, 244, 251, 264, 274, 328, 350, 357, 375, 381, 404

Redeeming...16, 22, 112, 140, 157, 185, 187, 202, 205, 213, 230, 231, 235, 241, 243, 244, 258, 264, 277, 283, 284, 290, 292-295, 304, 308, 315, 320, 362, 375, 388, 394, 397, 402, 404

Restoring...52-56, 140-144, 225, 226, 229, 251, 274, 277, 289, 311, 330, 357

Reviving........................See *Revival.*

Sanctifying. .See *Gospel, Sanctifying and Saving.*

Sinning against........................140

Sovereign...14, 51, 132-134, 141-143, 164, 168, 180, 191, 202, 208, 213, 232, 234, 241, 264, 288, 289, 292-295, 308, 315, 320, 350, 354, 375, 397, 402

Sustaining...21, 44, 48, 65, 67, 68, 77, 79, 106, 107, 114-118, 121, 159, 174, 225, 226, 228, 234, 243, 251, 274, 277, 290, 304, 308, 320, 324, 328, 350, 354, 357, 381, 394, 397, 402, 404

Gratitude......................See *Thanksgiving.*

Guidance, Divine..............See *God, Our Guide.*

Guilt:

Burden of................See *Sin, Conviction of.*

Expiated...See *Christ, Atonement of;* and *Salvation.*

Pardoned...See *Pardon; Salvation;* and *Sin, Salvation from.*

Happiness...See *Blessedness; Joy;* and *Righteous, Blessedness of.*

Harvest Songs...167, 169, 171, 176-178, 286, 393, 402

Heart:

Broken and Contrite...91, 140, 141, 143, 144, 402, 403

Claimed of God...6, 57, 59, 83, 140-144, 174, 254, 354-356, 383, 384

Evil, Hard, and Stubborn...21, 23, 93, 156, 165, 213, 254, 255

God the Strength of...18, 19, 22, 95, 203, 354-356, 389, 390

Good, Perfect, Pure, and Upright...22, 26, 33, 35, 57, 59, 69, 70, 83, 89, 92, 94, 122, 140-142, 144, 155, 201, 204, 215, 225, 227, 229, 253, 271, 298, 299, 305, 321, 322, 325, 326, 328, 333, 334, 354-356, 366

Searching of.............31, 32, 69, 70, 383, 384

Heathen...See *Missions, Royalty of Christ,* and *Salvation.*

Heaven...28-33, 52-56, 71, 94, 125, 159, 160, 202, 203, 249. See also *Aspirations, For Heaven.*

Hell..................................16, 20, 136

Holiness:

Of Christians...76, 89, 91, 140-144, 252, 260, 271, 321, 328, 333, 335, 336, 341. See also *Aspirations, For Holiness; Righteous;* and *Salvation.*

Of God.................See *God, Holiness of.*

Holy Spirit, The...85, 141-143, 255, 287, 389-391. See also *Aspirations, Bible,* and *God.*

Home, Our Eternal..........247. See also *Heaven.*

Home Life....................271, 305, 359, 360

Hope...87, 103, 104, 106, 114-120, 161, 162, 191, 209, 213, 247, 326, 327, 330, 331, 335, 362-365, 400

Index of Subjects

Index of Subjects

Index of Subjects

Index of Subjects

Index of Subjects

THE
DOCTRINAL STANDARDS,
LITURGY, AND
CHURCH ORDER

THE CATECHISM,

OR

METHOD OF INSTRUCTION IN THE CHRISTIAN RELIGION.

AS THE SAME IS TAUGHT IN THE REFORMED CHURCHES AND SCHOOLS IN HOLLAND AND IN AMERICA.

··◁▱▷··

I. LORD'S DAY.

Question 1. What is thy only comfort in life and death?

Answer. That I with *a* body and soul, both in life and death, *b* am not my own, but belong *c* unto my faithful Savior Jesus Christ; who, with his precious *d* blood, hath fully *e* satisfied for all my sins, and delivered *f* me from all the power of the devil; and so preserves me *g* that without the will of my heavenly Father, not a hair *h* can fall from my head; yea, that all things must be *i* subservient to my salvation, and therefore, by his Holy Spirit, he also assures me *j* of eternal life, and makes *k* me sincerely willing and ready, henceforth, to live unto him.

a 1 Cor. 6 19, 20. *b* Rom. 14:7, 8, 9. *c* 1 Cor. 3:23. *d* 1 Pet. 1:18, 19. *e* 1 John 1:7. *f* 1 John 3:8. Heb. 2:14, 15. *g* John 6:39 and 10:28, 29. *h* Luke 21:18. Matt. 10:30. *i* Rom. 8:28. *j* 2 Cor. 1:22, and 5:5. *k* Rom. 8:14, and 7:22.

Q. 2. How many things are necessary for thee to know, that thou, enjoying this comfort, mayest live and die happily?

A. Three; *l* the first, how great *m* my sins and miseries are; the second, how I may be delivered *n* from all my sins and miseries; the third, how I shall express my gratitude *o* to God for such deliverance.

l Luke 24:47. *m* 1 Cor. 6:10, 11. John 9:41. Rom. 3:10, 19. *n* John 17:3. Eph. 5:8, 9, 10.

THE FIRST PART—OF THE MISERY OF MAN.

II. LORD'S DAY.

Q. 3. Whence knowest thou thy misery?

A. Out of the law of God.*a*

a Rom. 3:20

Q. 4. What doth the law of God require of us?

A. Christ teaches us that briefly, Matt. 22:37-40, "Thou shalt love the Lord thy God with all thy heart, with all thy soul, and with all thy mind, and with all thy strength. *b* This is the first and the great commandment; and the second is like unto it, Thou shalt love thy neighbor as thyself. On these two commandments hang all the law and the prophets."

b Luke 10:27.

Q. 5. Canst thou keep all these things perfectly?

A. In no wise; *c* for I am prone by nature to hate God and my neighbor.*d*

c Rom. 3:10. *1* John 1:8. *d* Rom. 8:7. Tit. 3:3.

III. LORD'S DAY.

Q. 6. Did God then create man so wicked and perverse?

A. By no means; but God created man good, *a* and after his own image, in *b* true righteousness and holiness, that he might rightly know God his Creator, heartily love him and live with him in eternal happiness to glorify and praise him.*c*

a Gen. 1:31. *b* Gen. 1:26, 27. Col. 3:10. Eph. 4:24. *c* Eph. 1:6. 1 Cor. 6:20.

Q. 7. Whence then proceeds this depravity of human nature?

A. From the fall and disobedience of our first parents, Adam and Eve, *d* in Paradise; hence our nature is become so corrupt, that we are all conceived and born in sin.*e*

d Gen. 3:6. Rom. 5:12, 18, 19. *e* Psa. 51:5. Gen. 5:3.

Q. 8. Are we then so corrupt that we are wholly incapable of doing any good, and inclined to all wickedness?

A. Indeed we are; *f* except we are regenerated by the Spirit of God.*g*

f Gen. 6:5. Job 14.4, and 15:14, 16. *g* John 3:5. Eph. 2:5.

IV. LORD'S DAY.

Q. 9. Doth not God then do injustice to man, by requiring from him in his law, that which he cannot perform?

A. Not at all; *a* for God made man capable *b* of performing it; but man, by the instigation *c* of the devil, and his own wilful disobedience, *d* deprived himself and all his posterity of those divine gifts.

a Eccl. 7:29. *b* John 8:44. 2 Cor. 11:3. *c* Gen. 3:4, 7. *d* Rom. 5:12.

Q. 10. Will God suffer such disobedience and rebellion to go unpunished?

A. By no means; *e* but is terribly displeased *f* with our original as well as actual sins; and will punish them in his just judgment temporally and eternally, as he hath declared, *g* "Cursed is every one that continueth not in all things, which are written in the book of the law, to do them."

e Psa. 5:5. *f* Rom. 1.18. Deut. 28.15. Heb. 9:27. *g* Deut. 27:26. Gal. 3:10.

Q. 11. Is not God then also merciful?

A. God is indeed merciful, *h* but also just; *i* therefore his justice requires, *j* that sin which is committed against the most high majesty of God, be also punished with extreme, that is, with everlasting *k* punishment of body and soul.

h Ex. 34:6. *i* Ex. 20:5. Job 34:10, 11. *j* Psa. 5:5, 6. *k* Gen. 2:17 Rom. 6:23.

THE SECOND PART—OF MAN'S DELIVERANCE.

V. LORD'S DAY.

Q. 12. Since then, by the righteous judgment of God, we deserve temporal and eternal punishment, is there no way by which we may escape that punishment, and be again received into favor?

A. God will have his justice *a* satisfied: and therefore we must make this full *b* satisfaction, either by ourselves, or by another.

a Ex. 20:5. *b* Deut. 24.16. 2 Cor. 5 14, 15.

Q. 13. Can we ourselves then make this satisfaction?

A. By no means; *c* but on the contrary we *d* daily increase our debt.

c Job 9:2, 3, and 15 14, 15, 16. *d* Mat. 6.12. Isa. 64 6.

Q. 14. Can there be found anywhere, one, who is a mere creature, able to satisfy for us?

A. None; for, first, God will not *e* punish any other creature for the sin which man hath committed; and further, no mere creature can sustain the burden of God's eternal wrath against sin, so as to *f* deliver others from it.

e Ezek. 18:20. *f* Rev. 5:3. Psa. 49 8, 9.

Q. 15. What sort of a mediator and deliverer then must we seek for?

A. For one who is very man, *g* and perfectly righteous; and yet more powerful than all creatures; that is, one who is also very *h* God.

g 1 Cor. 15:21. Rom. 8:3. *h* Rom. 9:5. Isa. 7:14.

VI. LORD'S DAY.

Q. 16. Why must he be very man, and also perfectly righteous?

A. Because the justice of God requires that the same human nature which hath sinned, should *a* likewise make satisfaction for sin; and one, who is himself a sinner, *b* cannot satisfy for others.

a Rom. 5:12, 15. *b* 1 Pet. 3:18. Isa. 53:11.

Q. 17. Why must he in one person be also very God?

A. That he might, by the power of his Godhead *c* sustain in his human nature, the burden of God's wrath; and might *d* obtain for, and restore to us, righteousness and life.

Q. 18. Who then is that Mediator, who is in one person both very God, and a real righteous man?

A. Our Lord Jesus Christ: *e* "who of God is made unto *f* us wisdom, and righteousness, and sanctification, and redemption."

Q. 19. Whence knowest thou this?

A. From the holy gospel, which God himself first revealed in Paradise; *g* and afterwards published by the patriarchs *h* and prophets, and represented by the sacrifices *i* and other ceremonies of the law; and lastly, has fulfilled it *j* by his only begotten Son.

VII. LORD'S DAY.

Q. 20. Are all men then, as they perished in Adam, saved by Christ?

A. No; only *a* those who are ingrafted into him, *b* and receive all his benefits, by a true faith.

Q. 21. What is true faith?

A. True faith is not only a **certain** knowledge, *c* whereby I hold for truth all that God has revealed to us in his word, but also an assured *d* confidence, which the Holy *e* Ghost works by the gospel, *f* in my heart; that not only to others, but to me also, *g* remission of sin, everlasting righteousness *h* and salvation, are freely given by God, *i* merely of grace, only for the sake of Christ's merits.

Q. 22. What is then necessary for a christian to believe?

A. All things *j* promised us in the gospel, which the articles of our catholic undoubted christian faith briefly teach us.

Q. 23. What are these articles?

A. I. I believe in God the Father, Almighty, Maker of heaven and earth:

II. And in Jesus Christ, his only begotten Son, our Lord:

III. Who was conceived by the Holy Ghost, born of the Virgin Mary:

IV. Suffered under Pontius Pilate; was crucified, dead, and buried: He descended into hell:

V. The third day he rose again from the dead:

VI. He ascended into heaven, and sitteth at the right hand of God the Father Almighty:

VII. From thence he shall come to judge the quick and the dead:

VIII. I believe in the Holy Ghost:

IX. I believe an holy catholic church: the communion of saints:

X. The forgiveness of sins:

XI. The resurrection of the body:

XII. And the life everlasting. AMEN.

VIII. LORD'S DAY.

Q. 24. How are these articles divided?

A. Into three parts; the first is of God the Father, and our creation; *a* the second of God the Son, and our redemption; *b* the third of God the Holy Ghost, and our sanctification. *c*

---

c 1 Pet. 3:18. Acts 2:24. Isa. 53:8. *d* 1 John 1:2. Jer. 23:6. 2 Tim. 1:10. John 6:51.

e Mat. 1:23. 1 Tim. 3:16. Luke 2:11. *f* 1 Cor. 1:30.

g Gen. 3:15. *h* Gen. 22:17, 18, and 28:14. Rom. 1:2. Heb. 1:1. *i* Heb. 5:46. Heb. 10:7, 8. *j* Rom. 10:4. Heb. 13:8.

a Mat. 1:21. Isa. 53:11. *b* John 1:12, 13. Rom. 11:20. Heb. 10:39.

c John 6:69. John 17:3. Heb. 11:3, 6. *d* Eph. 3:12. *e* Rom. 4:16, 20, 21. Heb. 11:1. Eph. 3:12. Rom. 1:16. 1 Cor. 1:21. Acts 16:14. Mat. 16:17. John 3:5. *f* Rom. 10:14, 17. Mat. 9:2. *g* Rom. 5:1. *h* Gal 2:20. *i* Rom. 3:24, 25, 26.

j John 20:31 Mat. 28:19, 20.

a Gen. 1. *b* 1 Pet. 1:18, 19. *c* 1 Pet. 1:21, 22.

d Deut. 6.4. e Gen.
1:26. Isa. 61:1.
John 14:16, 17. 1
John 5:7. John
1.13. Mat. 28:19.
2 Cor. 13:14.

Q. 25. Since there is but one only d divine essence, why speakest thou of Father, Son, and Holy Ghost?

A. Because God hath so e revealed himself in his word, that these three distinct persons are the one only true and eternal God.

OF GOD THE FATHER.

IX. LORD'S DAY.

Q. 26. What believest thou when thou sayest, "I believe in God the Father, Almighty, Maker of heaven and earth"?

a Gen. 1, and 2.
Psa. 33:6. b Psa.
115.3. Mat. 10:29.
Heb. 1.3. John
5 17. c John 1:12,
16. Rom. 8.15, 16.
Gal. 4 5, 6. Eph.
1 5. 1 John 3:1.
d Psa. 55.22. Mat.
6.26. e Rom. 8:28,
and 4:21. f Rom.
10:12. Mat. 6 26,
and 7:9, 10, 11.

A. That the eternal Father of our Lord Jesus Christ (who a of nothing made heaven and earth, with all that is in them; who likewise upholds and b governs the same by his eternal counsel and providence) is for the sake of Christ his Son, my God and my Father; on whom I rely so entirely, that I have no doubt, but he will provide me with all things necessary c for soul and body: and further, that he will make whatever evils he sends upon me, in this valley of tears d turn out to my advantage; for he is able to do it, being Almighty e God, and willing, being a f faithful Father.

X. LORD'S DAY.

Q. 27. What dost thou mean by the providence of God?

a Acts 17:25, 26,
27, 28. b Heb. 1 3.
c Jer. 5:24. d Acts
14:17. e John 9:3.
f Prov. 22 2. Job.
1 21. g Mat 10 29,
30. Eph. 1 11.

A. The almighty and everywhere present power of God; a whereby, as it were by his hand, he b upholds and governs heaven, earth, and all creatures; so that herbs and grass, rain c and drought, fruitful d and barren years, meat and drink, e health and sickness, f riches and poverty, yea, and all things g come, not by chance, but by his fatherly hand.

Q. 28. What advantage is it to us to know that God has created, and by his providence doth still uphold all things?

h Rom. 5.3. Psa
39.10 i Deut. 8 10.
1 Thes. 5 18. j
Rom 5.3, 4, 5, 6.
k Rom. 8 38, 39
l Job. 1 12, and
2 6. Mat. 8 31.
Isa. 10 15

A. That we may be patient in adversity h; thankful i in prosperity; and that in all things, which may hereafter befall us, we place our firm j trust in our faithful God and Father, that nothing shall k separate us from his love; since all creatures are so in his hand, that without his will they l cannot so much as move.

OF GOD THE SON.

XI. LORD'S DAY.

Q. 29. Why is the Son of God called **Jesus**, that is a Savior?

a Mat. 1 21. b Acts
4 12.

A. Because he saveth us, and delivereth us from our a sins; and likewise, because we ought not to seek, neither can find b salvation in any other.

Q. 30. Do such then believe in Jesus the only Savior, who seek their salvation and welfare of saints, of themselves, or anywhere else?

c 1 Cor 1:13, 31.
Gal. 5.4. d Col.
2 20. Isa 9 6, 7.
Col. 1:19, 20.

A. They do not; for though they boast of him in words, yet in deeds they deny c Jesus the only deliverer and Savior; for one of these two things must be true, that either Jesus is not a complete Savior; or that they, who by a true faith receive this Savior, must find all things in him d necessary to their salvation.

XII. LORD'S DAY.

Q. 31. Why is he called Christ, that is anointed?

A. Because he is ordained of God the Father, and *a* anointed with the Holy Ghost, to be our *b* chief Prophet and Teacher, who has fully revealed to us the secret counsel and will of God concerning our redemption; and to be our only High Priest, *c* who by the one sacrifice of his body, has redeemed us, and makes continual *d* intercession with the Father for us; and also to be our eternal King, *e* who governs us by his word and Spirit, and who defends and *f* preserves us in (the enjoyment of) that salvation, he has purchased for us.

> *a* Heb. 1:9. *b* Deut. 18:18. Acts 3:22. John 1:18, and 15:15. Mat. 11:27. *c* Psa. 110:4. Heb. 7:21, and 10:14. *d* Rom. 8:34. *e* Psa. 2:6. Luke 1:33. *f* Mat. 28:18. John 10:28.

Q. 32. But why art thou called a christian?

A. Because I am a member of Christ *g* by faith, and thus am partaker *h* of his anointing; that so I may *i* confess his name, and present myself a living *j* sacrifice of thankfulness to him: and also that with a free and good conscience I may fight against sin and *k* Satan in this life: and afterwards *l* reign with him eternally, over all creatures.

> *g* 1 Cor. 6:15. *h* 1 John 2:27. Joel 2:28. *i* Mat. 10:32. *j* Rom. 12:1. *k* Eph. 6:11, 12. 1 Tim. 1:18, 19. *l* 2 Tim 2:12.

XIII. LORD'S DAY.

Q. 33. Why is Christ called the only begotten Son of God, since we are also the children of God?

A. Because Christ alone is the eternal and natural Son of *a* God; but we are children *b* adopted of God, by grace, for his sake.

> *a* John 1:1. Heb. 1:2. *b* Rom. 8:15, 16, 17. Eph. 1:5, 6.

Q. 34. Wherefore callest thou him our Lord?

A. Because he hath redeemed us, both soul and body, from all our sins, not with gold or silver, *c* but with his precious blood, and hath delivered us from all the power of the devil; and thus hath made us his own property.

> 1 Pet. 1:18, 19. 1 Cor. 6:20

XIV. LORD'S DAY.

Q. 35. What is the meaning of these words—"He was conceived by the Holy Ghost, born of the Virgin Mary"?

A. That God's eternal Son, who *a* is, and continueth true and eternal *b* God, took upon him the very nature of man, of the flesh and *c* blood of the Virgin Mary, by the operation of the Holy Ghost; *d* that he might also be the true seed of David, *e* like unto his brethren in all things, *f* sin excepted.

> *a* John 1:1. Col. 1:15. Psa. 2:7. *b* Rom. 9:5. 1 John 5:20. *c* John 1:14. Gal. 4:4. *d* Mat. 1:18. Luke 1:35 *e* Psa. 132:2. Acts 2:30. Rom. 1:3. *f* Phil. 2:7. Heb 4:15.

Q. 36. What profit dost thou receive by Christ's holy conception and nativity?

A. That he is our *g* Mediator; and with His innocence and perfect holiness, covers in the sight of *h* God, my sins, wherein I was conceived and brought forth.

> *g* Heb. 2:16, 17 *h* Psa. 32:1. 1 Cor. 1:30. Rom. 8:34.

XV. LORD'S DAY.

Q. 37. What dost thou understand by the words, "He suffered"?

A. That he, all the time that he lived on earth, but especially at the end of his life, *a* sustained in body and soul, the wrath of God against the sins of all mankind: that so by his passion, as the only *b* propitiatory sacrifice, he might redeem our body and soul from everlasting damnation, and obtain for us the favor of God, righteousness and eternal life.

> *a* 1 Pet. 2:24. Isa. 53:12. *b* 1 John 2:2. Rom. 3:25.

Q. 38. Why did he suffer under Pontius Pilate, as judge?

A. That he, being innocent, and yet condemned *c* by a temporal judge, might thereby free us from the severe judgment of God to which we were exposed.*d*

> *c* Luke 23:14. John 19:4. Psa. 69:4. *d* Gal. 3:13, 14.

Q. 39. Is there anything more in his being crucified, **than** if he had died some other death?

A. Yes [there is]; for thereby I am assured, that he took on him the curse which lay upon me; for the death of the cross was e accursed of God.

Deut. 21:23. Gal. 3:13.

XVI. LORD'S DAY.

Q. 40. Why was it necessary for Christ to humble himself even unto death?

A. Because with respect to the justice and truth of God, satisfaction for our sins could be made a no otherwise, than by the death of the Son b of God.

a Gen. 2:17. b Heb. 2:9 ,10. Phil. 2:8.

Q. 41. Why was he also "buried"?

A. Thereby to prove that he c was really dead.

c Acts 13:29. Mark 15:43,46

Q. 42. Since then Christ died for us, why must we also die?

A. Our death is not a satisfaction for our sins, but only an abolishing of sin, and a passage into d eternal life.

d John 5:24. Phil. 1:23.

Q. 43. What further benefit do we receive from the sacrifice and death of Christ on the cross?

A. That by virtue thereof, our old man is crucified, dead and e buried with him; that so the corrupt inclinations of the flesh may no more f reign in us; but that we may g offer ourselves unto him a sacrifice of thanksgiving.

e Rom. 6:6, 7 &c. f Rom. 6:12. g Rom. 12:1.

Q. 44. Why is there added, "he descended into hell"?

A. That in my greatest temptations, I may be assured, and wholly comfort myself in this, that my Lord Jesus Christ, by his inexpressible anguish, pains, terrors, and hellish agonies, in which he was plunged during all his sufferings, but especially on the cross, hath h delivered me from the anguish and torments of hell.

h Isa. 53:10. Mat. 7:46.

XVII. LORD'S DAY.

Q. 45. What doth the resurrection of Christ profit us?

A. First, by his resurrection he has overcome death, that he might a make us partakers of that righteousness which he had purchased for us by his death; secondly, we are also by his power b raised up to a new life; and lastly, the resurrection of Christ is a c sure pledge of our blessed resurrection.

a 1 Cor. 15:16. b Rom. 6:4. Col. 3:1, &c. c 1 Cor. 15. Rom. 8:11.

XVIII. LORD'S DAY.

Q. 46. How dost thou understand these words, "he ascended into heaven"?

A. That Christ, in sight of his disciples, was a taken up from earth into heaven; and that he continues b there for our interest, until he comes again to judge the quick and the dead.

a Acts 1:9. Mark 16:19. b Heb. 4:14. Rom. 8:34. Eph. 4:10.

Q. 47. Is not Christ then with us even to the end of the world, as he hath promised?

A. Christ is very man and very God; with respect to his c human nature, he is no more on earth; but with respect to his Godhead, majesty, grace and spirit, he is at no time absent from us.

c Acts 3:21. John 3:13. John 16:28. Mat. 28:20.

Q. 48. But if his human nature is not present, wherever his Godhead is, are not then these two natures in Christ separated from one another?

A. Not at all, for since the Godhead is illimitable and d omnipresent, it must necessarily follow that e the same is beyond the limits of the human nature he assumed, and yet is nevertheless in this human nature, and remains personally united to it.

d Acts 7:49. Mat. 24:30. e Mat. 28:20. John 16:28, and 17:11. John 3:13.

Q. 49. Of what advantage to us is Christ's ascension into heaven?

A. First, that he is our *g* advocate in the presence of his Father in heaven; secondly, that we have our flesh in heaven as a sure pledge that he, as the head, will also *h* take up to himself, us, his members; thirdly, that he *i* sends us his Spirit as an earnest, by whose power we "seek the things which are above, where Christ sitteth on the right hand of God, *j* and not things on earth."

g Heb. 9:24. 1 John 2:2. Rom. 8:34. *h* John 14:2. Eph. 2:6. *i* John 14:16. 2 Cor. 1:22. 2 Cor. 5:5. *j* Col. 3:1. Phil. 3:20.

XIX. LORD'S DAY.

Q. 50. Why is it added, "and sitteth at the right hand of God"?

A. Because Christ is ascended into heaven for this end, that he might *a* appear as head of his church, by whom the Father *b* governs all things.

a Eph. 1:20, 21, 22. Col. 1:18. *b* Mat. 28:18. John 5:22.

Q. 51. What profit is this glory of Christ, our head, unto us?

A. First, that by his Holy Spirit he *c* pours out heavenly graces upon us his members; and then that by his power he defends *d* and preserves us against all enemies.

c Eph. 4:8. *d* Psa. 2:9. John 10:28.

Q. 52. What comfort is it to thee that "Christ shall come again to judge the quick and the dead"?

A. That in all my sorrows and persecutions, with uplifted head *e* I look for the very same person, who before offered himself for my sake, to the tribunal of God, and has removed all curse from me, to come as judge from heaven: who shall cast all his *f* and my enemies into everlasting condemnation, but shall translate *g* me with all his chosen ones to himself, into heavenly joys and glory.

e Luke 21:28. Rom. 8:23, 24. 1 Thes. 4:16. *f* 2 Thes. 1:6, 7, 8, 9. Mat. 25:41. *g* Mat. 25:34.

OF GOD THE HOLY GHOST.

XX. LORD'S DAY.

Q. 53. What dost thou believe concerning the Holy Ghost?

A. First, that he is true and co-eternal God with the Father and the *a* Son; secondly, that he is also given *b* me, to *c* make me by a true faith, partaker of Christ and all his benefits, that he may *d* comfort me and *e* abide with me for ever.

a Gen. 1:2. Isa. 48:16. 1 Cor. 3:16. *b* Mat. 28:19. 2 Cor. 1:22. *c* Gal. 3:14. 1 Pet. 1:2. *d* Acts 9:31. *e* John 14:16. 1 Pet. 4:14.

XXI. LORD'S DAY.

Q. 54. What believest thou concerning the "holy catholic church" of Christ?

A. That the Son of God *a* from the *b* beginning to the end of the world, gathers, *c* defends, and *d* preserves to himself by his *e* Spirit and word, out of the *f* whole human race, a *g* church chosen to everlasting life, agreeing in true faith; and that I am and for ever shall remain, a *h* living member thereof.

a John 10:11. *b* Gen. 26:4. *c* Rom. 9:24. Eph. 1:10. *d* John 10:16. *e* Isa. 59:21. *f* Deut. 10:14, 15. *g* Acts 13:48. *h* 1 Cor. 1:8, 9. Rom. 8:35, &c.

Q. 55. What do you understand by "the communion of saints"?

A. First, that all and every one, who believes, being members of Christ, are in common, *i* partakers of him, and of all his riches and gifts; secondly, that every one must know it to be his duty, readily and *j* cheerfully to employ his gifts, for the advantage and salvation of other members.

i John 1:3, 4, Rom. 8:32. 1 Cor. 12:13. *j* 1 Cor. 13:5. Phil. 2:4, 5, 6.

Q. 56. What believest thou concerning "the forgiveness of sins"?

A. That God, for the sake of *k* Christ's satisfaction, will no more *l* remember my sins, neither my corrupt nature, against which I have to struggle all my life long; but will graciously impute to me the righteousness of Christ, that I may never be *m* condemned before the tribunal of God.

k 1 John 2:2. 2 Cor 5:19, 21. *l* Jer. 31:34. Psa. 103:3, 4, 10, 11. Rom. 8:1, 2, 3. *m* John 3:18.

XXII. LORD'S DAY.

Q. 57. What comfort doth the "resurrection of the body" afford thee?

a Luke 23:43. Phil. 1:23. *b* 1 Cor. 15:53. Job 19:25, 26.

A. That not only my soul after this life shall be immediately taken *a* up to Christ its head; but also, that this my body, being raised by the power of Christ, shall be reunited with my soul, and *b* made like unto the glorious body of Christ.

Q. 58. What comfort takest thou from the article of "life everlasting"?

c 2 Cor. 5:2, 3, 6. Rom. 14:17. *d* Psa. 10:11. *e* 1 Cor. 2:9.

A. That *c* since I now feel in my heart the beginning of eternal joy, after this life, *d* I shall inherit perfect salvation, which *e* "eye hath not seen, nor ear heard, neither hath it entered into the heart of man" to conceive, and that, to praise God therein for ever.

XXIII. LORD'S DAY.

Q. 59. But what doth it profit thee now that thou believest all this?

a Rom. 5:1. Rom. 1:17. John 3:36.

A. That I am righteous in Christ, before God, and an heir of eternal life.*a*

Q. 60. How art thou righteous before God?

b Rom. 3:22, &c. Gal. 2:16. Eph. 2:8, 9. *c* Rom. 3:9, &c. *d* Rom. 7:23. *e* Rom. 3:24. *f* Tit. 3:5. Eph. 2:8, 9. *g* Rom. 4:4, 5. 2 Cor. 5:19. *h* 1 John 2:1. *i* Rom. 3:24, 25. *j* 2 Cor. 5:21. *k* Rom. 3:28. ohn 3:18.

A. Only *b* by a true faith in Jesus Christ; so that, though my conscience accuse me, that I have grossly transgressed all the commandments of God, and *c* kept none of them, and am still *d* inclined to all evil; notwithstanding, God, without any *e* merit of mine, but only of mere *f* grace, grants *g* and *h* imputes to me, the perfect *i* satisfaction, righteousness and holiness of Christ; even so, as if I never had had, nor committed any sin: yea, as if I had fully *j* accomplished all that obedience which Christ has accomplished for me; *k* inasmuch as I embrace such benefit with a believing heart.

Q. 61. Why sayest thou, that thou art righteous by faith only?

l Psa. 16:2. Eph. 2:8, 9. *m* 1 Cor. 1:30. 1 Cor. 2:2. *n* 1 John 5:10.

A. Not that I am acceptable to God, on account of the *l* worthiness of my faith; but because only the satisfaction, righteousness, and holiness of Christ, is my righteousness before *m* God; and that I cannot receive *n* and apply the same to myself any other way than by faith only.

XXIV. LORD'S DAY.

Q. 62. But why cannot our good works be the whole, or part of our righteousness before God?

a Gal. 3:10. Deut. 17:26. *b* Isa. 64:6.

A. Because, that the righteousness, which can be approved of before the tribunal of God, must be absolutely perfect, and in all respects *a* conformable to the divine law; and also, that our best works in this life are all imperfect and *b* defiled with sin.

Q. 63. What! do not our good works merit, which yet God will reward in this and in a future life?

c Luke 17:10.

A. This reward is not of merit, but of grace.*c*

Q. 64. But doth not this doctrine make men careless and profane?

d Mat. 7:17, 18. John 15:5.

A. By no means: for it is impossible that those, who are implanted into Christ by a true faith, should not bring forth fruits of *d* thankfulness.

OF THE SACRAMENTS.

XXV. LORD'S DAY.

Q. 65. Since then we are made partakers of Christ and all his benefits by faith only, whence doth this faith proceed?

A. From the Holy Ghost, who works *a* faith in our hearts by the preaching of the gospel, and *b* confirms it by the use of the sacraments.

a Eph. 2:8, and 6:23. Phil. 1:29. *b* Mat. 28:19. Rom. 4:11.

Q. 66. What are the sacraments?

A. The sacraments are holy visible signs and seals, appointed of God for this end, that by the use thereof, he may the more fully declare and seal to us the promise of the gospel, viz., that he grants us freely the remission of sin, and *c* life eternal, for the sake of that one sacrifice of Christ, accomplished on the cross.

c Gen. 17:11. Rom. 4:11. Ex. 12. Lev. 6:25. Acts 22:16, and 2:38. Mat. 26:28.

Q. 67. Are both word and sacraments, then, ordained and appointed for this end, that they may direct our faith to the sacrifice of Jesus Christ on the cross, as the only ground of our salvation?

A. Yes, indeed: for the Holy Ghost teaches us in the gospel, and assures us by the sacraments, *d* that the whole of our salvation depends upon that one sacrifice of Christ which he offered for us on the cross.

d Rom. 6:3. Gal. 3:27.

Q. 68. How many sacraments has Christ instituted in the new covenant, or testament?

A. *e* Two: namely, holy baptism, and the holy supper.

1 Cor. 10:2, 3, 4.

OF HOLY BAPTISM.

XXVI. LORD'S DAY.

Q. 69. How art thou admonished and assured by holy baptism, that the one sacrifice of Christ upon the cross is of real advantage to thee?

A. Thus: 'That Christ appointed *a* this external washing with water, adding thereto this *b* promise, that I am as certainly washed by his blood and Spirit from all the pollution of my soul, that is, from all my sins, as I am *c* washed externally with water, by which the filthiness of the body is commonly washed away.

a Mat. 28:19. Acts 2:38. *b* Mark 16: 16. Mat. 3:11. Rom. 6:3. *c* Mark 1:4. Luke 3:3.

Q. 70. What is it to be washed with the blood and Spirit of Christ?

A. It is to receive of God the remission of sins, freely, for the sake of Christ's blood, which he *d* shed for us by his sacrifice upon the cross; and also to be renewed by the Holy Ghost, and sanctified to be members of Christ, that so we may more and more die unto sin, and *e* lead holy and unblamable lives.

d Heb. 12:24. 1 Pet. 1:2. *e* John 1:33. Rom. 6:4. Col. 2:11.

Q. 71. Where has Christ promised us, that he will as certainly wash us by his blood and Spirit, as we are washed with the water of baptism?

A. In the institution of baptism, which is thus expressed: " *f* Go ye, therefore, and teach all nations, baptizing them in the name of the Father, and of the Son, and of the Holy Ghost *g*," "he that believeth, and is baptized, shall be saved; but he that believeth not, shall be damned." This promise is also repeated, where the scripture calls baptism the *h* washing of regeneration, and the washing *i* away of sins.

f Mat. 28:19. *g* Mark 16:16. *h* Tit. 3:5. *i* Acts 22:16.

XXVII. LORD'S DAY.

Q. 72. Is then the external baptism with water the washing away of sin itself?

a Mat. 3:11. 1 Pet. 3:21. *b* 1 John 1:7. 1 Cor. 6:11.

A. Not at all: for the *a* blood of Jesus Christ only, and the Holy Ghost cleanse us from all *b* sin.

Q. 73. Why then doth the Holy Ghost call baptism "the washing of regeneration," and "the washing away of sins"?

c Rev. 1:5. 1 Cor. 6:11. *d* Mark 16:16. Gal. 3:27.

A. God speaks thus not without great cause, to-wit, not only thereby to teach us, that as the filth of the body is purged away by water, so our sins are *c* removed by the blood and Spirit of Jesus Christ; but especially that by *d* this divine pledge and sign he may assure us, that we are spiritually cleansed from our sins as really, as we are externally washed with water.

Q. 74. Are infants also to be baptized?

e Gen. 17:7. Acts 2:39. *f* 1 Cor. 7:14. Joel 2:16. *g* Mat. 19:14. *h* Luke 1: 14, 15. Psa. 22:10. Acts 2:39. *i* Acts 10:47. 1 Cor. 12: 13, and 7:14. *j* Gen. 17:14. *k* Col. 2:11, 12, 13.

A. Yes: for since they, as well as the adult, are included in the *e* covenant and *f* church of God; and since *g* redemption from sin by the blood of Christ, and the *h* Holy Ghost, the author of faith, is promised to them no less than to the adult; they must therefore by baptism, as a sign of the covenant, be also admitted into the christian church; and be distinguished *i* from the children of unbelievers as was done in the old covenant or testament by *j* circumcision, instead of which *k* baptism is instituted in the new covenant.

OF THE HOLY SUPPER OF OUR LORD JESUS CHRIST.

XXVIII. LORD'S DAY.

Q. 75. How art thou admonished and assured in the Lord's Supper, that thou art a partaker of that one sacrifice of Christ, accomplished on the cross, and of all his benefits?

a Mat. 26:26, 27, 28. Mark 14:22, 23, 24. Luke 22:19, 20. 1 Cor. 10:16, 17, and 11:23, 24, 25.

A. Thus: That Christ has commanded me and all believers, to eat of this broken bread, and to drink of this cup, in remembrance of him, *a* adding these promises: first, that his body was offered and broken on the cross for me, and his blood shed for me, as certainly as I see with my eyes, the bread of the Lord broken for me, and the cup communicated to me; and further, that he feeds and nourishes my soul to everlasting life, with his crucified body and shed blood, as assuredly as I receive from the hands of the minister, and taste with my mouth the bread and cup of the Lord, as certain signs of the body and blood of Christ.

Q. 76. What is it then to eat the crucified body, and drink the shed blood of Christ?

b John 6:35, 40, 47, 48, 50, 51, 53, 54. *c* John 6:55, 56. *d* Acts 3:21, and 1:9, 10, 11. 1 Cor. 11:26. *e* Eph. 5:29, 30, 31, 32. 1 Cor. 6:15, 17, 19. 1 John 3:24. *f* John 6:56, 57, 58. Eph. 4:15, 16,

A. It is not only to embrace with a believing heart all the sufferings and death of Christ, and thereby to *b* obtain the pardon of sin, and life eternal; but also, besides that, to become more and more *c* united to his sacred body, by the Holy Ghost, who dwells both in Christ and in us; *d* so that we, though Christ is in heaven and we on earth, are notwithstanding "Flesh of his flesh, and bone of *e* his bone"; and that we live, *f* and are governed forever by one spirit, as members of the same body are by one soul.

Q. 77. Where has Christ promised that he will as certainly feed and nourish believers with his body and blood, as they eat of this broken bread, and drink of this cup?

A. In the institution of the supper, which is thus expressed: g "The Lord Jesus, the same night in which he was betrayed, took bread, and when he had given thanks, he brake it, and said: eat, this is my body, which is broken for you; this do in remembrance of me. After the same manner also he took the cup, when he had supped, saying: this h cup is the new testament in my blood; i this do ye, as often as ye drink it, in remembrance of me. For, as often as ye eat this bread, and drink this cup, ye do show the Lord's death till he come."

This promise is repeated by the holy apostle Paul, where he says: j "The cup of blessing which we bless, is it not the communion of the blood of Christ? The bread which we break, is it not the communion of the body of Christ? For we, being many, are one bread and one body; because we are all partakers of that one bread."

g 1 Cor. 11:23. Mat. 26:26. Mark 14:22. Luke 22:19. *h* Ex. 24:8. Heb. 9:20. *i* Ex. 13:9. 1 Cor. 11:26. *j* 1 Cor. 10:16, 17.

XXIX. LORD'S DAY.

Q. 78. Do then the bread and wine become the very body and blood of Christ?

A. Not at all: a but as the water in baptism is not changed into the blood of Christ, neither is the washing away of sin itself, being only the sign and confirmation thereof appointed of God; so the bread in the Lord's supper is not changed into the very b body of Christ; though agreeably to the c nature and properties of sacraments, it is called the body of Christ Jesus.

a 1 Cor. 10:1, 2, 3, 4. 1 Pet.3:21. John 6:35, 62, 63. *b* 1 Cor. 10:16, &c., and 11:20, &c. *c* Gen. 17:10, 11, 14. Ex. 12:26, 27, 43, 48. Acts 7:8. Mat. 26:26. Mark 14:24.

Q. 79. Why then doth Christ call the bread his body, and the cup his blood, or the new covenant in his blood; and Paul the "communion of the body and blood of Christ"?

A. Christ speaks thus, not without great reason, namely, not only thereby to teach us, that as bread and wine support this temporal life, so his crucified body and shed blood are the true meat and drink, whereby our souls are d fed to eternal life; but more especially by these visible signs and pledges to assure us, that we are as really partakers of his true body and blood (by the operation of the Holy Ghost) as we e receive by the mouths of our bodies these holy signs in remembrance of him; and that all his sufferings f and obedience are as certainly ours, as if we had in our own persons suffered and made satisfaction for our sins to God.

d John 6:51, 55, 56. *e* 1 Cor. 10:16, 17, and 11:26, 27, 28. Eph. 5:30. *f* Rom. 5:9, 18, 19, and 8:4.

XXX. LORD'S DAY.

Q. 80. What difference is there between the Lord's supper and the popish mass?

A. The Lord's supper testifies to us, that we have a full pardon of all sin a by the only sacrifice of Jesus Christ, which he himself has once accomplished on the cross; and, that we by the Holy Ghost are ingrafted b into Christ, who, according to his human nature is now not on earth, but in c heaven, at the right hand of God his Father, and will there d be worshipped by us: — but the mass teaches, that the living and dead have not the pardon of sins through the sufferings of Christ, unless Christ is also daily offered for them by the priests; and further, that Christ is bodily under the form of bread and wine, and therefore is to be worshipped in them; so that the mass, at bottom, is nothing else than a e denial of the one sacrifice and sufferings of Jesus Christ, and an accursed idolatry

a Heb. 7:27, and 9:12, 26. Mat. 26:28. Luke 22:19, 20. 2 Cor. 5:21. *b* 1 Cor. 6 and 17, and 12:13. *c* Heb. 1:3, and 8:1, &c. *d* John 4:21, 22, 23. Col. 3:1. Phil. 3: 20. Luke 24:52, 53. Acts 7:55. *e* Isa. 1:11, 14. Mat. 15:9. Col. 2:22, 23. Jer. 2:13.

g Mat. 5:3, 6. Luke 7:37, 38, and 15: 18, 19. b Psa. 103: 3. i Psa. 116:12, 13, 14. 1 Pet. 2:11, 12. j 1 Cor. 10:20, &c., and 11:28, &c. Tit. 1:16. Psa. 50: 15, 16.

Q. 81. For whom is the Lord's supper instituted?
A. For those who are truly sorrowful *g* for their sins, and yet trust that these are forgiven them for the sake of Christ; and that their remaining infirmities *h* are covered by his passion and death; and who also earnestly *i* desire to have their faith more and more strengthened, and their lives more holy; but hypocrites, and such as turn not to God with sincere hearts, eat and *j* drink judgment to themselves.

Q. 82. Are they also to be admitted to this supper, who, by confession and life, declare themselves unbelieving and ungodly?

k 1 Cor. 10:21, and 11:30, 31. Isa. 1: 11, 13. Jer. 7:21. Psa. 50:16, 22. l Mat. 18:17, 18.

A. No; for by this, the covenant of God would be profaned, and his wrath *k* kindled against the whole congregation; therefore it is the duty of the christian church, according to the appointment of *l* Christ and his apostles, to exclude such persons, by the keys of the kingdom of heaven, till they show amendment of life.

XXXI. LORD'S DAY.

Q. 83. What are *a* the keys of the kingdom of heaven?

a Mat. 16:19. b John 20, 23. c Mat. 18:15-18.

A. The preaching *b* of the holy gospel, and christian discipline, *c* or excommunication out of the christian church; by these two, the kingdom of heaven is opened to believers, and shut against unbelievers.

Q. 84. How is the kingdom of heaven opened and shut by the preaching of the holy gospel?

d Mat. 28:19. e John 3:18, 36. Mark 16:16. f 2 Thes. 1:7, 8, 9. g John 20:21, 22, 23. Mat. 16:19. Rom. 2:2, 13-17.

A. Thus: when according to the command of *d* Christ, it is declared and publicly testified to all and every believer, that, whenever they *e* receive the promise of the gospel by a true faith, all their sins are really forgiven them of God, for the sake of Christ's merits; and on the contrary, when it is declared and testified to all unbelievers, and such as do not sincerely repent, that they stand exposed to the wrath of God, and eternal *f* condemnation, so long as they are *g* unconverted: according to which testimony of the gospel, God will judge them, both in this, and in the life to come.

Q. 85. How is the kingdom of heaven shut and opened by christian discipline?

h Mat. 18:15. i Cor. 5:12. j Mat. 18:15-18. k Rom. 12:7, 8, 9. 1 Cor. 12:28. 1 Tim. 5:17. 2 Thes. 3:14. l Mat. 18:17. 1 Cor. 5:3, 4, 5. m 2 Cor. 2:6, 7, 8, 10, 11. Luke 15:18.

A. Thus: when according *h* to the command of Christ, those, who under the name of christians, maintain doctrines, or practices *i* inconsistent therewith, and will not, after having been often brotherly admonished, renounce their errors and wicked course of life, are complained of to the church, *j* or to those, who are thereunto *k* appointed by the church; and if they despise their admonition, *l* are by them forbidden the use of the sacraments; whereby they are excluded from the christian church, and by God himself from the kingdom of Christ; and when they promise and show real amendment, are again *m* received as members of Christ and his church.

THE THIRD PART—OF THANKFULNESS.

XXXII. LORD'S DAY.

Q. 86. Since then we are delivered from our misery, merely of grace, through Christ, without any merit of ours, why must we still do good works?

a 1 Cor. 6:19, 20. Rom. 6:13, and 12: 1, 2. 1 Pet. 2:5, 9, 10. b Mat. 5:16. 1 Pet. 2:12. c 2 Pet. 1:10. Gal. 5:6, 24. d 1 Pet. 3:1, 2. Mat. 5:16. Rom. 14:19.

A. Because Christ, having redeemed and delivered us by his blood, also renews us by his Holy Spirit, after his own image; that so we may testify, by the whole of our conduct, our gratitude *a* to God for his blessings, and that he may be *b* praised by us; also, that every one may be *c* assured in himself of his faith, by the fruits thereof; and that, by our godly conversation, others may be *d* gained to Christ.

Q. 87. Cannot they then be saved, who, continuing in their wicked and ungrateful lives, are not converted to God?

A. By no means; for the holy scripture declares *e* that no unchaste person, idolator, adulterer, thief, covetous man, drunkard, slanderer, robber, or any such like, shall inherit the kingdom of God.

e 1 Cor. 6:9, 10. Eph. 5:5, 6. 1 John 3:14, 15. Gal. 5:21.

XXXIII. LORD'S DAY.

Q. 88. Of how many parts doth the true conversion of man consist?

A. Of two parts; of *a* the mortification of the old, and the quickening of the new man.

a Rom. 6:4, 5, 6. Eph. 4:22, 23. Col. 3:5. 1 Cor. 5:7.

Q. 89. What is the mortification of the old man?

A. It is a *b* sincere sorrow of heart, that we have provoked God by our sins; and more and more to hate and flee from them.

b Psa. 51:3, 8, 17. Luke 15:18. Rom. 8:13. Joel 1:12, 13.

Q. 90. What is the quickening of the new man?

A. It is a sincere joy of heart in God, through Christ, *c* and with love and *d* delight to live according to the will of God in all good works.

c Rom. 5:1, 2, and 14:17. Isa. 57:15. *d* Rom. 6:10, 11 1 Pet. 4:2. Gal. 2:20.

Q. 91. But what are good works?

A. Only those which proceed from a true *e* faith, are performed according to the *f* law of God, and to his *g* glory; and not such as are *h* founded on our imaginations, or the institutions of men.

e Rom. 14:23. *f* 1 Sam. 15:22. Eph. 2:2, 10. *g* 1 Cor. 10:31. *h* Deut. 12: 32. Ezek. 20:18. Mat. 15:9.

XXXIV. LORD'S DAY.

Q. 92. What is the law of God?

A. God spake all these words, Exodus 20, Deut. 5, saying: I am the Lord thy God, which hath brought thee out of the land of Egypt, out of the house of bondage.

I. Thou shalt have no other gods before me.

II. Thou shalt not make unto thyself any graven image, nor the likeness of any thing that is in heaven above, or in the earth beneath, or in the water under the earth. Thou shalt not bow down thyself to them, nor serve them; for I, the Lord thy God, am a jealous God, visiting the iniquity of the fathers upon the children, unto the third and fourth generation of them that hate me, and showing mercy unto thousands of them that love me, and keep my commandments.

III. Thou shalt not take the name of the Lord thy God in vain; for the Lord will not hold him guiltless, that taketh his name in vain.

IV. Remember the Sabbath day, to keep it holy; six days shalt thou labor and do all thy work; but the seventh day is the Sabbath of the Lord thy God; in it thou shalt do no manner of work, thou, nor thy son, nor thy daughter, thy man servant, nor thy maid servant, nor thy cattle, nor thy stranger that is within thy gates. For in six days the Lord made heaven and earth, the sea, and all that in them is, and rested the seventh day: wherefore the Lord blessed the Sabbath day, and hallowed it.

V. Honor thy father and thy mother, that thy days may be long in the land which the Lord thy God giveth thee.

VI. Thou shalt not kill.

VII. Thou shalt not commit adultery.

VIII. Thou shalt not steal.

IX. Thou shalt not bear false witness against thy neighbor.

X. Thou shalt not covet thy neighbor's house; thou shalt not covet thy neighbor's wife, nor his man servant, nor his maid servant, nor his ox, nor his ass, nor any thing that is thy neighbor's.

a Ex. 34:28, 29. b Deut. 4:13, and 10:3, 4.

Q. 93. How are these commandments divided?

A. Into two a tables; the b first of which teaches us how we must behave towards God; the second, what duties we owe to our neighbor.

c 1 Cor. 6:9, 10, and 10:7, 14. d Lev. 18:21. Deut. 18:10, 11, 12. e Mat. 4:10. Rev. 19:10. f John 17:3. g Jer. 17:5, 7. h Heb. 10:36. Col. 1:11. Rom. 5:3, 4. Phil. 2:14. i 1 Pet. 5:5, 6. j Psa. 104 27. Isa. 45:7. James 1:17. k Deut. 6:5. Mat. 22:37. l Deut. 6:5. Mat. 10:28. m Mat. 4:10. n Mat. 5:29, 30. Acts 5:29. Mat. 10:37. o Mat. 5:19.

Q. 94. What doth God enjoin in the first commandment?

A. That I, as sincerely as I desire the salvation of my own soul, avoid and flee from all idolatry, c sorcery, d soothsaying, superstition, e invocation of saints, or any other creatures; and learn f rightly to know the only true God; g trust in him alone, with humility h and patience i submit to him; j expect all good things from him only; k love, l fear, and m glorify him with my whole heart; so that I renounce n and forsake all creatures, rather than o commit even the least thing contrary to his will.

Q. 95. What is idolatry?

A. Idolatry is, instead of, or besides that one true God, who has manifested himself in his word, to contrive, or have any other object, in which men place their trust.p

p 2 Chron. 16:12. Phil. 3:18, 19. Gal. 4:8. Eph. 2:12.

XXXV. LORD'S DAY.

Q. 96. What doth God require in the second commandment?

A. That we in no wise a represent God by images, nor worship b him in any other way than he has commanded in his word.

a Deut. 4:15. Isa. 40:18. Rom. 1:23, &c. b 1 Sam. 15:23. Deut. 12:30.

Q. 97. Are images then not at all to be made?

A. God neither can, nor c may be represented by any means: but as to creatures; though they may be represented, yet God forbids to make, or have any resemblance of them, either in order to worship them d or to serve God by them.

c Deut. 4:15, 16. Isa. 46 5. Rom. 1:23. d Ex. 23:24, and 34:13, 14. Numb. 33:52. Deut. 7:5.

Q. 98. But may not images be tolerated in the churches, as books to the laity?

A. No: for we must not pretend to be wiser than God, who will have his people e taught, not by dumb images, f but by the lively preaching of his word.

e 2 Tim. 3:16. 2 Pet. 1:19. f Jer. 10:1, &c. Hab. 2:18, 19.

XXXVI. LORD'S DAY.

Q. 99. What is required in the third commandment?

A. That we, not only by cursing or a perjury, but also by b rash swearing, must not profane or abuse the name of God; nor by silence or connivance be partakers of these horrible sins in others; and, briefly, that we use the holy name of c God no otherwise than with fear and reverence; so that he may be rightly d confessed and e worshipped by us, and be glorified in all our words and works.

a Lev. 24:11, and 19:12. Mat. 5:37. Lev. 5:4. b Isa. 45:23, 24. c Mat. 10:32. d 1 Tim. 2:8. e 1 Cor. 3:16 17.

Q. 100. Is then the profaning of God's name, by swearing and cursing, so heinous a sin, that his wrath is kindled against those who do not endeavor, as much as in them lies, to prevent and forbid such cursing and swearing?

A. It undoubtedly is, f for there is no sin greater or more provoking to God, than the profaning of his name; and therefore he has commanded this g sin to be punished with death.

f Lev. 5:1. g Lev. 24:15.

XXXVII. LORD'S DAY.

Q. 101. May we then swear religiously by the name of God?

A. Yes: either when the magistrates demand it of the subjects; or when necessity requires us thereby to confirm a fidelity and truth to the glory of God, and the safety of our neighbor: for such an oath is b founded on God's word, and therefore was justly c used by the saints, both in the Old and New Testament.

a Ex. 22:11. Neh. 13:25. b Deut. 6: 13. Heb. 6:16. c Gen. 21:24. Jos. 9:15, 19. 1 Sam. 24:22. 2 Cor. 1:23. Rom. 1:9.

Q. 102. May we also swear by saints or any other creatures?
A. No; for a lawful oath is calling upon God, as the only one who knows the heart, that he will bear witness to the truth, and punish me if I swear *d* falsely; which honor is *e* due to no creature.

d 2 Cor. 1:23.
e Mat. 5:34, 35.

XXXVIII. LORD'S DAY.

Q. 103. What doth God require in the fourth commandment?
A. First, that the ministry of the gospel and the schools be *a* maintained; and that I, especially on the sabbath, *b* that is, on the day of rest, *c* diligently frequent *d* the church of God, to hear his word, to use the sacraments, *e* publicly to call upon the Lord, and contribute to the relief of the *f* poor, as becomes a christian. Secondly, that all the days of my life I cease from my evil works, and yield myself to the Lord, to work by his Holy Spirit in me: and thus *g* begin in this life the eternal sabbath.

a Deut. 12:19. Tit. 1:5. 1 Tim. 3:14, 15. 1 Cor. 9:11. 2 Tim. 2:2, and 1 Tim. 3:15. *b* Lev. 23:3. *c* Acts 2:42, 46. 1 Cor. 14:19, 29, 31. *d* 1 Cor. 11:33. *e* 1 Tim. 2:1, *f* 1 Cor. 16:2. *g* Isa. 66:23.

XXXIX. LORD'S DAY.

Q. 104. What doth God require in the fifth commandment?
A. That I show all honor, love and fidelity, to my father and mother, and all in authority over me, and *a* submit myself to their good instruction and correction, with due obedience; and also patiently bear with their *b* weaknesses and infirmities, since it pleases *c* God to govern us by their hand.

a Eph. 6:1, 2, &c. Col. 3:18, 20. Eph. 5:22. Rom. 1:31. *b* Prov. 23:22. *c* Eph. 6:5, 6. Col. 3:19, 21. Rom. 13:1-8. Mat. 22:21.

XL. LORD'S DAY.

Q. 105. What doth God require in the sixth commandment?
A. That neither in thoughts, nor words, nor gestures, much less in deeds, I dishonor, hate, wound, or *a* kill my neighbor, by myself or by another; but that I lay *b* aside all desire of revenge: also, that I *c* hurt not myself, nor wilfully expose myself to any danger. Wherefore also the magistrate *d* is armed with the sword, to prevent murder.

a Mat. 5:21, 22. Prov. 12:18. Mat. 26:52. *b* Eph. 4:26. Rom. 12:19. Mat. 5:39, 40. *c* Mat. 4:5, 6, 7. Col. 2:23. *d* Gen. 9:6. Mat. 26:52. Rom. 13:4.

Q. 106. But this commandment seems only to speak of murder?
A. In forbidding murder, God teaches us, that he abhors the causes thereof, such as *e* envy, *f* hatred, anger, and desire of revenge; and that *g* he accounts all these as murder.

e James 1:20. Gal. 5:20. *f* Rom. 1:29. 1 John 2:9. *g* 1 John 3:15.

Q. 107. But is it enough that we do not kill any man in the manner mentioned above?
A. No: for when God forbids envy, hatred, and anger, he commands us to *h* love our neighbor as ourselves; to show *i* patience, peace, *j* meekness, *k* mercy, and all kindness, towards him, *l* and prevent his hurt as much as in us lies; and that we *m* do good, even to our enemies.

h Mat. 22:39, and 7:12. *i* Rom. 12:10. *j* Eph. 4:2. Gal. 6:1, 2. Mat. 5:5. Rom. 12:18. *k* Ex. 23:5. *l* Mat. 5:45. *m* Rom. 12:20.

XLI. LORD'S DAY.

Q. 108. What doth the seventh commandment teach us?
A. That all uncleanness is accursed *a* of God: and that therefore we must with all our hearts *b* detest the same, and live *c* chastely and temperately, whether in *d* holy wedlock, or in single life.

a Lev. 18:27. *b* Deut. 29:20-23. *c* 1 Thes. 4:3, 4. *d* Heb. 13:4. 1 Cor. 7:4-9.

Q. 109. Doth God forbid in this commandment, only adultery, and such like gross sins?
A. Since both our body and soul are temples of the Holy Ghost, he commands us to preserve them pure and holy: therefore he forbids all unchaste actions, *e* gestures, words, thoughts, *f* desires, and whatever *g* can entice men thereto.

e Eph. 5:3. 1 Cor. 6:18. *f* Mat. 5:28. *g* Eph. 5:18. 1 Cor. 15:33.

XLII. LORD'S DAY.

Q. 110. What doth God forbid in the eighth commandment?

A. God forbids not only those *a* thefts, and *b* robberies, which are punishable by the magistrate; but he comprehends under the name of theft all wicked tricks and devices, whereby we design to *c* appropriate to ourselves the goods which belong to our neighbor: whether it be by force, or under the appearance of right, as by unjust *d* weights, ells, *e* measures, fraudulent merchandise, false coins, *f* usury, or by any other way forbidden by God; as also all *g* covetousness, all abuse and waste of his gifts.

Q. 111. But what doth God require in this commandment?

A. That I promote the advantage of my neighbor in every instance I can or may; and deal with him as I *h* desire to be dealt with by others: further also that I faithfully labor, so that I *i* may be able to relieve the needy.

XLIII. LORD'S DAY.

Q. 112. What is required in the ninth commandment?

A. That I bear false witness *a* against no man, nor falsify *b* any man's words; that I be no backbiter, *c* nor slanderer; that I do not judge, nor join *d* in condemning any man rashly, or unheard; but that I *e* avoid all sorts of lies and deceit, as the proper works *f* of the devil, unless I would bring down upon me the heavy wrath of God; likewise, that in judgment and all other dealings I love the truth, speak it uprightly *g* and confess it; also that I defend and promote, *h* as much as I am able, the honor and good character of my neighbor.

XLIV. LORD'S DAY.

Q. 113. What doth the tenth commandment require of us?

A. That even the smallest inclination or thought, contrary to any of God's commandments, never rise in our hearts; but that at all times we hate all sin with our whole heart, *a* and delight in all righteousness.

Q. 114. But can those who are converted to God perfectly keep these commandments?

A. No: but even the holiest men, while in this life, have only a small beginning of this *b* obedience; yet so, that with a *c* sincere resolution they begin to live, not only according to some, but all the commandments of God.

Q. 115. Why will God then have the ten commandments so strictly preached, since no man in this life can keep them?

A. First, that all our lifetime we may learn *d* more and more to know our sinful nature, and thus become the more earnest in seeking the remission of sin, *e* and righteousness in Christ; likewise, that we constantly endeavor and pray to God for the grace of the Holy Spirit, that we may become more and more conformable to the image of God, till we arrive at the perfection proposed to us, in a life to come.*f*

OF PRAYER.

XLV. LORD'S DAY.

Q. 116. Why is prayer necessary for christians?

A. Because it is the chief part of *a* thankfulness which God requires of us: and also, because God will give his grace and Holy Spirit to those only, who with sincere desires continually ask them of him, and *b* are thankful for them.

Marginal references:

a 1 Cor. 6:10. *b* 1 Cor. 5:10. *c* Luke 3:14. 1 Thes. 4:6. *d* Prov. 11:1. *e* Ezek. 45:9, 10, 11. Deut. 25:13. *f* Psa. 15:5. Luke 6:35. *g* 1 Cor. 6:10.

h Mat. 7:12. *i* Prov. 5:16. Eph. 4:28.

a Prov. 19:5, 9, and 21:28. *b* Psa. 15:3. *c* Rom. 1:29, 30. *d* Mat. 7:1, &c. Luke 6:37. *e* Lev. 19:11. *f* Prov. 12:22, and 13:5. *g* 1 Cor. 13:6. Eph. 4:25. *h* 1 Pet. 4:8.

a Rom. 7:7, &c.

b Rom. 7:14. *c* Rom. 7:22, 15, &c. James 3:2.

d 1 John 1:9. Rom. 3:20, and 5:13, and 7:7. *e* Rom. 7:24. *f* 1 Cor. 9:24. Phil. 3:12, 13, 14.

a Psa. 50:14, 15. *b* Mat. 7:7, *c*. Luke 11:9, 13. Mat. 13:12. Psa. 50:15.

Q. 117. What are the requisites of that prayer, which is acceptable to God, and which he will hear?

A. First, that we from the heart pray to the one true God only, who hath *c* manifested himself in his word, for all things, he hath commanded us to ask of him; *d* secondly, that we rightly and thoroughly know our need and misery, that so we may *e* deeply humble ourselves in the presence of his divine majesty; thirdly, that we be fully persuaded that he, notwithstanding that we are *f* unworthy of it, will, for the sake of Christ our Lord, certainly *g* hear our prayer, as he has *h* promised us in his word.

Q. 118. What hath God commanded us to ask of him?

A. All *i* things necessary for soul and body; which Christ our Lord has comprised in that prayer he himself *j* has taught us.

Q. 119. What are the words of that prayer?

A. Our Father which art in heaven, Hallowed be thy name. Thy kingdom come. Thy will be done on earth, as it is in heaven. Give us this day our daily bread. And forgive us our debts, as we forgive our debtors. And lead us not into temptation, but deliver us from evil. For thine is the kingdom, and the power, and the glory, for ever. Amen.

XLVI. LORD'S DAY.

Q. 120. Why hath Christ commanded us to address God thus: "Our Father"?

A. That immediately, in the very beginning of our prayer, he might excite in us a childlike reverence for, and confidence in God, which are the foundation of our prayer: namely, that God is become our Father in Christ, *a* and will much less deny us what we ask of him in true faith, than our parents *b* will refuse us earthly things.

Q. 121. Why is it here added, "Which art in heaven"?

A. Lest we should form any *c* earthly conceptions of God's heavenly majesty, and that we *d* may expect from his almighty power all things necessary for soul and body.

XLVII. LORD'S DAY.

Q. 122. Which is the first petition?

A. *a* "Hallowed be thy name"; that is, grant us, first, rightly *b* to know thee, and to *c* sanctify, glorify and praise thee, in all thy works, in which thy power, wisdom, goodness, justice, mercy and truth, are clearly displayed; and further also, that we may so order and direct our whole lives, our thoughts, words and actions, that thy name may never be blasphemed, but rather *d* honored and praised on our account.

XLVIII. LORD'S DAY.

Q. 123. Which is the second petition?

A. *a* "Thy kingdom come"; that is, rule us so by thy word and Spirit, that we may *b* submit ourselves more and more to thee; preserve and *c* increase thy church; destroy the *d* works of the devil, and all violence which would exalt itself against thee; and also, all wicked counsels devised against thy holy word; till the full *e* perfection of thy kingdom take place, *f* wherein 'hou shalt be all in all.

XLIX. LORD'S DAY.

Q. 124. Which is the third petition?

A. *a* **"Thy will be done on earth as it is in heaven";** that is, grant that we and all men may renounce *b* our own will, and without murmuring *c* obey thy will, which is only good; that so every one may attend to, and *d* perform the duties of his station and calling, as willingly and faithfully as the *e* angels do in heaven.

a Mat. 6:10. *b* Mat. 16:24. Tit. 2:12. *c* Luke 22: 42. *d* 1 Cor. 7:24. Eph. 4:1. *e* Psa. 103:20.

L. LORD'S DAY.

Q. 125. Which is the fourth petition?

A. *a* **"Give us this day our daily bread";** that is, be pleased to provide us with all things *b* necessary for the body, that we may thereby acknowledge thee to be the only fountain of all *c* good, and that neither our care nor industry, nor even thy gifts, can *d* profit us without thy blessing; and therefore that we may withdraw our trust from all creatures, and place *e* it alone in thee.

a Mat. 6:11. *b* Psa. 145:15. Mat. 6:25, &c. *c* Acts 17:25, and 14:17. *d* 1 Cor. 15:58. Deut. 8:3. Psa. 127:1, 2. *e* Psa. 62:11, and 55: 22.

LI. LORD'S DAY.

Q. 126. Which is the fifth petition?

A. *a* **"And forgive us our debts as we forgive our debtors";** that is, be pleased for the sake of Christ's blood, *b* not to impute to us poor sinners, our transgressions, nor that depravity, which always cleaves to us; even as we feel this evidence of thy grace in us, that it is our firm resolution from the heart to *c* forgive our neighbor.

a Mat. 6:12. *b* Psa. 51:1. 1 John 2:1, 2. *c* Mat. 6:14, 15.

LII. LORD'S DAY.

Q. 127. Which is the sixth petition?

A. *a* **"And lead us not into temptation, but deliver us from evil";** that is, since we are so weak in ourselves, that we cannot stand *b* a moment; and besides this, since our mortal enemies, *c* the devil, the *d* world, and our own *e* flesh, cease not to assault us, do thou therefore preserve and strengthen us by the power of thy Holy Spirit, that we may not be overcome in this spiritual warfare, *f* but constantly and strenuously may resist our foes, till at last we *g* obtain a complete victory.

a Mat. 6:13. *b* Rom. 8:26. Psa. 103:14. *c* 1 Pet. 5:8. *d* Eph. 6:12. John 15:19. Rom. 7:23. Gal. 5:17. *f* Mat. 26: 41. Mark 13:33. *g* 1 Thes. 3:13, and 5:23.

Q. 128. How dost thou conclude thy prayer?

A. *h* **"For thine is the kingdom, and the power, and the glory, for ever";** that is, all these we ask of thee, because thou, being our King and almighty, art willing and able to *i* give us all good; and all this we pray for, that thereby not we, but thy holy name, *j* may be glorified for ever.

h Mat. 6:13. *i* Rom. 10:12. 2 Pet. 2:9. *j* John 14:13. Psa. 115:1. Phil. 4:20.

Q. 129. What doth the word "Amen" signify?

A. *k* "Amen" signifies, it shall truly and certainly be: for my prayer is more assuredly heard of God, than I feel in my heart that I desire these things of him.

k 2 Cor. 1:20. 2 Tim. 2:13.

A COMPENDIUM

OF THE CHRISTIAN RELIGION.

··◁▮▷··

Question 1. How many things are necessary for thee to know, that thou enjoying real comfort mayest live and die happily?

Answer: Three: first, how great my sins and miseries are; the second, how I may be delivered from all my sins and miseries; the third, how I shall express my gratitude to God for such deliverance.

THE FIRST PART.

OF THE MISERY OF MAN

Q. 2. Whence knowest thou thy misery?

A. Out of the law of God.

Q. 3. What hath God commanded thee in his law?

A. That is contained in the ten commandments, which he hath revealed in Scripture, as follows:

Exodus 20 and Deut. 5: 6, 7, etc. I am the Lord thy God, which have brought thee out of the land of Egypt, out of the house of bondage.

I. Thou shalt have no other gods before me.

II. Thou shalt not make unto thee any graven image, nor any likeness of any thing, that is in heaven above, or that is in the earth beneath, or that is in the water under the earth. Thou shalt not bow down thyself to them, nor serve them: for I, the Lord thy God, am a jealous God, visiting the iniquity of the fathers upon the children, unto the third and fourth generation of them that hate me, and showing mercy unto thousands of them that love me, and keep my commandments.

III. Thou shalt not take the name of the Lord thy God in vain: for the Lord will not hold him guiltless, that taketh his name in vain.

IV. Remember the Sabbath day, to keep it holy: six days shalt thou labor and do all thy work; but the seventh day is the Sabbath of the Lord thy God; in it thou shalt not do any work, thou, nor thy son, nor thy daughter, thy man-servant, nor thy maid-servant, nor thy cattle, nor thy stranger that is within thy gates; for in six days the Lord made heaven and earth, the sea, and all that in them is, and rested the seventh day: wherefore the Lord blessed the Sabbath day, and hallowed it.

V. Honor thy father and thy mother, that thy days may be long upon the land, which the Lord thy God giveth thee.

VI. Thou shalt not kill.

VII. Thou shalt not commit adultery.

VIII. Thou shalt not steal.

IX. Thou shalt not bear false witness against thy neighbor.

X. Thou shalt not covet thy neighbor's house; thou shalt not covet thy neighbor's wife, nor his man-servant, nor his maid-servant, nor his ox, nor his ass, nor anything that is thy neighbor's.

Q. 4. How are the ten commandments divided?

A. Into two tables.

Q. 5. Which is the sum of what God requires of thee in the four commandments of the first table?

A. That I love the Lord my God, with all my heart, with all my soul, with all my mind, and with all my strength: this is the first and great commandment.

Q. 6. Which is the sum of what God commands thee in the six commandments of the second table?

A. That I love my neighbor as myself: on these two commandments hang the whole law and the prophets.

Q. 7. Canst thou keep all these things perfectly?

A. In no wise: for I am prone by nature to hate God and my neighbor; and to transgress the commandments of God in thought, word, and deed.

Q. 8. Hath God created thee naturally so wicked and perverse?

A. By no means: but he created me good and after his own image, in the true knowledge of God, in righteousness and in holiness.

Q. 9. Whence then proceeds that depravity which is in thee?

A. From the fall and disobedience of Adam and Eve in Paradise; hence our nature is become so corrupt, that we are all conceived and born in sin.

Q. 10. What was that disobedience?

A. That they did eat of the fruit of the tree, which God had forbidden them.

Q. 11. Does the disobedience of Adam concern us?

A. Certainly: for he is the father of us all; and we have all sinned in him.

Q. 12. Are we then incapable of doing any good of ourselves, and prone to all manner of wickedness?

A. Indeed we are: unless we are regenerated by the Spirit of God.

Q. 13. Will God suffer such disobedience and corruption to go unpunished?

A. By no means: but in his just judgment will punish them, both in time and eternity, as it is written: "Cursed is every one that continueth not in all things, which are written in the book of the law, to do them."

THE SECOND PART.

OF MAN'S DELIVERANCE.

Q. 14. By what means canst thou escape this punishment, and be again received into favor?

A. By such a Mediator, who is in one person very God, and a real righteous man.

Q. 15. Who is that Mediator?

A. Our Lord Jesus Christ, who in one person is true God, and a real righteous man.

Q. 16. Could not the angels be our mediators?

A. No; for they are neither God nor man.

Q. 17. Cannot the saints be our mediators?

A. No; for they themselves have sinned, and have obtained salvation by no other means, than through this Mediator.

Q. 18. Shall all men then be saved by the Mediator, Jesus, as they are all condemned in Adam?

A. No; but those only who receive him by a true faith; as it is written, John 3:16: "For God so loved the world, that he gave his only begotten Son, that whosoever believeth in him should not perish, but have everlasting life."

Q. 19. What is true faith?

A. It is a certain knowledge of God, and of his promises revealed to us in the gospel, and an hearty confidence that all my sins are forgiven me, for Christ's sake.

Q. 20. What is the sum of that which God has promised in the gospel, and commanded us to believe?

A. That is comprehended in the twelve articles of the catholic christian Faith, which are as follows:

1. I believe in God the Father, Almighty, Maker of heaven and earth;

2. And in Jesus Christ, his only begotten Son, our Lord;

3. Who was conceived by the Holy Ghost, born of the Virgin Mary;

4. Suffered under Pontius Pilate, was crucified, dead and buried, he descended into hell;

5. The third day he rose again from the dead;

6. He ascended into heaven, and sitteth at the right hand of God, the Father Almighty;

7. From thence he shall come to judge the quick and the dead.

8. I believe in the Holy Ghost.

9. I believe an holy catholic church; the communion of saints;

10. The forgiveness of sins;

11. The resurrection of the body;

12. And the life everlasting.

Q. 21. When you profess to believe in God the Father, and the Son, and the Holy Ghost, do you mean three Gods thereby?

A. In no wise; for there is but one only true God.

Q. 22. Why do you then name three, the Father, the Son, and the Holy Ghost?

A. Because God has so revealed himself in his word, that these three distinct persons, are the only one and true God, and we also are baptized in the name of the Father, and of the Son, and of the Holy Ghost.

Q. 23. What believest thou when thou sayest: "I believe in God the Father, Almighty, Maker of heaven and earth"?

A. That the eternal Father of our Lord Jesus Christ, who of nothing made heaven and earth, and still upholds them by his providence, is my God and Father, for Christ his Son's sake.

Q. 24. What believest thou when thou sayest: "And in Jesus Christ his only begotten Son, our Lord"?

A. That Jesus Christ is the eternal and only son of the Father, co-essential with God the Father, and the Holy Ghost.

Q. 25. Do you not believe that he also became man?

A. Yes: for he was conceived by the Holy Ghost, and born of the Virgin Mary.

Q. 26. Is his Godhead then changed into humanity?

A. No; for the Godhead is immutable.

Q. 27. How is he then become man?

A. By assuming the human nature into a personal union with his divine.

Q. 28. Did he then bring his human nature from heaven?

A. No; but he took it on him of the Virgin Mary, by the operation of the Holy Ghost, and is thus become like unto his brethren in all things, sin excepted. Heb. 2:17 and 4:15.

Q. 29. Why is he called Jesus, that is, Savior?

A. Because he saves his people from their sins.

Q. 30. Is there no other Savior?

A. No; for there is none other name under heaven given among men, whereby we must be saved, than the name of Jesus. Acts 4:12.

Q. 31. Why is he called Christ, that is, anointed?

A. Because he was anointed with the Holy Ghost, and ordained by God the Father, to be our chief Prophet, our only High Priest, and our eternal King.

Q. 32. What then hath Jesus Christ done to save us?

A. He has suffered for us, was crucified and died, was buried and descended into hell, that is, he suffered the torments of hell, and thus became obedient to his Father, that he might deliver us from the temporal and eternal punishment due to sin.

Q. 33. In which nature hath he suffered?

A. Only in his human nature, that is, in soul and body.

Q. 34. What hath then his Godhead contributed thereto?

A. His Godhead, by its power, in such wise strengthened the assumed human nature, that it could bear the burden of God's wrath against sin, and deliver us from it.

Q. 35. Did Christ then remain under the power of death?

A. No; but he rose from the dead the third day for our justification. Rom. 4:25.

Q. 36. Where is Christ now, as to his human nature?

A. He is ascended into heaven, and sits at the right hand of God the Father; that is, exalted in the highest glory, far above all creatures. Eph. 1:20, 21.

Q. 37. To what end is he there so highly exalted?

A. Particularly that he might from thence govern His Church, and there be our intercessor with the Father.

Q. 38. Is he not with us then even unto the end of the world, as he hath promised us? Matt. 28:20.

A. With respect to his Godhead, majesty, grace and spirit, he is never absent from us; but with respect to his human nature, he remains in heaven, until he shall come again to judge the quick and the dead.

Q. 39. What do you believe concerning the Holy Ghost?

A. That he is the true and co-eternal God with the Father and the Son; and that he being given to me of the Father, through Christ, regenerates me and leads me into all truth, comforts me, and will abide with me forever.

Q. 40. What believest thou concerning the holy catholic church?

A. That the Son of God gathers by his word and Spirit out of the whole human race, those, who are chosen to eternal life, to be a church to himself; of which I believe I am, and always shall remain a living member.

Q. 41. Where doth he gather his church?

A. Where God's word is purely preached, and the holy sacraments administered according to the institution of Christ.

Q. 42. What benefits doth Christ bestow on his church?

A. He grants her remission of sins, the resurrection of the body, and eternal life.

Q. 43. What doth it profit thee now that thou believest all this?

A. That I am righteous in Christ before God. Rom. 5:10.

Q. 44. How art thou righteous before God?

A. Only by a true faith in Jesus Christ.

Q. 45. How is it to be understood that thou art justified by faith only?

A. Thus: that the perfect satisfaction and righteousness of Christ alone are imputed to me of God, by which my sins are forgiven me, and I become an heir of everlasting life; and that I cannot receive that righteousness by any other means than by faith.

Q. 46. Why cannot our good works be our righteousness before God, or some part thereof?

A. Because even our best works, in this life, are imperfect, and polluted with sins.

Q. 47. Do our good works then merit nothing, which yet God will reward in this, and in a future life?

A. This reward is not given out of merit, but of grace.

Q. 48. Who worketh that faith in thee?

A. The Holy Ghost.

Q. 49. By what means?

A. By the hearing of the word preached. Rom. 10:14-17.

Q. 50. How does he strengthen that faith?

A. By the same word preached, and by the use of the holy sacraments.

Q. 51. What are the sacraments?

A. They are holy signs and seals instituted by God, thereby to assure us, that he of grace grants us remission of sins, and life eternal, for the sake of that one sacrifice of Christ finished on the cross.

Q. 52. How many sacraments hath Christ instituted in the New Testament?

A. Two: holy baptism, and the holy supper.

Q. 53. Which is the outward sign in baptism?

A. The water, with which we are baptized in the name of the Father, and of the Son, and of the Holy Ghost.

Q. 54. What doth that signify and seal?

A. The washing away of sins by the blood and Spirit of Jesus Christ.

Q. 55. Where hath Christ promised and assured us of this?

A. In the institution of baptism; which is as follows: "Go ye into all the world, and preach the gospel to every creature. He that believeth and is baptized shall be saved, but he that believeth not, shall be damned."

Q. 56. Are infants also to be baptized?

A. Yes; for they, as well as the adult, are comprehended in the covenant of God, and in his church.

Q. 57. What is the outward sign in the Lords' supper?

A. The broken bread that we eat, and the poured out wine which we drink, in remembrance of the sufferings and death of Christ.

Q. 58. What is thereby signified and sealed?

A. That Christ, with his crucified body and shed blood, feeds and nourishes our souls to everlasting life.

Q. 59. Where hath Christ promised such things to us?

A. In the institution of the Lord's Supper, which is thus expressed, by St. Paul, 1 Cor. 11:23, 24, 25, 26: "For I have received of the Lord, that which also I delivered unto you, that the Lord Jesus the same night in which he was betrayed, took bread; and when he had given thanks, brake it, and said, take, eat; this is my body, which is broken for you; this do in remembrance of me. After the same manner also he took the cup, when he had supped, saying, this cup is the new testament in my blood: this do ye, as oft as ye drink it, in remembrance of me. For as often as ye eat this bread, and drink this cup, ye do show the Lord's death till he come."

Q. 60. Is the bread changed into the body of Christ, and the wine into his blood?

A. No; no more than the water in baptism is changed into the blood of Christ.

Q. 61. After what manner must you examine yourself before you come to the Lord's supper?

A. 1. I must examine whether I abhor myself for my sins, and humble myself before God on account of them. 2. Whether I believe and trust that all my sins are forgiven me for Christ's sake. 3. Whether I also have a sincere resolution henceforward, to walk in all good works.

Q. 62. May those be admitted to the Lord's supper, who teach false doctrines, or lead offensive lives?

A. No; lest the covenant of God be profaned, and his wrath kindled against the whole church.

Q. 63. How must we then deal with such persons?

A. According to the appointment given us by Christ, Matt. 18:15, 16, 17: "If thy brother shall trespass against thee, go and tell him his fault between thee and him alone; if he shall hear thee, thou hast gained thy brother; but if he will not hear thee, then take with thee one or two more, that in the mouth of two or three witnesses every word may be established; and if he shall neglect to hear them, tell it unto the church; but if he neglect to hear the church, let him be unto thee as an heathen man and a publican."

THE THIRD PART.

OF THE GRATITUDE WE OWE TO GOD FOR REDEMPTION.

Q. 64. Since we are saved merely of grace through Christ, why must we then yet do good works?

A. Not to merit heaven thereby (which Christ has done), but because this is commanded me of God.

Q. 65. What purpose then do your good works answer?

A. That I may thereby testify my thankfulness to God for all his benefits, and that he may be glorified by me; and that also I may be assured of the sincerity of my faith, by good works, as the fruits thereof, and that my neighbors may be edified thereby and gained to Christ.

Q. 66. Shall they also be saved who do no good works?

A. No; for the Scripture says, that neither fornicators, nor idolaters, nor adulterers, nor whoremongers, nor thieves, nor covetous, nor drunkards, nor revilers, nor robbers, nor such like, shall inherit the kingdom of God, 1 Cor. 6:9 and 10, unless they turn to the Lord.

Q. 67. Wherein doth the conversion of man consist?

A. In a hearty repentance, and avoiding of sin, and in an earnest desire after, and doing all good works.

Q. 68. What are good works?

A. Only those, which proceed from a true faith; are done according to the law of God, and to his glory; and not those which are founded on human institutions, or on our own imaginations.

Q. 69. Can they, who are converted to God, perfectly keep the law?

A. Not at all; but even the most holy men, as long as they are in this life, have only a small beginning of this obedience; yet so, that they with a sincere resolution begin to live not only according to some, but according to all the commandments of God, as they also constantly pray to God that they may daily increase therein.

Q. 70. To whom must we pray for this?

A. Not to any creature, but to God alone, who can help us, and will hear us for Jesus Christ's sake.

Q. 71. In whose name must we pray to God?

A. Only in the name of Christ, John 16:23, and not in the name of any saints.

Q. 72. What must we pray to God for?

A. For all things necessary for soul and body, which Christ our Lord has comprised in the prayer, he himself has taught us.

Q. 73. What are the words of that prayer?

A. Our Father which art in heaven, hallowed be thy name. Thy kingdom come. Thy will be done on earth, as it is in heaven. Give us this day our daily bread. And forgive us our debts, as we forgive our debtors. And lead us not into temptation, but deliver us from evil. For thine is the kingdom, and the power, and the glory, forever. Amen.

Q. 74. What do you desire of God in this prayer?

A. 1. That all things which tend to the glory of God, may be promoted, and whatsoever is repugnant thereto, or contrary to his will, may be prevented. 2. That he may provide me with all things necessary for the body, and as to my soul, preserve me from all evil, which might in any wise be detrimental to my salvation. Amen.

THE CONFESSION OF FAITH

REVISED IN THE NATIONAL SYNOD, HELD AT DORDRECHT,
IN THE YEARS 1618 AND 1619

··◁▥▷··

ARTICLE I—That there is One Only God.

We all believe with the heart, and confess with the mouth, that there is one only simple and spiritual Being, which we call God; and that he is eternal, incomprehensible, invisible, immutable, infinite, almighty, perfectly wise, just, good, and the overflowing fountain of all good.

II.—By what means God is made known unto us.

We know him by two means: first, by the creation, preservation and government of the universe; which is before our eyes as a most elegant book, wherein all creatures, great and small, are as so many characters leading us to contemplate the invisible things of God, namely, his power and divinity, as the apostle Paul saith, Rom. 1:20. All which things are sufficient to convince men, and leave them without excuse. Secondly, he makes himself more clearly and fully known to us by his holy and divine Word, that is to say, as far as is necessary for us to know in this life, to his glory and our salvation.

III.—Of the written Word of God.

We confess that this Word of God was not sent, nor delivered by the will of man, but that holy men of God spake as they were moved by the Holy Ghost, as the apostle Peter saith. And that afterwards God, from a special care, which he has for us and our salvation, commanded his servants, the prophets and apostles, to commit his revealed word to writing; and he himself wrote with his own finger, the two tables of the law. Therefore we call such writings holy and divine Scriptures.

IV.—Canonical Books of the Holy Scripture.

We believe that the Holy Scriptures are contained in two books, namely, the Old and New Testament, which are canonical, against which nothing can be alleged. These are thus named in the Church of God. The books of the Old Testament are, the five books of Moses, viz.: Genesis, Exodus, Leviticus, Numbers, Deuteronomy; the books of Joshua, Ruth, Judges, the two books of Samuel, the two of the Kings, two books of the Chronicles, commonly called Paralipomenon, the first of Ezra, Nehemiah, Esther, Job, the Psalms of David, the three books of Solomon, namely, the Proverbs, Ecclesiastes, and the Song of Songs; the four great prophets Isaiah, Jeremiah, Ezekiel and Daniel; and the twelve lesser prophets, namely, Hosea, Joel, Amos, Obadiah, Jonah, Micah, Nahum, Habakkuk, Zephaniah, Haggai, Zechariah, and Malachi.

Those of the New Testament are the four evangelists, viz.: Matthew, Mark, Luke, and John; the Acts of the Apostles; the fourteen epistles of the apostle Paul, viz.: one to the Romans, two to the Corinthians, one to the Galatians, one to the Ephesians, one to the Philippians, one to the Colossians, two to the Thessalonians, two to Timothy, one to Titus, one to Philemon, and one to the Hebrews; the seven epistles of the other apostles, namely, one of James, two of Peter, three of John, one of Jude; and the Revelation of the apostle John.

V.—From whence the Holy Scriptures derive their dignity and authority.

We receive all these books, and these only, as holy and canonical, for the regulation, foundation, and confirmation of our faith; believing without any doubt, all things contained in them, not so much because the Church receives and approves them as such, but more especially because the Holy Ghost witnesseth in our hearts, that they are from God, whereof they carry the evidence in themselves. For the very blind are able to perceive that the things foretold in them are fulfilling.

VI.—The difference between the canonical and apocryphal books.

We distinguish those sacred books from the apochryphal, viz.: the third book of Esdras, the books of Tobias, Judith, Wisdom, Jesus Syrach, Baruch, the appendix to the book of Esther, the Song of the three Children in the Furnace, the history of Susannah, of Bell and the Dragon, the prayer of Manasses, and the two books of the Maccabees. All of which the Church may read and take instruction from, so far as they agree with the canonical books; but they are far from having such power and efficacy, as that we may from their testimony confirm any point of faith, or of the christian religion; much less detract from the authority of the other sacred books.

VII.—The sufficiency of the Holy Scriptures, to be the only rule of faith.

We believe that those Holy Scriptures fully contain the will of God, and that whatsoever man ought to believe, unto salvation, is sufficiently taught therein. For, since the whole manner of worship, which God requires of us, is written in them at large, it is unlawful for any one, though an apostle, to teach otherwise than we are now taught in the Holy Scriptures: nay, though it were an angel from heaven, as the apostle Paul saith. For, since it is forbidden, to add unto or take away anything from the word of God, it doth thereby evidently appear, that the doctrine thereof is most perfect and complete in all respects. Neither do we consider of equal value any writing of men, however holy these men may have been, with those divine Scriptures, nor ought we to consider custom, or the great multitude, or antiquity, or succession of times and persons, or councils, decrees or statutes, as of equal value with the truth of God, for the truth is above all; for all men are of themselves liars, and more vain than vanity itself. Therefore, we reject with all our hearts, whatsoever doth not agree with this infallible rule, which the apostles have taught us, saying, Try the spirits whether they are of God. Likewise, if there come any unto you, and bring not this doctrine, receive him not into your house.

VIII.—That God is one in Essence, yet nevertheless distinguished in three Persons.

According to this truth and this Word of God, we believe in one only God, who is the one single essence, in which are three persons, really, truly, and eternally distinct, according to their incommunicable properties; namely, the Father, and the Son, and the Holy Ghost. The Father is the cause, origin and beginning of all things visible and invisible; the Son is the word, wisdom, and image of the Father; the Holy Ghost is the eternal power and might, proceeding from the Father and the Son. Nevertheless God is not by this distinction divided into three, since the Holy Scriptures teach us, that the Father. and the Son, and the Holy Ghost, have each his personality, distinguished by their properties; but in such wise that these three persons are but one only God. Hence then, it is evident, that the Father is not the Son, nor the Son the Father, and likewise the Holy Ghost is neither the Father nor the Son. Nevertheless these persons thus distinguished are not divided, nor intermixed: for the Father hath not assumed the flesh, nor hath the Holy Ghost, but the Son only. The Father hath never been without his Son, or without his Holy Ghost. For they are all three co-eternal and co-essential. There is neither first nor last: for they are all three one, in truth, in power, in goodness, and in mercy.

IX.—The proof of the foregoing article of the Trinity of persons in one God.

All this we know, as well from the testimonies of holy writ, as from their operations, and chiefly by those we feel in ourselves. The testimonies of the Holy Scriptures, that teach us to believe this Holy Trinity are written in many places of the Old Testament, which are not so necessary to enumerate, as to choose them out with discretion and judgment. In Genesis, chap. 1:26, 27, God saith: Let us make man in our image, after our likeness, etc. So God created man in his own image, male and female created he them. And Gen. 3:22. Behold the man is become as one of us. From this saying, let us make man in our image, it appears that there are more persons than one in the Godhead; and when he saith, God created, he signifies the unity. It is true he doth not say how many persons there are, but that, which appears to us somewhat obscure in the Old Testament, is very plain in the New. For when our Lord was baptized in Jordan, the voice of the Father was heard, saying, This is my beloved Son: the Son was seen in the water, and the Holy Ghost appeared in the shape of a dove. This form is also instituted by Christ in the baptism of all believers. Baptize all nations, in the name of the Father, and of the Son, and of the Holy Ghost. In the Gospel of Luke, the angel Gabriel thus addressed Mary, the mother of our Lord, The Holy Ghost shall come upon thee, and the power of the Highest shall overshadow thee, therefore also that holy thing, which shall be born of thee, shall be called the Son of God: likewise, the grace of our Lord Jesus Christ, and the love of God, and the communion of the Holy Ghost be with you. And there are three that bear record in heaven, the Father, the Word, and the Holy Ghost, and these three are one. In all which places we are fully taught, that there are three persons in one only divine essence. And although this doctrine far surpasses all human understanding, nevertheless, we now believe it by means of the Word of God, but expect hereafter to enjoy the perfect knowledge and benefit thereof in Heaven. Moreover, we must observe the particular offices and operations of these three persons towards us. The Father is called our Creator, by his power; the Son is our Savior and Redeemer, by his blood; the Holy Ghost is our Sanctifier, by his dwelling in our hearts. This doctrine of the Holy Trinity, hath always been defended and maintained by the true Church, since the time of the apostles, to this very day, against the Jews, Mohammedans, and some false christians and heretics, as Marcion, Manes, Praxeas, Sabellius, Samosatenus, Arius, and such like, who have been justly condemned by the orthodox fathers. Therefore, in this point, we do willingly receive the three creeds, namely, that of the Apostles, of Nice, and of Athanasius: likewise that, which, conformable thereunto, is agreed upon by the ancient fathers.

X. — That Jesus Christ is true and eternal God.

We believe that Jesus Christ, according to his divine nature, is the only begotten Son of God, begotten from eternity, not made nor created (for then he should be a creature), but co-essential and co-eternal with the Father, the express image of his person, and the brightness of his glory, equal unto him in all things. He is the Son of God, not only from the time that he assumed our nature, but from all eternity, as these testimonies, when compared together, teach us. Moses saith, that God created the world; and John saith, that all things were made by that Word, which he calleth God. And the apostle saith, that God made the worlds by his Son; likewise, that God created all things by Jesus Christ. Therefore it must needs follow, that he, who is called God, the Word, the Son, and Jesus Christ, did exist at that time, when all things were created by him. Therefore the prophet Micah saith, His goings forth have been from of old, from everlasting. And the apostle: He hath neither beginning of days, nor end of life. He therefore is that true, eternal, and almighty God, whom we invoke, worship and serve.

XI.—That the Holy Ghost is true and eternal God.

We believe and confess also, that the Holy Ghost, from eternity, proceeds from the Father and Son; and therefore neither is made, created, nor begotten, but only proceedeth from both; who in order is the third person of the Holy Trinity; of one and the same essence, majesty and glory with the Father, and the Son: and therefore, is the true and eternal God, as the Holy Scriptures teach us.

XII.—Of the Creation.

We believe that the Father, by the Word, that is, by his Son, hath created of nothing, the heaven, the earth, and all creatures, as it seemed good unto him, giving unto every creature its being, shape, form, and several offices to serve its Creator. That he doth also still uphold and govern them by his eternal providence, and infinite power, for the service of mankind, to the end that man may serve his God. He also created the angels good, to be his messengers and to serve his elect; some of whom are fallen from that excellency, in which God created them, into everlasting perdition; and the others have, by the grace of God, remained steadfast and continued in their primitive state. The devils and evil spirits are so depraved, that they are enemies of God and every good thing, to the utmost of their power, as murderers, watching to ruin the Church and every member thereof, and by their wicked stratagems to destroy all; and are, therefore, by their own wickedness, adjudged to eternal damnation, daily expecting their horrible torments. Therefore we reject and abhor the error of the Sadducees, who deny the existence of spirits and angels: and also that of the Manichees, who assert that the devils have their origin of themselves, and that they are wicked of their own nature, without having been corrupted.

XIII.—Of Divine Providence.

We believe that the same God, after he had created all things, did not forsake them, or give them up to fortune or chance, but that he rules and governs them according to his holy will, so that nothing happens in this world without his appointment: nevertheless, God neither is the author of, nor can be charged with, the sins which are committed. For his power and goodness are so great and incomprehensible, that he orders and executes his work in the most excellent and just manner, even then, when devils and wicked men act unjustly. And, as to what he doth surpassing human understanding, we will not curiously inquire into, farther than our capacity will admit of; but with the greatest humility and reverence adore the righteous judgments of God, which are hid from us, contenting ourselves that we are disciples of Christ, to learn only those things which he has revealed to us in his Word, without transgressing these limits. This doc-

trine affords us unspeakable consolation, since we are taught thereby that nothing can befall us by chance, but by the direction of our most gracious and heavenly Father; who watches over us with a paternal care, keeping all creatures so under his power, that not a hair of our head (for they are all numbered), nor a sparrow, can fall to the ground, without the will of our Father, in whom we do entirely trust; being persuaded, that he so restrains the devil and all our enemies, that without his will and permission, they cannot hurt us. And therefore we reject that damnable error of the Epicureans, who say that God regards nothing, but leaves all things to chance.

XIV.—Of the Creation and Fall of man, and his Incapacity to perform what is truly good.

We believe that God created man out of the dust of the earth, and made and formed him after his own image and likeness, good, righteous, and holy, capable in all things to will, agreeably to the will of God. But being in honor, he understood it not, neither knew his excellency, but willfully subjected himself to sin, and consequently to death, and the curse, giving ear to the words of the devil. For the commandment of life, which he had received, he transgressed; and by sin separated himself from God, who was his true life, having corrupted his whole nature; whereby he made himself liable to corporal and spiritual death. And being thus become wicked, perverse, and corrupt in all his ways, he hath lost all his excellent gifts, which he had received from God, and only retained a few remains thereof, which, however, are sufficient to leave man without excuse; for all the light which is in us is changed into darkness, as the Scriptures teach us, saying: The light shineth in darkness, and the darkness comprehendeth it not: where St. John calleth men darkness. Therefore we reject all that is taught repugnant to this, concerning the free will of man, since man is but a slave to sin; and has nothing of himself, unless it is given from heaven. For who may presume to boast, that he of himself can do any good, since Christ saith, No man can come to me, except the Father, which hath sent me, draw him? Who will glory in his own will, who understands, that to be carnally minded is enmity against God? Who can speak of his knowledge, since the natural man receiveth not the things of the spirit of God? In short, who dare suggest any thought, since he knows that we are not sufficient of ourselves to think anything as of ourselves, but that our sufficiency is of God? And therefore what the apostle saith ought justly to be held sure and firm, that God worketh in us both to will and to do of his good pleasure. For there is no will nor understanding, conformable to the divine will and understanding, but what Christ hath wrought in man; which he teaches us, when he saith, Without me ye can do nothing.

XV.—Of Original Sin.

We believe that, through the disobedience of Adam, original sin is extended to all mankind; which is a corruption of the whole nature, and an hereditary disease, wherewith infants themselves are infected even in their mother's womb, and which produceth in man all sorts of sin, being in him as a root thereof; and therefore is so vile and abominable in the sight of God, that it is sufficient to condemn all mankind. Nor is it by any means abolished or done away by baptism; since sin always issues forth from this woeful source, as water from a fountain; notwithstanding it is not imputed to the children of God unto condemnation, but by his grace and mercy is forgiven them. Not that they should rest securely in sin, but that a sense of this corruption should make believers often to sigh, desiring to be delivered from this body of death. Wherefore we reject the error of the Pelagians, who assert that sin proceeds only from imitation.

XVI.—Of Eternal Election.

We believe that all the posterity of Adam being thus fallen into perdition and ruin, by the sin of our first parents, God then did manifest himself such as he is; that is to say, merciful and just: Merciful, since he delivers and preserves from this perdition all, whom he, in his eternal and unchangeable counsel of mere goodness, hath elected in Christ Jesus our Lord, without any respect to their works: Just, in leaving others in the fall and perdition wherein they have involved themselves.

XVII.—Of the Recovery of Fallen Man.

We believe that our most gracious God, in his admirable wisdom and goodness, seeing that man had thus thrown himself into temporal and eternal death, and made himself wholly miserable, was pleased to seek and comfort him, when he trembling fled from his presence, promising him that he would give his Son, who should be made of a woman, to bruise the head of the serpent, and would make him happy.

XVIII.—Of the Incarnation of Jesus Christ.

We confess, therefore, that God did fulfill the promise, which he made to the fathers, by the mouth of his holy prophets, when he sent into the world, at the time appointed by him, his own, only-begotten and eternal Son, who took upon him the form of a servant, and became like unto man, really assuming the true human nature, with all its infirmities, sin excepted, being conceived in the womb of the blessed Virgin Mary, by the power of the Holy Ghost, without the means of man, and did not only assume human nature as to the body, but also a true human soul, that he might be a real man. For since the soul was lost as well as the body, it was necessary that he should take both upon him, to save both. Therefore we confess (in opposition to the heresy of the Anabaptists, who deny that Christ assumed human flesh of his mother) that Christ is become a partaker of the flesh and blood of the children; that he is a fruit of the loins of David after the flesh; made of the seed of David according to the flesh; a fruit of the womb of the Virgin Mary, made of a woman, a branch of David; a shoot of the root of Jesse; sprung from the tribe of Judah; descended from the Jews according to the flesh; of the seed of Abraham, since he took on him the seed of Abraham, and became like unto his brethren in all things, sin excepted, so that in truth he is our **Immanuel**, that is to say, God with us.

XIX.—Of the union and distinction of the two Natures in the person of Christ.

We believe that by this conception, the person of the Son is inseparably united and connected with the human nature; so that there are not two Sons of God, nor two persons, but two natures united in one single person: yet, that each nature retains its own distinct properties. As then the divine nature hath always remained uncreated, without beginning of days or end of life, filling heaven and earth: so also hath the human nature not lost its properties, but remained a creature, having beginning of days, being a finite nature, and retaining all the properties of a real body. And though he hath by his resurrection given immortality to the same, nevertheless he hath not changed the reality of his human nature; forasmuch as our salvation and resurrection also depend on the reality of his body. But these two natures are so closely united in one person, that they were not separated even by his death. Therefore that which he, when dying, commended into the hands of his Father, was a real human spirit, departing from his body. But in the meantime the divine nature always remained united with the human, even when he lay in the grave. And the Godhead did not cease to be in him, any more than it did when he was an infant, though it did not so clearly manifest itself for a while. Wherefore we confess, that he is **very God, and very Man**: very God by his power to conquer death; and very man that he might die for us according to the infirmity of his flesh.

XX.—That God hath manifested his justice and mercy in Christ.

We believe that God, who is perfectly merciful and just, sent his Son to assume that nature, in which the disobedience was committed, to make satisfaction in the same, and to bear the punishment of sin by his most bitter passion and death. God therefore manifested his justice against his Son, when he laid our iniquities upon him; and poured forth his mercy and goodness on us, who were guilty and worthy of damnation, out of mere and perfect love, giving his Son unto death for us, and raising him for our justification, that through him we might obtain immortality and life eternal.

XXI.—Of the satisfaction of Christ, our only High Priest, for us.

We believe that Jesus Christ is ordained with an oath to be an everlasting High Priest, after the order of Melchisedec; and that he hath presented himself in our behalf before the Father, to appease his wrath by his full satisfaction, by offering himself on the tree of the cross, and pouring out his precious blood to purge away our sins; as the prophets had foretold. For it is written: He was wounded for our transgressions, he was bruised for our iniquities: the chastisement of our peace was upon him, and with his stripes we are healed. He was brought as a lamb to the slaughter, and numbered with the transgressors, and condemned by Pontius Pilate as a malefactor, though he had first declared him innocent. Therefore: he restored that which he took not away, and suffered, the just for the unjust, as well in his body as in his soul, feeling the terrible punishment which our sins had merited; insomuch that his sweat became like unto drops of blood falling on the ground. He called out, my God, my God, why hast thou forsaken me? and hath suffered all this for the remission of our sins. Wherefore we justly say with the apostle Paul: that we know nothing, but Jesus Christ, and him crucified; we count all things but loss and dung for the excellency of the knowledge of Christ Jesus our Lord, in whose wounds we find all manner of consolation. Neither is it necessary to seek or invent any other means of being reconciled to God, than this only sacrifice, once offered, by which believers are made perfect forever. This is also the reason why he was called by the angel of God, **Jesus**, that is to say, **Savior**, because he should save his people from their sins.

XXII.—Of Faith in Jesus Christ.

We believe that, to attain the true knowledge of this great mystery, the Holy Ghost kindleth in our hearts an upright faith, which embraces Jesus Christ, with all his merits, appropriates him, and seeks nothing more besides him. For it must needs follow, either that all things, which are requisite to our salvation, are not in Jesus Christ, or if all things are in him, that then those who possess Jesus Christ through faith, have complete salvation in him. Therefore, for any to assert, that Christ is not sufficient, but that something more is required besides him, would be too gross a blasphemy: for hence it would follow, that Christ was but half a Savior. Therefore we justly say with Paul, that we are justified by faith alone, or by faith without works. However, to speak more clearly, we do not mean, that faith itself justifies us, for it is only an instrument with which we embrace Christ our Righteousness. But Jesus Christ, imputing to us all his merits, and so many holy works which he has done for us, and in our stead, is our Righteousness. And faith is an instrument that keeps us in communion with him in all his benefits, which, when become ours, are more than sufficient to acquit us of our sins.

XXIII.—Of Justification.

We believe that our salvation consists in the remission of our sins for Jesus Christ's sake, and that therein our righteousness before God is implied: as David and Paul teach us, declaring this to be the happiness of man, that God imputes righteousness to him without works. And the same apostle saith, that we are justified freely by his grace, through the redemption which is in Jesus Christ. And therefore we always hold fast this foundation, ascribing all the glory to God, humbling ourselves before him, and acknowledging ourselves to be such as we really are, without presuming to trust in any thing in ourselves, or in any merit of ours, relying and resting upon the obedience of Christ crucified alone, which becomes ours, when we believe in him. This is sufficient to cover all our iniquities, and to give us confidence in approaching to God; freeing the conscience of fear, terror and dread, without following the example of our first father, Adam, who, trembling, attempted to cover himself with fig-leaves. And verily if we should appear before God, relying on ourselves, or on any other creature, though ever so little, we should, alas! be consumed. And therefore every one must pray with David: O Lord, enter not into judgment with thy servant: for in thy sight shall no man living be justified.

XXIV.—Of man's Sanctification and Good Works.

We believe that this true faith being wrought in man by the hearing of the Word of God, and the operation of the Holy Ghost, doth regenerate and make him a new man, causing him to live a new life, and freeing him from the bondage of sin. Therefore it is so far from being true, that this justifying faith makes men remiss in a pious and holy life, that on the contrary without it they would never do anything out of love to God, but only out of self-love or fear of damnation. Therefore it is impossible that this holy faith can be unfruitful in man: for we do not speak of a vain faith, but of such a faith, which is called in Scripture, a faith that worketh by love, which excites man to the practice of those works, which God has commanded in his Word. Which works, as they proceed from the good root of faith, are good and acceptable in the sight of God, forasmuch as they are all sanctified by his grace: howbeit they are of no account towards our justification. For it is by faith in Christ that we are justified, even before we do good works; otherwise they could not be good works, any more than the fruit of a tree can be good, before the tree itself is good. Therefore we do good works, but not to merit by them, (for what can we merit?) nay, we are beholden to God for the good works we do, and not he to us, since it is he that worketh in us both to will and to do of his good pleasure. Let us therefore attend to what is written: when ye shall have done all those things which are commanded you, say, we are unprofitable servants; we have done that which was our duty to do. In the meantime, we do not deny that God rewards our good works, but it is through his grace that he crowns his gifts. Moreover, though we do good works, we do not found our salvation upon them; for we do no work but what is polluted by our flesh, and also punishable; and although we could perform such works, still the remembrance of one sin is sufficient to make God reject them. Thus then we would always be in doubt, tossed to and fro without any certainty, and our poor consciences continually vexed, if they relied not on the merits of the suffering and death of our Savior.

XXV.—Of the abolishing of the Ceremonial Law.

We believe, that the ceremonies and figures of the law ceased at the coming of Christ, and that all the shadows are accomplished; so that the use of them must be abolished amongst christians; yet the truth and substance of them remain with us in Jesus Christ, in whom they have their completion. In the meantime, we still use the testimonies taken out of the law and the prophets, to confirm us in the doctrine of the gospel, and to regulate our life in all honesty, to the glory of God, according to his will.

XXVI.—Of Christ's Intercession.

We believe that we have no access unto God, but alone through the only Mediator and Advocate, Jesus Christ the righteous, who therefore became man, having united in one person the divine and human natures, that we men might have access to the divine Majesty, which access would otherwise be barred against us. But this Mediator, whom the Father has appointed between him and us, ought in no wise to affright us by his majesty, or cause us to seek another according to our fancy. For there is no creature either in heaven or on earth who loveth us more than Jesus Christ; who, though he was in the form of God, yet made himself of no reputation, and took upon him the form of a man, and of a servant for us, and was made like unto his brethren in all things. If then we should seek for another Mediator, who would be well affected towards us, whom could we find, who loved us more than he, who laid down his life for us, even when we were his enemies? And if we seek for one who hath power and majesty, who is there that has so much of both as he who sits at the right hand of his Father, and who hath all power in heaven and on earth? And who will sooner be heard than the own well beloved Son of God? Therefore it was only through distrust that this practice of dishonoring, instead of honoring the saints, was introduced, doing that, which they never have done, nor required, but have on the contrary steadfastly rejected according to their bounden duty, as appears by their writings. Neither must we plead here our unworthiness; for the meaning is not that we should offer our prayers to God on the ground of our own worthiness but only on the ground of the excellency and worthiness of the Lord Jesus Christ, whose righteousness is become ours by faith. Therefore the apostle, to remove this foolish fear, or rather mistrust from us, justly saith, that Jesus Christ was made like unto his brethren in all things, that he might be a merciful and faithful High Priest, to make reconciliation for the sins of the people. For in that he himself hath suffered, being tempted, he is able to succor them that are tempted; and further to encourage us, he adds, seeing then that we have a great High Priest, that is passed into the heavens, Jesus the Son of God, let us hold fast our profession. For we have not an high priest which cannot be touched with the feeling of our infirmities; but was in all points tempted like as we are, yet without sin. Let us therefore come boldly unto the throne of grace, that we may obtain mercy, and find grace to help in time of need. The same apostle saith, having boldness to enter into the holiest, by the blood of Jesus; let us draw near with a true heart in full assurance of faith, etc. Likewise, Christ hath an unchangeable priesthood, wherefore he is able also to same them to the uttermost, that come unto God by him, seeing he ever liveth to make intercession for them. What more can be required? since Christ himself saith, I am the way and the truth, and the life: no man cometh unto the Father but by me. To what purpose should we then seek another advocate, since it has pleased God, to give us his own Son as an advocate? Let us not forsake him to take another, or rather to seek after another, without ever being able to find him; for God well knew, when he gave him to us, that we were sinners. Therefore according to the command of Christ, we call upon the heavenly Father through Jesus Christ our own Mediator, as we are taught in the Lord's prayer; being assured that whatever we ask of the Father in his name. will be granted us.

XXVII.—Of the Catholic Christian Church.

We believe and profess, one catholic or universal Church, which is an holy congregation, of true Christian believers, all expecting their salvation in Jesus Christ, being washed by his blood, sanctified and sealed by the Holy Ghost. This Church hath been from the beginning of the world, and will be to the end thereof; which is evident from this, that Christ is an eternal King, which, without subjects, cannot be. And this holy Church is preserved or supported by God, against the rage of the whole world; though she sometimes (for a while) appears very small, and in the eyes of men, to be reduced to nothing: as during the perilous reign of Ahab, the Lord reserved unto him seven thousand men, who had not bowed their knees to Baal. Furthermore, this holy Church is not confined, bound, or limited to a certain place or to certain persons, but is spread and dispersed over the whole world; and yet is joined and united with heart and will, by the power of faith, in one and the same spirit.

XXVIII.—That every one is bound to join himself to the true Church.

We believe, since this holy congregation is an assembly of those who are saved, and that out of it there is no salvation, that no person of whatsoever state or condition he may be, ought to withdraw himself, to live in a separate state from it; but that all men are in duty bound to join and unite themselves with it; maintaining the unity of the Church; submitting themselves to the doctrine and discipline thereof; bowing their necks under the yoke of Jesus Christ; and as mutual members of the same body, serving to the edification of the brethren, according to the talents God has given them. And that this may be the more effectually observed, it is the duty of all believers, according to the word of God, to separate themselves from all those who do not belong to the Church, and to join themselves to this congregation, wheresoever God hath established it, even though the magistrates and edicts of princes were against it, yea, though they should suffer death or any other corporal punishment. Therefore all those, who separate themselves from the same, or do not join themselves to it, act contrary to the ordinance of God.

XXIX.—Of the marks of the true Church, and wherein she differs from the false Church.

We believe, that we ought diligently and circumspectly to discern from the Word of God which is the true Church, since all sects which are in the world assume to themselves the name of the Church. But we speak not here of hypocrites, who are mixed in the Church with the good, yet are not of the Church, though externally in it; but we say that the body and communion of the true Church must be distinguished from all sects, who call themselves the Church. The marks, by which the true Church is known, are these: if the pure doctrine of the gospel is preached therein; if she maintains the pure administration of the sacraments as instituted by Christ; if church discipline is exercised in punishing of sin: in short, if all things are managed according to the pure Word of God, all things contrary thereto rejected, and Jesus Christ acknowledged as the only Head of the Church. Hereby the true Church may certainly be known, from which no man has a right to separate himself. With respect to those, who are members of the Church, they may be known by the marks of Christians: namely, by faith; and when they have received Jesus Christ the only Savior, they avoid sin, follow after righteousness, love the true God and their neighbor, neither turn aside to the right or left, and crucify the flesh with the works thereof. But this is not to be understood, as if there did not remain in them great infirmities; but they fight against them through the Spirit, all the days of their life, continually taking their refuge in the blood, death, passion and obedience of our Lord Jesus Christ, "in whom they have remission of sins, through faith in him." As for the false Church, she ascribes more power and authority to herself and her ordinances than to the Word of God, and will not submit herself to the yoke of Christ. Neither does she administer the sacraments as appointed by Christ in his Word, but adds to and takes from them, as she thinks proper; she relieth more upon men than upon Christ; and persecutes those, who live holily according to the Word of God, and rebuke her for her errors, covetousness, and idolatry. These two Churches are easily known and distinguished from each other.

XXX.—Concerning the Government of, and Offices in the Church.

We believe, that this true Church must be governed by that spiritual policy which our Lord hath taught us in his Word; namely, that there must be ministers or pastors to preach the Word of God, and to administer the sacraments; also elders and deacons, who, together with the pastors, form the council of the Church: that by these means the true religion may be preserved, and the true doctrine everywhere propagated, likewise transgressors punished and restrained by spiritual means: also that the poor and distressed may be relieved and comforted, according to their necessities. By these means everything will be carried on in the Church with good order and decency, when faithful men are chosen, according to the rule prescribed by St. Paul in his Epistle to Timothy.

XXXI.—Of the Ministers, Elders, and Deacons.

We believe, that the ministers of God's Word, and the elders and deacons, ought to be chosen to their respective offices by a lawful election by the Church, with calling upon the name of the Lord, and in that order which the Word of God teacheth. Therefore every one must take heed, not to intrude himself by indecent means, but is bound to wait till it shall please God to call him; that he may have testimony of his calling, and be certain and assured that it is of the Lord. As for the ministers of God's Word, they have equally the same power and authority wheresoever they are, as they are all ministers of Christ, the only universal Bishop, and the only Head of the Church. Moreover, that this holy ordinance of God may not be violated or slighted, we say that every one ought to esteem the ministers of God's Word, and the elders of the Church, very highly for their work's sake, and be at peace with them without murmuring, strife or contention, as much as possible.

XXXII.—Of the Order and Discipline of the Church.

In the meantime we believe, though it is useful and beneficial, that those, who are rulers of the Church, institute and establish certain ordinances among themselves for maintaining the body of the Church; yet they ought studiously to take care, that they do not depart from those things which Christ, our only Master, hath instituted. And therefore, we reject all human inventions, and all laws, which man would introduce into the worship of God, thereby to bind and compel the conscience in any manner whatever. Therefore we admit only of that which tends to nourish and preserve concord, and unity, and to keep all men in obedience to God. For this purpose, ex-communication or church discipline is requisite, with the several circumstances belonging to it, according to the Word of God.

XXXIII.—Of the Sacraments.

We believe, that our gracious God, on account of our weakness and infirmities hath ordained the sacraments for us, thereby to seal unto us his promises, and to be pledges of the good will and grace of God toward us, and also to nourish and strengthen our faith; which he hath joined to the Word of the gospel, the better to present to our senses, both that which he signifies to us by his Word, and that which he works inwardly in our hearts, thereby assuring and confirming in us the salvation which he imparts to us. For they are visible signs and seals of an inward and invisible thing, by means whereof God worketh in us by the power of the Holy Ghost. Therefore the signs are not in vain or insignificant, so as to deceive us. For Jesus Christ is the true object presented by them, without whom they would be of no moment. Moreover, we are satisfied with the number of sacraments which Christ our Lord hath instituted, which are two only, namely, the sacrament of baptism, and the holy supper of our Lord Jesus Christ.

XXXIV.—Of Holy Baptism.

We believe and confess that Jesus Christ, who is the end of the law, hath made an end, by the shedding of his blood, of all other sheddings of blood which men could or would make as a propitiation or satisfaction for sin: and that he, having abolished circumcision, which was done with blood, hath instituted the sacrament of baptism instead thereof; by which we are received into the Church of God, and separated from all other people and strange religions, that we may wholly belong to him, whose ensign and banner we bear: and which serves as a testimony to us, that he will forever be our gracious God and Father. Therefore he has commanded all those, who are his, to be baptized with pure water, "in the name of the Father, and of the Son, and of the Holy Ghost": thereby signifying to us, that as water washeth away the filth of the body, when poured upon it, and is seen on the body of the baptized, when sprinkled upon him; so doth the blood of Christ, by the power of the Holy Ghost, internally sprinkle the soul, cleanse it from its sins, and regenerate us from children of wrath, unto children of God. Not that this is effected by the external water, but by the sprinkling of the precious blood of the Son of God; who is our Red Sea, through which we must pass, to escape the tyranny of Pharaoh, that is, the devil, and to enter into the spiritual land of Canaan. Therefore the ministers, on their part, administer the sacrament, and that which is visible, but our Lord giveth that which is signified by the sacrament, namely, the gifts and invisible grace; washing, cleansing and purging our souls of all filth and unrighteousness; renewing our hearts, and filling them with all comfort; giving unto us a true assurance of his fatherly goodness; putting on us the new man, and putting off the old man with all his deeds. Therefore we believe, that every man, who is earnestly studious of obtaining life eternal, ought to be but once baptized with this only baptism, without ever repeating the same: since we cannot be born twice. Neither doth this baptism only avail us, at the time when the water is poured upon us, and received by us, but also through the whole course of our life; therefore we detest the error of the Anabaptists, who are not content with the one only baptism they have once received, and moreover condemn the baptism of the infants of believers, whom we believe ought to be baptized and sealed with the sign of the covenant, as the children in Israel formerly were circumcised, upon the same promises which are made unto our children. And indeed Christ shed his blood no less for the washing of the children of the faithful, than for adult persons; and therefore they ought to receive the sign and sacrament of that, which Christ hath done for them; as the Lord commanded in the law, that they

should be made partakers of the sacrament of Christ's suffering and death, shortly after they were born, by offering for them a lamb, which was a sacrament of Jesus Christ. Moreover, what circumcision was to the Jews, that baptism is to our children. And for this reason Paul calls baptism the circumcision of Christ.

XXXV.—Of the Holy Supper of our Lord Jesus Christ.

We believe and confess, that our Savior Jesus Christ did ordain and institute the sacrament of the holy supper, to nourish and support those whom he hath already regenerated, and incorporated into his family, which is his Church. Now those, who are regenerated, have in them a twofold life, the one corporal and temporal, which they have from the first birth, and is common to all men: the other spiritual and heavenly, which is given them in their second birth, which is effected by the word of the gospel, in the communion of the body of Christ; and this life is not common, but is peculiar to God's elect. In like manner God hath given us, for the support of the bodily and earthly life, earthly and common bread, which is subservient thereto, and is common to all men, even as life itself. But for the support of the spiritual and heavenly life, which believers have, he hath sent a living bread, which descended from heaven, namely, Jesus Christ, who nourishes and strengthens the spiritual life of believers, when they eat him, that is to say, when they apply and receive him by faith in the spirit. Christ, that he might represent unto us this spiritual and heavenly bread, hath instituted an earthly and visible bread, as a sacrament of his body, and wine as a sacrament of his blood, to testify by them unto us, that, as certainly as we receive and hold this sacrament in our hands, and eat and drink the same with our mouths, by which our life is afterwards nourished, we also do as certainly receive by faith (which is the hand and mouth of our soul) the true body and blood of Christ our only Savior in our souls, for the support of our spiritual life. Now, as it is certain and beyond all doubt, that Jesus Christ hath not enjoined to us the use of his sacraments in vain, so he works in us all that he represents to us by these holy signs, though the manner surpasses our understanding, and cannot be comprehended by us, as the operations of the Holy Ghost are hidden and incomprehensible. In the meantime we err not, when we say, that what is eaten and drunk by us is the proper and natural body, and the proper blood of Christ. But the manner of our partaking of the same, is not by the mouth, but by the spirit through faith. Thus then, though Christ always sits at the right hand of his Father in the heavens, yet doth he not therefore cease to make us partakers of himself by faith. This feast is a spiritual table, at which Christ communicates himself with all his benefits to us, and gives us there to enjoy both himself, and the merits of his sufferings and death, nourishing, strengthening and comforting our poor comfortless souls by the eating of his flesh, quickening and refreshing them by the drinking of his blood. Further, though the sacraments are connected with the thing signified, nevertheless both are not received by all men: the ungodly indeed receives the sacrament to his condemnation, but he doth not receive the truth of the sacrament. As Judas, and Simon the sorcerer, both indeed received the sacrament, but not Christ, who was signified by it, of whom believers only are made partakers. Lastly, we receive this holy sacrament in the assembly of the people of God, with humility and reverence, keeping up amongst us a holy remembrance of the death of Christ our Savior, with

thanksgiving: making there confession of our faith, and of the Christian religion. Therefore no one ought to come to this table without having previously rightly examined himself; lest by eating of this bread and drinking of this cup, he eat and drink judgment to himself. In a word, we are excited by the use of this holy sacrament, to a fervent love towards God and our neighbor. Therefore we reject all mixtures and damnable inventions, which men have added unto, and blended with the sacraments, as profanations of them: and affirm that we ought to rest satisfied with the ordinance which Christ and his apostles have taught us, and that we must speak of them in the same manner as they have spoken.

XXXVI.—Of Magistrates.

We believe that our gracious God, because of the depravity of mankind, hath appointed kings, princes and magistrates, willing that the world should be governed by certain laws and policies; to the end that the dissoluteness of men might be restrained, and all things carried on among them with good order and decency. For this purpose he hath invested the magistracy with the sword, for the punishment of evil-doers, and for the protection of them that do well. And their office is, not only to have regard unto, and watch for the welfare of the civil state; but also that they protect the sacred ministry; and thus may remove and prevent all idolatry and false worship;* that the kingdom

---

*This phrase, touching the office of the magistracy in its relation to the Church, proceeds on the principle of the Established Church, which was first applied by Constantine and afterwards also in many Protestant countries. History, however, does not support the principle of State domination over the Church, but rather the separation of Church and State. Moreover, it is contrary to the New Dispensation that authority be vested in the State to arbitrarily reform the Church, and to deny the Church the right of independently conducting its own affairs as a distinct territory alongside the State. The New Testament does not subject the Christian Church to the authority of the State that it should be governed and extended by political measures, but to our Lord and King only as an independent territory alongside and altogether independent of the State, that it may be governed and edified by its office-bearers and with spiritual weapons only. Practically all Reformed churches have repudiated the idea of the Established Church, and are advocating the autonomy of the churches and personal liberty of conscience in matters pertaining to the service of God.

"The Christian Reformed Church in America, being in full accord with this view, feels constrained to declare that it does not conceive of the office of the magistracy in this sense, that it be in duty bound to also exercise political authority in the sphere of religion, by establishing and maintaining a State Church, advancing and supporting the same as the only true Church, and to oppose, to persecute and to destroy by means of the sword all the other churches as being false religions; and to also declare that it does positively hold that, within its own secular sphere, the magistracy has a divine duty towards the first table of the Law as well as towards the second; and furthermore that both State and Church as institutions of God and Christ have mutual rights and duties appointed them from on high, and therefore have a very sacred reciprocal obligation to meet through the Holy Spirit, who proceeds from Father and Son. They may not, however, encroach upon each other's territory. The Church has rights of sovereignty in its own sphere as well as the State."

Acta. Synod. 1910.

of anti-christ may be thus destroyed and the kingdom of Christ promoted. They must therefore countenance the preaching of the Word of the gospel everywhere, that God may be honored and worshipped by every one, as he commands in his Word. Moreover, it is the bounden duty of every one, of what state, quality, or condition soever he may be, to subject himself to the magistrates; to pay tribute, to show due honor and respect to them, and to obey them in all things which are not repugnant to the Word of God; to supplicate for them in their prayers, that God may rule and guide them in all their ways, and that we may lead a quiet and peaceable life in all godliness and honesty. Wherefore we detest the Anabaptists and other seditious people, and in general all those who reject the higher powers and magistrates, and would subvert justice, introduce community of goods, and confound that decency and good order, which God hath established among men.

XXXVII.—Of the Last Judgment.

Finally we believe, according to the Word of God, when the time appointed by the Lord (which is unknown to all creatures) is come, and the number of the elect complete, that our Lord Jesus Christ will come from heaven, corporally and visibly, as he ascended, with great glory and majesty to declare himself judge of the quick and the dead; burning this old world with fire and flame, to cleanse it. And then all men will personally appear before this great judge, both men and women and children, that have been from the beginning of the world to the end thereof, being summoned by the voice of the archangel, and by the sound of the trumpet of God. For all the dead shall be raised out of the earth, and their souls joined and united with their proper bodies, in which they formerly lived. As for those who shall then be living, they shall not die as the others, but be changed in the twinkling of an eye, and from corruptible, become incorruptible. Then the books (that is to say the consciences) shall be opened, and the dead judged according to what they shall have done in this world, whether it be good or evil. Nay, all men shall give an account of every idle word they have spoken, which the world only counts amusement and jest: and then the secrets and hypocrisy of men shall be disclosed and laid open before all. And therefore the consideration of this judgment, is justly terrible and dreadful to the wicked and ungodly, but most desirable and comfortable to the righteous and elect: because then their full deliverance shall be perfected, and there they shall receive the fruits of their labor and trouble which they have borne. Their innocence shall be known to all, and they shall see the terrible vengeance which God shall execute on the wicked, who most cruelly persecuted, oppressed and tormented them in this world; and who shall be convicted by the testimony of their own consciences, and being immortal, shall be tormented in that everlasting fire, which is prepared for the devil and his angels. But on the contrary, the faithful and elect shall be crowned with glory and honor; and the Son of God will confess their names before God his Father, and his elect angels; all tears shall be wiped from their eyes; and their cause which is now condemned by many judges and magistrates, as heretical and impious, will then be known to be the cause of the Son of God. And for a gracious reward, the Lord will cause them to possess such a glory, as never entered into the heart of man to conceive. Therefore we expect that great day with a most ardent desire to the end that we may fully enjoy the promises of God in Christ Jesus our Lord. AMEN.

"Even so, come, Lord Jesus."—Rev. 22:20,

CANONS

RATIFIED IN THE NATIONAL SYNOD OF THE

REFORMED CHURCH,

Held at Dordrecht, in the years 1618 and 1619.

••◁▥▷••

FIRST HEAD OF DOCTRINE.

••◁▥▷••

OF DIVINE PREDESTINATION.

Article 1. As all men have sinned in Adam, lie under the curse, and are deserving of eternal death, God would have done no injustice by leaving them all to perish, and delivering them over to condemnation on account of sin, according to the words of the apostle, Rom. 3:19, "that every mouth may be stopped, and all the world may become guilty before God." And verse 23: "for all have sinned, and come short of the glory of God." And Rom. 6:23: "for the wages of sin is death."

Article 2. But in this the love of God was manifested, that he sent his only begotten Son into the world, that whosoever believeth on him should not perish, but have everlasting life. 1 John 4:9. John 3:16.

Article 3. And that men may be brought to believe, God mercifully sends the messengers of these most joyful tidings, to whom he will and at what time he pleaseth; by whose ministry men are called to repentance and faith in Christ crucified. Rom. 10: 14, 15. "How then shall they call on him in whom they have not believed? And how shall they believe in him of whom they have not heard? And how shall they hear without a preacher? And how shall they preach except they be sent?"

Article 4. The wrath of God abideth upon those who believe not this gospel. But such as receive it, and embrace Jesus the Savior by a true and living faith, are by him delivered from the wrath of God, and from destruction, and have the gift of eternal life conferred upon them.

Article 5. The cause or guilt of this unbelief as well as of all other sins, is no wise in God, but in man himself; whereas faith in Jesus Christ, and salvation through him is the free gift of God, as it is written: "By grace ye are saved through faith, and that not of yourselves, it is the gift of God." Eph. 2:8. "And unto you it is given in the behalf of Christ, not only to believe on him," etc. Phil. 1:29.

Article 6. That some receive the gift of faith from God, and others do not receive it proceeds from God's eternal decree, "For known unto God are all his works from the beginning of the world," Acts 15:18. "Who worketh all things after the counsel of his will," Eph. 1:11. According to which decree, he graciously softens the hearts of the elect, however obstinate, and inclines them to believe, while he leaves the non-elect in his just judgment to their own wickedness and obduracy. And herein is especially displayed the profound, the merciful, and at the same time the righteous discrimination between men, equally involved in ruin; or that decree of election and reprobation, revealed in the Word of God, which though men of perverse, impure and unstable minds wrest to their own destruction, yet to holy and pious souls affords unspeakable consolation.

Article 7. Election is the unchangeable purpose of God, whereby, before the foundation of the world, he hath out of mere grace, according to the sovereign good pleasure of his own will, chosen, from the whole human race, which had fallen through their own fault, from their primitive state of rectitude, into sin and destruction, a certain number of persons to redemption in Christ, whom he from eternity appointed the Mediator and Head of the elect, and the foundation of Salvation.

This elect number, though by nature neither better nor more deserving than others, but with them involved in one common misery, God hath decreed to give to Christ, to be saved by him, and effectually to call and draw them to his communion by his Word and Spirit, to bestow upon them true faith, justification and sanctification; and having powerfully preserved them in the fellowship of his Son, finally, to glorify them for the demonstration of his mercy, and for the praise of his glorious grace; as it is written: "According as he hath chosen us in him, before the foundation of the world, that we should be holy, and without blame before him in love; having predestinated us unto the adoption of children by Jesus Christ to himself, according to the good pleasure of his will, to the praise of the glory of his grace, wherein he hath made us accepted in the beloved." Eph. 1:4, 5, 6. And elsewhere: "Whom he did predestinate, them he also called, and whom he called, them he also justified, and whom he justified them he also glorified." Rom. 8:30.

Article 8. There are not various decrees of election, but one and the same decree respecting all those, who shall be saved, both under the Old and New Testament: since the scripture declares the good pleasure, purpose and counsel of the divine will to be one, according to which he hath chosen us from eternity, both to grace and glory, to salvation and the way of salvation, which he hath ordained that we should walk therein.

Article 9. This election was not founded upon foreseen faith, and the obedience of faith, holiness, or any other good quality or disposition in man, as the pre-requisite, cause or condition on which it depended; but men are chosen to faith and to the obedience of faith, holiness, etc., therefore election is the fountain of every saving good; from which proceed faith, holiness, and the other gifts of salvation, and finally eternal life itself, as its fruits and effects, according to that of the apostle: "He hath chosen us (not because we were) but that we should be holy, and without blame, before him in love." Eph. 1:4.

Article 10. The good pleasure of God is the sole cause of this gracious election; which doth not consist herein, that out of all possible qualities and actions of men God has chosen some as a condition of salvation; but that he was pleased out of the common mass of sinners to adopt some certain persons as a peculiar people to himself, as it is written, "For the children being not yet born neither having done any good or evil," etc., it was said (namely to Rebecca): "the elder shall serve the younger; as it is written, Jacob have I loved, but Esau have I hated." Rom 9:11, 12, 13. "And as many as were ordained to eternal life believed." Acts 13:48.

Article 11. And as God himself is most wise, unchangeable, omniscient and omnipotent, so the election made by him can neither be interrupted nor changed, recalled or annulled; neither can the elect be cast away, nor their number diminished.

Article 12. The elect in due time, though in various degrees and in different measures, attain the assurance of this their eternal and unchangeable election, not by inquisitively prying into the secret and deep things of God, but by observing in themselves with a spiritual joy and holy pleasure, the infallible fruits of election pointed out in the Word of God—such as a true faith in Christ, filial fear, a godly sorrow for sin, a hungering and thirsting after righteousness, etc.

Article 13. The sense and certainty of this election afford to the children of God additional matter for daily humiliation before him, for adoring the depth of his mercies, for cleansing themselves, and rendering grateful returns of ardent love to him, who first manifested so great love towards them. The consideration of this doctrine of election is so far from encouraging remissness in the observance of the divine commands, or from sinking men in carnal security, that these, in the just judgment of God, are the usual effects of rash presumption, or of idle and wanton trifling with the grace of election, in those who refuse to walk in the ways of the elect.

Article 14. As the doctrine of divine election by the most wise counsel of God, was declared by the prophets, by Christ himself, and by the apostles, and is clearly revealed in the Scriptures, both of the Old and New Testament, so it is still to be published in due time and place in the Church of God, for which it was peculiarly designed, provided it be done with reverence, in the spirit of discretion and piety, for the glory of God's most holy name, and for enlivening and comforting his people, without vainly attempting to investigate the secret ways of the Most High. Acts 20:27; Rom. 11:33, 34; 12:3; Heb. 6:17, 18.

Article 15. What peculiarly tends to illustrate and recommend to us the eternal and unmerited grace of election, is the express testimony of sacred Scripture, that not all, but some only are elected, while others are passed by in the eternal decree; whom God, out of his sovereign, most just, irreprehensible and unchangeable good pleasure, hath decreed to leave in the common misery into which they have wilfully plunged themselves, and not to bestow upon them saving faith and the grace of conversion; but permitting them in his just judgment to follow their own ways, at last for the declaration of his justice, to condemn and perish them forever, not only on account of their unbelief, but also for all their other sins. And this is the decree of reprobation which by no means makes God the author of sin (the very thought of which is blasphemy), but declares him to be an awful, irreprehensible, and righteous judge and avenger thereof.

Article 16. Those who do not yet experience a lively faith in Christ, an assured confidence of soul, peace of conscience, an earnest endeavor after filial obedience, and glorying in God through Christ, efficaciously wrought in them, and do nevertheless persist in the use of the means which God hath appointed for working these graces in us, ought not to be alarmed at the mention of reprobation, nor to rank themselves among the reprobate, but diligently to persevere in the use of means, and with ardent desires, devoutly and humbly to wait for a season of richer grace. Much less cause have they to be terrified by the doctrine of reprobation, who, though they seriously desire to be turned to God, to please him only, and to be delivered from the body of death, cannot yet reach that measure of holiness and faith to which they aspire; since a merciful God has promised that he will not quench the smoking flax, nor break the bruised reed. But this doctrine is justly terrible to those, who, regardless of God and of the Savior Jesus Christ, have wholly given themselves up to the cares of the world, and the pleasures of the flesh, so long as they are not seriously converted to God.

Article 17. Since we are to judge of the will of God from his Word, which testifies that the children of believers are holy, not by nature, but in virtue of the covenant of grace, in which they, together with the parents, are comprehended, godly parents have no reason to doubt of the election and salvation of their children, whom it pleaseth God to call out of this life in their infancy.

Article 18. To those who murmur at the free grace of election, and just severity of reprobation, we answer with the apostle: "Nay, but, O man, who art thou that repliest against God?" Rom. 9:30, and quote the language of our Savior: "Is it not lawful for me to do what I will with mine own?" Matt. 20:15. And therefore with holy adoration of these mysteries, we exclaim in the words of the apostle: "O the depth of the riches both of the wisdom and knowledge of God! how unsearchable are his judgments, and his ways past finding out! For who hath known the mind of the Lord, or who hath been his counsellor? or who hath first given to him, and it shall be recompensed unto him again? For of him, and through him, and to him are all things: to whom be glory for ever.—Amen."

The true doctrine concerning Election and Rejection having been explained, the Synod rejects the errors of those:

I.

Who teach: That the will of God to save those who would believe and would persevere in faith and in the obedience of faith, is the whole and entire decree of election unto salvation, and that nothing else concerning this decree has been revealed in God's Word.

For these deceive the simple and plainly contradict the Scriptures, which declare that God will not only save those who will believe, but that he has also from eternity chosen certain particular persons to whom above others he in time will grant both faith in Christ and perseverance; as it is written: "I manifested thy name unto the men whom thou gavest me out of the world." John 17:6. "And as many as were ordained to eternal life believed," Acts 13:48. And: "Even as he chose us in him before the foundation of the world, that we should be holy and without blemish before him in love." Eph. 1:4.

II.

Who teach: That there are various kinds of election of God unto eternal life: the one general and indefinite, the other particular and definite; and that the latter in turn is either incomplete, revocable, non-decisive and conditional, or complete, irrevocable, decisive and absolute. Likewise: that there is one election unto faith, and another unto salvation, so that election can be unto justifying faith, without being a decisive election unto salvation. For this is a fancy of men's minds, invented regardless of the Scriptures, whereby the doctrine of election is corrupted, and this golden chain of our salvation is broken: "And whom he foreordained, them he also called; and whom he called, them he also justified; and whom he justified, them he also glorified." Rom. 8:30.

III.

Who teach: That the good pleasure and purpose of God, of which Scripture makes mention in the doctrine of election, does not consist in this, that God chose certain persons rather than others, but in this that he chose out of all possible conditions (among which are also the works of the law), or out of the whole order of things, the act of faith which from its very nature is undeserving, as well as its incomplete obedience, as a condition of salvation, and that he would graciously consider this in itself as a complete obedience and count it worthy of the reward of eternal life. For by this injurious error the pleasure of God and the merits of Christ are made of none effect, and men are drawn away by useless questions from the truth of gracious justification and from the simplicity of Scripture, and this declaration of the Apostle is charged as untrue: "Who saved us, and called us with a holy calling, not according to our works, but according to his own purpose and grace, which was given us in Christ Jesus before times eternal." 2 Tim. 1:9.

IV.

Who teach: That in the election unto faith this condition is beforehand demanded, viz., that man should use the light of nature aright, be pious, humble, meek, and fit for eternal life, as if on these things election were in any way dependent. For this savors of the teaching of Pelagius, and is opposed to the doctrine of the apostle, when he writes: "Among whom we also all once lived in the lust of our flesh, doing the desires of the flesh and of the mind, and were by nature children of wrath, even as the rest; but God being rich in mercy, for his great love wherewith he loved us, even when we were dead through our trespasses, made us alive together with Christ (by grace have ye been saved), and raised us up with him, and made us to sit with him in heavenly places, in Christ Jesus; that in the ages to come he might show the exceeding riches of his grace in kindness towards us in Christ Jesus; for by grace have ye been saved through faith; and that not of yourselves, it is the gift of God; not of works, that no man should glory." —Eph. 2:3-9.

V.

Who teach: That the incomplete and non-decisive election of particular persons to salvation occurred because of a foreseen faith, conversion, holiness, godliness, which either began or continued for some time; but that the complete and decisive election occurred because of foreseen perseverance unto the end in faith, conversion, holiness and godliness; and that this is the gracious and evangelical worthiness, for the sake of which he who is chosen, is more worthy than he who is not chosen; and that therefore faith, the obedience of faith, holiness, godliness and perseverance are not fruits of the unchangeable election unto glory, but are conditions, which, being required beforehand, were foreseen as being met by those who will be fully elected, and are causes without which the unchangeable election to glory does not occur.

This is repugnant to the entire Scripture, which constantly inculcates this and similar declarations: Election is not out of works, but of him that calleth. Rom. 9:11. "And as many as were ordained to eternal life believed," Acts 13:48. "He chose us in him before the foundation of the world, that we should be holy," Eph. 1:4. "Ye did not choose me, but I chose you," John 15:16. "But if it be of grace, it is no more of works," Rom. 11:6. "Herein is love, not that we loved God, but that he loved us, and sent his Son," 1 John 4:10.

VI.

Who teach: That not every election unto salvation is unchangeable, but that some of the elect, any decree of God notwithstanding, can yet perish and do indeed perish. By which gross error they make God to be changeable, and destroy the comfort which the godly obtain out of the firmness of their election, and contradict the Holy Scripture, which teaches, that the elect can not be led astray. Matt. 24:24; that Christ does not lose those whom the Father gave him. John 6:39; and that God hath also glorified those whom he foreordained, called and justified. Rom. 8:30.

VII.

Who teach: That there is in this life no fruit and no consciousness of the unchangeable election to glory, nor any certainty, except that which depends on a changeable and uncertain condition. For not only is it absurd to speak of an uncertain certainty, but also contrary to the experience of the saints, who by virtue of the consciousness of their election rejoice with the Apostle and praise this favor of God, Eph. 1; who according to Christ's admonition rejoice with his disciples that their names are written in heaven, Luke 10:20; who also place the consciousness of their election over against the fiery darts of the devil, asking: "Who shall lay anything to the charge of God's elect?" Rom. 8:33.

VIII.

Who teach: That God, simply by virtue of his righteous will, did not decide either to leave anyone in the fall of Adam and in the common state of sin and condemnation, or to pass anyone by in the communication of grace which is necessary for faith and conversion. For this is firmly decreed: "He hath mercy on whom he will, and whom he will he hardeneth," Rom. 9:18. And also this: "Unto you it is given to know the mysteries of the kingdom of heaven, but to them it is not given," Matt. 13:11. Likewise: "I thank thee, O Father, Lord of heaven and earth, that thou didst hide these things from the wise and understanding, and didst reveal them unto babes; yea, Father, for so it was well-pleasing in thy sight," Matt. 11:25, 26.

IX.

Who teach: That the reason why God sends the gospel to one people rather than to another is not merely and solely the good pleasure of God, but rather the fact that one people is better and worthier than another to whom the gospel is not communicated. For this Moses denies, addressing the people of Israel as follows: "Behold unto Jehovah thy God belongeth heaven and the heaven of heavens, the earth, with all that is therein. Only Jehovah had a delight in thy fathers to love him, and he chose their seed after them, even you above all peoples, as at this day," Deut. 10: 14, 15. And Christ said: "Woe unto thee, Chorazin! woe unto thee, Bethsaida! for if the mighty works had been done in Tyre and Sidon which were done in you, they would have repented long ago in sackcloth and ashes." Matt. 11:21.

SECOND HEAD OF DOCTRINE.

OF THE DEATH OF CHRIST, AND THE REDEMPTION OF MEN THEREBY.

Article 1. God is not only supremely merciful, but also supremely just. And his justice requires (as he hath revealed himself in his Word), that our sins committed against his infinite majesty should be punished, not only with temporal, but with eternal punishment, both in body and soul; which we cannot escape, unless satisfaction be made to the justice of God.

Article 2. Since therefore we are unable to make that satisfaction in our own persons, or to deliver ourselves from the wrath of God, he hath been pleased in his infinite mercy to give his only begotten Son, for our surety, who was made sin, and became a curse for us and in our stead, that he might make satisfaction to divine justice on our behalf.

Article 3. The death of the Son of God is the only and most perfect sacrifice and satisfaction for sin; and is of infinite worth and value, abundantly sufficient to expiate the sins of the whole world.

Article 4. This death derives its infinite value and dignity from these considerations, because the person who submitted to it was not only really man, and perfectly holy, but also the only begotten Son of God, of the same eternal and infinite essence with the Father and the Holy Spirit, which qualifications were necessary to constitute him a Savior for us; and because it was attended with a sense of the wrath and curse of God due to us for sin.

Article 5. Moreover, the promise of the gospel is, that whosoever believeth in Christ crucified, shall not perish, but have everlasting life. This promise, together with the command to repent and believe, ought to be declared and published to all nations, and to all persons promiscuously and without distinction, to whom God out of his good pleasure sends the gospel.

Article 6. And, whereas many who are called by the gospel, do not repent, nor believe in Christ, but perish in unbelief; this is not owing to any defect or insufficiency in the sacrifice offered by Christ upon the cross, but is wholly to be imputed to themselves.

Article 7. But as many as truly believe, and are delivered and saved from sin and destruction through the death of Christ, are indebted for this benefit solely to the grace of God, given them in Christ from everlasting, and not to any merit of their own.

Article 8. For this was the sovereign counsel, and most gracious will and purpose of God the Father, that the quickening and saving efficacy of the most precious death of his Son should extend to all the elect, for bestowing upon them alone the gift of justifying faith, thereby to bring them infallibly to salvation: that is, it was the will of God, that Christ by the blood of the cross, whereby he confirmed the new covenant, should effectually redeem out of every people, tribe, nation, and language, all those, and those only, who were from eternity chosen to salvation, and given to him by the Father; that he should confer upon them faith, which together with all the other saving gifts of the Holy Spirit, he purchased for them by his death; should purge them from all sin, both original and actual, whether committed before or after believing; and having faithfully preserved them even to the end, should at last bring them free from every spot and blemish to the enjoyment of glory in his own presence forever.

Article 9. This purpose proceeding from everlasting love towards the elect, has from the beginning of the world to this day been powerfully accomplished, and will henceforward still continue to be accomplished, notwithstanding all the ineffectual opposition of the gates of hell, so that the elect in due time may be gathered together into one, and that there never may be wanting a church composed of believers, the foundation of which is laid in the blood of Christ, which may steadfastly love, and faithfully serve him as their Savior, who as a bridegroom for his bride, laid down his life for them upon the cross, and which may celebrate his praises here and through all eternity.

The true doctrine having been explained, the Synod **rejects** the errors of those:

I.

Who teach: That God the Father has ordained his Son to the death of the cross without a certain and definite decree to save any, so that the necessity, profitableness and worth of what Christ merited by his death might have existed, and might remain in all its parts complete, perfect and intact, even if the merited redemption had never in fact been applied to any person. For this doctrine tends to the despising of the wisdom of the Father and of the merits of Jesus Christ, and is contrary to Scripture. For thus saith our Savior: "I lay down my life for the sheep, and I know them," John 10:15, 27. And the prophet Isaiah saith concerning the Savior: "When thou shalt make his soul an offering for sin, he shall see his seed, he shall prolong his days, and the pleasure of Jehovah shall prosper in his hand," Is. 53:10. Finally, this contradicts the article of faith according to which we believe the catholic christian church.

II.

Who teach: That it was not the purpose of the death of Christ that he should confirm the new covenant of grace through his blood, but only that he should acquire for the Father the mere right to establish with man such a covenant as he might please, whether of grace or of works. For this is repugnant to Scripture which teaches that Christ has become the Surety and Mediator of a better, that is, the new covenant, and that a testament is of force where death has occurred. Heb. 7:22; 9:15, 17.

III.

Who teach: That Christ by his satisfaction merited neither salvation itself for anyone, nor faith, whereby this satisfaction of Christ unto salvation is effectually appropriated; but that he merited for the Father only the authority or the perfect will to deal again with man, and to prescribe new conditions as he might desire, obedience to which, however, depended on the free will of man, so that it therefore might have come to pass that either none or all should fulfill these conditions. For these adjudge too contemptuously of the death of Christ, do in no wise acknowledge the most important fruit or benefit thereby gained, and bring again out of hell the Pelagian error.

IV.

Who teach: That the new covenant of grace, which God the Father, through the mediation of the death of Christ, made with man, does not herein consist that we by faith, in as much as it accepts the merits of Christ, are justified before God and saved, but in the fact that God having revoked the demand of perfect obedience of faith, regards faith itself and the obedience of faith, although imperfect, as the perfect obedience of the law, and does esteem it worthy of the reward of eternal life through grace. For these contradict the Scriptures: "Being justified freely by his grace through the redemption that is in Christ Jesus; whom God set forth to be a propitiation through faith in his blood," Rom. 3:24, 25. And these proclaim, as did the wicked Socinus, a new and strange justification of man before God, against the consensus of the whole church.

V.

Who teach: That all men have been accepted unto the state of reconciliation and unto the grace of the covenant, so that no one is worthy of condemnation on account of original sin, and that no one shall be condemned because of it, but that all are free from the guilt of original sin. For this opinion is repugnant to Scripture which teaches that we are by nature children of wrath. Eph. 2:3.

VI.

Who use the difference between meriting and appropriating, to the end that they may instill into the minds of the imprudent and inexperienced this teaching that God, as far as he is concerned, has been minded of applying to all equally the benefits gained by the death of Christ; but that, while some obtain the pardon of sin and eternal life, and others do not, this difference depends on their own free will, which joins itself to the grace that is offered without exception, and that it is not dependent on the special gift of mercy, which powerfully works in them, that they rather than others should appropriate unto themselves this grace. For these, while they feign that they present this distinction, in a sound sense, seek to instill into the people the destructive poison of the Pelagian errors.

VII.

Who teach: That Christ neither could die, needed to die, nor did die for those whom God loved in the high-est degree and elected to eternal life, and did not die for these, since these do not need the death of Christ. For they contradict the Apostle, who declares: "Christ loved me, and gave himself for me," Gal. 2:20. Likewise: "Who shall lay any thing to the charge of God's elect? It is God that justifieth; who is he that condemneth? It is Christ Jesus that died," Rom. 8: 33, 34, viz., for them; and the Savior who says: "I lay down my life for the sheep," John 10:15. And: "This is my commandment, that ye love one another, even as I have loved you. Greater love hath no man than this, that a man lay down his life for his friends," John 15:12, 13.

———·❆ ❆·———

THIRD AND FOURTH HEADS OF DOCTRINE.

··❂❧❂··

OF THE CORRUPTION OF MAN, HIS CONVERSION TO GOD, AND THE MANNER THEREOF.

Article 1. Man was originally formed after the image of God. His understanding was adorned with a true and saving knowledge of his Creator, and of spiritual things; his heart and will were upright; all his affections pure; and the whole man was holy; but revolting from God by the instigation of the devil, and abusing the freedom of his own will, he forfeited these excellent gifts; and on the contrary entailed on himself blindness of mind, horrible darkness, vanity and perverseness of judgment, became wicked, rebellious, and obdurate in heart and will, and impure in his affections.

Article 2. Man after the fall begat children in his own likeness. A corrupt stock produced a corrupt offspring. Hence all the posterity of Adam, Christ only excepted, have derived corruption from their original parent, not by imitation, as the Pelagians of old asserted, but by the propagation of a vicious nature.

Article 3. Therefore all men are conceived in sin, and by nature children of wrath, incapable of saving good, prone to evil, dead in sin, and in bondage thereto, and without the regenerating grace of the Holy Spirit, they are neither able nor willing to return to God, to reform the depravity of their nature, nor to dispose themselves to reformation.

Article 4. There remain, however, in man since the fall, the glimmerings of natural light, whereby he retains some knowledge of God, of natural things, and of the differences between good and evil, and discovers some regard for virtue, good order in society, and for maintaining an orderly external deportment. But so far is this light of nature from being sufficient to bring him to a saving knowledge of God, and to true conversion, that he is incapable of using it aright even in things natural and civil. Nay further, this light, such as it is, man in various ways renders wholly polluted, and holds it in unrighteousness, by doing which he becomes inexcusable before God.

Article 5. In the same light are we to consider the law of the decalogue, delivered by God to his peculiar people the Jews, by the hands of Moses. For though it discovers the greatness of sin, and more and more convinces man thereof, yet as it neither points out a remedy, nor imparts strength to extricate him from misery, and thus being weak through the flesh, leaves the transgressor under the curse, man cannot by this law obtain saving grace.

Article 6. What therefore neither the light of nature, nor the law could do, that God performs by the operation of the Holy Spirit through the word or ministry of reconciliation: which is the glad tidings concerning the Messiah, by means whereof, it hath pleased God to save such as believe, as well under the Old, as under the New Testament.

Article 7. This mystery of his will God discovered to but a small number under the Old Testament; under the New, (the distinction between various peoples having been removed), he reveals himself to many, without any distinction of people. The cause of this dispensation is not to be ascribed to the superior worth of one nation above another, nor to their making a better use of the light of nature, but results wholly from the sovereign good pleasure and unmerited love of God. Hence they, to whom so great and so gracious a blessing is communicated, above their desert, or rather notwithstanding their demerits, are bound to acknowledge it with humble and grateful hearts, and with the apostle to adore, not curiously to pry into the severity and justice of God's judgments displayed to others, to whom this grace is not given.

Article 8. As many as are called by the gospel, are unfeignedly called. For God hath most earnestly and truly declared in his Word, what will be acceptable to him; namely, that all who are called, should comply with the invitation. He, moreover, seriously promises eternal life, and rest, to as many as shall come to him, and believe on him.

Article 9. It is not the fault of the gospel, nor of Christ, offered therein, nor of God, who calls men by the gospel, and confers upon them various gifts, that those who are called by the ministry of the word, refuse to come, and be converted: the fault lies in themselves; some of whom when called, regardless of their danger, reject the word of life; others, though they receive it, suffer it not to make a lasting impression on their heart; therefore, their joy, arising only from a temporary faith, soon vanishes, and

they fall away; while others choke the seed of the word by perplexing cares, and the pleasures of this world, and produce no fruit.—This our Savior teaches in the parable of the sower. Matt. 13.

Article 10. But that others who are called by the gospel, obey the call, and are converted, is not to be ascribed to the proper exercise of free will, whereby one distinguishes himself above others, equally furnished with grace sufficient for faith and conversions, as the proud heresy of Pelagius maintains; but it must be wholly ascribed to God, who as he has chosen his own from eternity in Christ, so he confers upon them faith and repentance, rescues them from the power of darkness, and translates them into the kingdom of his own Son, that they may show forth the praises of him, who hath called them out of darkness into his marvelous light; and may glory not in themselves, but in the Lord according to the testimony of the apostles in various places.

Article 11. But when God accomplishes his good pleasure in the elect, or works in them true conversion, he not only causes the gospel to be externally preached to them, and powerfully illuminates their minds by his Holy Spirit, that they may rightly understand and discern the things of the Spirit of God; but by the efficacy of the same regenerating Spirit, pervades the inmost recesses of the man; he opens the closed, and softens the hardened heart, and circumcises that which was uncircumcised, infuses new qualities into the will, which though heretofore dead, he quickens; from being evil, disobedient, and refractory, he renders it good, obedient, and pliable; actuates and strengthens it, that like a good tree, it may bring forth the fruits of good actions.

Article 12. And this is the regeneration so highly celebrated in Scripture, and denominated a new creation: a resurrection from the dead, a making alive, which God works in us without our aid. But this is in no wise effected merely by the external preaching of the gospel, by moral suasion, or such a mode of operation, that after God has performed his part, it still remains in the power of man to be regenerated or not, to be converted.

or to continue unconverted; but it is evidently a supernatural work, most powerful, and at the same time most delightful, astonishing, mysterious, and ineffable; not inferior in efficacy to creation, or the resurrection from the dead, as the Scripture inspired by the author of this work declares; so that all in whose heart God works in this marvelous manner, are certainly, infallibly, and effectually regenerated, and do actually believe.—Whereupon the will thus renewed, is not only actuated and influenced by God, but in consequence of this influence, becomes itself active. Wherefore also, man is himself rightly said to believe and repent, by virtue of that grace received.

Article 13. The manner of this operation cannot be fully comprehended by believers in this life. Notwithstanding which, they rest satisfied with knowing and experiencing, that by this grace of God they are enabled to believe with the heart, and love their Savior.

Article 14. Faith is therefore to be considered as the gift of God, not on account of its being offered by God to man, to be accepted or rejected at his pleasure; but because it is in reality conferred, breathed, and infused into him; or even because God bestows the power or ability to believe, and then expects that man should by the exercise of his own free will, consent to the terms of salvation, and actually believe in Christ; but because he who works in man both to will and to do, and indeed all things in all, produces both the will to believe, and the act of believing also.

Article 15. God is under no obligation to confer this grace upon any; for how can he be indebted to man, who had no previous gifts to bestow, as a foundation for such recompense? Nay, who has nothing of his own but sin and falsehood? He therefore who becomes the subject of this grace, owes eternal gratitude to God, and gives him thanks forever. Whoever is not made partaker thereof, is either altogether regardless of these spiritual gifts, and satisfied with his own condition; or is in no apprehension of danger, and vainly boasts the possession of that which he has not. With respect to those who make an external profession of faith, and live regular lives, we are bound, after the example of the apostle, to judge and speak of them in the most favorable manner. For the secret recesses of the heart are unknown to us. And as to others, who have not yet been called, it is our duty to pray for them to God, who calls the things that are not, as if they were. But we are in no wise to conduct ourselves towards them with haughtiness, as if we had made ourselves to differ.

Article 16. But as man by the fall did not cease to be a creature, endowed with understanding and will, nor did sin which pervaded the whole race of mankind, deprive him of the human nature, but brought upon him depravity and spiritual death; so also this grace of regeneration does not treat men as senseless stocks and blocks, nor takes away their will and its properties, neither does violence thereto; but spiritually quickens, heals, corrects, and at the same time sweetly and powerfully bends it; that where carnal rebellion and resistance formerly prevailed, a ready and sincere spiritual obedience begins to reign; in which the true and spiritual restoration and freedom of our will consist. Wherefore unless the admirable author of every good work wrought in us, man could have no hope of recovering from his fall by his own free will, by the abuse of which, in a state of innocence, he plunged himself into ruin.

Article 17. As the almighty operation of God, whereby he prolongs and supports this our natural life, does not exclude, but requires the use of means, by which God of his infinite mercy and goodness hath chosen to exert his influence, so also the beforementioned supernatural operation of God, by which we are regenerated, in no wise excludes, or subverts the use of the gospel, which the most wise God has ordained to be the seed of regeneration, and food of the soul. Wherefore, as the apostles, and teachers who succeeded them, piously instructed the people concerning this grace of God, to his glory, and the abasement of all pride, and in the meantime, however, neglected not to keep them by the sacred precepts of the gospel in the exercise of the Word, sacraments and discipline; so even to this day, be it far from either instructors or instructed to presume to tempt God in the church by separating what he of his good pleasure hath most intimately joined together. For grace is conferred by means of admonitions; and the more readily we perform our duty, the more eminent usually is this blessing of God working in us, and the more directly is his work advanced; to whom alone all the glory both of means, and of their saving fruit and efficacy is forever due. Amen.

———

The true doctrine having been explained, the Synod rejects the errors of those:

I.

Who teach: That it cannot properly be said, that original sin in itself suffices to condemn the whole human race, or to deserve temporal and eternal punishment. For these contradict the Apostle, who declares: "Therefore as through one man sin entered into the world, and death through sin, and so death passed unto all men, for that all sinned," Rom. 5:12. And: "The judgment came of one unto condemnation," Rom. 5:16. And: "The wages of sin is death," Rom. 6:23.

II.

Who teach: That the spiritual gifts, or the good qualities and virtues, such as: goodness, holiness, righteousness, could not belong to the will of man when he was first created, and that these, therefore, could not have been separated therefrom in the fall. For such is contrary to the description of the image of God, which the Apostle gives in Eph. 4:24, where he declares that it consists in righteousness and holiness, which undoubtedly belong to the will.

III.

Who teach: That in spiritual death the spiritual gifts are not separate from the will of man, since the will in itself has never been corrupted, but only hindered through the darkness of the understanding and the irregularity of the affections; and that, these hindrances having been removed, the will can then bring into operation its native powers, that is, that the will of itself is able to will and to choose, or

not to will and not to choose, all manner of good which may be presented to it. This is an innovation and an error, and tends to elevate the powers of the free will, contrary to the declaration of the Prophet: "The heart is deceitful above all things, and it is exceedingly corrupt," Jer. 17:9; and of the Apostle: "Among whom (sons of disobedience) we also all once lived in the lusts of the flesh, doing the desires of the flesh and of the mind," Eph. 2:3.

IV.

Who teach: That the unregenerate man is not really nor utterly dead in sin, nor destitute of all powers unto spiritual good, but that he can yet hunger and thirst after righteousness and life, and offer the sacrifice of a contrite and broken spirit, which is pleasing to God. For these are contrary to the express testimony of Scripture. "Ye were dead through trespasses and sins," Eph. 2:1, 5; and: "Every imagination of the thought of his heart are only evil continually," Gen. 6:5; 8:21.

Moreover, to hunger and thirst after deliverance from misery, and after life, and to offer unto God the sacrifice of a broken spirit, is peculiar to the regenerate and those that are called blessed. Ps. 51:10, 19; Matt. 5:6.

V.

Who teach: That the corrupt and natural man can so well use the common grace (by which they understand the light of nature), or the gifts still left him after the fall, that he can gradually gain by their good use a greater, viz., the evangelical or saving grace and salvation itself. And that in this way God on his part shows himself ready to reveal Christ to all men, since he applies to all sufficiently and efficiently the means necessary to conversion. For the experience of all ages and the Scriptures do both testify that this is untrue. "He showeth his Word unto Jacob, his statutes and his ordinances unto Israel. He hath not dealt so with any nation: and as for his ordinances they have not known them," Ps. 147:19, 20. "Who in the generations gone by suffered all the nations to walk in their own way," Acts 14:16. And: "And they (Paul and his companions) having been forbidden of the Holy Spirit to speak the word in Asia, and when they were come over against Mysia, they assayed to go into Bithynia, and the Spirit suffered them not," Acts 16:6, 7.

VI.

Who teach: That in the true conversion of man no new qualities, powers or gifts can be infused by God into the will, and that therefore faith through which we are first converted, and because of which we are called believers, is not a quality or gift infused by God, but only an act of man, and that it can not be said to be a gift, except in respect of the power to attain to this faith. For thereby they contradict the Holy Scriptures, which declare that God infuses new qualities of faith, of obedience, and of the consciousness of his love into our hearts: "I will put my law in their inward parts, and in their hearts will I write it," Jer. 31:33. And: "I will pour water upon him that is thirsty, and streams upon the dry ground; I will pour my Spirit upon thy seed," Is. 44:3. And: "The love of God hath been shed abroad in our hearts through the Holy Spirit which hath been given us," Rom. 5:5. This is also repugnant to the continuous practice of the Church, which prays by the mouth of the Prophet thus: "Turn thou me, and I shall be turned," Jer. 31:18.

VII.

Who teach: That the grace whereby we are converted to God is only a gentle advising, or (as others explain it), that this is the noblest manner of working in the conversion of man, and that this manner of working, which consists in advising, is most in harmony with man's nature; and that there is no reason why this advising grace alone should not be sufficient to make the natural man spiritual, indeed, that God does not produce the consent of the will except through this manner of advising; and that the power of the divine working, whereby it surpasses the working of Satan, consists in this, that God promises eternal, while Satan promises only temporal goods. But this is altogether Pelagian and contrary to the whole Scripture which, besides this, teaches yet another and far more powerful and divine manner of the Holy Spirit's working in the conversion of man, as in Ezekiel: "A new heart also will I give you, and a new spirit will I put within you; and I will take away the stony heart out of your flesh, and I will give you a heart of flesh," Ezek. 36:26.

VIII.

Who teach: That God in the regeneration of man does not use such powers of his omnipotence as potently and infallibly bend man's will to faith and conversion; but that all the works of grace having been accomplished, which God employs to convert man, man may yet so resist God and the Holy Spirit, when God intends man's regeneration and wills to regenerate him, and indeed that man often does so resist that he prevents entirely his regeneration, and that it therefore remains in man's power to be regenerated or not. For this is nothing less than the denial of all the efficiency of God's grace in our conversion, and the subjecting of the working of Almighty God to the will of man, which is contrary to the Apostles, who teach: "That we believe according to the working of the strength of his power," Eph. 1:19. And: "That God fulfils every desire of goodness and every work of faith with power," 2 Thess. 1:11. And: "That his divine power hath given unto us all things that pertain unto life and godliness," 2 Peter 1:3.

IX.

Who teach: That grace and free will are partial causes, which together work the beginning of conversion, and that grace, in order of working, does not precede the working of the will; that is, that God does not efficiently help the will of man unto conversion until the will of man moves and determines to do this. For the ancient Church has long ago condemned this doctrine of the Pelagians according to the words of the Apostle: "So then it is not of him that willeth, nor of him that runneth, but of God that hath mercy," Rom. 9:16. Likewise: "For who maketh thee to differ? and what hast thou that thou didst not receive?" 1 Cor. 4:7. And: "For it is God who worketh in you both to will and to work, for his good pleasure," Phil. 2:13.

FIFTH HEAD OF DOCTRINE.

··◁▥▷··

OF THE PERSEVERANCE OF THE SAINTS.

Article 1. Whom God calls, according to his purpose, to the communion of his Son, our Lord Jesus Christ, and regenerates by the Holy Spirit, he delivers also from the dominion and slavery of sin in this life; though not altogether from the body of sin, and from the infirmities of the flesh, so long as they continue in this world.

Article 2. Hence spring daily sins of infirmity, and hence spots adhere to the best works of the saints; which furnish them with constant matter for humiliation before God, and flying for refuge to Christ crucified; for mortifying the flesh more and more by the spirit of prayer, and by holy exercises of piety; and for pressing forward to the goal of perfection, till being at length delivered from this body of death, they are brought to reign with the Lamb of God in heaven.

Article 3. By reason of these remains of indwelling sin, and the temptations of sin and of the world, those who are converted could not persevere in a state of grace, if left to their own strength. But God is faithful, who having conferred grace, mercifully confirms, and powerfully preserves them therein, even to the end.

Article 4. Although the weakness of the flesh cannot prevail against the power of God, who confirms and preserves true believers in a state of grace, yet converts are not always so influenced and actuated by the Spirit of God, as not in some particular instances sinfully to deviate from the guidance of divine grace, so as to be seduced by, and comply with the lusts of the flesh; they must, therefore, be constant in watching and prayer, that they be not led into temptation. When these are neglected, they are not only liable to be drawn into great and heinous sins, by Satan, the world and the flesh, but sometimes by the righteous permission of God actually fall into these evils. This, the lamentable fall of David, Peter, and other saints described in Holy Scripture, demonstrates.

Article 5. By such enormous sins, however, they very highly offend God, incur a deadly guilt, grieve the Holy Spirit, interrupt the exercise of faith, very grievously wound their consciences, and sometimes lose the sense of God's favor, for a time, until on their returning into the right way of serious repentance, the light of God's fatherly countenance again shines upon them.

Article 6. But God, who is rich in mercy, according to his unchangeable purpose of election, does not wholly withdraw the Holy Spirit from his own people, even in their melancholy falls; nor suffers them to proceed so far as to lose the grace of adoption, and forfeit the state of justification, or to commit the sin unto death; nor does he permit them to be totally deserted, and to plunge themselves into everlasting destruction.

Article 7. For in the first place, in these falls he preserves in them the incorruptible seed of regeneration from perishing, or being totally lost; and again, by his Word and Spirit, certainly and effectually renews them to repentance, to a sincere and godly sorrow for their sins, that they may seek and obtain remission in the blood of the Mediator, may again experience the favor of a reconciled God, through faith adore his mercies, and henceforward more diligently work out their own salvation with fear and trembling.

Article 8. Thus, it is not in consequence of their own merits, or strength, but of God's free mercy, that they do not totally fall from faith and grace, nor continue and perish finally in their backslidings; which, with respect to themselves, is not only possible, but would undoubtedly happen; but with respect to God, it is utterly impossible, since his counsel cannot be changed, nor his promise fail, neither can the call according to his purpose be revoked, nor the merit, intercession and preservation of Christ be rendered ineffectual, nor the sealing of the Holy Spirit be frustrated or obliterated.

Article 9. Of this preservation of the elect to salvation, and of their perseverance in the faith, true believers for themselves may and do obtain assurance according to the measure of their faith, whereby they arrive at the certain persuasion, that they ever will continue true and living members of the church; and that they experience forgiveness of sins, and will at last inherit eternal life.

Article 10. This assurance, however, is not produced by any peculiar revelation contrary to, or independent of the Word of God; but springs from faith in God's promises, which he has most abundantly revealed in his Word for our comfort; from the testimony of the Holy Spirit, witnessing with our spirit, that we are children and heirs of God, Rom. 8:16; and lastly, from a serious and holy desire to preserve a good conscience, and to perform good works. And if the elect of God were deprived of this solid comfort, that they shall finally obtain the victory, and of this infallible pledge or earnest of eternal glory, they would be of all men the most miserable.

Article 11. The Scripture moreover testifies, that believers in this life have to struggle with various carnal doubts, and that under grievous temptations they are not always sensible of this full assurance of faith and certainty of persevering. But God, who is the Father of all consolation, does not suffer them to be tempted above that they are able, but will with the temptation also make a way to escape, that they may be able to bear it, 1 Cor. 10:13, and by the Holy Spirit again inspires them with the comfortable assurance of persevering.

Article 12. This certainty of perseverance, however, is so far from exciting in believers a spirit of pride, or of rendering them carnally secure, that on the contrary, it is the real source of humility, filial reverence, true piety, patience in every tribulation, fervent prayers, constancy in suffering, and in confessing the truth, and of solid rejoicing in God: so that the consideration of this benefit should serve as an incentive to the serious and constant practice of gratitude and good works, as appears from the testimonies of Scripture, and the examples of the saints.

Article 13. Neither does renewed confidence of persevering produce licentiousness, or a disregard to piety in those who are recovering from backsliding; but it renders them much more careful and solicitous to continue in the ways of the Lord, which he hath ordained, that they who walk therein may maintain an assurance of persevering, lest by abusing his fatherly kindness, God should turn away his gracious countenance from them, to behold which is to the godly dearer than life: the withdrawing whereof is more bitter than death, and they in consequence hereof should fall into more grievous torments of conscience.

Article 14. And as it hath pleased God, by the preaching of the gospel, to begin this work of grace in us, so he preserves, continues, and perfects it by the hearing and reading of his Word, by meditation thereon, and by the exhortations, threatenings, and promises thereof, as well as by the use of the sacraments.

Article 15. The carnal mind is unable to comprehend this doctrine of the perseverance of the saints, and the certainty thereof; which God hath most abundantly revealed in his Word, for the glory of his name, and the consolation of pious souls, and which he impresses upon the hearts of the faithful. Satan abhors it; the world ridicules it; the ignorant and hypocrite abuse, and heretics oppose it; but the spouse of Christ hath always most tenderly loved and constantly defended it, as an inestimable treasure; and God, against whom neither counsel nor strength can prevail, will dispose her to continue this conduct to the end. Now, to this one God, Father, Son, and Holy Spirit, be honor and glory, forever. AMEN.

The true doctrine having been explained, the Synod **rejects the errors** of those:

I.

Who teach: That the perseverance of the true believers is not a fruit of election, or a gift of God, gained by the death of Christ, but a condition of the new covenant, which (as they declare) man before his decisive election and justification must fulfill through his free will. For the Holy Scripture testifies that this follows out of election, and is given the elect in virtue of the death, the resurrection and intercession of Christ: "But the elect obtained it and the rest were hardened," Rom. 11:7. Likewise: "He that spared not his own Son, but delivered him up for us all, how shall he not also with him freely give us all things? Who shall lay anything to the charge of God's elect? It is God that justifieth; who is he that condemneth? It is Christ Jesus that died, yea rather, that was raised from the dead, who is at the right hand of God, who also maketh intercession for us. Who shall separate us from the love of Christ?" Rom. 8:32-35.

II.

Who teach: That God does indeed provide the believer with sufficient powers to persevere, and is ever ready to preserve these in him, if he will do his duty; but that through all things, which are necessary to persevere in faith and which God will use to preserve faith, are made use of, it even then ever depends on the pleasure of the will whether it will persevere or not. For this idea contains an outspoken Pelagianism, and while it would make men free, it makes them robbers of God's honor, contrary to the prevailing agreement of the evangelical doctrine, which takes from man all cause of boasting, and ascribes all the praise for this favor to the grace of God alone; and contrary to the Apostle, who declares: "That it is God, who shall also confirm you unto the end, that ye be unreprovable in the day of our Lord Jesus Christ." 1 Cor. 1:18.

III.

Who teach: That the true believers and regenerate not only can fall from justifying faith and likewise from grace and salvation wholly and to the end, but indeed often do fall from this and are lost forever. For this conception makes powerless the grace, justification, regeneration, and continued keeping by Christ, contrary to the expressed words of the Apostle Paul: "That while we were yet sinners Christ died for us. Much more then, being justified by his blood, shall

we be saved from the wrath of God through him," Rom. 5:8, 9. And contrary to the Apostle John: "Whosoever is begotten of God doeth no sin, because his seed abideth in him; and he can not sin, because he is begotten of God," 1 John 3:9. And also contrary to the words of Jesus Christ: "I give unto them eternal life; and they shall never perish, and no one shall snatch them out of my hand. My Father who hath given them to me, is greater than all; and no one is able to snatch them out of the Father's hand." John 10:28, 29.

IV.

Who teach: That true believers and regenerate can sin the sin unto death or against the Holy Spirit. Since the same Apostle John, after having spoken in the fifth chapter of his first epistle, vss. 16 and 17, of those who sin unto death and having forbidden to pray for them, immediately adds to this in vs. 18: "We know that whosoever is begotten of God sinneth not (meaning a sin of that character), but he that is begotten of God keepeth himself, and the evil one toucheth him not," 1 John 5:18.

V.

Who teach: That without a special revelation we can have no certainty of future perseverance in this life. For by this doctrine the sure comfort of the true believers is taken away in this life, and the doubts of the papist are again introduced into the church, while the Holy Scriptures constantly deduce this assurance, not from a special and extraordinary revelation, but from the marks proper to the children of God and from the constant promises of God. So especially the Apostle Paul: "No creature shall be able to separate us from the love of God, which is in Christ Jesus our Lord," Rom. 8:39. And John declares: "And he that keepeth his commandments abideth in him, and he in him. And hereby we know that he abideth in us, by the Spirit which he gave us." 1 John 3:24.

VI.

Who teach: That the doctrine of the certainty of perseverance and of salvation from its own character and nature is a cause of indolence and is injurious to godliness, good morals, prayers and other holy exercises, but that on the contrary it is praiseworthy to doubt. For these show that they do not know the power of divine grace and the working of the indwelling Holy Spirit. And they contradict the Apostle John, who teaches the opposite with express words in his first epistle: "Beloved, now are we the children of God, and it is not yet made manifest what we shall be. We know that, if he shall be manifested, we shall be like him; for we shall see him even as he is. And every one that hath this hope set on him purifieth himself, even as he is pure," 1 John 3:2, 3. Furthermore, these are contradicted by the example of the saints, both of the Old and the New Testament, who though they were assured of their perseverance and salvation, were nevertheless constant in prayers and other exercises of godliness.

VII.

Who teach: That the faith of those, who believe for a time, does not differ from justifying and saving faith except only in duration. For Christ himself, in Matt. 13:20, Luke 8:13, and in other places, evidently notes, besides this duration, a threefold difference between those who believe only for a time and true believers, when he declares that the former receive the seed in stony ground, but the latter in the good ground or heart; that the former are without root, but the latter have a firm root; that the former are without fruit, but that the latter bring forth their fruit in various measure, with constancy and steadfastness.

VIII.

Who teach: That it is not absurd that one having lost his first regeneration, is again and even often born anew. For these deny by this doctrine the incorruptibleness of the seed of God, whereby we are born again. Contrary to the testimony of the Apostle Peter: "Having been begotten again, not of corruptible seed, but of incorruptible," 1 Peter 1:23.

IX.

Who teach: That Christ has in no place prayed that believers should infallibly continue in faith. For they contradict Christ himself, who says: "I have prayed for thee (Simon), that thy faith fail not," Luke 22:32; and the Evangelist John, who declares, that Christ has not prayed for the Apostles only, but also for those who through their word would believe: "Holy Father, keep them in thy name," and: "I pray not that thou shouldest take them out of the world, but that thou shouldest keep them from the evil one," John 17:11, 15, 20.

————◄ ☧ ►————

CONCLUSION.

And this is the perspicuous, simple, and ingenuous declaration of the orthodox doctrine respecting the five articles which have been controverted in the Belgic churches; and the rejection of the errors, with which they have for some time been troubled. This doctrine, the Synod judges to be drawn from the Word of God, and to be agreeable to the confessions of the Reformed churches. Whence it clearly appears, that some whom such conduct by no means became, have violated all truth, equity, and charity, in wishing to persuade the public.

"That the doctrine of the Reformed churches concerning predestination, and the points annexed to it, by its own genius and necessary tendency, leads off the minds of men from all piety and religion; that it is an opiate administered by the flesh and the devil, and the stronghold of Satan, where he lies in wait for all; and from which he wounds multitudes, and mortally strikes through many with the darts both of despair and security; that it makes God the author of sin, unjust, tyrannical, hypocritical; that it is nothing more than interpolated Stoicism, Manicheism, Libertinism, Turcism; that it renders men carnally secure, since they are persuaded by it that nothing can hinder the salvation of the elect, let them live as they please; and therefore, that they may safely perpetrate every species of the most atrocious crimes; and that, if the reprobate should even perform truly all the works of the saints, their obedience would not in the least contribute to their salvation; that the same doctrine teaches, that God, by a mere arbitrary act of his will, without the least respect or view to any sin, has predestinated the greatest part of the world to eternal damnation; and, has created them for this very purpose; that in the same manner in which the election is the fountain and the cause of faith and good works, reprobation is the cause of unbelief and impiety; that many children of the faithful are torn, guiltless, from their mothers' breasts, and tyrannically plunged into hell; so that, neither baptism, nor the prayers of the Church at their baptism, can at all profit by them;" and many other things of the same kind, which the Reformed Churches not only do not acknowledge, but even detest with their whole soul. Wherefore, this Synod of Dort, in the name of the Lord, conjures as many as piously call upon the name of our Savior Jesus Christ, to judge of the faith of the Reformed Churches, not from the calumnies, which, on every side, are heaped upon it; nor from the private expressions of a few among ancient and modern teachers, often dishonestly quoted, or corrupted, and wrested to a meaning quite foreign to their intention; but from the public confessions of the Churches themselves, and from the declaration of the orthodox doctrine, confirmed by the unanimous consent of all and each of the members of the whole Synod. Moreover, the Synod warns calumniators themselves, to consider the terrible judgment of God which awaits them, for bearing false witness against the confessions of so many Churches, for distressing the conciences of the weak; and for laboring to render suspected the society of the truly faithful. Finally, this Synod exhorts all their brethren in the gospel of Christ, to conduct themselves piously and religiously in handling this doctrine, both in the universities and churches; to direct it, as well in discourse, as in writing, to the glory of the Divine Name, to holiness of life, and to the consolation of afflicted souls; to regulate, by the Scripture, according to the analogy of faith, not only their sentiments, but also their language; and, to abstain from all those phrases which exceed the limits necessary to be observed in ascertaining the genuine sense of the holy Scriptures; and may furnish insolent sophists with a just pretext for violently assailing, or even vilifying, the doctrine of the Reformed Churches.

May Jesus Christ, the Son of God, who, seated at the Father's right hand, gives gifts to men, sanctify us in the truth, bring to the truth those who err, shut the mouths of the calumniators of sound doctrine, and endue the faithful minister of his Word with the spirit of wisdom and discretion, that all their discourses may tend to the glory of God, and the edification of those who hear them. AMEN.

That this is our faith and decision we certify by subscribing our names.

Here follow the names, not only of President, Assistant President, and Secretaries of the Synod, and of the Professors of Theology in the Dutch Churches, but of all the Members who were deputed to the Synod, as the Representatives of their respective Churches, that is, of the Delegates from Great Britain, the Electoral Palatinate, Hessia, Switzerland, Wetteraw,—the Republic and Church of Geneva,—The Republic and Church of Bremen,—The Republic and Church of Emden,—The Duchy of Gelderland and of Zutphen,—South Holland,—North Holland,—Zeeland,—The Province of Utrecht,—Friesland,—Transylvania,—The State of Groningen and Omland, — Drent, — The French Churches.

LITURGY

··◇◦◇··

FORM FOR THE ADMINISTRATION OF BAPTISM.

The principal parts of the doctrine of holy baptism are these three:

First. That we with our children are conceived and born in sin, and therefore are children of wrath, in so much that we cannot enter into the kingdom of God, except we are born again. This, the dipping in, or sprinkling with water teaches us, whereby the impurity of our souls is signified, and we admonished to loathe, and humble ourselves before God, and seek for our purification and salvation without ourselves.

Secondly. Holy baptism witnesseth and sealeth unto us the washing away of our sins through Jesus Christ. Therefore we are baptized in the name of the Father, and of the Son, and of the Holy Ghost. For when we are baptized in the name of the Father, God the Father witnesseth and sealeth unto us, that he doth make an eternal covenant of grace with us, and adopts us for his children and heirs, and therefore will provide us with every good thing, and avert all evil or turn it to our profit. And when we are baptized in the name of the Son, the Son sealeth unto us, that he doth wash us in his blood from all our sins, incorporating us into the fellowship of his death and resurrection, so that we are freed from all our sins, and accounted righteous before God. In like manner, when we are baptized in the name of the Holy Ghost, the Holy Ghost assures us, by this holy sacrament, that he will dwell in us, and sanctify us to be members of Christ, applying unto us, that which we have in Christ, namely, the washing away of our sins, and the daily renewing of our lives, till we shall finally be presented without spot or wrinkle among the assembly of the elect in life eternal.

Thirdly. Whereas in all covenants, there are contained two parts: therefore are we by God through baptism, admonished of, and obliged unto new obedience, namely, that we cleave to this one God, Father, Son, and Holy Ghost; that we trust in him, and love him with all our hearts, with all our souls, with all our mind, and with all our strength; that we forsake the world, crucify our old nature, and walk in a new and holy life.

And if we sometimes through weakness fall into sin, we must not therefore despair of God's mercy, nor continue in sin, since baptism is a seal and undoubted testimony, that we have an eternal covenant of grace with God

I. TO INFANTS OF BELIEVERS.

And although our young children do not understand these things, we may not therefore exclude them from baptism, for as they are without their knowledge, partakers of the condemnation in Adam, so are they again received unto grace in Christ; as God speaketh unto Abraham, the father of all the faithful, and therefore unto us and our children (Gen. 17:7), saying, "I will establish my covenant between me and thee, and thy seed after thee, in their generations, for an everlasting covenant; to be a God unto thee, and to thy seed after thee." This also the Apostle Peter testifieth, with these words (Acts 2:39), "For the promise is unto you and to your children, and to all that are afar off, even as many as the Lord our God shall call." Therefore God formerly commanded them to be circumcised, which was a seal of the covenant, and of the righteousness of faith; and therefore Christ also embraced them, laid his hands upon them and blessed them (Mark 10).

Since then baptism is come in the place of circumcision, therefore infants are to be baptized as heirs of the kingdom of God, and of his covenant. And parents are in duty bound, further to instruct their children herein, when they shall arrive to years of discretion.

That therefore this holy ordinance of God may be administered to his glory, to our comfort, and to the edification of his Church, let us call upon his holy name.

PRAYER.

O Almighty and eternal God, Thou, who hast according to thy severe judgment punished the unbelieving and unrepentant world with the flood, and hast according to thy great mercy saved and protected believing Noah and his family; Thou, who hast drowned the obstinate Pharaoh and his host in the Red Sea, and hast led thy people Israel through the midst of the Sea upon dry ground, by which baptism was signified—we beseech thee, that Thou wilt be pleased of thine infinite mercy, graciously to look upon these children, and incorporate them by thy Holy Spirit, into thy Son Jesus Christ, that they may be buried with him into his death, and be raised with him in newness of life; that they may daily follow him, joyfully bearing their cross, and cleave unto him in true faith, firm hope, and ardent love; that they may, with a comfortable sense of thy favor, leave this life, which is nothing but a continual death, and at the last day, may appear without terror before the judgment seat of Christ thy Son, through Jesus Christ our Lord, who with thee and the Holy Ghost, one only God, lives and reigns forever. Amen.

An exhortation to the Parents.

Beloved in the Lord Jesus Christ, you have heard that baptism is an ordinance of God, to seal unto us and to our seed his covenant; therefore it must be used for that end, and not out of custom or superstition. That it may then be manifest, that you are thus minded, you are to answer sincerely to these questions:

First. Whether you acknowledge, that although our children are conceived and born in sin, and therefore are subject to all miseries, yea, to condemnation itself; yet that they are sanctified* in Christ, and therefore, as members of his Church ought to be baptized?

Secondly. Whether you acknowledge the doctrine which is contained in the Old and New Testament, and in the articles of the Christian faith, and which is taught here in this Christian Church, to be the true and perfect† doctrine of salvation?

Thirdly. Whether you promise and intend to see these children, when come to the years of discretion (whereof you are either parent or witness), instructed and brought up in the aforesaid doctrine, or help or cause them to be instructed therein, to the utmost of your power?

Answer. Yes.

Then the Minister of God's Word, in baptizing, shall say, N., I baptize thee in the name of the Father, and of the Son, and of the Holy Ghost. Amen.

THANKSGIVING.

Almighty God and merciful Father, we thank and praise thee, that Thou hast forgiven us, and our children, all our sins, through the blood of thy beloved Son Jesus Christ, and received us through thy Holy Spirit as members of thine only begotten Son, and adopted us to be thy children, and sealed and confirmed the same unto us by holy baptism; we beseech thee, through the same Son of thy love, that Thou wilt be pleased always to govern these baptized children by thy Holy Spirit, that they may be piously and religiously educated, increase and grow up in the Lord Jesus Christ, that they then may acknowledge thy fatherly goodness and mercy, which Thou hast shown to them and us, and live in all righteousness, under our only Teacher, King and High Priest, Jesus Christ; and manfully fight

*My children. Ezek. 16:21. They are holy. 1 Cor. 7:14.

†Dutch—Volkomene—complete.

against, and overcome sin, the devil and his whole dominion, to the end that they may eternally praise and magnify thee, and thy Son Jesus Christ, together with the Holy Ghost, the one only true God. Amen.

II. TO ADULT PERSONS.

However children of Christian parents (although they understand not this mystery) must be baptized by virtue of the covenant; yet it is not lawful to baptize those who are come to years of discretion, except they first be sensible of their sins, and make confession both of their repentance and faith in Christ. For this cause did not only John the Baptist preach (according to the command of God) the baptism of repentance, and baptized, for the remission of sins, those who confessed their sins (Mark 1 and Luke 3); but our Lord Jesus Christ also commanded his disciples to teach all nations, and then to baptize them, in the name of the Father, and of the Son, and of the Holy Ghost (Matt. 28, Mark 16), adding this promise: "He that believeth and is baptized shall be saved." According to which rule, the Apostles, as appeareth from Acts 2, 10 and 16, baptized none who were of years of discretion, but such as made confession of their faith and repentance. Therefore it is not lawful now to baptize any other adult person, than such as have been taught the mysteries of holy baptism, by the preaching of the gospel, and are able to give an account of their faith by the confession of the mouth.

That therefore this holy ordinance of God may be administered to his glory, to our comfort, and to the edification of his Church, let us call upon his holy name:

O Almighty and eternal God, Thou, who hast according to thy severe judgment punished the unbelieving and unrepentant world with the flood, and hast according to thy great mercy saved and protected believing Noah and his family; Thou, who hast drowned the obstinate Pharaoh and his host in the Red Sea, and hast led thy people Israel through the midst of the Sea upon dry ground, by which baptism is signified—we beseech thee, that

Thou wilt, be pleased of thine infinite mercy, graciously to look upon this person, and incorporate him by thy Holy Spirit into thy Son Jesus Christ, that he may be buried with him into his death, and be raised with him in newness of life; that he may daily follow him, joyfully bearing his cross, and cleave unto him in true faith, firm hope, and ardent love; that he may with a comfortable sense of thy favor, leave this life, which is nothing but a continual death, and at the last day, may appear without terror before the judgment seat of Christ thy Son, through Jesus Christ our Lord, who with thee and the Holy Ghost, one only God, lives and reigns forever. Amen.

Since therefore thou, N., art also desirous of holy baptism, to the end, that it may be to thee a seal of thine ingrafting into the Church of God; that it may appear that thou dost not only receive the Christian religion, in which thou hast been privately instructed by us and of which also thou hast made confession before us, but that thou (through the grace of God), intendest and purposest to lead a life according to the same, thou art sincerely to give answer before God and his Church.

First. Dost thou believe in the only true God, distinct in three persons, Father, Son, and Holy Ghost, who has made heaven and earth, and all that in them is, of nothing, and still maintains and governs them, insomuch that nothing comes to pass, either in heaven or on earth, without his divine will?

Answer. Yes.

Secondly. Dost thou believe that thou art conceived and born in sin, and therefore art a child of wrath by nature, wholly incapable of doing any good, and prone to all evil; and that thou hast frequently, in thought, word and deed, transgressed the commandments of the Lord: and whether thou art heartily sorry for these sins?

Answer. Yes.

Thirdly. Dost thou believe that Christ, who is the true and eternal God, and very man, who took his human nature on him out of the flesh and blood of the Virgin Mary, is given thee of God, to be thy Savior, and that thou dost receive by this faith, remission of sins in his blood, and that thou art made by the power of the Holy Ghost, a member of Jesus Christ and his Church?

Answer. Yes.

Fourthly. Dost thou assent to all the articles of the Christian religion, as they are taught here, in this Christian Church, according to the Word of God; and purpose steadfastly to continue in the same doctrine to the end of thy life; and also dost thou reject all heresies and schisms, repugnant to this doctrine, and promise to persevere in the communion of the Christian Church, not only in the hearing of the Word, but also in the use of the Lord's Supper?

Answer. Yes.

Fifthly. Hast thou taken a firm resolution always to lead a Christian life; to forsake the world and its evil lusts, as is becoming the members of Christ and his Church; and to submit thyself to all Christian admonitions?

Answer. Yes.

The good and great God mercifully grant his grace and blessing to this thy purpose, through Jesus Christ. Amen.

THANKSGIVING.

Almighty God and merciful Father, we thank and praise thee, that thou hast forgiven us and our children all our sins, through the blood of thy Son Jesus Christ, and received us through thy Holy Spirit, as members of thine only begotten Son, and adopted us to be thy children, and sealed and confirmed the same unto us by holy baptism. We beseech thee, through the same Son of thy love, that thou wilt be pleased always to govern this baptized person by thy Holy Spirit, that he may lead a christian and godly life, and increase and grow up in the Lord Jesus Christ, that he may acknowledge thy fatherly goodness and mercy, which thou hast shown to him and to us, and live in all righteousness, under our only Teacher, King, and High Priest, Jesus Christ; and that he may manfully fight against and overcome sin, the devil and his whole dominion, to the end that he may eternally praise and magnify thee, and thy Son Jesus Christ together with the Holy Ghost, the one only true God. Amen.

PUBLIC
CONFESSION
of FAITH

Questions and Answer.

(Before or after the sermon, the minister requests those who intend to make public confession of their faith to arise and to reply to the following questions:)

1. Do you acknowledge the doctrine contained in the Old and New Testaments and in the Articles of the Christian faith and taught here in this Christian Church to be the true and complete doctrine of salvation?

2. Have you resolved by the grace of God to adhere to this doctrine; to reject all heresies repugnant thereto and to lead a new, godly life?

3. Will you submit to church government, and in case you should become delinquent (which may God graciously forbid) to church discipline?

    Answer: Yes.

FORM FOR THE ADMINISTRATION OF THE LORD'S SUPPER.

Beloved in the Lord Jesus Christ, attend to the words of the institution of the Holy Supper of our Lord Jesus Christ, as they are delivered by the holy Apostle Paul. 1 Cor. 11:23-30.

"For I have received of the Lord, that which also I delivered unto you, that the Lord Jesus, the same night in which he was betrayed, took bread; and when he had given thanks, he brake it, and said, Take, eat; this is my body which is broken for you, this do in remembrance of me. And after the same manner also, he took the cup, when he had supped, saying, This cup is the new testament in my blood; this do ye, as oft as ye drink it in remembrance of me; for as oft as ye eat this bread, and drink this cup, ye do show the Lord's death till he come. Wherefore, whosoever shall eat this bread, and drink this cup of the Lord unworthily, shall be guilty of the body and blood of the Lord. But let a man examine himself, and so let him eat of that bread, and drink of that cup; for he that eateth and drinketh unworthily, eateth and drinketh damnation* to himself, not discerning the Lord's body.

That we may now celebrate the Supper of the Lord to our comfort, it is above all things necessary,

First. Rightly to examine ourselves.

Secondly. To direct it to that end for which Christ hath ordained and instituted the same, namely, to his remembrance.

The true **examination** of ourselves consists of these three parts:

First. That every one consider by himself, his sins and the curse due to him for them, to the end that he may abhor and humble himself before God: considering that the wrath of

*Dutch, Oordeel—English, Judgment, condemnation.

God against sin is so great, that (rather than it should go unpunished) he hath punished the same in his beloved Son Jesus Christ, with the bitter and shameful death of the cross.

Secondly. That every one examine his own heart, whether he doth believe this faithful promise of God, that all his sins are forgiven him only for the sake of the passion and death of Jesus Christ, and that the perfect righteousness of Christ is imputed and freely given him as his own, yea, so perfectly, as if he had satisfied in his own person for all his sins, and fulfilled all righteousness.

Thirdly. That every one examine his own conscience, whether he purposeth henceforth to show true thankfulness to God in his whole life, and to walk uprightly before him; as also, whether he hath laid aside unfeignedly all enmity, hatred, and envy, and doth firmly resolve henceforward to walk in true love and peace with his neighbor.

All those, then, who are thus disposed, God will certainly receive in mercy, and count them worthy partakers of the table of his Son Jesus Christ. On the contrary, those who do not feel this testimony in their hearts, eat and drink judgment to themselves.

Therefore, we also, according to the command of Christ and the Apostle Paul, admonish all those who are defiled with the following sins, to keep themselves from the table of the Lord, and declare to them that they have no part in the kingdom of Christ; such as all idolaters, all those who invoke deceased saints, angels or other creatures; all those who worship images; all enchanters, diviners, charmers, and those who confide in such enchantments; all despisers of God, and of his Word, and of the holy sacraments; all blasphemers; all those who are given to raise discord, sects and mutiny in Church or State; all perjured persons; all those who are **disobedient to their parents and su-**

periors; all murderers, contentious persons, and those who live in hatred and envy against their neighbors; all adulterers, whoremongers, drunkards, thieves, usurers, robbers, gamesters, covetous, and all who lead offensive lives.

All these, while they continue in such sins, shall abstain from this meat (which Christ hath ordained only for the faithful), lest their judgment and condemnation be made the heavier.

But this is not designed (dearly beloved brethren and sisters in the Lord), to deject the contrite hearts of the faithful, as if none might come to the supper of the Lord, but those who are without sin; for we do not come to this supper, to testify thereby that we are perfect and righteous in ourselves; but on the contrary, considering that we seek our life out of ourselves in Jesus Christ, we acknowledge that we lie in the midst of death; therefore, notwithstanding we feel many infirmities and miseries in ourselves, as namely, that we have not perfect faith, and that we do not give ourselves to serve God with that zeal as we are bound, but have daily to strive with the weakness of our faith, and the evil lusts of our flesh; yet, since we are (by the grace of the Holy Spirit) sorry for these weaknesses, and earnestly desirous to fight against our unbelief, and to live according to all the commandments of God: therefore we rest assured that no sin or infirmity, which still remaineth against our will, in us, can hinder us from being received of God in mercy, and from being made worthy partakers of this heavenly meat and drink.

Let us now also consider, to what end the Lord hath instituted his Supper, namely, that we do it in remembrance of him. Now after this manner are we to remember him by it:

First. That we are confidently persuaded in our hearts, that our Lord Jesus Christ (according to the promises made to our forefathers in the Old Testament) was sent of the Father into the world; that he assumed our flesh and blood; that he bore for us the wrath of God (under which we should have perished everlastingly) from the beginning of his incarnation, to the end of his life upon earth; and that he hath fulfilled, for us, all obedience to the divine law, and

righteousness; especially, when the weight of our sins and the wrath of God pressed out of him the bloody sweat in the garden, where he was bound that we might be freed from our sins; that he afterwards suffered innumerable reproaches, that we might never be confounded; that he was innocently condemned to death, that we might be acquitted at the judgment-seat of God; yea, that he suffered his blessed body to be nailed on the cross—that he might fix thereon the handwriting of our sins; and hath also taken upon himself the curse due to us, that he might fill us with his blessings: and hath humbled himself unto the deepest reproach and pains of hell, both in body and soul, on the tree of the cross, when he cried out with a loud voice, "My God, my God! why hast thou forsaken me?" that we might be accepted of God and never be forsaken of him: and finally confirmed with his death and shedding of his blood, the new and eternal testament, that covenant of grace and reconciliation when he said: "It is finished."

Secondly. And that we might firmly believe that we belong to this covenant of grace, the Lord Jesus Christ, in his last Supper, took bread, and when he had given thanks, he brake it, and gave it to his disciples and said, "Take, eat, this is my body which is broken for you, this do in remembrance of me; in like manner also after supper he took the cup, gave thanks and said, Drink ye all of it; this cup is the new testament in my blood, which is shed for you and for many, for the remission of sins; this do ye as often as ye drink it in remembrance of me": that is, as often as ye eat of this bread and drink of this cup, you shall thereby as by a sure remembrance and pledge, be admonished and assured of - this my hearty love and faithfulness towards you; that, whereas you should otherwise have suffered eternal death, I have given my body to the death of the cross, and shed my blood for you; and as certainly feed and nourish your hungry and thirsty souls with my crucified body, and shed blood, to everlasting life, as this bread is broken before your eyes, and this cup is given to you, and you eat and drink the same with your mouth, in remembrance of me.

From this institution of the Holy Supper of our Lord Jesus Christ, we see that he directs our faith and trust to his perfect sacrifice (once offered on the cross) as to the only ground and foundation of our salvation, wherein he is become to our hungry and thirsty souls, the true meat and drink of life eternal. For by his death he hath taken away the cause of our eternal death and misery, namely, sin, and obtained for us the quickening Spirit, that we by the same (who dwelleth in Christ as in the head, and in us as his members), might have true communion with him, and be made partakers of all his blessings, of life eternal, righteousness and glory.

Besides, that we by this same Spirit may also be united as members of one body in true brotherly love, as the holy Apostle saith, "For we, being many, are one bread and one body; for we are all partakers of that one bread." For as out of many grains one meal is ground, and one bread baked, and out of many berries being pressed together, one wine floweth, and mixeth itself together; so shall we all, who by a true faith are ingrafted into Christ, be altogether one body, through brotherly love, for Christ's sake, our beloved Savior, who hath so exceedingly loved us, and not only show this in word, but also in very deed towards one another.

Hereto assist us, the Almighty God and Father of our Lord Jesus Christ through his Holy Spirit. AMEN.

That we may obtain all this, let us humble ourselves before God, and with true faith implore his grace.

PRAYER.

O most merciful God and Father, we beseech thee, that Thou wilt be pleased in this Supper (in which we celebrate the glorious remembrance of the bitter death of thy beloved Son Jesus Christ) to work in our hearts through the Holy Spirit, that we may daily more and more with true confidence, give ourselves up unto thy Son Jesus Christ, that our afflicted and contrite hearts, through the power of the Holy Ghost, may be fed and comforted with his true body and blood; yea, with him, true God and man, that only heavenly bread; and that we may no longer live in our sins, but he in us, and we in him, and thus truly be made partakers of the new and everlasting covenant of grace. That me may not doubt but Thou wilt forever be our gracious Father, nevermore imputing our sins unto us, and providing us with all things necessary, as well for the body as the soul, as thy beloved children and heirs; grant us also thy grace, that we may take up our cross cheerfully, deny ourselves, confess our Savior, and in all tribulations, with uplifted heads expect our Lord Jesus Christ from heaven, where he will make our mortal bodies like unto his most glorious body, and take us unto him in eternity.

Our Father which are in heaven. Hallowed be thy name. Thy kingdom come. Thy will be done in earth, as it is in heaven. Give us this day our daily bread. And forgive us our debts, as we forgive our debtors. And lead us not into temptation, but deliver us from evil: For thine is the kingdom, and the power and the glory, for ever.

Strengthen us also by this Holy Supper in the catholic undoubted christian faith, whereof we make confession with our mouths and hearts, saying:

I believe in God the Father, Almighty, Maker of heaven and earth; and in Jesus Christ his only Son our Lord; who was conceived by the Holy Ghost, born of the virgin Mary, suffered under Pontius Pilate, was crucified, dead and buried, he descended into hell: the third day he rose again from the dead, he ascended into heaven, and sitteth at the right hand of God the Father Almighty; from thence he shall come to judge the quick and the dead.

I believe in the Holy Ghost; I believe an holy catholic church; the communion of saints; the forgiveness of sins; the resurrection of the body; and the life everlasting. Amen.

That we may be now fed with the true heavenly bread, Christ Jesus, let us not cleave with our hearts unto the external bread and wine, but lift them up on high in heaven, where Christ

Jesus is our Advocate, at the right hand of his heavenly Father, whither all the articles of our faith lead us; not doubting, but we shall as certainly be fed and refreshed in our souls through the working of the Holy Ghost, with his body and blood, as we receive the holy bread and wine in remembrance of him.

In breaking and distributing the bread, the Minister shall say:

The bread which we break, is the communion of the body of Christ.

And when he giveth the cup:

The cup of blessing, which we bless, is the communion of the blood of Christ.

(During the communion, there shall or may be devoutly sung, a psalm, or some chapter read, in remembrance of the death of Christ, as the 53rd chapter of Isaiah, the 13th, 14th, 15th, 16th, 17th, and 18th chapters of John, or the like.)

After the Communion the Minister shall say:

Beloved in the Lord, since the Lord hath now fed our souls at this table, let us therefore jointly praise his holy name with thanksgiving, and every one say in his heart, thus:

Bless the Lord, O my soul; and all that is within me, bless his holy name.

Bless the Lord, O my soul, and forget not all his benefits.

Who forgiveth all thine iniquities; who healeth all thy diseases.

Who redeemeth thy life from destruction, who crowneth thee with loving kindness and tender mercies.

The Lord is merciful and gracious, slow to anger and plenteous in mercy.

He hath not dealt with us after our sins, nor rewarded us according to our iniquities.

For as the heaven is high above the earth, so great is his mercy towards them that fear him.

As far as the East is from the West, so far hath he removed our transgressions from us.

Like as a father pitieth his children, so the Lord pitieth them that fear him.

Who hath not spared his own Son, but delivered him up for us all, and given us all things with him. Therefore God commendeth therewith his love towards us, in that while we were yet sinners, Christ died for us; much more then, being now justified in his blood, we shall be saved from wrath through him: for, if, when we were enemies, we were reconciled to God by the death of his Son; much more being reconciled, we shall be saved by his life. Therefore shall my mouth and heart show forth the praise of the Lord from this time forth forever more. AMEN.

Let every one say with an attentive heart:

THANKSGIVING.

O! Almighty, merciful God and Father, we render thee most humble and hearty thanks, that Thou hast of thy infinite mercy, given us thine only begotten Son, for a Mediator and a sacrifice for our sins, and to be our meat and drink unto life eternal, and that Thou givest us lively faith, whereby we are made partakers of such great benefits. Thou hast also been pleased, that thy beloved Son Jesus Christ should institute and ordain his Holy Supper for the confirmation of the same. Grant, we beseech thee, O faithful God and Father, that through the operation of thy Holy Spirit, the commemoration of the death of our Lord Jesus Christ may tend to the daily increase of our faith, and saving fellowship with him, through Jesus Christ thy Son, in whose name we conclude our prayers, saying:

Our Father, etc.

FORM OF EXCOMMUNICATION.

Beloved in the Lord Jesus Christ; it is known unto you, that we have several times, and by several methods declared unto you the great sin committed, and the heinous offence given by our fellow-member N., to the end that he, by your christian admonition and prayers to God, might be brought to repentance, and so be freed from the bonds of the devil (by whom he is held captive), and recovered by the will of the Lord. But we cannot conceal from you, with great sorrow, that no one has yet appeared before us, who hath in the least given us to understand that he, by the frequent admonitions given him, (as well in private as before witnesses, and in the presence of many), is come to any remorse for his sins, or hath shown the least token of true repentance. Since then he daily aggravates his sin, (which in itself is not small), by his stubbornness, and since we have signified unto you the last time, that in case he did not repent, after such patience shown him by the Church, we should be under the disagreeable necessity of being further grieved for him, and come to the last remedy: wherefore we at this present are necessitated to proceed to this excommunication according to the command and charge given us by God in his holy Word; to the end that he may hereby be made (if possible) ashamed of his sins, and likewise that we may not by this rotten and as yet incurable member, put the whole body of the Church in danger, and that God's name may not be blasphemed.

Therefore we, the ministers and rulers of the Church of God, being here assembled in the name and authority of our Lord Jesus Christ, declare before you all, that for the aforesaid reasons we have excommunicated, and by these, do excommunicate N. from the Church of God, and from fellowship with Christ, and the holy sacraments, and from all the spiritual blessings and benefits, which God promiseth to and bestows upon his Church, so long as he obstinately and impenitently persists in his sins, and is therefore to be accounted by you as a heathen man and a publican, according to the command of Christ (Matt. 18), who saith, that whatsoever his ministers bind on earth, shall be bound in heaven.

Further we exhort you, beloved Christians, to keep no company with him, that he may be ashamed; yet count him not as an enemy, but at all times admonish him as you would a brother. In the meantime let every one take warning by this and such like examples; to fear the Lord, and diligently take heed unto himself, If he thinketh he standeth, lest he fall; but having true fellowship with the Father and his Son Jesus Christ, together with all faithful Christians, remain steadfast therein to the end, and so obtain eternal salvation. You have seen, beloved brethren and sisters, in what manner this our excommunicated brother has begun to fall, and by degrees is come to ruin; observe therefore, how subtle Satan is, to bring man to destruction, and to withdraw him from all salutary means of salvation: guard then, against the least beginnings of evil, "and laying aside," according to the exhortation of the apostle, "every weight and the sin which doth so easily beset us, let us run with patience the race that is set before us, looking unto Jesus the author and finisher of our faith; be sober, watch and pray, lest you enter into temptation. Today, if you will hear the voice of the Lord, harden not your hearts, but work out your own salvation with fear and trembling;" and every one repent of his sins, lest our God humble us again and that we be obliged to bewail some one of you; but that you may with one accord, living in all godliness, be our crown and joy in the Lord.

Since it is God who worketh in us, both to will and to do of his good pleasure, let us call upon his holy name with confession of our sins, saying:

O! Righteous God and merciful Father, we bewail our sins before thy high majesty, and acknowledge that we have deserved the grief and sorrow caused unto us by the cutting off of this our late fellow-member; yea, we all deserve, shouldst Thou enter into judgment with us, by reason of our great transgressions, to be cut off and banished from thy presence.—But O Lord, Thou art merciful unto us for Christ's sake; forgive us our trespasses, for we heartily repent of them, and daily work in our hearts a greater measure of sorrow for them; that we may, fearing thy judgments which thou executest against the stiff-necked, endeavor to please thee; grant us to avoid all pollution of the world, and those who are cut off from the communion of the Church, that we may not make ourselves partakers of their sins; and that he who is excommunicated may become ashamed of his sins; and since thou desirest not the death of a sinner, but that he may repent and live, and the bosom of thy Church is always open for those, who turn away from their wickedness; we therefore humbly beseech thee, to kindle in our hearts a pious zeal, that we may labor, with good christian admonitions and examples, to bring again this excommunicated person on the right way, together with all those, who, through unbelief or dissoluteness of life, go astray.

Give thy blessing to our admonitions, that we may have reason thereby to rejoice again in him, for whom we must now mourn, and that thy holy name may be praised, through our Lord Jesus Christ, who hath taught us to pray:

Our Father, etc.

——— ·⳩· ———

FORM OF READMITTING EXCOMMUNICATED PERSONS.

Beloved in the Lord, it is known to you, that some time ago our fellow-member N., was cut off from the Church of Christ; we cannot now conceal from you, that he, by the above-mentioned remedy, as also by the means of good admonitions and your christian prayers, is come so far, that he is ashamed of his sins, praying us to be re-admitted into the communion of the Church.

Since we, then, by virture of the command of God, are in duty bound to receive such persons with joy, and it being necessary that good order should be used therein, we therefore give you to understand hereby, that we purpose to loose again the aforementioned excommunicated person from the bond of excommunication, the next time when by the grace of God we celebrate the Supper of the Lord, and receive him again into the communion of the Church; except any one of you, in the meantime, shall show just cause why this ought not to be done, of which you must give notice to us in due time. In the meantime, let every one thank the Lord, for the mercy shown this poor sinner, beseeching him to perfect his work in him to his eternal salvation. Amen.

Afterwards, if no impediment be alleged, the Minister shall proceed to the re-admission of the excommunicated sinner, in the following manner:

Beloved Christians, we have the last time informed you of the repentance of our fellow-member N. to the end, that he might with your foreknowledge be again received into the Church of Christ: and whereas no one has alleged anything why his re-admission ought not to take place, we therefore at present purpose to proceed to the same.

Our Lord Jesus Christ (Matt. 18), having confirmed the sentence of his Church, in the excommunicating of impenitent sinners, declareth immediately thereupon, "that whatsoever his ministers shall loose on earth, shall be loosed in heaven"; whereby he giveth to understand, that when any person is cut off from his Church, he is not deprived of all hopes of salvation; but can again be loosed from the bonds of condemnation. Therefore, since God declares in his word, that he takes no pleasure in the death of a sinner, but that he turn from his wickedness and live, so the church always hopes for the repentance of the backslidden sinner, and keepeth her bosom open to receive the penitent; accordingly the apostle Paul (1 Cor. 5), commanded the Corinthian (whom he had declared ought to be cut off from the Church) to be again received and comforted, since being reproved by many, he was come to the knowledge of his sins: to the end that he should not be swallowed up with overmuch sorrow (2 Cor. 2).

Secondly. Christ teacheth us in the aforementioned text, that the sentence of absolution, which is passed upon such a penitent sinner according to the Word of God, is counted sure and firm by the Lord; therefore, no one ought to doubt in the least, who truly repents, that he is assuredly received by God in mercy, as Christ saith (John 20), "Whosesoever sins ye remit, they are remitted unto them."

But now to proceed to the matter in hand: I ask thee, N., whether thou dost declare here with all thine heart before God and his Church; that thou art sincerely sorry for the sin and stubbornness, for which thou hast been justly cut off from the Church? whether thou dost also truly believe, that the Lord hath forgiven thee, and doth forgive thy sins for Christ's sake, and that thou therefore art desirous to be re-admitted into the Church of Christ, promising henceforth to live in all godliness according to the command of the Lord?

Answer. Yes, verily.

Then the Minister shall further say:
We then, here assembled in the name and authority of the Lord Jesus Christ, declare thee, N., to be absolved from the bonds of excommunication; and do receive thee again into the Church of the Lord, and declare unto thee that thou art in the communion of Christ and of the holy sacraments, and of all the spiritual blessings and benefits of God, which he promiseth to and bestoweth upon his Church: may the eternal God preserve thee therein to the end, through his only begotten Son Jesus Christ. Amen.

Be therefore assured in thy heart, my beloved brother, that the Lord hath again received thee in mercy. Be diligent henceforward to guard thyself against the subtlety of Satan, and the wickedness of the world, to the end, that thou mayest not fall again into sin: love Christ, for many sins are forgiven thee.

And you, beloved Christians, receive this your brother, with hearty affection; be glad that he was dead and is alive, he was lost and is found; rejoice with the angels of heaven, over this sinner who repenteth: count him no longer as a stranger, but as a fellow-citizen with the saints, and of the household of God.

And whereas we can have no good of ourselves, let us, praising and magnifying the Lord Almighty, implore his mercy, saying:

Gracious God and Father, we thank thee through Jesus Christ, that thou hast been pleased to give this our fellow-brother repentance unto life, and us cause to rejoice in his conversion. We beseech thee, show him thy mercy, that he may become more and more assured in his mind of the remission of his sins, and that he may receive from thence inexpressible joy and delight, to serve thee. And whereas he hath heretofore by his sins offended many, grant that he may, by his conversion, edify many. Grant also that he may steadfastly walk in thy ways to the end: and may we learn from this example, that with thee is mercy, that thou mayest be feared; and that we, counting him for our brother and co-heir of life eternal, may jointly serve thee with filial fear and obedience all the days of our life, through Jesus Christ, our Lord, in whose name we thus conclude our prayer: Our Father, etc.

FORM OF ORDINATION OF THE MINISTERS OF GOD'S WORD.

The sermon and the usual prayers being finished, the Minister shall thus speak to the congregation:

Beloved brethren, it is known unto you, that we have, at three different times, published the name of our brother N., here present, to learn whether any person had aught to offer concerning his doctrine or life, why he might not be ordained to the ministry of the Word. And whereas no one hath appeared before us, who hath alleged anything lawful against his person, we shall therefore at present, in the name of the Lord, proceed to his ordination; for which purpose, you N., and all those who are here present, shall first attend to a short declaration taken from the word of God, touching the institution and the office of pastors and ministers of God's Word; where, in the first place, you are to observe, that God our heavenly Father, willing to call and gather a Church from amongst the corrupt race of men unto life eternal, doth by a particular mark of his favor use the ministry of men therein.

Therefore, Paul saith, that the Lord Jesus Christ hath given some apostles and some prophets, and some evangelists, and some pastors and ministers; for the perfecting of the saints, for the work of the ministry, for the edifying of the body of Christ. Here we see that the holy apostle among other things saith, that the pastoral office is an institution of Christ.

What this holy office enjoins, may easily be gathered from the very name itself; for as it is the duty of a common shepherd, to feed, guide, protect and rule the flock committed to his charge; so it is with regard to these spiritual shepherds, who are set over the Church, which God calleth unto salvation, and counts as sheep of his pasture. The pasture, with which these sheep are fed, is nothing else but the preaching of the gospel, accompanied with prayer, and the administration of the holy sacraments; the same word of God is likewise the staff with which the flock is guided and ruled, consequently it is evident, that the office of pastors and ministers of God's word is,

First. That they faithfully explain to their flock, the Word of the Lord, revealed by the writings of the prophets and the apostles; and apply the same as well in general as in particular, to the edification of the hearers; instructing, admonishing, comforting and reproving, according to every one's need; preaching repentance towards God, and reconciliation with him through faith in Christ; and refuting with the Holy Scriptures, all schisms and heresies which are repugnant to the pure doctrine. All this is clearly signified to us in Holy Writ, for the Apostle Paul saith, "that these labor in the Word"; and elsewhere he teacheth, that this must be done "according to he measure or rule of faith"; he writes also, that a pastor "must hold fast and right divide the faithful and sincere word which is according to the doctrine": likewise, he that prophesieth (that is, preacheth God's Word), speaketh unto men to edification, and exhortation and comfort. In another place he proposes himself as a pattern to pastors, declaring that he hath publicly, and from house to house, taught and testified repentance toward God, and faith toward our Lord Jesus Christ. But particularly we have a clear description of the office, and ministers of God's Word (2 Cor. 5:18, 19, 20), where the apostle thus speaketh, "And all things are of God, who hath reconciled us to himself by Jesus Christ, and hath given to us (namely, to the apostles and pastors) the ministry of reconciliation; to-wit, that God was in Christ reconciling the world unto himself, not imputing their trespasses unto them, and hath committed unto us the word of reconciliation. Now then we are ambassadors for Christ, as though God did beseech you by us; we pray you in Christ's stead, be ye reconciled to God." Concerning the refutation of false doctrine, the same apostle saith (Titus 1:9): "That a minister must hold fast the faithful Word of God, that he may be able by sound doctrine, both to exhort and convince the gainsayers."

Secondly. It is the office of the Ministers, publicly to call upon the name of the Lord in behalf of the whole congregation; for that which the apostles say, we will give ourselves continually to prayer and to the ministry of the word, is common to these pastors with the apostles; to which St. Paul alluding, thus speaketh to Timothy: "I exhort therefore, that first of all supplications, prayers, intercessions, and giving of thanks be made for all men; for kings, and for all that are in authority," etc. (1 Tim. 2:1 and 2).

Thirdly. Their office is to administer the sacraments, which the Lord hath instituted as seals of his grace: as is evident from the command given by Christ to the apostles, and in them to all pastors: "Baptize them in the name of the Father, and of the Son, and of the Holy Ghost." Likewise: "for I have received of the Lord, that which also I delivered unto you, that the Lord Jesus the same night in which he was betrayed," etc.

Finally, it is the duty of the Ministers of the Word, to keep the Church of God in good discipline, and to govern it in such a manner as the Lord hath ordained; for Christ having spoken of the Christian discipline, says to his apostles, whatsoever ye shall bind on earth shall be bound in heaven. And Paul will have the ministers to know how to rule their own house, since they otherwise neither can provide for, nor rule the Church of God. This is the reason why the pastors are in Scripture called stewards of God, and bishops, that is, overseers and watchmen, for they have the oversight of the house of God, wherein they are conversant, to the end that everything may be transacted with good order and decency; and also to open and shut, with the keys of the kingdom of heaven, committed to them, according to the charge given them by God.

From these things may be learned, what a glorious work the ministerial office is, since so great things are effected by it; yea, how highly necessary it is for man's salvation, which is also the reason why the Lord will have such an office always to remain. For Christ said when he sent forth his apostles to officiate in his holy function, Lo, I am always with you, even unto the end of the world; where we see his pleasure is, that this holy office (for the persons to whom he here speaketh, could not live to the end of the world) should always be maintained on earth. And therefore Paul exhorteth Timothy, to commit that which he had heard of him, to faithful men, who are able to teach others, and he also, having ordained Titus minister, further commanded him to ordain elders in every city. (Titus 1:5.)

Forasmuch, therefore as we, for the maintaining of this office in the Church of God, are now to ordain a new minister of the Word, and having sufficiently spoken of the office of such persons, therefore you N., shall answer to the following questions, which shall be proposed to you, to the end that it may appear to all here present, that you are inclined to accept of this office as above described.

First. I ask thee, whether thou feelest in thy heart that thou art lawfully called of God's Church, and therefore of God himself, to this holy ministry?

Secondly. Whether thou dost believe the books of the Old and New Testament to be the only Word of God and the perfect doctrine unto salvation, and dost reject all doctrine repugnant thereto?

Thirdly. Whether thou dost promise faithfully to discharge thy office, according to the same doctrine as above described, and to adorn it with a godly life: also, to submit thyself, in case thou shouldest become delinquent either in life or doctrine, to ecclesiastical admonition, according to the public ordinance of the churches?

Answer. Yes, truly, with all my heart.

Then the Minister, who demanded those questions of him, while he and other Ministers who are present, shall lay their hands* on his head, shall say:

God our heavenly Father, who hath called thee to his holy ministry, enlighten thee with his Holy Spirit, strengthen thee with his hand, and so govern thee in thy ministry, that thou

---

*This ceremony shall not be used in the case of those who have before been in the ministry.

mayest decently and fruitfully walk therein, to the glory of his name, and the propagation of the kingdom of his Son Jesus Christ. Amen.

Then the Minister shall, from the pulpit, exhort the ordained Minister, and the congregation in the following manner:

"Take heed, therefore, beloved brother, and fellow-servant in Christ, unto thyself and to all the flock, over which the Holy Ghost hath made thee overseer, to feed the Church of God which he hath purchased with his own blood: love Christ and feed his sheep, taking the oversight of them not by constraint, but willingly; not for filthy lucre, but of a ready mind, neither as being lord over God's heritage, but as an example to the flock. Be an example of believers, in word, in conversation, in charity, in spirit, in faith, in purity. Give attendance to reading, to exhortation, to doctrine. Neglect not the gift that is in thee, meditate upon those things, give thyself wholly to them, that thy profiting may appear to all; take heed to thy doctrine, and continue steadfast therein. Bear patiently all sufferings, and oppressions, as a good soldier of Jesus Christ, for in doing this thou shalt both save thyself and them that hear thee. And when the chief Shepherd shall appear, thou shalt receive a crown of glory that fadeth not away."

"And you likewise, beloved Christians, receive this your minister in the Lord with all gladness, 'and hold such in reputation.' Remember that God himself through him speaketh unto and beseecheth you. Receive the Word, which he, according to the Scripture, shall preach unto you, 'not as the word of man, but (as it is in truth) the Word of God.' Let the feet of those, that preach the gospel of peace, and bring glad tidings of good things, be beautiful and pleasant unto you. Obey them that have the rule over you, and submit yourselves; for they watch for your souls, as they that must give account; that they may do it with joy, and not with grief: for that is unprofitable for you. If you do these things, it shall come to pass, that the peace of God shall enter into your houses, and that you who receive this man in the name of a prophet, shall receive a prophet's reward, and through his preaching, believing in Christ, shall through Christ, inherit life eternal."

Since no man is of himself fit for any of these things, let us call upon God with thanksgiving.

Merciful Father, we thank thee that it pleaseth thee, by the ministry of men, to gather a Church to thyself unto life eternal, from amongst the lost children of men; we bless thee for so graciously providing the Church in this place with a faithful minister; we beseech thee to qualify him daily more and more by the Holy Spirit, for the ministry to which thou hast ordained and called him; enlighten his understanding to comprehend thy holy Word, and give him utterance, that he may boldly open his mouth, to make known and dispense the mysteries of the gospel. Endue him with wisdom and valor, to rule the people aright over which he is set, and to preserve them in christian peace, to the end that thy Church under his administration and by his good example, may increase in number and in virtue. Grant him courage to bear the difficulties and troubles which he may meet with in his ministry, that being strengthened by the comfort of thy Spirit, he may remain steadfast to the end, and be received with all faithful servants into the joy of his master. Give thy grace also to this people and Church, that they may becomingly deport themselves towards this their minister; that they may acknowledge him to be sent of thee; that they may receive his doctrine with all reverence, and submit themselves to his exhortations. To the end that they may, by his word, believing in Christ, be made partakers of eternal life. Hear us, O Father, through thy beloved Son, who hath taught us to pray:

Our Father, etc.

FORM OF ORDINATION
OF ELDERS AND DEACONS.

When ordained at the same time. But if they are ordained separately this form shall be used as occasion requires.

Beloved Christians, you know that we have several times published unto you the names of our brethren here present, who are chosen to the office of elders and deacons in this Church, to the end that we might know whether any person had aught to allege, why they should not be ordained in their respective offices; and whereas no one hath appeared before us, who hath alleged anything lawful against them, we shall therefore at present, in the name of the Lord, proceed to their ordination.

But first, you, who are to be ordained, and all those who are here present, shall attend to a short declaration from the word of God concerning the institution and the office of elders and deacons.

Of the **elders** is to be observed, that the word elder or eldest (which is taken from the Old Testament, and signifieth a person who is placed in an honorable office of government over others), is applied to two sorts of persons who minister in the Church of Jesus Christ: for the apostle saith, "the elders that rule well, shall be counted worthy of double honor, especially they who labor in the Word and doctrine." Hence it is evident that there were two sorts of elders in the Apostolic Church, the former whereof did labor in the Word and doctrine, and the latter did not. The first were the ministers of the Word and pastors, who preached the gospel and administered the sacraments; but the others, who did not labor in the Word, and still did serve in the Church, bore a particular office, namely, they had the oversight of the Church, and ruled the same with the ministers of the Word. For Paul, Rom. chap. 12, having spoken of the ministry of the word, and also of the office of distribution or deaconship, speaketh afterwards particularly of this office, saying, "he that ruleth let him do it with diligence"; likewise, in another place he counts government among the gifts and offices which God hath instituted in the Church: 1 Cor. 12. Thus we see that these sorts of ministers are added to the others who preach the gospel, to aid and assist them, as in the Old Testament the common Levites were to the priests in the service of the tabernacle, in those things which they could not perform alone: notwithstanding the offices always remained distinct one from the other. Moreover, it is proper that such men should be joined to the ministers of the Word in the government of the Church, to the end, that thereby all tyranny and lording may be kept out of the Church of God, which may sooner creep in, when the government is placed in the hands of one alone, or of a very few. And thus the ministers of the Word, together with the elders, form a body or assembly, being as a council of the Church, representing the whole Church; to which Christ alludes when he saith, "Tell the Church"—which can in no wise be understood of all and every member of the Church in particular, but very properly of those who govern the Church, out of which they are chosen.

Therefore, in the **first** place, the office of elders is, together with the ministers of the Word, to take the oversight of the Church, which is committed to them, and diligently to look, whether every one properly deports himself in his confession and conversation; to admonish those who behave themselves disorderly, and to prevent, as much as possible, the sacraments from being profaned: also to act (according to the Christian discipline) against the impenitent, and to receive the penitent again into the bosom of the Church, as doth not only appear from the above mentioned saying of Christ, but also from many other places of Holy Writ, as 1 Cor. chap. 5, and 2 Cor. chap. 2, that these things are not alone intrusted to one or two persons, but to many who are ordained thereto.

Secondly. Since the apostle enjoineth, that all things shall be done decently and in order, amongst Christians, and that no other persons ought to serve in the Church of Christ, but those who are lawfully called, according to the christian ordinance, therefore it is also the duty of the elders to pay regard to it, and in all occurrences, which relate to the welfare and good order of the Church, to be assistant with their good counsel and advice, to the ministers of the Word, yea, also to serve all Christians with advice and consolation.

Thirdly. It is also the duty particularly to have regard unto the doctrine and conversation of the ministers of the Word, to the end that all things may be directed to the edification of the Church; and that no strange doctrine be taught, according to that which we read, Acts 20, where the apostle exhorteth to watch diligently against the wolves, which might come into the sheepfold of Christ; for the performance of which, the elders are in duty bound diligently to search the Word of God, and continually be meditating on the mysteries of faith.

Concerning the **deacons:** of the origin and institution of their office we may read, Acts 6, where we find that the apostles themselves did in the beginning serve the poor, "At whose feet was brought the price of the things that were sold: and distribution was made unto every man, according as he had need. But afterwards, when a murmuring arose, because the widows of the Grecians were neglected in the daily ministrations," men were chosen (by the advice of the apostles) who should make the service of the poor their peculiar business, to the end that the apostles might continually give themselves to prayer, and to the ministry of the Word. And this has been continued from that time forward in the Church, as appears from Rom. 12, where the apostle, speaking of this office, saith, "he that giveth, let him do it with simplicity." And 1 Cor. 12:28 speaking of helps, he means those, who are appointed in the Church to help and assist the poor and indigent in time of need.

From which passage we may easily gather, what the deacon's office is, namely, that they in the **first** place collect and preserve with the greatest fidelity and diligence, the alms and goods which are given to the poor: yea, to do their utmost endeavors, that many good means be procured for the relief of the poor.

The **second** part of their office consists in distribution, wherein are not only required discretion and prudence to bestow the alms only on objects of charity, but also cheerfulness and simplicity to assist the poor with compassion and hearty affection: as the apostle requires, Rom., chap 12; and 2 Cor., chap. 9. For which end it is very beneficial, that they do not only administer relief to the poor and indigent with external gifts, but also with comfortable words from Scripture.

To the end therefore, beloved brethren, N. N., that every one may hear, that you are willing to take your respective offices upon you, ye shall answer to the following questions:

And in the **first** place I ask you, both elders and deacons, whether you do not feel in your hearts, that ye are lawfully called of God's Church, and consequently of God himself, to these your respective holy offices?

Secondly. Whether ye believe the books of the Old and New Testament to be the only Word of God, and the perfect doctrine of salvation, and do reject all doctrines repugnant thereto?

Thirdly. Whether ye promise, agreeably to said doctrine, faithfully, according to your ability, to discharge your respective offices, as they are here described? ye elders in the government of the Church together with the ministers of the Word: and ye deacons in the ministration to the poor? Do ye also jointly promise to walk in all godliness, and to submit yourself, in case ye should become remiss in your duty, to the admonition of the Church?—Upon which they shall answer: Yes.

Then the Minister shall say:

The Almighty God and Father, replenish you all with his grace, that ye may faithfully and fruitfully discharge your respective offices. Amen.

The Minister shall further exhort them, and the whole congregation, in the following manner:

Therefore, ye **elders,** be diligent in the government of the Church, which is committed to you, and the ministers of the Word. Be also, as watchmen over the house and city of God, faithful to admonish and to caution every one against his ruin. Take heed that purity of doctrine and godliness of life be maintained in the Church, of God. And, ye **deacons,** be diligent in collecting the alms, prudent and cheerful in the distribution of the same: assist the oppressed, provide for the true widows and orphans, show liberality unto all men, but especially to the household of faith.

Be ye all with one accord faithful in your offices, and hold the mystery of the faith in a pure conscience, being good examples unto all the people. In so doing you will purchase to yourselves a good degree, and great boldness in the faith, which is in Christ Jesus, and hereafter enter into the joy of our Lord. On the other hand, beloved Christians, receive these men as the servants of God: count the elders that rule well worthy of double honor, give yourselves willingly to their inspection and government. Provide the deacons with good means to assist the indigent. Be charitable, ye rich, give liberally, and contribute willingly. And, ye poor, be poor in spirit, and deport yourselves respectfully towards your benefactors, be thankful to them, and avoid murmuring: follow Christ, for the food of your souls, but not for bread. "Let him that hath stolen (or who hath been burdensome to his neighbors) steal no more: but rather let him labor, working with his hands the things which are good, that he may give to him that needeth." Each of you, doing these things in your respective callings, shall receive of the Lord, the reward of righteousness. But since we are unable of ourselves, let us call upon the name of the Lord saying:

O Lord God and heavenly Father, we thank thee that it hath pleased thee, for the better edification of thy Church, to ordain in it, besides the ministers of the Word, rulers and assistants, by whom thy Church may be preserved in peace and prosperity, and the indigent assisted; and that Thou hast at present granted us in this place, men, who are of good testimony, and we hope endowed with thy Spirit. We beseech thee, replenish them more and more with such gifts as are necessary, for them in their ministration; with the gifts of wisdom, courage, discretion, and benevolence, to the end that every one may, in his respective office, acquit himself as is becoming; the elders in taking diligent heed unto the doctrine and conversation, in keeping out the wolves from the sheepfold of thy beloved Son; and in admonishing and reproving disorderly persons. In like manner, the deacons in carefully receiving, and liberally and prudently distributing of the alms to the poor, and in comforting them with thy holy Word. Give grace both to the elders and deacons, that they may persevere in their faithful labor, and never become weary by reason of any trouble, pain or persecution of the world. Grant also especially thy divine grace to this people, over whom they are placed, that they may willingly submit themselves to the good exhortations of the elders, counting them worthy of honor for their work's sake; give also unto the rich, liberal hearts towards the poor, and to the poor grateful hearts towards those who help and serve them; to the end that every one acquitting himself of his duty, thy holy name may thereby be magnified, and the kingdom of thy Son Jesus Christ, enlarged, in whose name we conclude our prayers, saying: "Our Father," etc.

———— ·⟨ ⟩· ————

FORM FOR THE INSTALLATION OF PROFESSORS OF THEOLOGY.

Beloved brethren, it is known unto you that our brother in the holy ministry, N. N., has been called by our last Synod to the important office of professor of theology at our Theological Seminary. To our joy he has accepted this call, and we are now assembled to install him in office. For which purpose we request thee, brother N. N., to arise and to listen to that which belongs to this office, and is placed by the Lord and the Church in thy charge.

Since our God, who is rich in mercy, has chosen in his great love a Church unto himself for the inheritance of eternal life, and will gather this Church through his Spirit and Word to the fellowship of his Son, in the unity of true faith, and to the increase of the knowledge of his will, so it pleases him to call men by his Holy Spirit, who as ministers of the Word are to preach the glad tidings of salvation among those who already belong to the Church and among those outside, who are yet without the knowledge of God's ways.

The first messengers of peace in the days of the New Testament were immediately taught by our Lord Jesus Christ, and were by him personally trained and sent. After the outpouring of the Holy Spirit he gave them great diversities of extraordinary gifts and knowledge of the mysteries of salvation of sinners and the upbuilding of saints. Because these extraordinary methods, however, lasted only as long as the Lord judged them to be necessary for the founding of his Church among the nations, the necessity was soon felt of training youths and men for the holy ministry under the ordinary dispensation of the Spirit by the regular methods of eduction. And this especially in virtue of what Paul wrote in 2 Tim. 2:2, "And the things which thou hast heard from me among many witnesses, the same commit thou to faithful men, who shall be able to teach others also." The Apostle here points to what he had himself done and what he required of his disciple Timothy.

In obedience to this apostolic direction this training was originally done by learned and capable overseers of the Church. Later the schools of Alexandria, Antioch, and other important cities were especially engaged in this work. And when towards the end of the middle ages and in the sixteenth and seventeenth centuries universities arose in various places, theology was not incorporated merely as a faculty with other faculties, but usually recognized as Queen of Sciences. This was the more easily done because the Church, both Roman Catholic and Protestant, exercised authority over or concerned itself with everything.

As long as a university is founded on the basis of Holy Scripture, accepts the confession of a certain denomination, and this denomination has part control in the appointing of professors of theology, it can not be disapproved of that future ministers of the Word should receive their education at such an institution.

Since, however, Paul in Rom. 3:2 expressly declares that the Church of the Old Dispensation, and therefore also the Church of the New Dispensation, was given the special prerogative that to her were intrusted the oracles of God, it follows therefore that the Church has a divine mission to proclaim the word of God, to collect from the Word of God her standards of faith, to study theology according to these words, and further to advance what is in direct connection with this study.

Conscious of this calling our Church has also established a Theological School and called the reverend brother N. N. to devote his talents to this School.

In behalf of our Church the Curators charge thee, esteemed brother, with the task of instructing and establishing in the knowledge of God's Word, the students who hope once to minister in his Church. Expound to them the mysteries of the faith; caution them in regard to the errors and heresies of the old, but especially of the new day; seek to explain how they not alone as teachers are to instruct but also as pastors are to shepherd the flock of the Lord. Assist in maintaining order and discipline among the disciples, that our Seminary may continue to enjoy the respect, the support, the appreciation, the love and the prayer of the Church. Be a good example to the students, that they may not only profit from thy learning, but also find in thee a living illustration of the power and practice of true godliness.

Be engaged in all of this according to the measure of the gifts God gave thee, in dependence on the Lord's help and the light of the Holy Spirit.

And that it may now publicly appear that thou, highly esteemed brother, art thus disposed, thou art to answer the following questions:

First. I ask thee, dost thou feel in thy heart that thou art lawfully called of God's Church and therefore of God himself to this office?

Secondly. Dost thou believe the books of the Old and New Testament to be the only Word of God? Dost thou reject all doctrine repugnant thereto, and dost thou accept the doctrinal standards of the Christian Reformed Church as the truest expression of the doctrine of salvation?

Thirdly. Dost thou promise faithfully to discharge thy office according to the same doctrine above described, and to adorn it with a godly life?

Fourthly. Dost thou promise to submit thyself, in case thou shouldest become delinquent, either in life or doctrine, to the ordinance of the Church, and if necessary, to Church discipline?

Answer: Yes, with all my heart.

————◄ ☙ ►————

FORM OF ORDINATION OF MISSIONARIES.

Beloved in our Lord and Savior and all here present.

It is known to you that our brother N. N., called by the...............................
as missionary minister of the Word among the Heathen (Dispersed), (and recently examined by the Classis of ....) is now to be publicly ordained (installed) as missionary.

We, therefore, request thee, beloved brother N. N., to arise and to attend to a short declaration touching the office of missionary ministers of the Word.

Since our God, according to his infinite mercy, has chosen a Church unto everlasting life, and gathers it by his blessed gospel, out of every nation, and of all tribes and peoples and tongues, unto the fellowship of his Son, in unity of the true faith, therefore our risen Savior has ordained an office and has called men, to carry the message of salvation to all peoples, commanding his apostles, and in them all lawful ministers of the Word: "Go ye into all the world, and preach the gospel to every creature." Mark 16:15. For he that ascended far above all the heavens, that he might fulfill all things, gave some to be apostles; and some prophets; and some evangelists; and some pastors and teachers; for the perfecting of the saints, unto the work of ministering, unto the building up of the body of Christ. And the Apostles, responding to this, went forth into the world declaring the whole counsel of God, particularly repentance, and remission of sins, through faith in Jesus Christ, testifying: "for God so loved the world, that He gave his only begotten Son, that whosoever believeth in Him should not perish, but have eternal life." John 3:16. "But all things are

of God who reconciled us to himself through Christ, and gave unto us the ministry of reconciliation: to-wit, that God was in Christ reconciling the world unto himself, not reckoning unto them their trespasses; and hath committed unto us the word of reconciliation. We are ambassadors, therefore, on behalf of Christ, as though God were entreating by us: we beseech you on behalf of Christ, be ye reconciled to God." 2 Cor. 5.

Without this word of reconciliation, faith in Christ and consequently salvation, is and remains forever impossible, for Holy Scripture says, Acts 4:12: "And in none other is there salvation: for neither is there any other name under heaven, that is given among men, wherein we must be saved"; and elsewhere: Rom. 10:14, 15, 17: "How shall they believe in him of whom they have not heard? and how shall they hear without a preacher? and how shall they preach, except they be sent? So then, faith cometh by hearing, and hearing by the Word of God."

Although all ministers of the Word have in common, that to them is committed the preaching of the Gospel, the administration of the Sacraments, the government of the Church, and the maintenance of christian discipline, yea, all, that, according to the Word of God belongs to the office of pastor and teacher: and although from the difference of field of labor no difference is resulting, concerning office, authority or dignity, since all possess the same mission, the same office and the same authority, yet notwithstanding this, it is necessary that some labor in the congregations already established, while others are called and sent to preach the Gospel to those without, in order to bring them to Christ. And let each man abide in that calling wherein he was called by the Church of God and consequently by God himself and whereunto each has received gifts, until it pleases the Lord to lead him along a lawful way to a different field of labor.

UNTO THE HEATHEN

That unto the **Heathen** also these glad tidings must be brought appears plainly from Matt. 28:19, "Go ye therefore, and teach all nations, baptizing them in the name of the Father, and of the Son, and of the Holy Ghost; teaching them to observe all things whatsoever I have commanded you."

The same was revealed to Peter by showing him as it were a great sheet let down by four corners upon the earth, wherein were all manner of beasts, and thereupon commanding him to go down to the Gentile Cornelius, saying: "Arise, and get thee down, and go with them, nothing doubting; for I have sent them," Acts 10:20. Likewise he spoke to Paul in a vision in the temple: "Depart: for I will send thee forth far hence unto the Gentiles." Acts 22:21.

This divine charge was also carried out by the church of Antioch, when they, after fasting and prayer, laid their hands upon Barnabas and Saul and sent them away to preach the gospel also unto the Gentiles, Acts 13. And when they on their first missionary journey had arrived at Antioch in Pisidia they testified to the contradicting Jews: "Lo, we turn to the Gentiles. For so hath the Lord commanded us, saying: I have set thee for a light of the Gentiles; that thou shouldest be for salvation unto the uttermost part of the earth."

And besides all this it is evident that the work of missions is the task of the Church since the Lord Jesus himself calls his Church the salt of the earth, and says: "Ye are the light of the world. A city on a hill cannot be hid. Neither do men light a lamp, and put it under the bushel, but on the stand." Matt. 5.

UNTO THE DISPERSED

That unto the **Dispersed** also these glad tidings must be brought is plainly inferred from what God says in Ezekiel 34:11-16: "For thus saith the Lord God: Behold, I myself, even I, will search for my sheep, and will seek them out. As a shepherd seeketh out his flock in the day that he is among his sheep that are scattered abroad, so will I seek out my sheep; and I will deliver them out of all places whither they have been scattered in the cloudy and dark day. And I will bring them out from the peoples, and gather them from the countries, and will bring them into their own land; and I will feed them upon the mountains of Israel, by the watercourses, and in all the inhabited places of the country. I will feed them with good pasture, and upon the mountains of the height of Israel shall their fold be: there shall they lie down in a good fold, and on fat pasture shall they feed upon the mountains of Israel. I myself will feed my sheep, and I will cause them to lie down, saith the Lord God. I will seek that which was lost, and will bring again that which was driven away, and will bind up that which was broken, and will strengthen that which was sick. I will feed them in judgment."

That the Lord does this by means of his servants, is clearly shown by the way wherein God, in the same chapter, rebukes the unfaithful shepherds: "Neither have ye brought again that which was driven away," and expresses his holy indignation because: "My sheep wandered through all the mountains, and upon every high hill: yea, my sheep were scattered upon all the face of the earth; and there was none that did search or seek after them." Ezek. 34:4, 6.

The same also follows from the fact that Jesus who Himself was sent "to the lost sheep of the House of Israel," calls the Church the salt of the earth, while besides all this, the example of the Apostle Paul teaches us plainly that it is our high calling to bring the bread of life to our dispersed brethren after the flesh everywhere, and therefore certainly first of all in our own country, to gather them, if possible, as congregations of our Lord.

And since thou, beloved brother, art now called and art now being sent to labor among the **Heathen (Dispersed)**, thou art to consider which important duties are thereby devolving upon thee:

In the **first** place thou art to bring to their attention by all fit and lawful means, the glad tidings that Jesus Christ has come into the world to save sinners. All thine actions, thy speaking and thy silence, yea, all thine influence is to co-operate to recommend the gospel of Christ. Let thy conversation be without covetousness; abhor that which is evil; cleave to that which is good, that thou mayest be able to say with the Apostle Paul, 1 Cor. 9: 19, 22, 27: "For though I was free from all men I brought myself under bondage to all, that I might gain the more. . . . I am become all things to all men, that I may by all means save some. I buffet my body, and bring it into bondage: lest by any means, after that I have preached to others, I myself should be rejected."

Secondly, thou art holden, if it pleases God to make thy work fruitful unto the gathering of a church, to administer the Sacrament of Holy Baptism according to the institution of the Lord and the requirement of the covenant.

Furthermore, thou art called wherever it is necessary and possible to ordain elders and deacons even as Paul charged Titus, chapter 1:5, saying: "For this cause left I thee in Crete, that thou shouldest set in order the things that were wanting, and appoint elders in every city, as I gave thee charge." But lay hands hastily on no man.

Moreover, there is committed unto thee, as minister of Christ and steward of the mysteries of God, the administering of the Holy Supper of the Lord according to the institution of Christ.

Besides this, there is commended unto thee the maintaining of christian discipline in the midst of the congregation, by faithful use of the keys of the Kingdom, as our Lord Jesus has spoken: "Go, show him his fault, between thee and him alone," etc. And afterward: "Verily I say unto you, what things soever ye shall bind on earth, shall be bound in heaven."

And finally, beloved brother, be a faithful servant of Jesus Christ, and a careful shepherd of the flock. "Preach the Word; be urgent in season, out of season; reprove, rebuke, exhort, with all longsuffering and teaching, . . . be an example to them that believe, in word, in manner of life, in love, in faith, in purity." . . . "Give heed to reading, to exhortations, to teaching. Neglect not the gift that is in thee." . . . "Be diligent in these things; give thyself wholly to them; that thy progress may be manifest unto all. Take heed to thyself, and to thy teaching. Continue in these things; for in doing this thou shalt save both thyself and them that hear thee." (2 Tim. 4:2 and 1 Tim. 4:12b, 16.)

And that now everyone present may hear, beloved brother, that thou art willing, and ready to undertake the ministry of the Word among the **Heathen (Dispersed),** thou art requested to answer sincerely the following questions:

First. I ask thee whether thou feelest in thy heart that thou art lawfully called of God's Church and therefore of God himself, to this holy ministry?

Secondly. Whether thou dost believe the books of the Old and New Testament to be the only Word of God, and the perfect doctrine unto salvation, and dost reject all doctrines repugnant thereto?

Thirdly. Whether thou dost promise faithfully to discharge thine office, according to the same doctrine as above described, and to adorn it with a godly life; also, to submit thyself, in case thou shouldest become delinquent either in life or doctrine, to ecclesiastical admonition, according to the public ordinance of the churches?

Answer. Yes, truly, with all my heart.

Then the Minister, who demanded those questions of him, while he and other Ministers who are present, shall lays their hands* on his head, shall say:

"Go then, beloved brother, and teach all nations, baptizing them in the name of the Father and of the Son, and of the Holy Ghost. God our heavenly Father, who hath called thee to his holy ministry, enlighten thee with his Holy Spirit, strengthen thee with his hand and so govern thee in thy ministry, that thou mayest decently and fruitfully walk therein, to the glory of his Name, and the propagation of the Kingdom of his Son Jesus Christ." Amen.

*This ceremony shall not be used in the case of those who have before been in the Ministry.

FORM FOR THE CONFIRMATION OF MARRIAGE BEFORE THE CHURCH.

Whereas married persons are generally, by reason of sin, subject to many troubles and afflictions; to the end that you N. and N., who desire to have your marriage bond publicly confirmed, here in the name of God, before this Church, may also be assured in your hearts of the certain assistance of God in your afflictions, hear therefore from the Word of God, how honorable the marriage state is, and that it is an institution of God, which is pleasing to him. [Wherefore he also will (as he hath promised) bless and assist the married persons, and on the contrary, judge and punish whoremongers and adulterers.]

I. In the first place you are to know, that God our Father, after he had created heaven and earth, and all that in them is, made man in his own image and likeness, that he should have dominion over the beasts of the field, over the fish of the sea, and over the fowls of the air. And after he had created man, he said, "It is not good that man should be alone, I will make him an helpmeet for him. And the Lord caused a deep sleep to fall upon Adam, and he slept; and he took one of his ribs, and closed up the flesh instead thereof. And the rib which the Lord God had taken from man, made he a woman, and brought her unto the man. And Adam said, this is now bone of my bone, and flesh of my flesh: she shall be called woman, because she was taken out of man. Therefore shall a man leave his father, and his mother, and shall cleave unto his wife, and they two shall be one flesh." Therefore ye are not to doubt, but that the married state is pleasing to the Lord, since he made unto Adam his wife, brought and gave her himself to him to be his wife; witnessing thereby that he doth yet as with his hand bring unto every man his wife. For this reason the Lord Jesus Christ did also highly honor it with his presence, gifts and miracles, in Cana of Galilee, to show thereby that this holy state ought to be kept honorably by all, and that he will aid and protect married persons, even when they are least deserving it.

[But that you may live godly in this state, you must know the reasons, wherefore God hath instituted the same. The first reason is, that each faithfully assist the other, in all things that belong to this life, and a better.

Secondly. That they bring up the children, which the Lord shall give them, in the true knowledge and fear of God, to his glory, and their salvation.

Thirdly. That each of them, avoiding all uncleanness and evil lusts, may live with a good and quiet conscience.

For, to avoid fornication, let every man have his own wife, and every woman her own husband; insomuch that all, who are come to their years, and have not the gift of continence, are bound by the command of God, to enter into the marriage state, with knowledge and consent of parents, or guardians and friends; so that the temple of God, which is our body, may not be defiled; for, whosoever defileth the temple of God, him shall God destroy.]

II. Next, you are to know, how each is bound to behave respectively towards the other, according to the word of God.

First. You, who are the bridegroom, must know, that God hath set you to be the head of your wife, that you, according to your ability, shall lead her with discretion; instructing, comforting, protecting her, as the head rules the body; yea, as Christ is the head, wisdom, consolation and assistance to his Church. Besides, you are to love your wife as your own body, as Christ hath loved his Church: you shall not be bitter against her, but dwell with her as a man of understanding, giving honor to the wife as the weaker vessel, considering that ye are joint heirs of the grace of life, that your prayers be not hindered. And since it is God's command, "that the man shall eat his bread in the sweat of his face," therefore you are to labor diligently and faithfully, in the calling wherein God hath set you, that you may maintain your household honestly, and likewise have something to give to the poor.

In like manner, must you, who are the bride, know how you are to carry yourself towards your husband, according to the Word of God. You are to love your lawful husband, to honor and fear him, as also to be obedient unto him in all lawful things, as to your Lord, as the body is obedient to the head, and the Church to Christ. You shall not exercise any dominion over your husband, but be silent: for Adam was first created, and then Eve, to be an help to Adam; and after the fall, God said to Eve, and in her to all women, "your will shall be subject to your husband." [You shall not resist this ordinance of God, but be obedient to the word of God, and follow the examples of godly women, who trusted in God, and were subject to their husbands; "as Sarah was obedient to Abraham, calling him her lord": you shall also be an help to your husband in all good and lawful things, looking to your family, and walking in all honesty and virtue, without worldly pride, that you may give an example to others of modesty.]

Wherefore you N. and you N., having now understood that God hath instituted marriage, and what he commands you therein; are you willing thus to behave yourselves in this holy state, as you here do confess before this christian assembly, and desirous that you be confirmed in the same?

Answer. Yes.

Whereupon the Minister shall say:

I take you all, who are met here to witness, that there is brought no lawful impediment.

Further to the married persons.

Since then it is fit that you be furthered in this your work, the Lord God confirm your purpose, which he hath given you; and your beginning be in the name of the Lord, who made heaven and earth.

Hereupon they shall join hands together, and the Minister speak first to the bridegroom.

N. Do you acknowledge here before God and this his holy Church, that you have taken, and do take to your lawful wife, N., here present, promising her never to forsake her; to love her faithfully, to maintain her, as a faithful and pious husband is bound to do to his lawful wife; that you will live holily with her; keeping faith and truth to her in all things according to the holy gospel?

Answer. Yes.

Afterwards to the bride.

N. Do you acknowledge here before God, and this his holy Church, that you have taken, and do take to your lawful husband, N., here present, promising to be obedient to him, to serve and assist him, never to forsake him, to live holily with him, keeping faith and truth to him in all things, as a pious and faithful wife is bound to her lawful husband according to the holy gospel?

Answer. Yes.

Then the Minister shall say:

The Father of all mercies, who of his grace hath called you to this holy state of marriage, bind you in true love and faithfulness, and grant you his blessing. Amen.

Hear now from the Gospel, how firm the bond of marriage is, as described, Matt. 19:3-9:

"The Pharisees also came unto him, tempting him, and saying unto him, Is it lawful for a man to put away his wife for every cause? And he answered and said unto them, Have ye not read, that he which made them at the beginning made them male and female, and said, For this cause shall a man leave father and mother, and shall cleave to his wife: and they twain shall be one flesh? Wherefore they are no more twain, but one flesh. What therefore God hath joined together, let not man put asunder. They say unto him, Why did Moses then command to give a writing of divorcement, and to put her away? He saith unto them, Moses because of the hardness of your hearts suffered you to put away your wives; but from the beginning it was not so. And I say unto you, Whosoever shall put away his wife, except it be for fornication, and shall marry another, committeth adultery: and whoso marrieth her which is put away doth commit adultery."

Believe these words of Christ, and be certain and assured, that your Lord God hath joined you together in this holy state. You are therefore to receive whatever befalls you therein, with patience and thanksgiving, as from the hand of God, and thus all things will turn to your advantage and salvation. Amen.

PRAYER.

Almighty God, Thou, who dost manifest thy goodness and wisdom in all thy works and ordinances; and from the beginning hast said, that it is not good that man be alone and therefore hast created him a helpmeet to be with him, and ordained that they who were two should be one, and who dost also punish all impurity; we pray thee, since Thou hast called and united these two persons in the holy state of marriage, that Thou wilt give them thy Holy Spirit, so that they in true love and firm faith my live holy according to thy divine will and resist all evil. Wilt Thou also bless them as Thou hast blessed the believing fathers, thy friends and faithful servants, Abraham, Isaac and Jacob; in order that they, as co-heirs of the covenant which Thou hast established with these fathers, may bring up their children, which Thou wilt be pleased to give them, in the fear of the Lord, to the honor of thy holy name, to the edification of thy Church and to the extension of the holy gospel. Hear us, Father of all mercy, for the sake of Jesus Christ, thy beloved Son, our Lord, in whose name we conclude our prayer: Our Father, who art in heaven, etc.

Hearken now to the promise of God, from Psalm 128: "Blessed is every one that feareth the Lord, that walketh in his ways. For thou shalt eat the labor of thine hands: happy shalt thou be, and it shall be well with thee. Thy wife shall be as a fruitful vine by the sides of thine house; thy children like olive plants round about thy table. Behold, that thus shall the man be blessed that feareth the Lord. The Lord shall bless thee out of Zion: and thou shalt see the good of Jerusalem all the days of thy life; yea, thou shalt see thy children's children, and peace upon Israel."

The Lord our God replenish you with his grace, and grant that ye may long live together in all godliness and holiness. Amen.

THE CONSOLATION OF THE SICK.

Which is an Instruction in Faith, and the Way of Salvation to prepare Believers to die willingly.

Since Adam was created just and good, that is to say, holy, righteous and immortal, and dominion given him over all the creatures which God had created; and whereas he did not long remain in this state, but has through the subtilty of the Devil and his own rebellion fallen from this excellent glory, whereby he hath brought upon us the misery of temporal and eternal death; this is the original sin of which David speaks in the

Ps. 51. v. 5.   51st Psalm, saying, I was shapen in iniquity and in sin did my mother conceive me: In like manner Paul saith to the Romans,

Rom. 5:12.   That by one man sin entered into the world, and death by sin, and death passed upon all men, for that all have sinned. For as soon as Adam was thus fallen, he immediately came under a certain curse, as we read in Genesis, where God saith,

Gen. 3:17,19.   Cursed is the ground for thy sake, in sorrow shalt thou eat of it all the days of thy life, in the sweat of thy face shalt thou eat bread, till thou return unto the ground; for out of it wast thou taken: For dust thou art, and unto dust shalt thou return. Whence we certainly know, that all things which receive life,

Ps. 89.48.
Eccl. 9:5.
Heb. 13:14.   must once die: This David clearly testifies, saying, What man is he that liveth, and shall not see death? For Solomon saith, The living know that they shall die. (Hebrews.) For here we have no continuing city, but we seek one to come. And to

Heb. 9:27.
2 Sam. 14:14.   the Hebrews, That it is appointed unto men once to die, and after this the judgment. For as the Scripture saith: We must needs all die, and are as water spilt on the ground, which cannot

Job 9:25.   be gathered up again. For our days (saith Job) are like the days of an hireling, and swifter than a post. And we pass away (saith David) like a stream, yea like a leaf which the wind driveth away, and a withered stalk and a garment moth-

Eccl. 12:7.   eaten. For the dust must return to the earth, as it was, and the spirit unto God who gave it; as Job saith, We are ashes

Jam. 4:14.   and must return to ashes. Likewise James saith, That man's life is even a vapour that appeareth for a little time and then vanisheth away. Yea our time passeth away as a cloud and is consumed like a mist, and vanisheth as a shadow. And Peter also

1 Peter 1:24.   saith (quoting from Isaiah), That all flesh is as grass, and all the glory of men, as the flower of grass; the grass withereth, and the flower thereof falleth away. Again Jesus Syrach saith, This is the old covenant, you must die;—the one today and the other tomorrow, like as green leaves upon a tree, some fall off, and others grow again: Thus it goeth with mankind, some

Eccl. 3:1, 2.   die and some are born. As Solomon saith, To every thing there is a season, a time to be born, and a time to die.

And this time is in the hands of the Lord, as Job saith, Man

Job 14:5.   hath his appointed time, the number of his months are with him, he has appointed our bounds that we cannot pass. Which

Acts 17:26.   Paul also saith, That God hath determined the times before appointed, and the bounds of their habitation. And David saith,

Ps. 39:5.   That our days are as an hand-breadth by the Lord, and our age is as nothing before him: How vain are all men who live so unconcerned? For our days are lighter than a weaver's shuttle, and swifter than a post. Moreover we are here only pilgrims and strangers for a short time. For the days of our years are threescore years and ten, and if by reason of strength they be fourscore years, yet is their strength, labour and sorrow; for it is soon cut off, and we fly away. And when we live long we live a hundred years: As drops of water are to the sea, so are our years to eternity. And Peter saith, That one day is with the Lord as a thousand years, and a thousand years as one day, even so are our years to eternity.

Whereas then we must all die, according to holy Scripture, who would not earnestly wish for death, when we behold in what state and ruin we are plunged through Adam, namely, in all unrighteousness, misery and trouble; inasmuch that we are wicked, and inclined to wickedness from our very infancy. For as Paul saith, We are by nature the children of wrath, and reprobate unto every good work, having nothing of ourselves but sin. And David also saith, There is none that doth good, they are all gone aside, they are all-together become filthy. For the good that we would, we do not, by reason of sin that dwelleth in us. Of this inherent sin, David witnesseth, That we are conceived and born in sin, and proceed in the same. For the inclination of men's hearts is to evil from their youth.

Since we thus lie under the wrath of God, and in the shadow of death, yea in hell and damnation, therefore Christ the light of the world appeared unto us, and the sun of righteousness is risen: Who was delivered for our offences, and was raised again for our justification, and hath also quickened us when we were dead in sin, and hath forgiven us our sins, and blotted out the hand-writing of ordinances that was against us, and took it out of the way, and nailed it on the cross; whereby he hath triumphed over all our enemies, as death, Satan, hell and the curse of the law, as God hath spoken by the Prophet Hosea, O death, where is thy sting? O grave, where is thy victory? Thanks be to God, which giveth us the victory, through our Lord Jesus Christ, who hath also (according to the promise of God) bruised the head of the Devil, in whose power we were kept captives, by reason of the transgressions of sin.

God to the end that he might deliver us therefrom, hath given us his dearest pledge, namely his only beloved Son in whom the Father is well pleased, and commands us to hear him. Whom he hath given for a propitiation and a ransom. For God so loved the world, that he gave his only begotten Son; that whosoever believeth in him should not perish, but have everlasting life. Also in this was manifested the love of God towards us, because that God sent his only begotten Son into the world, that we might live through him. And this is life eternal (saith Christ), that they might know thee the only true God, and Jesus Christ whom thou hast sent. He is the true Messiah, who came into the world in the fullness of time, true God to crush the power of the Devil; and true man to be our mediator before God, that he might deliver those who were captive under the law. He is that lamb without blemish, that was wounded and offered for our transgressions, to be a propitiation for all our sins, as Isaiah clearly testifies. And he who was rich, for our sakes became poor, that we through his poverty might be rich, for he hath given unto us, all his goods, all his benefits, all his righteousness, merits and holiness. Therefore we must embrace him in faith, and be thankful to him with love and obedience. And who would not love him who first loved us? in that when we were yet his enemies, he delivered and reconciled us, how much

Margin references:
Job. 7:6.
Job. 9:25.
Heb. 11:13.

Ps. 90:10.

2 Peter 3:8.

Eph. 2:3.
Tit. 1:16.
Ps. 14:1.

Rom. 7:19.
Ps. 51.

Rom. 4:25.

Col. 2:14.

1 Cor. 15:55, 57.

John 3:16.

1 John 4:9.

John 1:17, 3.

2 Cor. 8.

Rom. 5:18.

John 15:13.

more being reconciled, shall we be saved by his life? For how can one have greater love, than to lay down his life for his friends? Which Christ as a good shepherd has done, who hath been obedient to his Father, unto death, even the death of the cross, and was made a little lower than the angels, for the suffering of death, crowned with glory and honour; that he by the grace of God should taste death for every man. Also he is the true Samaritan who poured oil and wine in our wounds, that is to say, he hath poured out his precious blood for our sins, and bought us with such a precious price. For we are not (saith Peter) redeemed with gold or silver, but with the precious blood of Christ, as of a lamb without blemish and without spot. For we are not redeemed by the blood of goats or calves, but by his own blood he entered in once into the holy place, having obtained eternal redemption for us: Who hath also delivered us from the power of darkness, and hath translated us into the kingdom of his dear Son, in whom we have the redemption through his blood, even the forgiveness of sins.

Phil. 2:8.
Heb. 2:9.

Luke 10:34.

1 Pet. 1:18, 19.

Heb. 9:12.

Col. 1:13, 14.

Since we certainly know this, that we only obtain eternal salvation, without our merits (for we have none, wherefore we are unprofitable servants), through the death and resurrection of Christ, we must therefore come boldly unto the throne of grace, that we may obtain mercy, and find grace to help in time of need. And since we always stand in need of help, we must go unto him; for he saith, by the Prophet David, Call upon me in the day of trouble, and I will deliver thee. And although a mother might forsake her child, yet will I never forsake thee, as Christ himself saith in the gospel: Come unto me all ye that labor and are heavy laden and I will give you rest, and ye shall find rest unto your souls. To whom else should we go? He has the words of eternal life, and life is made manifest in him. He is that heavenly manna, which eternally satisfies our souls, that heavenly bread of which he that eateth through faith, shall never hunger, and whosoever drinketh of his blood shall never thirst.

Heb. 4:16.

Ps. 50:15.

Mat. 11:28, 29.

John 6:68.

Again Christ saith by the Apostle John, Let him that is a-thirst, come and take the water of life freely: He that believeth on me, as the Scripture hath said, out of this belly shall flow rivers of living water, which are the operations of the Holy Ghost: Whosoever drinketh of that living water, shall never thirst, for the water that I shall give him, shall be in him a well of water springing up into everlasting life. As God hath said by the Prophet Isaiah, Ho, every one that thirsteth, come ye to the waters, and he that hath no money, come ye, buy and eat; yea come, buy wine and milk, without money and without price. Therefore let us go to this fountain for our refreshment, and not to broken wells which contain no water, For of his fullness have we all received grace for grace: For the law was given by Moses, but grace and truth came by Jesus Christ.

Rev. 22:17.
John 7:38.

John 4:14.

Isa. 55:1.

John 1:16, 17.

He is the true mediator who stands between God and us, to be our advocate against all our accusers: For there is one mediator between God and man, the man Christ Jesus. For this cause he is also a mediator of the New Testament, that by means of death, for the redemption of the transgressions that were under the first testament, they which are called might receive the promise of an eternal inheritance. Wherefore he is able also to save them to the uttermost, that come unto God by him, seeing he ever liveth to make intercession for us; with which the Apostle John agreeing, saith, If any man sin, we have an advocate with the Father, Jesus Christ the righteous. He is the propitiation for our sins: And not for ours only, but also for the

1 Tim. 2:5.
Heb. 9:15.

Heb. 7:25.

1 John 2:1, 2.

sins of the whole world: Namely for all peoples and nations of the whole world, who sincerely repent and turn themselves to God: For the lamb was slain, from the beginning of the world for believers, as Christ himself saith, That Abraham saw his day and was glad.

John 8:56, 5.

Thus we see that God is no respecter of persons. For God is not only the God of the Jews, but of the Gentiles also: Namely he is a God who justifies the circumcision by faith, and uncircumcision through faith; for he hath justified us by faith, without the deeds of the law, after which manner David also speaks, that salvation is only come unto the man to whom God imputeth righteousness without works, where he saith, Blessed is he whose transgression is forgiven, whose sin is covered. Blessed is the man unto whom the Lord imputeth not iniquity.

Acts 10:34.
Rom. 3:29, 30.

Ps. 32:1, 2.

Therefore being justified by faith, we have peace with God, through our Lord Jesus Christ, by whom we have a certain access into the holy place, by his blood, whereby he hath made peace between God and us; for he is our true peace, wherefore we have nothing to fear. For Paul saith, If God be for us who can be against us? Who shall lay any thing to the charge of God's elect? It is God that justifieth, who is he that condemneth? It is Christ that died, yea rather that is risen again, who is even at the right hand of God, who maketh intercession for us; who shall separate us from the love of Christ? shall tribulation, or distress, or persecution, or famine, or nakedness, or peril or sword? Therefore though we have the daily actual and other sins remaining in us, we must not despair. For the Prophet Isaiah saith, Though your sins be as scarlet, they shall be as white as snow; though they be red like crimson, they shall be as wool. And this is done through Jesus Christ, who hath washed away our sins by his blood, of which baptism is a sign; and the Lord's Supper is a token unto us, that we are redeemed by the sacrifice of Christ once offered on the cross, that he might deliver us from the wrath to come, and all iniquity; and purify unto himself a peculiar people, zealous of good works, by which the Lord may be praised.

Rom. 5 1.

Rom. 8:31, 33, 34, 35.

Isa 1 18.

Tit. 2:24.

We then knowing for certain, that we are reconciled to God by Jesus Christ, ought (according to the word of God) to have an earnest desire of being delivered from this mortal body, by which we must come to that glorious inheritance of all the children of God, which is prepared for us in heaven. This, Paul, that chosen vessel of God, desired, when he saith, O wretched man that I am, who shall deliver me from the body of this death? Moreover he saith, We know that if our own earthly house of this tabernacle were dissolved, we have a building of God, eternal in the heavens; for in this we groan, earnestly desiring to be clothed upon, with our house which is from heaven, and we are always confident, knowing that whilst we are at home in the body, we are absent from the Lord; therefore we are willing rather to be absent from the body, and to be present with the Lord. Again Paul saith, We know that the whole creation groaneth with us, and not only they, but we ourselves groan within ourselves, who have the first fruits of the spirit, waiting for the adoption, to wit the redemption of our body. And since we are pilgrims and strangers, who would not desire to be at home in his native country? For here we walk in absence, and in faith, but not in sight. For now we see through a glass darkly, but then face to face, as he is. Who would not long after this sight, since we see that the holy men of God have craved after it? As we read in the 42nd Psalm, As the hart panteth after the water brooks, so panteth my soul

Rom. 7 24.

2 Cor 5 1.

2 Cor. 5 2, 6, 8.

Rom. f 22.

1 Cor. 13:12.

after thee, O God! My soul thirsteth for God, for the living God; when shall I come and appear before God? My tears have been my meat, day and night, while they continually say unto me, where is thy God? This unutterable glorious sight of God is so great (as the prophet saith), That eye hath not seen, nor ear heard, neither hath entered into the heart of man the things which God hath prepared for them that love him. Again David saith, that a day in the courts of the Lord, is better than a thousand; yea I had rather be a door-keeper in the house of God, than to dwell long in the tents of wickedness. How amiable are thy tabernacles, O Lord of Host! Blessed are they that dwell in thy house: They will be still praising thee. And they shall be abundantly satisfied with the fatness of thy house, and thou shalt make them drink of the river of thy pleasures. For with thee is the fountain of life, in thy light shall we see light; this is the delightful mansion, of which Christ spake by John, In my Father's house are many mansions, if it were not so, I would have told you. I go to prepare a place for you, I come again and receive you unto myself, that where I am there may ye be also; namely in the new Jerusalem, which has no need of the sun, neither of the moon, for the glory of God lightens it, and the lamb is the light thereof. There God will wipe all tears away from our eyes, and death shall be no more: Which is the last enemy that God will trample under his feet. There God hath prepared a glorious wedding, where we shall sit at the table of the Lord, together with Abraham, Isaac and Jacob: And blessed are they who are called to this wedding or supper.

We cannot come to this supper by any other means than through death, therefore Paul saith, For to me to live is Christ, and to die is gain. And as soon as the faithful depart from hence, they enter into eternal rest, as Christ saith, Where I am, there shall also my servant be: Again, He that heareth my Word and believeth on him that sent me, hath everlasting life, and shall not come into condemnation, but is passed from death unto life. Which is also plainly to be observed in the malefactor, when he prayed and said, Lord remember me when thou comest into thy kingdom. Upon which Christ answered him, Today shalt thou be with me in Paradise: Therefore Paul justly said (agreeable to this), I desire to depart and to be with Christ. Solomon likewise saith, That dust must return to the earth as it was, and the spirit unto God who gave it. Which also evidently appears in the example of Enoch and Elias, who were both taken up into heaven, where our citizenshp and conversation is: from whence also we look for the Savior, the Lord Jesus Christ, who shall change our vile body, that it may be fashioned like unto his glorious body.

And we cannot arrive to this state of glory, unless through much tribulation, of which Jesus Syrach elegantly speaks: My son (saith he), if thou come to serve the Lord, prepare thy soul for temptation: In which thou shalt also rejoice, thou who hast for a short time, mourned with much temptation. But the God of all grace, who hath called us unto his eternal glory by Christ Jesus, after that ye have suffered a while will make you perfect, establish, strengthen, settle you. Again Paul saith, If so be that we suffer with Christ, we shall also be glorified together. For the sufferings of this present time, are not to be compared with the glory which shall be revealed to us. For our affliction is temporal and light, but worketh an eternal and exceeding weight of glory. And David said, Weeping may endure for a night, but joy cometh in the morning. Therefore rejoice, that when his glory shall be revealed ye may be glad also with

Marginal references:
Isa. 64:4.
1 Cor. 2:9.

Ps. 84:10.
Ps. 34:1, 4.
Ps. 36:8, 9.

John 14:2, 3.

Rev. 21:23.

Phil. 1:21.

John 12:26.
John 5:24.

Luke 23:42, 43.

Phil. 1:23.
Eccl. 12:7.

Phil. 3:20, 21.

1 Pet. 5:10.

Rom. 8:17, 18.

2 Cor. 4:17.

Ps. 30:5.

1 Pet. 4:13.

exceeding joy: Christ hath also suffered without the gate, therefore let us also go forth unto him without the camp, bearing his reproach. For herein hath Christ left us an example, that we should follow his steps. Again Peter saith, "Forasmuch then, as Christ hath suffered for us in the flesh, arm yourselves likewise with the same mind: For he that suffers in the flesh ceaseth from sin. Moreover the Apostle James also saith, My beloved brethren, count it all joy when you fall in divers temptations. And Paul likewise saith, We glory in tribulations, knowing that tribulation worketh patience, and patience, experience; and experience hope, and hope maketh not ashamed. For which reason we must not despise the chastening of the Lord, when we are rebuked of him; for whom the Lord loveth he chasteneth, and he scourgeth, every son whom he receiveth; which may be seen at large in the 12th chapter of the Epistle to the Hebrews, Be therefore patient, and stablish your hearts, for the coming of the Lord draweth nigh. Take also the prophets for an example of suffering affliction, and of patience; we count them happy which endure, for we have heard of the patience of Job, and have seen the end of the Lord, who have left us an example of perseverance. For we see that Christ for the suffering of death, hath been crowned with never fading honour. Therefore Christ also saith, He that endureth to the end shall be saved: And the Apostle Paul saith, I have fought a good fight, I have finished my course, I have kept the faith, henceforth there is laid up for me a crown of righteousness, which the Lord shall give me; and not only to me, but unto all them that love his appearing. Likewise James saith, Blessed is the man that endureth temptation, for when he is tried, he shall receive the crown of life, which the Lord hath promised to them, that love him.

To obtain this crown of righteousness, we must manfully fight against all our enemies, who attack us on all sides: Particularly against the wiles of the Devil, against which put on the whole armour of God, with which you will be able to withstand the Devil and all his might. Peter speaking of his fight saith, That the Devil walketh about as a roaring lion seeking whom he may devour: Whom resist steadfast in the faith, and he will flee from you. This victory and resistance we have of God through Christ, who tramples the Devil under our feet, in whose power and bonds we were bound. He is the prince of this world whom Christ hath cast out; and we have likewise through him obtained the victory, and are also through faith made partakers of him. He is the old serpent who seeks to devour us, who did devour our first parents, and who still bites us in the heel, wherefore he is called a murderer from the beginning.

Therefore we must be diligent on our guard against his wiles, as Peter saith, Be sober and watch unto prayer. For as Christ saith, We know neither the day nor the hour wherein the Lord will come. But this ye know that, if the good man of the house had known what hour the thief would come, he would have watched. Be ye ready therefore also, for the Son of Man will come at an hour when we watch not, but begin to beat our fellow-servants, and to eat and drink with the drunkards; then the Lord will come, and cut us in sunder, and our portion will be with the hypocrites: there will be weeping and gnashing of teeth, there the worm never dieth, and the fire is not quenched. For we certainly know that the day of the Lord will come as a thief in the night, when we shall say, Peace and safety, then sudden destruction will come upon us, as travail upon a woman with child. Therefore take heed to yourselves lest at any time

Heb. 13:12, 13.

1 Pet. 2.21.
1 Pet. 4:1.

Jam. 1:2.

Rom. 5.3, 4, 5

Jam. 5:8, 10, 11.

Heb. 2.9.
Mat. 10:22.
2 Tim. 4.7, 8.

Jam. 1.12.

1 Pet. 5:8, 9.

1 Pet. 4:7.

Mat. 25 13.
Luke 12 39.
Luke 12 40, 45, 46.

Mark 9:44.

2 Pet. 3:10.

Luke 21:34.

Luke 21:35, 36.

your hearts be overcharged with surfeiting and drunkenness and cares of this life, and so that day come upon you unawares. For as a snare, or as lightning which comes suddenly, shall it come on us all. Watch therefore and pray always, that ye may be accounted worthy to escape all these things, that shall come to pass, and to stand undaunted before the Son of Man.

But this worthiness to stand before the Son of Man consists in a pure undefiled and immovable faith which worketh through love, by which we receive and embrace Christ with all his merits and benefits. Which faith we must show by a pure life. As Mat. 5:8. James saith, And of this purity Christ speaks by Matthew, Blessed are the pure in heart, for they shall see God. And the Mat. 15:19, 20. principal purity lies in the heart, for as Christ saith, Out of the heart proceed evil thoughts, murders, adulteries, fornications, thefts, false witness and blasphemies: these things defile man. Gal. 5:22, 23. Therefore the fruits of the spirit follow, which are, love, joy, peace, long suffering, gentleness, goodness, faith, meekness, chastity, righteousness, and truth. Therefore unless we are Mat. 3:3. born again, we cannot see the kingdom of God. Yea as Christ saith, Except ye repent and become as children (to wit in sin) Mark 10:14. ye shall not enter into the kingdom of heaven. There shall Rev. 21:27. nothing enter into it that defileth, neither whatsoever worketh abomination, or maketh a lie, as Paul likewise clearly testifieth.

Since then the law of God requires this perfection of us, as it is written, Cursed is every one who doth not keep the whole Jam. 2:10. law; as James also saith, Whosoever offendeth in one point, he is guilty of all. Again whosoever doth the law, shall live by it: But we do not keep the least commandment perfectly. As the wise man saith, When we imagine to have done we only begin (and in case we did do it, we only do our duty), wherefore we are by the law condemned in God's righteous judgment; for this we have a sure remedy and cure, namely Christ who Gal. 3:13. hath redeemed us (as Paul saith) from the curse of the law, and hath satisfied the righteousness of God for us, making reconciliation; and who hath broken down the wall which was between us, namely the law, contained in ordinances, and forgiven us our sins, and torn the hand-writing of them, and nailed it to the cross: For this great love of Christ, we ought also to love him, and to be thankful to him, with good works, and verily to believe in him, for the gift of these excellent benefits: For he that cometh to God, must believe that he is a Heb. 11:6. rewarder of them that seek him; for the just shall live by his Heb. 2:4. faith. Therefore we conclude that a man is justified by faith, Rom. 3:28. without the deeds of the law; and although we suffer a little with Christ, we must not despair, for we see that Christ himself when he was smote for our sins, did not smite again, but suffered patiently.

And if the ungodly live in great prosperity, as David and the prophets testify, we must not marvel, neither stumble, but comfort ourselves, being assured that their end is everlasting death. He lets them go as sheep to the slaughter, therefore it is to be wondered at that the faithful meet with still more crosses in comparison to the glorious joy which is prepared for them, and on the contrary, that the ungodly have still more prosperity, than they have, in comparison to the dreadful damnation which attends them. Therefore if the trial of believers is not alike, so neither shall the resurrection of the dead be alike.

And in this we have great comfort, that all believers will rise at the last day; of which Paul reasoning, saith, If the dead rise not, then is not Christ risen, then is our preaching vain, and we are found false witnesses of God. The manner of our resurrection we may read in the 37th chapter of Ezekiel, how that we shall rise with flesh and bones. And Job also saith, I know that my redeemer liveth, and will hereafter raise me up out of the earth, and that I shall be covered with my skin, and in my own flesh, see God; likewise the Prophet Isaiah saith, that the earth and the sea shall give up the dead which have slept in them, for Christ is the resurrection, the first of them that slept. But you must not be ignorant concerning them which are asleep, that ye sorrow not even as others, which have no hope. For if we believe that Jesus died and rose again, even so those also which sleep in Jesus, will God bring with him, for this we say as a true word of God; that we which are alive and remain unto the coming of the Lord, shall not prevent them which are asleep, for the Lord himself, shall descend from heaven with a shout, with the voice of the archangel, and with the trump of God, and the dead in Christ shall rise first; then we which are alive and remain, shall be caught up together with them in the clouds, to meet the Lord in the air. Where we must appear before the judgment seat of Christ: Where every one will receive according to that he hath done, whether it be good or bad. Then Christ will separate the sheep from the goats, and the sheep will be set on his right hand, who shall hear the delightful voice, Come ye blessed, inherit the kingdom of my Father prepared for you from the foundation of the world. There we shall stand with greater confidence against those who have distressed us: Then we shall shine forth as the sun in the kingdom of our Father, there we shall come to the hope of an innumerable company of angels. There we shall reign from eternity to eternity, Amen.

Blessed are they whose names are written in the Book of Life.

1 Cor. 15.

Job 19.

1 Thess. 4, 13-17.

2 Cor. 5. 10.

——————◁ ▷·————— —

CHURCH ORDER

····◁║▷····

ARTICLE 1.

For the maintenance of good order in the Church of Christ it is necessary that there should be: offices, assemblies, supervision of doctrine, sacraments and ceremonies, and Christian discipline; of which matters the following articles treat in due order.

OF THE OFFICES.

ARTICLE 2.

The offices are of four kinds: of the Ministers of the Word, of the Professors of Theology, of the Elders, and of the Deacons.

ARTICLE 3.

No one, though he be a Professor of Theology, Elder or Deacon, shall be permitted to enter upon the Ministry of the Word and the Sacraments without having been lawfully called thereunto. And when any one acts contrary thereto, and after being frequently admonished does not desist, the Classis shall judge whether he is to be declared a schismatic or is to be punished in some other way.

ARTICLE 4.

The lawful calling of those who have not been previously in office, consists:

First, in the ELECTION by the Consistory and the Deacons, after preceding prayers, with due observance of the regulations established by the consistory for this purpose, and of the ecclesiastical ordinance, that only those can for the first time be called to the Ministry of the Word who have been declared eligible by the churches, according to the rule in this matter; and furthermore with the advice of Classis or of the counselor appointed for this purpose by the Classis;

Secondly, in the EXAMINATION both of doctrine and life which shall be conducted by the Classis, to which the call must be submitted for approval, and which shall take place in the presence of three Delegates of Synod from the nearest Classes;

Thirdly, in the APPROBATION by the members of the calling church, when, the name of the minister having been announced for two successive Sundays, no lawful objection arises; which approbation, however, is not required in case the election takes place with the co-operation of the congregation by choosing out of a nomination previously made.

Finally, in the public ORDINATION in the presence of the presence of the congregation, which shall take place with appropriate stipulations and interrogations, admonitions and prayers and imposition of hands by the officiating minister (and by other ministers who are present) agreeably to the Form for that purpose.

ARTICLE 5.

Ministers already in the Ministry of the Word, who are called to another congregation, shall likewise be called in the aforesaid manner by the Consistory and the Deacons, with observance of the regulations made for the purpose by the Consistory and of the general ecclesiastical ordinances for the eligibility of those who have served outside of the Christian Reformed Church and for the repeated calling of the same Minister during the same vacancy; further, with the advice of the Classis or of the counselor, appointed by the Classis, and with the approval of the Classis or of the Delegates appointed by the Classis, to whom the ministers called show good ecclesiastical testimonials of doctrine and life, with the approval of the members of the calling congregation, as stated in Article 4; whereupon the minister called shall be installed with appropriate stipulations and prayers agreeably to the Form for this purpose.

ARTICLE 6.

No Minister shall be at liberty to serve in institutions of mercy or otherwise, unless he be previously admitted in accordance with the preceding articles, and he shall, no less than others, be subject to the Church Order.

ARTICLE 7.

No one shall be called to the Ministry of the Word, without his being stationed in a particular place, except he be sent to do church extension work.

ARTICLE 8.

Persons who have not pursued the regular course of study in preparation for the Ministry of the Word, and have therefore not been declared eligible according to Article 4, shall not be admitted to the Ministry unless there is assurance of their exceptional gifts, godliness, humility, modesty, common sense and discretion, as also gifts of public address. When such persons present themselves for the Ministry, the Classis (if the [particular] Synod approve) shall first examine them, and further deal with them as it shall deem edifying, according to the general regulations of the churches.

ARTICLE 9.

Preachers without fixed charge, or others who have left some sect, shall not be admitted to the Ministry in the Church until they have been declared eligible, after careful examination, by the Classis, with the approval of Synod.

ARTICLE 10.

A Minister, once lawfully called, may not leave the congregation with which he is connected, to accept a call elsewhere, without the consent of the Consistory, together with the Deacons, and knowledge on the part of the Classis; likewise no other church may receive him until he has presented a proper certificate of dismission from the church and the Classis where he served.

ARTICLE 11.

On the other hand, the Consistory, as representing the congregation, shall also be bound to provide for the proper support of its Ministers, and shall not dismiss them from service without the knowledge and approbation of the Classis and of the Delegates of the (particular) Synod.

ARTICLE 12.

Inasmuch as a Minister of the Word, once lawfully called as described above, is bound to the service of the Church for life, he is not allowed to enter upon a secular vocation except for such weighty reasons as shall receive the approval of the Classis.

ARTICLE 13.

Ministers, who by reason of age, sickness, or otherwise, are rendered incapable of performing the duties of their Office, shall nevertheless retain the honor and title of a Minister, and the Church which they have served shall provide honorably for them in their need (likewise for the orphans and widows of Ministers) out of the common fund of the Churches, according to the general ecclesiastical ordinances in this matter.

ARTICLE 14.

If any Minister, for the aforesaid or any other reason, is compelled to discontinue his service for a time, which shall not take place without the advice of the Consistory, he shall nevertheless at all times be and remain subject to the call of the congregation.

ARTICLE 15.

No one shall be permitted, neglecting the Ministry of his Church or being without a fixed charge, to preach indiscriminately without the consent and authority of Synod or Classis. Likewise, no one shall be permitted to preach or administer the Sacraments in another Church without the consent of the Consistory of that Church.

ARTICLE 16.

The office of the Minister is to continue in prayer and in the Ministry of the Word, to dispense the Sacraments, to watch over his brethren, the Elders and Deacons, as well as the Congregation, and finally, with the Elders, to exercise church discipline and to see to it that everything is done decently and in good order.

ARTICLE 17.

Among the Ministers of the Word equality shall be maintained with respect to the duties of their office and also in other matters as far as possible according to the judgment of the Consistory, and if necessary, of the Classis; which equality shall also be maintained in the case of the Elders and the Deacons.

ARTICLE 18.

The office of the Professors of Theology is to expound the Holy Scripture and to vindicate sound doctrine against heresies and errors.

ARTICLE 19.

The Churches shall exert themselves, as far as necessary, that there may be students supported by them to be trained for the Ministry of the Word.

ARTICLE 20.

Students who have received permission according to the rule in this matter, and persons who have according to Article 8 been judged competent to be prepared for the Ministry of the Word, shall, for their own training, and for the sake of becoming known to the Congregations, be allowed to speak a word of edification in the meetings for public worship.

ARTICLE 21.

The Consistories shall see to it that there are good Christian Schools in which the parents have their children instructed according to the demands of the Covenant.

ARTICLE 22.

The Elders shall be chosen by the judgment of the Consistory and the Deacons according to the regulations for that purpose established by the Consistory. In pursuance of these regulations, every church shall be at liberty, according to its circumstances, to give the members an opportunity to direct attention to suitable persons, in order that the Consistory may thereupon either present to the congregation for election as many elders as are needed, that they may, after they are approved by it, unless any obstacle arise, be installed with public prayers and stipulations; or present a double number to the congregation and thereupon install the one-half chosen by it, in the aforesaid manner, agreeably to the Form for this purpose.

ARTICLE 23.

The office of the Elders, in addition to what was said in Article 16 to be their duty in common with the Minister of the Word, is to take heed that the Ministers, together with their fellow-Elders and the Deacons, faithfully discharge their office, and both before and after the Lord's Supper, as time and circumstances may demand, for the edification of the churches to visit the families of the Congregation, in order particularly to comfort and instruct the members, and also to exhort others in respect to the Christian Religion.

ARTICLE 24.

The Deacons shall be chosen, approved and installed in the same manner as was stated concerning the Elders.

ARTICLE 25.

The office peculiar to the Deacons is diligently to collect alms and other contributions of charity, and after mutual counsel, faithfully and diligently to distribute the same to the poor as their needs may require it; to visit and comfort the distressed and to exercise care that the alms are not misused; of which they shall render an account in Consistory, and also (if anyone desires to be present) to the Congregation, at such a time as the Consistory may see fit.

ARTICLE 26.

In places where others are devoting themselves to the care of the poor, the Deacons shall seek a mutual understanding with them to the end that the alms may all the better be distributed among those who have the greatest need. Moreover, they shall make it possible for the poor to make use of institutions of mercy, and to that end they shall request the Board of Directors of such institutions to keep in close touch with them. It is also desirable that the Deaconates assist and consult one another, especially in caring for the poor in such institutions.

ARTICLE 27.

The Elders and Deacons shall serve two or more years according to local regulations, and a proportionate number shall retire each year. The retiring officers shall be succeeded by others unless the circumstances and the profit of any church, in the execution of Articles 22 and 24, render a re-election advisable.

ARTICLE 28.

The Consistory shall take care, that the churches for the possession of their property, and the peace and order of their meetings can claim the protection of the Authorities; it should be well understood, however, that for the sake of peace and material possession they may never suffer the royal government of Christ over His Church to be in the least infringed upon.

——————·◖ ◗·——————

OF THE ECCLESIASTICAL ASSEMBLIES.

ARTICLE 29.

Four kinds of ecclesiastical assemblies shall be maintained: the Consistory, the Classis (the Particular Synod), and the General Synod.

ARTICLE 30.

In these assemblies ecclesiastical matters only shall be transacted and that in an ecclesiastical manner. In major assemblies only such matters shall be dealt with as could not be finished in minor assemblies, or such as pertain to the Churches of the major assembly in common.

ARTICLE 31.

If any one complain that he has been wronged by the decision of a minor assembly, he shall have the right to appeal to a major ecclesiastical assembly, and whatever may be agreed upon by a majority vote shall be considered settled and binding, unless it be proved to conflict with the Word of God or with the Articles of the Church Order, as long as they are not changed by a General Synod.

ARTICLE 32.

The proceedings of all assemblies shall begin by calling upon the Name of God and be closed with thanksgiving.

ARTICLE 33.

Those who are delegated to the assemblies shall bring with them their credentials and instructions, signed by those sending them, and they shall have a vote in all matters, except such as particularly concern their persons or churches.

ARTICLE 34.

In all assemblies there shall be not only a president, but also a clerk to keep a faithful record of all important matters.

ARTICLE 35.

The office of the president is to state and explain the business to be transacted, to see to it that everyone observe due order in speaking, to silence the captious and those who are vehement in speaking; and to properly discipline them if they refuse to listen. Furthermore his office shall cease when the assembly arises.

ARTICLE 36.

The Classis has the same jurisdiction over the Consistory as the Particular Synod has over the Classis and the General Synod over the Particular.

ARTICLE 37.

In all Churches there shall be a Consistory composed of the Ministers of the Word and the Elders, who at least in larger congregations, shall, as a rule, meet once a week. The Minister of the Word (or the Ministers, if there be more than one, in turn) shall preside and regulate the proceedings. Whenever the number of Elders is small, the Deacons may be added to the consistory by local regulation; this shall invariably be the rule where the number is less than three.

ARTICLE 38.

In places where the Consistory is to be constituted for the first time or anew, this shall not take place except with the advice of the Classis.

ARTICLE 39.

Places where as yet no Consistory can be constituted shall be placed under the care of a neighboring Consistory.

ARTICLE 40.

The Deacons shall meet, wherever necessary, every week to transact the business pertaining to their office, calling upon the Name of God; whereunto the Ministers shall take good heed and if necessary they shall be present.

ARTICLE 41.

The classical meetings shall consist of neighboring churches that respectively delegate, with proper credentials, a minister and an elder to meet at such time and place as was determined by the previous classical meeting. Such meetings shall be held at least once in three months, unless great distances render this inadvisable. In these meetings the ministers shall preside in rotation, or one shall be chosen to preside; however, the same minister shall not be chosen twice in succession.

Furthermore, the president shall, among other things, put the following questions to the delegates of each church:

1. Are the consistory meetings held in your church?

2. Is church discipline exercised?

3. Are the poor and the Christian schools cared for?

4. Do you need the judgment and help of the Classis for the proper government of your church?

And finally, at one but the last meeting and, if necessary, at the last meeting before the (Particular) Synod, delegates shall be chosen to attend said Synod.

ARTICLE 42.

Where in a church there are more Ministers than one, also those not delegated according to the foregoing article shall have the right to attend Classis with advisory vote.

ARTICLE 43.

At the close of the Classical and other major assemblies, Censure shall be exercised over those, who in the meeting have done something worthy of punishment, or who have scorned the admonition of the minor assemblies.

ARTICLE 44.

The Classis shall authorize at least two of her oldest, most experienced and most competent Ministers to visit all the Churches once a year and to take heed whether the Minister and the Consistory faithfully perform the duties of their office, adhere to sound doctrine, observe in all things the adopted order, and properly promote as much as lies in them, through word and deed, the upbuilding of the congregation, in particular of the youth, to the end that they may in time fraternally admonish those who have in anything been negligent, and may by their advice and assistance help direct all things unto the peace, upbuilding, and greatest profit of the churches. And each Classis may continue these visitors in service as long as it sees fit, except where the visitors themselves request to be released for reasons of which the Classis shall judge.

ARTICLE 45.

It shall be the duty of the church in which the Classis and likewise the (Particular) or General Synod meets to furnish the following meeting with the minutes of the preceding.

ARTICLE 46.

Instructions concerning matters to be considered in major assemblies shall not be written until the decision of previous Synods touching these matters have been read, in order that what was once decided be not again proposed, unless a revision be deemed necessary.

ARTICLE 47.

(Every year [or if need be oftener] four or five or more neighboring Classes shall meet as a Particular Synod, to which each Classis shall delegate two Ministers and two Elders. At the close of both the Particular and the General Synod, some church shall be empowered to determine with advice of Classis, the time and place of the next Synod.)

ARTICLE 48.

(Each Synod shall be at liberty to solicit and hold correspondence with its neighboring Synod or Synods in such manner as they shall judge most conducive to general edification.)

ARTICLE 49.

(Each Synod shall delegate some to execute everything ordained by Synod both as to what pertains to the Government and to the respective Classes, resorting under it, and likewise to supervise together or in smaller number all examinations of future Ministers. And, moreover, in all other eventual difficulties they shall extend help to the Classes in order that proper unity, order and soundness of doctrine may be maintained and established. Also they shall keep proper record of all their actions to report thereof to Synod, and if it be demanded, give reasons. They shall also not be discharged from their service before and until Synod itself discharges them.)

ARTICLE 50.

The General Synod shall ordinarily meet once every two years unless there be urgent need to shorten the time.

To this Synod three Ministers and three Elders out of every Classis shall be delegated. If it becomes necessary in the opinion of at least three Classes to call a meeting of Synod within two years, the local church designated for this purpose shall determine time and place.

ARTICLE 51.

The Missionary Work of the Church is regulated by the General Synod in a Mission Order.

ARTICLE 52.

Inasmuch as different languages are spoken in the churches, the necessary translations shall be made in the ecclesiastical assemblies, and in the publication of recommendations, instructions and decisions.

———— ·‹ ›· ————

OF DOCTRINES, SACRAMENTS AND OTHER CEREMONIES.

ARTICLE 53.

The Ministers of the Word of God and likewise the Professors of Theology (which also behooves the other Professors and School Teachers) shall subscribe to the Three Formulas of Unity, namely, the Belgic Confession of Faith, the Heidelberg Catechism, and the Canons of Dordrecht, 1618-'19, and the Ministers of the Word who refuse to do so shall de facto be suspended from their office by the Consistory or Classis until they shall have given a full statement, and if they obstinately persist in refusing, they shall be deposed from their office.

ARTICLE 54.

Likewise the Elders and Deacons shall subscribe to the aforesaid Formulas of Unity.

ARTICLE 55.

To ward off false doctrines and errors that multiply exceedingly through heretical writings, the Ministers and Elders shall use the means of teaching, of refutation, or warning, and of admonition, as well in the Ministry of the Word as in Christian teaching and family-visiting.

ARTICLE 56.

The Covenant of God shall be sealed unto the children of Christians by Baptism, as soon as the administration thereof is feasible, in the public assembly when the Word of God is preached.

ARTICLE 57.

The Ministers shall do their utmost to the end that the father present his child for Baptism.

ARTICLE 58.

In the ceremony of Baptism, both of children and of adults, the Minister shall use the respective forms drawn up for the administration of this Sacrament.

ARTICLE 59.

Adults are through Baptism incorporated into the Christian Church, and are accepted as members of the Church, and are therefore obliged also to partake of the Lord's Supper, which they shall promise to do at their Baptism.

ARTICLE 60.

The names of those baptized, together with those of the parents, and likewise the date of birth and baptism, shall be recorded.

ARTICLE 61.

None shall be admitted to the Lord's Supper except those who according to the usage of the Church with which they unite themselves have made a confession of the Reformed Religion, besides being reputed to be of a godly walk, without which those who come from other Churches shall not be admitted.

ARTICLE 62.

Every Church shall administer the Lord's Supper in such a manner as it shall judge most conducive to edification; provided, however, that the outward ceremonies as prescribed in God's Word be not changed and all superstition be avoided, and that at the conclusion of the sermon and the usual prayers, the Form for the Administration of the Lord's Supper, together with the prayer for that purpose, shall be read.

ARTICLE 63.

The Lord's Supper shall be administered at least every two or three months.

ARTICLE 64.

The administration of the Lord's Supper shall take place only there where there is supervision of Elders, according to the ecclesiastical order and in a public gathering of the Congregation.

ARTICLE 65.

Funeral sermons or funeral services shall not be introduced.

ARTICLE 66.

In time of war, pestilence, national calamities, and other great afflictions, the pressure of which is felt throughout the Churches, it is fitting that the Classes proclaim a Day of Prayer.

ARTICLE 67.

The Churches shall observe, in addition to the Sunday, also Christmas, Good Friday, Easter, Ascension Day, Pentecost, the Day of Prayer, the National Thanksgiving Day, and Old and New Year's Day.

ARTICLE 68.

The Ministers shall on Sunday explain briefly the sum of Christian Doctrine comprehended in the Heidelberg Catechism so that as much as possible the explanation shall be annually completed, according to the division of the Catechism itself, for that purpose.

ARTICLE 69.

In the Churches only the 150 Psalms of David, the Ten Commandments, the Lord's Prayer, the Twelve Articles of Faith, the Songs of Mary, Zacharias and Simeon, the Morning and Evening Hymns, and the Hymn of Prayer before the sermon shall be sung.

ARTICLE 70.

Since it is proper that the matrimonial state be confirmed in the presence of Christ's Church, according to the Form for that purpose, the Consistories shall attend to it.

———— ·◁ ▷· ————

OF CENSURE AND ECCLESIASTICAL ADMONITION.

ARTICLE 71.

As Christian Discipline is of a spiritual nature, and exempts no one from Civil trial or punishment by the Authorities, so also besides Civil punishment there is need of Ecclesiastical Censures, to reconcile the sinner with the Church and his neighbor and to remove the offense out of the Church of Christ.

ARTICLE 72.

In case any one errs in doctrine or offends in conduct as long as the sin is of a private character, not giving public offense, the rule clearly prescribed by Christ in Matth. 18 shall be followed.

ARTICLE 73.

Secret sins of which the sinner repents, after being admonished by one person in private or in the presence of two or three witnesses, shall not be laid before the Consistory.

ARTICLE 74.

If any one, having been admonished in love concerning a secret sin by two or three persons, does not give heed, or otherwise has committed a public sin, the matter shall be reported to the Consistory.

ARTICLE 75.

The reconciliation of all such sins as are of their nature of a public character, or have become public because the admonition of the Church was despised, shall take place (upon sufficient evidence of repentance) in such a manner as the Consistory shall deem conducive to the edification of each Church. Whether in particular cases this shall take place in public, shall, when there is a difference of opinion about it in the Consistory, be considered with the advice of two neighboring Churches or of the Classis.

ARTICLE 76.

Such as obstinately reject the admonition of the Consistory, and likewise those who have committed a public or otherwise gross sin, shall be suspended from the Lord's Supper. And if he, having been suspended, after repeated admonitions, shows no signs of repentance, the Consistory shall at last proceed to the extreme remedy, namely, excommunication, agreeably to the form adopted for that purpose according to the Word of God. But no one shall be excommunicated except with consent of the Classis.

ARTICLE 77.

After the suspension from the Lord's Table, and subsequent admoni-tions, and before proceeding to excommunication, the obstinacy of the sinner shall be publicly made known to the congregation, the offense explained, together with the care bestowed upon him, in reproof, suspension from the Lord's Supper, and repeated admonition, and the congregation shall be exhorted to speak to him and to pray for him. There shall be three such admonitions. In the first the name of the sinner shall not be mentioned that he be somewhat spared. In the second, with the consent of the Classis, his name shall be mentioned. In the third the congregation shall be informed that (unless he repent) he will be excluded from the fellowship of the Church, so that his excommunication, in case he remains obstinate, may take place with the tacit approbation of the Church. The interval between the admonitions shall be left to the discretion of the Consistory.

ARTICLE 78.

Whenever anyone who has been excommunicated desires to become reconciled to the Church in the way of repentance, it shall be announced to the Congregation, either before the celebration of the Lord's Supper, or at some other opportune time, in order that (in as far as no one can mention anything against him to the contrary) he may with profession of his conversion be publicly reinstated, according to the Form for that purpose.

ARTICLE 79.

When Ministers of the Divine Word, Elders or Deacons, have committed any public, gross sin, which is a disgrace to the Church, or worthy of punishment by the Authorities, the Elders and Deacons shall immediately by preceding sentence of the Consistory thereof and of the nearest Church, be suspended or expelled from their office, but the Ministers shall only be suspended. Whether these shall be entirely deposed from office, shall be subject to the judgment of the Classis, with the advice of the Delegates of the (Particular) Synod mentioned in Article 11.

ARTICLE 80.

Furthermore among the gross sins, which are worthy of being punished with suspension or deposition from office, these are the principal ones: false doctrine or heresy, public schism, public blasphemy, simony, faithless desertion of office or intrusion upon that of another, perjury, adultery, fornication, theft, acts of violence, habitual drunkenness, brawling, filthy lucre; in short, all sins and gross offenses, as render the perpetrators infamous before the world, and which in any private member of the Church would be considered worthy of excommunication.

ARTICLE 81.

The Ministers of the Word, Elders and Deacons, shall before the celebration of the Lord's Supper exercise Christian censure among themselves and in a friendly spirit admonish one another with regard to the discharge of their office.

ARTICLE 82.

To those who remove from the Congregation a letter or testimony concerning their profession and conduct shall be given by the Consistory, signed by two; or in the case of letters, which are given under the seal of the Church, signed by one.

ARTICLE 83.

Furthermore, to the poor, removing for sufficient reasons, so much money for traveling shall be given by the Deacons, as they deem adequate. The Consistory and the Deacons shall, however, see to it that they be not too much inclined to relieve their Churches of the poor, with whom they would without necessity burden other Churches.

ARTICLE 84.

No Church shall in any way lord it over other Churches, no Minister over other Ministers, no Elder or Deacon over other Elders or Deacons.

ARTICLE 85.

Churches whose usages differ from ours merely in non-essentials shall not be rejected.

ARTICLE 86.

These Articles, relating to the lawful order of the Church, have been so drafted and adopted by common consent, that they (if the profit of the Church demand otherwise) may and ought to be altered, augmented or diminished. However, no particular Congregation, Classis, (or Synod) shall be at liberty to do so, but they shall show all diligence in observing them, until it be otherwise ordained by the General Synod.

FORMULA OF SUBSCRIPTION

WE, the undersigned, Professors of The .... Reformed Church, Ministers of the Gospel, Elders and Deacons of

The .... Reformed congregation of ...., of the Classis of ....

do hereby sincerely and in good conscience before the Lord, declare by this, our subscription, that we heartily believe and are persuaded that all the articles and points of doctrine, contained in the Confession and Catechism of the Reformed Churches, together with the explanation of some points of the aforesaid doctrine, made by the National Synod of Dordrecht, 1618-'19, do fully agree with the Word of God.

We promise therefore diligently to teach and faithfully to defend the aforesaid doctrine, without either directly or indirectly contradicting the same, by our public preaching or writing.

We declare, moreover, that we not only reject all errors that militate against this doctrine and particularly those which were condemned by the above mentioned Synod, but that we are disposed to refute and contradict these, and to exert ourselves in keeping the Church free from such errors. And if hereafter any difficulties or different sentiments respecting the aforesaid doctrines should arise in our minds, we promise that we will neither publicly nor privately propose, teach, or defend the same, either by preaching or writing, until we have first revealed such sentiments to the consistory, Classis and Synod, that the same may be there examined, being ready always cheerfully to submit to the judgment of the consistory, Classis and Synod, under the penalty in case of refusal to be, by that very fact, suspended from our office.

And further, if at any time the consistory, Classis or Synod, upon sufficient grounds of suspicion and to preserve the uniformity and purity of doctrine, may deem it proper to require of us a further explanation of our sentiments respecting any particular article of the Confession of Faith, the Catechism, or the explanation of the National Synod, we do hereby promise to be always willing and ready to comply with such requisition, under the penalty above mentioned, reserving for ourselves, however, the right of an appeal, whenever we shall believe ourselves aggrieved by the sentence of the consistory, the Classis or the Synod, and until a decision is made upon such an appeal, we will acquiesce in the determination and judgment already passed.